The
CHESAPEAKE BAY
Book

A Complete Guide

The majestic great blue heron thrives in the Chesapeake's tidal marshes and bays.

THE
CHESAPEAKE BAY
BOOK

A Complete Guide

Second Edition

Allison Blake
with Tom Dove

Berkshire House Publishers
Lee, Massachusetts

Cover photography and frontispiece by David Trozzo. Front cover: Sailboats in Annapolis Harbor.

THE CHESAPEAKE BAY BOOK: A COMPLETE GUIDE
Copyright © 1992, 1996 by Berkshire House Publishers
Cover and interior photographs © 1992, 1996 by David Trozzo and other credited sources
Maps © 1992 by Alison Kolisar
Permission to use historic photographs was courteously granted by the Maryland State Archives, Annapolis.

_____ Library of Congress Cataloging-in-Publication data _____
Blake, Allison, 1960-
    The Chesapeake Bay book : a complete guide / Allison Blake with Tom Dove — 2nd ed.
        p.   cm. — (Great destinations series, ISSN 1056-7968)
Includes bibliographical references (p.   ) and index.
ISBN 0-936399-73-2
1. Chesapeake Bay Region (Md. and Va.)—Guidebooks. I. Dove, Tom. II. Title. III. Series.
F187.C5B54   1996
917.55'18043—dc20   95-21684
                                                                       CIP

Editor: Sarah Novak. Managing Editor: Philip Rich. Original design for Great Destinations™ series: Janice Lindstrom. Original design for cover: Jane McWhorter. Production services by Ripinsky & Company, Connecticut.

Berkshire House books are available at substantial discounts for bulk purchases by corporations and other organizations for promotions and premiums. Special personalized editions can also be produced in large quantities. For more information, contact:

Berkshire House Publishers
480 Pleasant St., Lee MA 01238
800-321-8526

Manufactured in the United States of America
First printing 1996
10 9 8 7 6 5 4 3 2 1

No complimentary meals or lodgings were accepted by the author and reviewers in gathering information for this work.

The <u>GREAT DESTINATIONS</u>™ Series

The Berkshire Book: A Complete Guide
The Santa Fe & Taos Book: A Complete Guide
The Napa & Sonoma Book: A Complete Guide
The Chesapeake Bay Book: A Complete Guide
The Coast of Maine Book: A Complete Guide
The Adirondack Book: A Complete Guide
The Aspen Book: A Complete Guide
The Charleston, Savannah & Coastal Islands Book:
  A Complete Guide
The Gulf Coast of Florida Book: A Complete Guide
The Central Coast of California Book : A Complete Guide
The Newport & Narragansett Bay Book: A Complete Guide
The Hamptons Book: A Complete Guide
Wineries of the Eastern States

The Great Destinations™ series features regions in the United States rich in natural beauty and culture. Each Great Destinations™ guidebook reviews an extensive selection of lodgings, restaurants, cultural events, historic sites, shops, and recreational opportunities, and outlines the region's natural and social history. Written by resident authors, the guides are a resource for visitor and resident alike. The books feature maps, photographs, directions to and around the region, lists of helpful phone numbers and addresses, and indexes.

Contents

CHAPTER ONE
"A Very Goodly Bay"
HISTORY
1

CHAPTER TWO
Of Ferries and Freeways
TRANSPORTATION
20

CHAPTER THREE
Bed & Breakfast & Boat
LODGING
00

CHAPTER FOUR
The Best of the Bay
CULTURE
75

CHAPTER FIVE
Catch of the Bay
RESTAURANTS & FOOD PURVEYORS
125

CHAPTER SIX
Water, Water Everywhere
RECREATION
174

CHAPTER SEVEN
Antiques, Boutiques, and Inlet Outlets
SHOPPING
224

CHAPTER EIGHT
The Right Connections
INFORMATION
253

CHAPTER NINE
Bay Neighbors
BALTIMORE AND NEARBY ATTRACTIONS
272

Acknowledgments

An undertaking such as *The Chesapeake Bay Book* requires the good will and hard work of many folks, from contributors to understanding day job bosses to families.

My thanks goes to Tom Dove, a noted boating writer from Kent Island who knows his way around good inns and restaurants, too. With the assistance of his wife, Pam, Tom researched the Eastern Shore for the Culture, Recreation, Shopping and Lodging chapters, and supplied the information about food purveyors and some topnotch restaurant reviews, too. Thanks also to tireless David Trozzo, whose relentless quest for the perfect pictures brings to you a taste of the Chesapeake that words cannot reflect.

Up in Baltimore, Joanna Sullivan researched the area's cultural attractions and B&Bs for a new feature in this edition, a "best-of" section describing the highlights of Baltimore and other Chesapeake neighbors.

Many thanks also to an excellent team of restaurant reviewers, many of whom joined me for a second tour of duty through the area's many culinary delights: Tom Marquardt in Annapolis, Anne Stinson in Easton and environs, Jay Votel up Chestertown way, Tracy Sahler in Salisbury, and Art Shettle, also of Salisbury. Jack Chamberlain down on the Northern Neck not only reviewed restaurants, but provided much-appreciated advice about that area, and Debbie Funk of Baltimore, with a little help from Joanna, reviewed that city's best.

Thanks to Anne Stinson for making the trek to write about Smith Island.

Thanks also to good friend and fact checker Kathy Edwards.

The folks at Berkshire House Publishers have always provided full support, particularly Sarah Novak, editor of editions one and two, and Philip Rich, managing editor.

I'd also like to thank the folks at *The Roanoke Times*, especially Beth Obenshain and Madelyn Rosenberg, for their support.

On behalf of Dave, thanks also to Kathy (who also skillfully tried her hand at restaurant reviewing) and Andrew. Thanks to Hannah Gillelan for last-minute virtual pinch-hitting, and to Bess Gillelan and Howard Gillelan for regional advice.

Most of all, my thanks goes to my mate and most trusted critic, Joshua Gillelan.

Introduction

Down on Kitty Duval Creek in Annapolis, the blue heron rules the marsh, even if the redwing blackbirds stake out cattail quadrants of their own. A barn owl lived one summer in the white boathouse across the way, and swooped by from time to time when we rowed past in the double-ended dory. An ambitious day in the dory finds us clear to the mouth of the river, where stands the famed Thomas Point Light. An unambitious day means poking around the cove around the corner. Afterwards, we'll order up a dozen crabs from the Maryland Watermen's Co-op. If it's Memorial Day, we'll pick 'em out in the backyard, looking up as the Blue Angels, in town for the Naval Academy graduation, scream overhead from time to time. If it's Saturday night, we might hop in the car and make it to Washington or Baltimore within an easy hour — sometimes, parking time included.

Therein lies a great beauty of life on the Chesapeake: it's the best of both worlds. You can live out of the way. You can live an urban life. Some people would rather be out of the way. They live in corners of the Eastern Shore, or down in Virginia's placid Northern Neck and Middle Peninsula. Urban dwellers who secretly wish they had the nerve to live there all the time keep big houses on the creeks and rivers and invite their friends down on weekends. Those of us who call out on the Chesapeake and Potomac Telephone Co. lines, or, as kids, wondered about that big "Chessie" cat on the Chesapeake & Ohio Railway cars, are here to report that the region is enormous and diverse.

Visitors wandering into Sister's Store down near Port Lookout, Maryland, right where the Potomac and Chesapeake meet, will find a Coke in the corner cooler and local friends talking around the cash register. Parked side by side out front will be somebody's pickup and a Volvo from the suburbs. It's a good couple of hours north to Annapolis, where Euro-style restaurants have moved into the historic district. Drive the same distance south to the Bay Bridge Tunnel, and you'll pass through the green rural tidewater, flat and calm and good bit more Tennessee Williams than you'll find at the head of the Bay in Havre de Grace. Up there, it's starting to feel ever so slightly Northeast industrial. Still, the sailors from Wilmington and Philadelphia bring the boat shoes; the Bay and the Susquehanna River meet at Havre de Grace and water is in view everywhere you turn.

And all that's only the Western Shore.

Old steamship lines served the Chesapeake Bay well into this century, a lifeline to history as rich as anywhere in this relatively young country. Forebears to oysters now ordered at the raw bar fed our native forebears; George Washington did sleep here, maybe in the very colonial four-poster in your room at the B&B.

And the Bay itself, which scientists know suffered from our early farming settlers, ecologically is turning around. The huge local and federal clean-up effort, rallied by a "Save the Bay" battle cry, is making headway. Back on Kitty Duval Creek, that means the redwing blackbirds shouldn't miss a migratory beat.

Allison Blake
Arundel on the Bay, Annapolis, Maryland

THE WAY THIS BOOK WORKS

Geographically, we've divided the Bay area like so: **Head of the Bay** starts past Aberdeen, Maryland, and circles around the top of the Bay to the Sassafras River, and includes historic Havre de Grace and Chesapeake City. Below the Head of the Bay, on the western side, we've designated the area south of the Magothy River to the Potomac, and west to Rte. 301, as the **Annapolis/Western Shore** area. Virginia's **Northern Neck/Middle Peninsula** area runs down to Gloucester Point, west to Rte. 301 at the northern end of the area, and Rte. 17 farther south.

Over on the other side of the Bay is the **Upper Eastern Shore**, from the Sassafras south to the Choptank, east to the Delaware line. South of the Choptank to Virginia's Cape Charles — with a side trip through Berlin to Assateague Island — is the **Lower Eastern Shore**.

Information is presented according to these five regions; within each region, town are listed alphabetically, with lodgings, restaurants, and other places of interest in each town also given alphabetically. The book covers sections of both Maryland and Virginia, of course, with Maryland having the greater percentage of territory and, therefore, entries. So whenever we cross the border into Virginia, we'll remind you, by specifying that in the address that accompanies each set of listings.

The helpful little blocks of salient information that accompany listings and reviews have been researched as close to publication as possible to be as up to date as possible. But we can't control changes in operating hours or prices. Please accept our apologies in advance for any details that may have changed, and be sure to call ahead when planning.

For the same reason, we've usually avoided listing specific prices, preferring instead to indicate a range of prices, explained below. (Restaurant prices cover an average dinner for one, including appetizer, entrée, and dessert, but not wine or cocktails.)

Price Codes:

	Lodging	*Dining*
Inexpensive:	Up to $55	Up to $15
Moderate:	$56 to $85	$16 to $22
Expensive:	$86 to $125	$23 to $32
Very Expensive:	$126 and above	$33 or more

Credit cards are abbreviated as follows:

AE:	American Express
C:	Choice
CB:	Carte Blanche
D:	Discover Card
DC:	Diner's Club
MC:	Master Card
V:	Visa

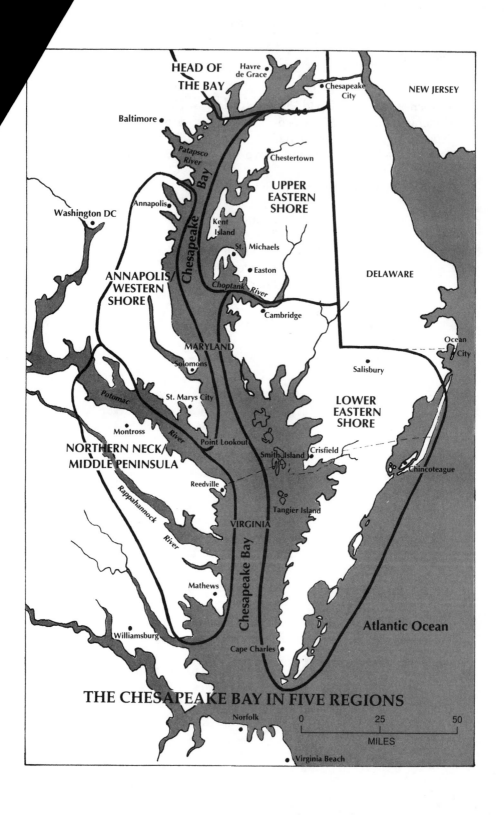

THE CHESAPEAKE BAY IN FIVE REGIONS

The
CHESAPEAKE BAY
Book
A Complete Guide

CHAPTER ONE
"A Very Goodly Bay"
HISTORY

There is but one entrance by Sea into this Country, and that is at the mouth of a very goodly Bay, 18 or 20 myles broad. The cape on the South is called Cape Henry, in honour of our most notable Prince. The North Edge is called Cape Charles, in honour of the worthy Duke of Yorke. Within is a country that may have the prerogative over the most pleasant places. Heaven and earth never agreed better to frame a place for man's habitation. Here are mountains, hills, plaines, valleyes, rivers, and brookes, all running into a faire Bay, compassed but for the mouth, with fruitful and delightsome land.

— Capt. John Smith, 1607

Maryland State Archives

Archaeologists digging in this cradle of U.S. history have unearthed countless remnants of an even deeper past. Layered in sand and clay along Chesapeake Bay shores are oyster shells, some thousands of years old. The largest cache was a 30-acre Indian shell midden spread across Pope's Creek, off the Potomac River. Long before Chesapeake watermen took up their tongs, the Bay was feeding her people.

An 1890 fleet of skipjacks — still the country's oldest fishing fleet under sail — stands at the dock in Cambridge, Maryland.

The Indians called her Chesapeake Bay, "the Great Shellfish Bay." In the 16th century, a Jesuit priest sailed through the Virginia capes described by John Smith and bestowed a second name: La Bahia de la Madre de Dios — the Bay of the Mother of God.

The Chesapeake has always looked after those who lived here. Just as the Indians thrived on Bay oysters, so early European settlers grew crops in rich Bay soil. As the Indians paddled canoes from encampment to encampment, so ferries linked later settlements.

Today, the waters of this ancient river valley fan out into a complex network of urban bridges and rural lanes. Here endures the heart of the modern mid-Atlantic megalopolis, and the soul of 19th-century fishing villages. U.S. history here is old; geological history is young.

The Chesapeake Bay is bookended by two major metropolitan areas in two states: Baltimore, Maryland's largest city, and Norfolk–Newport News–Hampton Roads in Virginia's Tidewater. Both are major Atlantic ports. Near John Smith's Virginia capes, now spanned by the 17.6-mile Chesapeake Bay Bridge-Tunnel, the Norfolk Naval Air Station presides over a strong Navy presence throughout Tidewater.

Increasingly, Canada geese winter on the Bay. These residents live at Blackwater National Wildlife Refuge.

David Trozzo

Much of Maryland's Western Shore life looks to urban centers, as city dwellers willing to endure the hour-long commute to Washington or Baltimore emigrate to Annapolis or Kent Island. For their highway-bound hours during the week, these government insiders are repaid with long sails on the Bay, or hours anchored in secluded "gunkholes," shallow coves where green and great blue herons fly from nearby marshes. On the Eastern Shore, fishing, farming, tourism, and the retirement business spur local economic life.

Up the Bay's major tributaries are the major cities of the region: Washington, DC, on the Potomac; Richmond, Virginia, on the James; and Baltimore, Maryland, on the Patapsco. Maryland's capital, Annapolis, stands at the mouth of the Severn River, near where the William Preston Lane Memorial Bridge, or Bay Bridge, links the Eastern and Western Shores.

Even as the Chesapeake is defined by her waters, so she is defined by her history. A stop at Maryland's Statehouse in Annapolis, where Washington resigned his Continental Army commission, is as integral to a Chesapeake country visit as a charter-boat fishing trip from Tilghman Island.

The first permanent colonial English settlement was here, at Jamestown, Virginia, in 1607. The first Catholic settlers landed farther north, on the Potomac, and established Maryland at St. Marys City in 1634. George Washington and his peers used the Bay first to transport their tobacco, the region's first sizable cash crop, and then to their military advantage as they plotted their navigational comings and goings during the Revolutionary War.

For all the Bay's history and enduring navigability, however, she shares a problem with virtually every other heavily populated estuary. A confluence of pressures has threatened the health of her rich waters since the European settlers chopped down forests to create fields to farm. Soil from the fertile lands lining the Bay's shores has slipped into the water, silting in harbors and obscuring marshy invertebrate nurseries. Damage has been compounded by 20th-century wastes: fertilizers, air pollution, and sewage.

Many say the magnificent Chesapeake is at the most crucial crossroads of her most recent geological incarnation. A massive assault against pollution is well underway, and is producing some good results. Perhaps, like the estuary's flushing by fresh water from the north and by saltwater tides from the south, the diverse mix of urban and rural can maintain a beneficial balance in La Bahia de la Madre de Dios.

NATURAL HISTORY

Cargo ships journeying the 200-mile length of the Chesapeake Bay travel in a deep channel that more than 10,000 years ago cradled the ancient Susquehanna River.

The mighty river flowed south to the ocean, drawing in the waters of many tributaries but for one independent soul: the present-day James River. Then came the great shift in the glaciers of the last Ice Age, when the thick sheets of ice that stopped just north of the Chesapeake region — in what is now northern Pennsylvania and New York state — began to melt under warming temperatures. As the Pleistocene Era ended, torrents of released water flowed, filling the oceans. The Susquehanna River valley flooded once, twice, and probably more, settling, eventually, within the bounds of the present-day Chesapeake Bay.

Scientists in late 1995 presented convincing evidence that 35 million years ago, a giant meteor — at least a mile in diameter — struck the earth at what is now the lower Bay. The impact formed a 55-mile-wide crater, the remains of which underlie the lower Bay and the nearby sea floor. Obviously, the consequences of this discovery for our understanding of the Bay's origins and geology will be far-reaching.

The Bay as it now exists is the largest estuary in the United States — some say all North America. Estuaries are schizophrenic bodies of water, mixing the fresh waters of inland mountain streams and rivers with salty ocean waters.

The undulating brew of fresh and salt stirs a habitat that supports a huge range of creatures. Clams, crabs, oysters, striped bass (known hereabouts as rockfish), menhaden, and more, have always thrived in these waters, living a solitary life in the deep as bottom dwellers, or bedding down in the shallows, or navigating north to the fresh water to spawn.

The Susquehanna River, supplying 50 percent of the Chesapeake's fresh water, flows into the head of the Bay. The Potomac adds another 20 percent. Even the renegade James River has joined the other Chesapeake tributaries, helping to nourish the vast mix of species living in the Bay.

An ever-popular family pastime: hunting for prehistoric shark teeth at Calvert Cliffs.

David Ropiski

Along the Western Shore of Maryland, about 80 miles south of Annapolis, solid evidence of a prehistoric past is layered within dramatic Calvert Cliffs. There lie the fossils of the 12- to 17-million-year-old forebears to the crab, menhaden, and oyster that now live in the Bay. The great white shark swam in the waters of a prehistoric Bay; crocodile, rhinoceros, and mastodon lived along the edge. Their teeth and bones are still pulled from these cliffs that were once the uplands of the ancient Susquehanna River Valley.

WHERE LAND AND WATER MEET

The modern-day Chesapeake boasts impressive statistics. The Bay surface is 2,200 square miles, but her 150 tributaries — including all manner of coves, creeks, and tidal rivers — double that area. The total system is filled by 18 trillion gallons of water, the fresher water in the upper Bay, the saltier farther south.

The Bay's width ranges from four miles at Annapolis to 30 miles at Point Lookout, Maryland, where the Potomac River meets the Bay, dividing Maryland and Virginia. Despite the enormity of this expansive body of water, the Chesapeake is surprisingly shallow. Its average depth is 21 feet, although at the so-called "Deep Trough," off Kent Island, depths reach 160 feet.

TOPOGRAPHY OF CHESAPEAKE BAY AREA

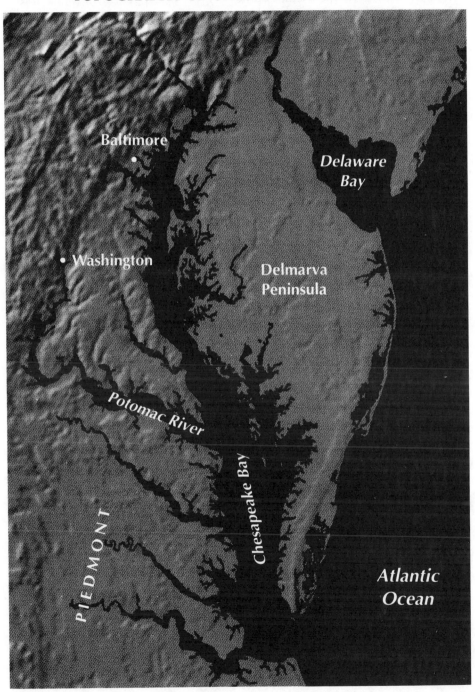

Beyond the waters of the Bay, within her 64,000-square-mile watershed, is geological diversity: the metamorphic rock of the Appalachian plateau, the weathered, iron-rich soil of the piedmont, and the sandy coastal plain.

Meanwhile, a shoreline that seems to snake forever along marshes, creeks, or mighty rivers amounts to as many miles as the number of history books that tell of this Bay. Estimates of total shoreline reach 6,000 miles. A variety of wildlife lives here. Muskrats were hunted and trapped commonly — and still are; but nutria, a similar South American species, have taken over much of their habitat since a few escaped from an Eastern Shore breeding operation back in the 1940s or '50s.

Overhead each fall come the migratory waterfowl — swans, Canada geese, brant, and, of course, ducks: mallards, pintail, canvasbacks, and teal — following the Atlantic flyway. The mighty osprey is common, back from its severely threatened status after the insecticide DDT was banned in the early '70s.

David Trozzo

Sunset over Blackwater National Wildlife Refuge, deep in Dorchester County's lowlands.

The Eastern Shore, in particular, historically has been a haven for hunters. Hunting is still popular, but so is birdwatching. Down in the lowlands of Dorchester County, the brackish marshes of Blackwater National Wildlife Refuge welcome the red-cockaded woodpecker, peregrine falcon, and the endangered bald eagle, which breeds here. The great horned owl likewise breeds in this marshy backwater, and the rare Delmarva fox squirrel also makes it his home.

The Chesapeake's salt marshes are crucial creature nurseries once thought to be useless. Here, as elsewhere in early America, settlers harvested "salt hay" for their livestock's winter food. Spartina grasses tough enough to withstand this strange habitat between land and sea grew profusely, sheltering molting blue crabs and protecting sea from land — and vice versa.

Talk to a salty waterman who has worked the Bay and her rivers for a few decades, though, and he'll tell you the once-prolific Bay grasses aren't what they once were. Environmentalists studying the Bay watch the grasses, known officially as "submerged aquatic vegetation," as a sort of clarity gauge of the Bay. Efforts to bring back these protectors have been fairly successful in recent years, giving fish and fowl, and even the shores of the Bay, one more ally against the rush of wind against bare sea and land.

Even with the decline in these marshy incubators, the Chesapeake as a fishery remains impressive. Its annual catch is third in the U.S., behind only the far larger waters of the Atlantic and Pacific oceans. Menhaden and blue crabs are the bulk of the take, although even the scavenging crab, mainstay of a Chesapeake summer diet, has become an object of some concern.

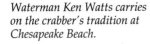

Waterman Ken Watts carries on the crabber's tradition at Chesapeake Beach.

David Trozzo

Many warn of the future overharvesting of these incredibly popular critters, whose numbers in the Bay declined by over one billion, to just over 600 million, between 1988-1989 and 1993-1994. The decline may be a natural drop in the life cycle of the population, which remains plentiful, scientists say. But since fishing pressures have increased at the same time, both Maryland and Virginia may take steps to limit commercial and recreational overharvesting. Meanwhile, tables still fill at Chesapeake crab houses, and recreational crabbers still take nets down to local piers.

The story of the formerly endangered rockfish could signal a brighter future for the blue crab. Commercial fishermen who had enjoyed steady catches of five million pounds of fish annually saw the stocks drop to two million pounds in the late 1970s. By 1985, Maryland imposed a fishing moratorium. Virginia followed in 1989. Since then, a limited catch-and-release season has expanded each year, and stocks were officially declared restored in January

1995 by the body that governs coastal catches, the Atlantic States Marine Fisheries Commission. Scientists continue to monitor the rockfish's cautious road to recovery — and devotees have been pleased to find this sweet, flavorful fish return to local menus.

One reason fishing pressures are up for the blue crab has been the plunge among the native oysters that breathed economic life into the Eastern Shore for decades. A century after they were first dangerously overfished, harvestable oysters have dropped to an all-time low. In recent years, a combination of threats has undermined efforts to help restore what were once bounteous oyster bars: overfishing, disease, habitat destruction, and pollution. Scientists debate just how to solve the dilemma — and not only to retain the popular, historic fishery. Oysters filter pollutants from the water, and may be a key to restoring the Bay's overall water quality.

As the oyster population has swelled and dropped, so has the Bay shoreline itself. The lapping and crashing of water against her edges have always caused erosion: marshes fill, harbors shift, and, over the years, islands and peninsulas have disappeared.

Colonial-era Sharp's Island, off the mouth of the Eastern Shore's Choptank River, was once the site of one of William Claiborne's string of trading posts founded in the 1630s. A 600-acre plantation was established here, but now it — and the entire island — is gone. Apparently, the island eroded away quickly, for there are old-timers along the Shore who still remember it. A similar fate befell Holland Island at Tangier Sound, once the site of a small village, home to 300. The shoreline began to slip by 1900, and its residents moved away two decades later.

SAVING THE BAY

Even as time and tide send shoreline slipping into the Bay, man's debris has followed. In addition to chemical fertilizers from farms throughout the vast watershed, waste discharged from aging sewage plants, until recently, flowed into the estuary. Industrial and residential development has likewise sped erosion. Waste-produced nutrients, primarily phosphorous and nitrogen, poured into the Bay, feeding algae blooms that cut oxygen and light to the flora and fauna on the Bay floor during the spring and summer. Air pollution adds as much as one-quarter of the nitrogen, scientists say.

Efforts to clean up Chesapeake Bay stretch back over decades, although formal federal and state programs weren't organized until 1977. In 1964, President Lyndon B. Johnson announced the federally supported beginnings of an effort to clean up the Potomac River, one of the Bay's best-known tributaries. The $1-billion project is considered a great success story, perhaps inspiration to the many agencies and organizations now spending millions of dollars and countless hours to save the Bay.

"Save the Bay" is the rallying cry for the non-profit Chesapeake Bay Foundation, even as continuing efforts by state and federal government programs are working to improve the Bay. Research begun in 1977 led to the Chesapeake Bay Agreement of 1983, signed by the states of Maryland, Virginia, and Pennsylvania, the District of Columbia, the Environmental Protection Agency, and the Chesapeake Bay Commission, a group of area legislators. The landmark agreement established the nuts-and-bolts programs for cleaning up a deteriorating habitat. At that point, the focus was on cleaning the Bay per se; an updated agreement in 1987 shifted the focus from improving water quality to conserving Bay flora and fauna. Now scientists are shifting their concerns not only to cleaning up air pollution harming the Bay, but also to projects for restoring wetlands, encouraging landowners to plant trees along watershed streams, and creating experimental oyster bars.

The results of the Bay cleanup are mixed: blue crab populations are currently cause for concern, but the submerged aquatic grasses have started to come back. Moratoriums on shad fishing seem to have prompted signs of improvement in those stocks, but they're still nowhere near healthy levels. Even as environmentalists see progress in the Bay's comeback, a new potential threat has surfaced from another source: Capitol Hill. In these times of fiscal austerity, program funding could be cut. What that means to the Bay, only time will tell.

Visitors, meanwhile, can expect to see enthusiastic local support for the Bay, from the annual Bay Bridge Walk from Annapolis to Kent Island in late spring, to Maryland's new "Treasure the Chesapeake" specialty license plates. Half the proceeds from sales of the special plates go to Bay cleanup efforts.

In the years since the cleanup began, the Bay's health has improved. Sailing and boating thrive; recreational fishers still go after bluefish or croaker. The central effort for all Bay lovers is to help restore the estuary and nurture it as the mid-Atlantic region continues to grow.

SOCIAL HISTORY

The first settlers of the Chesapeake region lived here during the last Ice Age. These paleo-Indians were hunters, following mammoth and bison on their migrations. The melting of the glaciers marked the beginning of the Archaic period, when these forebears of the Piscataway and Nanticoke tribes convened in villages, and began to eat oysters and other shell- and finfish from the Bay. About 3,000 years ago, they began to farm these shores, raising maize, ancestor of the Eastern Shore's now popular Silver Queen corn, and tobacco, which the English settlers later converted to the region's early economic foundation.

EARLY SETTLERS

Dutch and Spanish explorers of the 16th century were reportedly the first Europeans to sail into the Bay, and Vikings may have visited even earlier.

The first Europeans to settle permanently, however, were the English. In 1607, Capt. Christopher Newport left England, crossed the Atlantic to the West Indies, then sailed north into the Bay. He navigated up what would come to be called the James River. Those aboard Newport's three-ship fleet, the 49-foot *Discovery*, the 68-foot *Godspeed*, and the 111-foot *Susan Constant*, settled Jamestown.

The new colony, chartered by the Virginia Company, proved to be a near disaster. Hostile Indians and disease either drove off or killed many of the original settlers. Among the survivors was Capt. John Smith, by all accounts an adventurer. It was here that Smith's fabled rescue by the Indian maiden Pocahontas took place — an event recorded in Smith's journal, but questioned by scholars. As the story goes, the young captain was captured by Indians and taken to a village where the old "powhatan," or chief, was to preside over Smith's execution. Even as the Indian warriors threatened with raised clubs, the chief's young daughter threw herself upon the English captain, thus saving him from a brutal fate.

Smith was also the first Englishman to explore the Bay, and indeed charted it rather accurately. He set out from Jamestown on his exploration in 1608, accompanied by 14 men on an open barge. They sailed first up the "Easterne Shore," where sources of fresh water proved poor. While still in what came to be called Virginia, Smith wrote: ". . . the first people we saw were 2. grimme and stout Salvages upon Cape-Charles, with long poles like Javelings, headed with bone. They boldly demanded what we were, and what we would, but after many circumstances, they in time seemed very kinde. . . ."

Smith learned from them "such descriptions of the Bay, Isles, and rivers, that often did us exceeding pleasure." The party then went on across the Bay to its western shore, sailing as fast as they could ahead of a fearsome storm. "Such an extreame gust of wind, rayne, thunder, and lightening happened, that with great danger we escaped the unmercifull raging of that Ocean-like water," wrote Smith.

Early Jamestown survived as Virginia's colonial capital to the end of the 17th century. Meanwhile, English migration across the Atlantic continued. William Claiborne established his trading post at Kent Island, mid-Bay, in 1631, setting himself up to become arguably the first settler of Maryland. In ensuing years, on behalf of the Virginia Company, he provided ample rivalry for Maryland's "proprietors," or royal grant holders, the Calverts.

George Calvert, the first Lord Baltimore, hoped to settle his own "Avalon." He first sought to establish a colony in Newfoundland, but soon abandoned the harsh northern land. A second grant for a new colony passed to his son, the second Lord Baltimore, Cecil Calvert. The younger Calvert, a Catholic, knew that Virginia would not welcome the new settlement, and feared that enemies in England would try to undermine his colony. He put his younger brother, Leonard, in charge of the settlers who boarded the ships *Ark* and *Dove* and sailed off to found Maryland — named in honor of Charles I's queen — at St. Clement's Island, near the mouth of the Potomac.

The 128 hardy souls aboard the two ships landed on March 25, 1634, after taking a route similar to that taken by Christopher Newport. Upon landing, Leonard Calvert, as governor, led a party of men up the river to meet the "tayac," or leader, of the Piscataways. The tayac gave the settlers permission to settle where they would; their village was to become Maryland's first capital, St. Marys City. They also taught the English settlers how to farm unfamiliar lands in an unfamiliar climate.

Long before Europeans settled Chesapeake, woodland Indians lived here. Their tools are demonstrated at St. Marys City, site of Maryland's first capital.

David Trozzo

Among the Marylanders' first crops was tobacco, soon to be the staple of a Chesapeake economy, and already being harvested farther south along the Virginia Bay coast. In years that followed, farmers would discover just how damaging tobacco proved to be in costs to both the land and humans. The crop sapped the soil's nutrients. Without fertilizers, a field was used up after a couple of seasons, so more land constantly had to be cleared and planted. This called for labor. While some Englishmen indentured themselves to this life in exchange for trans-Atlantic passage to the colonies, tobacco farming was nevertheless responsible for the beginnings of African slave labor along the Chesapeake. By the late 17th century, wealthy planters had begun to "invest" in slaves as "assets."

Up and down the Chesapeake grew a tobacco coast, fueled by demand from English traders. From its beginnings as a friendly home to new settlers, the Bay grew into a seagoing highway for the burgeoning tobacco trade. Soon came fishing and boatbuilding.

A rural manorial society grew up around St. Marys City, which was never itself very large. Perhaps a dozen families lived within five square miles. Planters raised tobacco here, a fort was established, and government business eventually brought inns and stables. In 1650, about 100 miles to the north, a settlement was established near what is now Annapolis, named Providence. In 1695, the new governor, Francis Nicholson, moved Maryland's capital near the

Archaeologists unearth Maryland history at St. Marys City.

Dan Wolff

mouth of the Severn River, to Annapolis. By 1720, St. Marys City was gone. That colony's heyday has been re-created, however, in a living museum, complete with authentic pigs. Archaeological work continues on the site. Just recently, three lead coffins holding the remains of members of the Calvert clan were unearthed.

The Statehouse in Annapolis, the country's oldest capitol building in continuous use.

David Trozzo

Nicholson's Annapolis, considered America's first baroque-style city, is still evident: from two circles, State Circle and Church Circle, radiate the streets of today's historic district. Three statehouses have stood in State Circle, the most recent begun in 1772. This was the building used as the national capitol during the period of the Articles of Confederation, and is the state capitol in longest continual use. From the center of Church Circle rises the spire of St. Anne's Church, the third on the site since 1696.

Known also as "the Ancient City," Annapolis grew into a thriving late 17th- and 18th-century town. It became renowned as the social gathering spot for colonial gentlemen and ladies. Here, the Provincial Court and the Legislature met. Planters "wintered" here amid fashionable society; the witty men of the Tuesday Club gathered at the homes of its members for music and poetry.

Elsewhere in along the Chesapeake, seaport settlements were rising from the sandier Eastern Shore. Chestertown was established as a seaport and Kent county seat in 1706. Near the head of the Bay, "Baltimore Town" was first carved from 60 acres owned by the wealthy Carroll family in 1729. Those who couldn't survive the fluctuations of the tobacco market turned to tonging for oysters, fishing for herring, or to shipbuilding.

THE CHESAPEAKE IN WARTIME

During the Revolutionary War, Annapolis's central port location drew blockade runners and Continental colonels alike. Both Americans and British used the Bay to transport troops. War meetings that included the likes of George Washington and the Marquis de Lafayette were held beneath the Liberty Tree, still standing today on the campus of St. John's College, and thought to be 400 to 600 years old. (The college, founded in 1696 as King William's School, still holds graduation ceremonies there.)

The gardens at the home of William Paca, signer of the Declaration of Independence, were painstakingly reconstructed from archaeological digs.

David Trozzo

Three Annapolitans, Samuel Chase, William Paca, and Charles Carroll of Carrollton, signed the Declaration of Independence in 1776; their colonial-era homes have been preserved and are open for public tours. The war finally ended at Yorktown, Virginia, near Jamestown, in 1781. Reinforcements traveled south along the Bay to meet up with Washington's gathering troops, and French Admiral de Grasse barricaded the mouth of the Bay. Lord Cornwallis, the British commander, surrendered.

In 1783, during a meeting of the Continental Congress in the Maryland state-house in Annapolis, George Washington resigned his Army commission. Visitors may still see the chamber. This is also where the Treaty of Paris was ratified in 1784, formally ending the war. Likewise, Annapolis itself soon saw an end to its glittery social role. The city soon fell quiet, awakened only by the 1845 establishment of the U.S. Naval Academy, which overshadowed much of city life for at least the next century.

Peace with the British after the Revolution was short-lived. Soon came the War of 1812, the only war in U.S. history wherein unfriendly foreign troops reached our shores. The British established their operations center at Tangier Island, and many battles and skirmishes ensued upon the Bay. The citizens of the young nation were not eager to bow to the British, including those at the shipbuilding center of St. Michaels. Blockade runners routinely left the Eastern Shore port, and hostility ran high.

Late on the night of August 9, 1813, amid rumors of an impending British attack, the good citizens of St. Michaels blew out their lanterns. Just before dawn, the British attacked a nearby fort. The wily Shorefolk were ready. They hoisted their lanterns into the treetops, the British fired too high, and the town — except the now-renowned "Cannonball House" — was saved. For this, St. Michaels calls itself "The Town That Fooled the British."

A year later came the war's decisive battle. In September 1814, a man watched the fire of cannons and guns as the Americans successfully defended Fort McHenry, which guards the entrance to Baltimore Harbor. The next morning, Francis Scott Key saw a tattered U.S. flag flying and, inspired, penned the words to "The Star-Spangled Banner." It became the national anthem in 1931.

19TH-CENTURY LIFE

Once this second war ended, the denizens of 19th-century Chesapeake country turned to building their economy. Tobacco declined; shipbuilding grew. Smaller Chesapeake shore towns such as Chestertown and Annapolis lost commercial prominence to Baltimore, which grew into the Upper Bay region's major trade center. Steamships were launched, and the Baltimore & Ohio Railroad more speedily connected the region to points west. Exported were Eastern Shore—grown wheat and the watermen's catch of oysters, menhaden, and more.

By all accounts, there was no love lost between the landed gentry who controlled the region, and the Chesapeake watermen. These scrappy individualists may have been one-time small farmers down on their luck, or were descendants of released indentured servants who had once served the wealthy class.

Meanwhile, the shoals of the Chesapeake saw their first aids to navigation in this era. Lightships were sent out to warn passing ships of the worst sand bars. In 1819, Congress made provisions to set two lightships in Virginia waters.

The Drum Point screw-pile lighthouse early in the 20th century. It now stands at the Calvert Marine Museum.

Maryland State Archives

This experiment in safety was popular, and by 1833 ten lightships stood sentinel at the mouth of the Rappahannock River and elsewhere in the Bay. The mid-19th century saw construction of the distinctive screw-pile lighthouses, with their pilings that could be driven securely into the Bay bottom. Today, only three stand — two at maritime museums at Solomons and St. Michaels, Maryland, and one in action in the Bay just southeast of Annapolis, off Thomas Point. The Thomas Point Light was manned until automation came in 1986.

As the Bay became easier to travel, the people who spent the most time on the water discovered perhaps her greatest wealth. In the 19th century, demand increased for the famous Chesapeake oysters. Watermen went after them in an early ancestor to many "Bay-built" boat designs, the log canoe. Boats like the fast oceangoing schooners known as "Baltimore clippers" already were being built, but oyster dredging and tonging required boats that could skip over shoals, run fast, and allow a man to haul gear over the side. Log canoes have unusually low freeboard; crab pots and oyster tongs can be worked over their sides. These successors to Indian dug-out canoes were given sails and shallow-draft hulls to navigate shoals.

With their top-heavy sails and low sides, log canoes now present one of a yachtsman's greatest challenges. Shifting their weight just ahead of the wind, sailors race log canoes most summer weekends on the Eastern Shore.

The Bay's 120-year steamboat era, meanwhile, arrived in 1813, seven years after packets first carried passengers on a ship-and-stagecoach journey from Baltimore to Philadelphia. The steamboat *Chesapeake* paddled out of Baltimore Harbor on June 13, 1813, for Frenchtown, Maryland, a now-extinct town at the head of the Bay. Within a week, a trip was offered to Rock Hall, Maryland, on the Eastern Shore, for 75 cents. By 1848, the steamship company that came to be called the Old Bay Line ran the 200-mile length of the Bay, from Baltimore to Norfolk. Steamships ran in the Bay into the 1960s.

THE CIVIL WAR AND SLAVERY

Even as the Chesapeake Bay fueled a growing 19th-century economy, these were the years of growing North-South hostility. The Chesapeake region was largely slave-holding, although the nearby Mason-Dixon Line (the southern boundary of Pennsylvania) to the north beckoned many slaves to freedom. Historical accounts say this tended to moderate the behavior of many Maryland slave holders who feared their slaves would run away.

The history of slavery here had started with tobacco farming in the late 1600s; by 1770, tobacco exports reached 100 million pounds in the Western Shore region. When the tobacco trade declined in the 19th century, the services of many slaves were no longer needed. Abolitionist Quakers living in the Bay area campaigned to free many slaves, and free blacks were not uncommon in Annapolis and Baltimore in the first half of the 19th century. Many Eastern Shore watermen were free blacks, who mixed with white watermen in mutual contempt for the wealthy.

In 1817, abolitionist and writer Frederick Douglass was born into slavery in Talbot County, Maryland. As a boy, he worked at Wye Plantation, owned by Edward Lloyd V, the scion of a political dynasty in Maryland. Following alternately civil treatment in Baltimore and brutal treatment as an Eastern Shore field hand, Douglass escaped to Philadelphia at 21 and became a free man.

Because the upper reaches of the Bay were so close to freedom, the Underground Railroad thrived here. The best-known local conductor was Harriet Tubman, an escaped slave from Dorchester County, Maryland, who led nearly 300 slaves north during her career.

When the Civil War broke out in 1861, the Virginia half of the Chesapeake quickly turned to Richmond, located at the head of navigation of the James River. Maryland struggled over its political loyalties. Many Chesapeake families would be divided by the North-South rivalries.

Naval warfare changed forever on the waters of the Civil War Bay, when the *Monitor* and *Merrimack* met at Hampton Roads. The *Merrimack*, having been salvaged, rebuilt as an ironclad, and renamed *Virginia* by the Confederates, had already rammed and sunk the Union *Cumberland* and disabled the *Congress*, which burned and sank. The next day, the ironclad *Monitor*, with her two guns protected in a swiveling turret, arrived to engage the *Merrimack*'s fixed guns. Neither ship sank the other; neither side won, but the encounter was the first battle between armored battleships.

Ironically, when the Emancipation Proclamation went into effect in January 1863, slaves laboring on the Virginia shores of the Chesapeake were freed where federal law — via Union occupation — prevailed; slaves in Union Maryland were not. The Proclamation freed only those in the states "in rebellion against the United States." It wasn't until September 1864, when Maryland voted for its own new constitution, that those in bondage in the state were freed.

THE OYSTER BOOM

In the years before the war, shrewd Baltimore businessmen had opened oyster packing plants. With the war over, enterprising Chesapeake business was renewed. The fertile oyster bars of the Bay's famed shoals fueled a much-needed economic spurt for the Eastern Shore.

Chesapeake oyster production peaked at more than 11 million bushels during the great oyster boom of the 1870s. The Eastern Shore Railroad snaked down through the flatlands to Dorchester County, where one John Crisfield, former Maryland congressman, set about capitalizing on his new railroad.

At the head of Tangier Sound, where watermen were dredging or tonging millions of oysters from the rich waters, Crisfield built a town that still calls itself "Crab Capital of the World." The town was literally built upon millions of oyster shells. An enormous wharf stretched along Somer's Cove, and the railroad depot stood nearby. Shuckers and packers set to work once the daily catch was landed; the cargo was shipped out on the railroad line; newly developed refrigeration techniques kept it fresh on its way deep into the nation's interior.

Like Crisfield, Solomons, Maryland, sprang from the oyster rush. Isaac Solomon came from Baltimore, taking his patented pasteurizing canning process to the tiny village, where he set up a successful packing plant.

From this gold mine grew greed, and the famed Chesapeake Oyster Wars ensued. The oystermen — the tongers and dredgers, known as "drudgers" — battled over rights to oyster beds; tempers ran high and shots were fired. Maryland authorities, already funding an Oyster Navy to maintain some measure of decorum on the Bay, were angered that Virginia was not so helpful when it came to keeping its watermen within their boundaries — whatever exactly they were.

The Oyster Wars proved to be the catalyst that finally forced Maryland and Virginia to define their disputed Bay border. Three years of negotiations at the

A cast-off waterman's deadrise begins its evolutionary return to the sea.

David Trozzo

federal bargaining table set the boundary, in 1877, about where it is today. The southern shore of the Potomac was always the boundary between the two states, but how far down that shore the river ended and the Bay began — from which point to draw the line east, across the Bay — was subject to dispute. The two states agreed to draw the line across Smith's Point to Watkins Point on the Eastern Shore's Pocomoke River. Today, the boundary has been further refined: Maryland extends to the low-tide line of the river on the Virginia shore. Present-day Virginians at Colonial Beach accept this arrangement with ingenuity, playing the lottery of their own state in town, and betting on their neighbor's jackpot at the end of a long pier — the same device they resorted to decades ago when gambling was legal in southern Maryland.

CHESAPEAKE TOURISM

The late 19th century brought the first tourists to the Bay, lured by clever investors who built the first resorts. Vacationers from Baltimore and Philadelphia turned to the Chesapeake, staying at new hotels built at Betterton and Tolchester on Maryland's Eastern Shore. On the Western Shore, Chesapeake Beach, just south of the Anne Arundel–Calvert County line, was carved from the shore by businessmen from the Pennsylvania Railroad. A new station built there gave easy access to people from Baltimore and Washington, DC.

Until about 1920, the Bay and tributaries were the region's highways. Ferries connected to railroad lines crisscrossed the network of water and land, and steamships were everywhere. Farming and fishing supported much of the rural Western and Eastern shores, in both Maryland and Virginia. Following World War II, the Chesapeake region mirrored the rest of the country, as industry and shipping propelled Baltimore and Norfolk into a new prosperity.

The automobile, too, fueled change, and by the mid-20th century the time had come to span the Bay by highway. On October 1, 1949, construction of the Chesapeake Bay Bridge began. Less than three years later, on July 30, 1952, the $112-million, 4.3-mile bridge opened.

Over the next thirty years, travelers "discovered" the Eastern Shore as never before. As far south as Salisbury, Maryland, towns saw growth; Talbot and Kent counties in particular became home to many retirees from the cities.

Meanwhile, in 1964, the other end of the Bay was spanned. The spectacular Chesapeake Bay Bridge-Tunnel was more than three years in the making, at $200 million. The 17.6-mile corridor includes two mile-long tunnels and 12 miles of trestled roadway that alternately soar above, then dive beneath the Bay. Four manmade islands serve as supports between bridge and road, as the bridge-tunnel spans the entryway through which early explorers first found the Chesapeake.

What is the future of the Bay area? Apparently, it depends on the self-control of those who live here, and of those within the watershed that spreads to upstate New York, whose debris ultimately trickles into the Bay.

Annapolis, with ties to Baltimore and Washington, DC, increasingly is caught in the region's web of urban growth, yet manages to maintain its colonial charm. The Bay area still retains its rural places. Along the Northern Neck of Virginia, there are only a couple of convenience stores. Across the Bay, on the Eastern Shore, the old shipbuilding ports of Oxford and St. Michaels have new lives as quiet, colonial-style villages for people who have opted to escape the city.

The first English settlers, Protestant and Catholic, brought diversity when they came to live among the Native Americans already here. So it is today, as city dwellers and those who fall in love with "the land of pleasant living" move in among the old families whose forebears long ago planted and fished along the Chesapeake Bay.

CHAPTER TWO

Of Ferries and Freeways
TRANSPORTATION

The history of Chesapeake transportation is intimately tied to its vast inland sea, plied in ancient days by dugout canoes; later, by indigenous sailing craft; and today, by massive steel cargo ships or yachts.

For centuries, the Susquehannock, Wicomico, and Nanticoke Indians had the Bay to themselves. Then came Spanish explorers and the 17th-century Englishmen who settled first at Jamestown, Virginia, in 1607. Soon after the vessels *Ark* and *Dove* landed at St. Marys City, in 1634, commerce drove the development of a ferry system across the Bay's hundreds of rivers and creeks.

Maryland State Archives

In the heyday of the Chesapeake steamboats, tourists cruised the Bay aboard such classic vessels as the Dreamland, *on their way to Chesapeake Beach, pictured here, and other resort towns.*

By the late 1600s, ferries crossed the South River south of present-day Annapolis to deposit traders at London Town who swapped furs for supplies. In 1683, what is claimed to be the oldest passenger ferry in North America was established, with a run between Oxford and Bellevue on Maryland's Eastern Shore. It still makes the crossing.

The *Chesapeake* was the first steamship to sail from Baltimore, in 1813, using the Patapsco River as a 19th-century highway connecting the boat's route to now-extinct Frenchtown, on the Elk River. Passengers could disembark and cross to the Delaware Bay by stagecoach, then re-board a sailing packet for Philadelphia.

Despite the *Chesapeake*'s historic role on the water, however, it was the Baltimore Steam Packet Co. — known more commonly, even lovingly, as the Old Bay Line — that is synonymous with Bay transportation. The venerable company was launched in 1839, and operated its wooden, then steel, paddlewheel boats and steamships into the 1960s.

Meanwhile, as settlers, then colonists, planters, and watermen traversed the Bay, the 184.5-mile Chesapeake and Ohio Canal was completed in 1850 and first connected the Bay to the nation's interior. The C&O Canal paralleled the non-navigable section of the Potomac River above Washington, which is in turn strategically linked to the Bay by the navigable waters of the lower Potomac. The canal took 20 years to build, but was never really successful. Just about the time it opened, the first rails were laid for the Baltimore and Ohio Railroad.

The B&O was the first railroad to connect Bay country to the outside, but others soon came. Working in tandem with packet and steamship lines, railroads dramatically opened up the area. Stations opened deep into the Eastern Shore, at places like Crisfield, which boomed from oyster exports in the late 1800s.

The 4.3-mile William Preston Lane Memorial Bridge, known locally as the Chesapeake Bay Bridge, frames a familiar seascape for Chesapeake anglers.

David Trozzo

Steamships and ferries, railroads, and small roads all provided transport well into this century. Until 1952, a ferry crossed the Bay near Annapolis where the 4.3-mile William Preston Lane Memorial Bridge — known locally as the Chesapeake Bay Bridge — now stands. A single span first connected the isolated Eastern Shore to the "outside" in 1952. Later, a second span was added. Travel to the Shore and to Atlantic beaches by tourists and city dwellers boomed, eventually outgrowing the bridge and roadway system. In 1991, a new bridge replaced an old drawbridge at Kent Narrows, just east of the Bay Bridge, greatly easing traffic flow over the busy Narrows.

Not long after the Upper Bay was opened to cars, a feat of engineering did the same at the mouth of the Bay. Where Vikings once may have sailed, the Chesapeake Bay Bridge-Tunnel now stands. The massive 17.6-mile span alternates bridge and tunnel across four manmade islands to Cape Charles from the Virginia mainland, and there's talk of expansion.

Travelers can reach the gateway cities to the Chesapeake — Washington, DC, Baltimore, and Norfolk–Hampton Roads — by air, bus, or train. Once here, you'll need to rent a car to explore the small towns and back roads of the largely rural and spread-out Chesapeake region. Mass transportation outside the cities is generally poor, although some connections can be made.

GETTING TO THE CHESAPEAKE BAY AREA

BY AIR

Five major airports serve the region — one in Baltimore, two in the Washington, DC, area, and two more in Norfolk—Hampton Roads. Most major airlines serve the region. Arrangements may best be made by contacting your local travel agent.

Maryland

Baltimore-Washington International Airport, better known as BWI, is 25 miles north of Annapolis, about a 30-minute drive. Less than 15 minutes from

David Trozzo

Baltimore-Washington International Airport is home base for much of the Chesapeake's air travel traffic.

CHESAPEAKE BAY AREA ACCESS

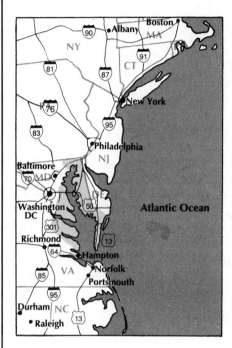

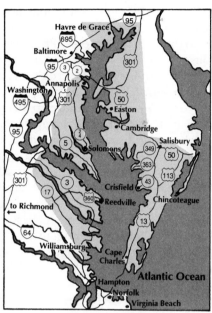

The approximate distances and driving times, at 50 MPH, from the following major cities to Annapolis are as follows:

CITY	MILES	HOURS
Atlanta	631	12.75
Boston	425	8.5
Chicago	706	14.0
Cincinnati	504	10.25
New York	216	4.5
Norfolk, Va.	204	4.25
Philadelphia	120	2.5
Pittsburgh	256	5.25
Richmond	133	2.5
Raleigh, N.C.	277	5.5

Baltimore's Inner Harbor, BWI is a major hub for *USAir*, but all major airlines fly in and out. For more information, contact BWI Airport at PO Box 8766, BWI Airport, MD 21240; 410-859-7111 (Baltimore area); 301-261-1000 or -1001 (Washington area); 1-800-435-9294.

A variety of shuttle and limousine services offer transport from the airport to cities and hotels nearby, including Annapolis. Also, cars for hire are available to the Eastern Shore — although travelers will pay a hefty price.

Buses to Baltimore operated by *Super Shuttle* (1-800-809-7080, 202-562-1234, 410-859-0803, 301-982-1234) run every half-hour, 6am to 11pm; $10 one-way or $15 round-trip. Shuttles to Annapolis run every two hours from 7am to 11pm; at $17 one-way, or $26 round-trip, per person.

Yellow Transportation Co. operates cars, shuttles, limos, and sedans out of the airport's ground transportation department, with access to downtown Washington, Baltimore, Annapolis, and points north of Baltimore, including Towson. Call for reservations, costs and schedules: 1-800-809-7080 or 202-562-1234 (Yellow operates through Super Shuttle). Travelers can also call *Private Car*, which can take you from BWI to any location. One to four passengers will pay $107 to go from the airport to Easton; 410-519-0000. Folks stopping over in Washington before heading to the Chesapeake leave BWI by shuttle bus, hourly from 5am to 12:30pm, for downtown hotels. Super Shuttle (see above) charges $19 one-way or $29 round-trip. Or, *Airport Connection* offers reasonably priced door-to-door service — generally $30 or less. 301-441-3108 or 1-800-284-6066 outside DC and Maryland.

Washington Metropolitan Area

Washington National Airport not only is convenient to Washington, but also connects to public transportation into Baltimore and Annapolis. Visitors will encounter heavy traffic on Friday afternoons, Sunday evenings, or Monday mornings, so plan accordingly. Most airlines fly in and out of this major airport. Write National Airport, Washington DC 20001, or call 703-419-8000.

Thirty miles west of Washington, in Chantilly, Virginia, is **Dulles International Airport**, often the airport of choice for international travelers. Write Dulles Airport, Chantilly VA 22021, or call 703-661-2700.

Many private cars and shuttles operate from the airport — check the Yellow Pages. A good choice is the *Washington Flyer*, "the official ground transportation of the Metropolitan Washington Airport Authority." It offers express bus service between both airports and Washington, and between the two airports. Also, it's also possible to get from Dulles to Annapolis and Baltimore by public transportation routes, since a few transportation systems link up. It sounds confusing but it's really not. Take the shuttle from Dulles to the West Falls Church Metro stop and catch the Orange Line. To reach Baltimore, transfer to the Red Line at the Metro Center, then switch at the Union Station stop to an Amtrak or MARC (Maryland Area Rail Commuter) train; they run frequently. To get to Annapolis, stay on the Orange Line to the far end, at New Carrollton's Amtrak-MARC station. It's about 20 miles west of Annapolis. Catch a bus to Annapolis. The bus is offered by Baltimore's Metropolitan Transit Authority. Schedules (clustered around rush hours) are available at 410-539-5000 (Mon.–Fri. 6am to 9pm).

Tidewater Virginia

Following a recent renovation, the former Patrick Henry International Airport in Newport News was renamed the **Newport News–Williamsburg International Airport.** Write 900 Bland Blvd., Newport News VA 23602, or call 804-877-0221. Transportation by shuttle, taxi, or limo from the airport is offered by *Williamsburg Limousine Service* to any location within Virginia. As always, prices vary. Call for reservations: 804-877-0279.

Norfolk International Airport is about a 30-minute drive from the Newport News airport in clear traffic; during rush hour, forget it (there's a tunnel under Hampton Roads involved). For information about the airport, write Norfolk VA 23518-5897 or call 804-857-3351 or 804-857-3200. To catch a ride from the airport, try the *Norfolk Airport Shuttle*, which offers transport to locations within about 60 miles of the city. Costs vary according to distance and the size of your party. For reservations and information: 804-857-1231.

FROM SMALL AIRPORTS

Charters, limited air shuttle service, and tie-downs are available at the following regional airports:

Bay Bridge Airport: Stevensville, Kent Island. Tie-downs and repairs (no charters or shuttles). 410-643-4364.

Easton Municipal Airport/Maryland Air and Jet Center: 410-822-0400.

Salisbury/Wicomico County Airport: Offers USAir Express shuttle service to Baltimore, Washington, Philadelphia, and Charlotte. USAir Express: 410-742-4190; airport: 410-548-4827. (Shuttle service to Charlotte is limited.)

Bowie Freeway Airport: 12 miles west of Annapolis. Hours are 8 to dark, daily (6 in winter, 8 in summer). Tie-downs and maintenance. 301-390-6424. Also offers airplane rides for tourists.

Lee Airport: Edgewater, Maryland, 2 miles south of Annapolis. Tie-downs, no charters. 410-956-2114.

BY AIRPORT RENTAL CAR

Since Baltimore's BWI and Washington's National Airport are only 35 miles apart, rental agencies usually allow cars rented at one airport to be returned to the other without extra charge. The policy tends to hold true between Dulles Airport and National or BWI, but we recommend checking with the individual companies to ensure they conform to this standard.

Expect to pay a large drop-off fee if renting in the Baltimore-Washington area and leaving via Norfolk or Newport News, if such an arrangement is allowed at all. Inquire with rental agents.

From BWI:

Alamo: 1-800-327-9633

Avis: 410-859-1680

Budget: 410-859-0850

Dollar: 410-684-3315

Hertz: 410-850-7400

National: 410-859-8860

From Dulles:

Avis: 703-661-3500

Bargain Buggies: 703-661-6780 (Less expensive used cars for folks who may not have abundant financial resources, including those under 25, who often have trouble renting cars.)

Budget: 703-437-9373

Thrifty: 703-471-4545 (for reservations, rates, etc.); 703-661-2100 (office in terminal)

From National:

Alamo: 703-684-0086

Budget: 703-419-1021

Dollar: 1-800-800-4000 (reservations); 703-519-8700 (office)

National: 202-783-1590

Thrifty: 703-838-6895

From Norfolk:

Avis: 804-855-1944

Alamo: 804-857-0754

Hertz: 804-857-1261

From Newport News/Williamsburg:

Avis: 804-877-0291

Budget: 804-874-5794

Enterprise: 804-782-9536

Hertz: 804-877-9229

National: 804-877-6486

Thrifty: 804-877-5745

Toll-Free Numbers:
Alamo: 1-800-327-9633
Avis: 1-800-331-1212
Dollar: 1-800-800-4000
Hertz: 1-800-654-3131
National: 1-800-227-7368
Thrifty: 1-800-367-2277
Budget: 1-800-437-4360

BY BUS

Those with either a slim wallet or a sense of adventure may want to reach the Bay area by bus — but be forewarned that service is extremely limited. Always call ahead. Greyhound offers toll-free schedule and fare information, often for local connecting lines as well as its own service, at 1-800-231-2222.

Maryland and Washington, DC

The Washington *Greyhound* terminal is at 1005 1st St. NE. To get from there to Annapolis, access the Washington Metro system at Union Station, ride the Red Line to Metro Center, and change to the Orange Line for New Carrollton, Maryland. Connect with a shuttle bus to Annapolis operated by the Baltimore Metropolitan Transit Authority. Schedules (clustered around rush hours) are available at 410-539-5000 (Mon.–Fri. 6am to 9pm). From Baltimore's bus station at 210 W. Fayette St., find *Trailways* connections to the Eastern Shore; call Greyhound for schedules and fares (1-800-231-2222; Baltimore, 410-752-0869; Washington, 202-289-5154).

To get around Annapolis, call the city's Dept. of Transportation, 410-263-7964, for schedule and fare information.

Local stations on the Eastern Shore with twice-a-day service by Trailways to and from Baltimore:

Cambridge: Sunburst Mobile, 2903 Ocean Gateway Dr., 410-228-4626
Salisbury: 350 Cypress St., 410-749-4121
Easton: Fast Stop Convenience, Rte. 50 & Cordova Rd., 410-822-3333

Virginia

For municipal service around Virginia's urban Tidewater, call:
Hampton–Newport News: Pentran, 804-723-3344.
Norfolk area: Tidewater Regional Transit, or TRT, 804-640-6200

Trailways takes three trips a day from Norfolk to Exmore, on Virginia's Eastern Shore, and back again. The bus stop is at Lloyd's Drug Store, 804-442-6267. Call Greyhound and Trailways in Norfolk, 804-627-7538; or Richmond, 804-254-5910.

BY CAR

From the North

From New York: South from the New Jersey Turnpike, cross the Delaware Memorial Bridge, then take I-95 to 896 S. toward Middletown, Delaware. Then pick up U.S. 301 south through the Upper Eastern Shore region. Head for Annapolis across the 4.3-mile-long William Preston Lane Memorial Bridge, or journey through the Shore region on Rte. 50 east.

Or, choose I-95 from Delaware. You're passing the head of the Chesapeake when you cross the Susquehanna River near Havre de Grace. (U.S. 40, a more congested road, parallels I-95 for most of the trip between the Maryland line and Baltimore.) Follow I-95 through the Baltimore Harbor Tunnel or the Fort McHenry Tunnel, or take I-695, the Baltimore Beltway, east and south to the Francis Scott Key Bridge over the Patapsco River. The bridge route takes about 20 minutes longer, but its high span provides a spectacular view of the city and its harbor, guarded by Fort McHenry in the fork of the river, to your right.

Either way, take the Beltway to I-97 for rapid access to Annapolis and points east and south.

From the Harrisburg, Pennsylvania, area: Take I-83, which crosses through rural Baltimore County to I-695, the Baltimore Beltway. Exit west on the Beltway and eventually you'll reach I-97, a direct connection to U.S. 50 just west of Annapolis.

From the West

From Pittsburgh: The Pennsylvania Turnpike connects with I-70 at Breezewood, Pennsylvania, which then drops south to Hancock, Maryland. This is your quickest route into the region. I-70 splits at Frederick, Maryland. For a scenic route to Frederick through rolling farmland, take Alternate U.S. 40. Just east of Frederick, the highway diverges. Reach Annapolis and the Eastern Shore by way of either Washington or Baltimore.

From Washington: The quickest way to Washington from the west is by I-270, but beware extended morning and evening rush hours along this bedroom community corridor. From I-270, take the Washington Beltway (I-495 E., becoming I-95 S.). Twenty miles after you leave I-270, look for John Hanson Highway, U.S. 50. Go east to Annapolis and, just beyond the city, reach the dual spans of the William Preston Lane Memorial Bridge, gateway to the Eastern Shore.

From Baltimore: Coming from the west, travel I-70 from Frederick to I-695, the Baltimore Beltway. For a slightly less hectic drive, take the exit for Rte. 40 E. just east of West Friendship to Md. 144, which cuts through the heart of Ellicott City, a restored mill and railroad town. Follow Rte. 40 E. to the Beltway.

To reach Annapolis, head south on the Beltway and follow signs for I-97. It's an easy alternative to the notoriously traffic-choked Washington Beltway.

Travel Tips for Drivers

Circumnavigating Washington, DC: Washington's famed **Capital Beltway** circles the city, but travelers will encounter other names for the highway. The eastern half of the elliptical roadway is known as I-95 N. and S. — even as it proceeds east and west. The western half is called I-495, and travelers headed clockwise will find the road referred to as W., N., and E. Locals refer to the clockwise route as the Beltway's "inner loop," while the counterclockwise route is the "outer loop."

Meanwhile, an anachronism rules the Beltway's southeastern corner — a drawbridge. The Woodrow Wilson Memorial Bridge across the Potomac, while offering a spectacular view of the river, opens only occasionally, but tired travelers weary of the highway may want to avoid the possibility.

Baltimore's Harbor Tunnel can get backed up, especially during rush hour — or the weekend rush to the Atlantic beaches. To bypass, take I-695 east to the Francis Scott Key Bridge. The trip is a bit longer, but the view is much better. And as long as we're talking summer weekends, consider crossing the William Preston Lane Memorial Bridge (aka the **Bay Bridge**) at Rte. 50 near Annapolis sometime other than a July Friday at 6pm, or an August Sunday right at 4.

From western Virginia, and Dulles Airport: Take I-66 east. The road connects with the Washington Beltway 7 miles east of Vienna, Virginia. Take the Beltway's inner loop north to I-95 to Baltimore; take the outer loop south to reach U.S. 50 and Annapolis. Rte. 50 E. crosses the Beltway just north of Cheverly, Maryland.

From the South

Coming north on I-95, which way you go depends on where in the area you're headed. To go directly to the Eastern Shore, pick up U.S. 13 in North Carolina to the Norfolk area, and follow the signs for the Chesapeake Bay Bridge-Tunnel (see "Getting Around the Chesapeake Area" below). Or continue on I-95 to Richmond, and take I-64 E. down the historic peninsula between the James and York rivers. At the end of the peninsula, the highway tunnels under the mouth of the James to Norfolk, where you can pick up the Bridge-Tunnel to the Eastern Shore.

If you're trying to get straight to the Annapolis area, take I-95 to I-495, the Washington Beltway. Go east to Rte. 50, then head east to Annapolis. Since the I-95/I-495 intersection often is traffic-choked, consider turning off I-95 30 miles north of Richmond, and follow Va. 207 northeast to Bowling Green. Here, pick up U.S. 301 N. Cross the Rappahannock River. You'll intersect with Va. Rte. 3, leading down the Northern Neck, between the Rappahannock and the Potomac. Bear right on U.S. 360 to Reedville on the Bay, or stay on 3 to Kilmarnock.

Or, back on Rte. 301, cross into Maryland over the only bridge downriver from Washington. Six miles later, Md. 234 E. connects to Md. 5 S. to Leonard-town and St. Marys City, from which you can wend your way up the Bay on Md. Rtes. 235, 4, and 2 past Solomons and Prince Frederick to Annapolis. For a more direct route, stay with U.S. 301, which merges with U.S. 50 E. 12 miles west of Annapolis. Expect a 20-mile stretch of heavy commercial development (and stop-and-go traffic) around Waldorf.

BY TRAIN

Amtrak renovated its classic Penn Station in Baltimore, at 1501 N. Charles St., as well as Union Station in Washington, DC. While waiting for your express *Metroliner* service to and from New York and other cities in the east, enjoy Union Station's elegant interior, with an array of shops, restaurants, and informal cafes.

Amtrak also operates a rail station at BWI Airport, a short ride from the ter-minal, on the line connecting Washington and Baltimore. For schedule and fare information, call 1-800-872-RAIL.

Direct access to the Chesapeake region, via Annapolis, is available during the work week from Amtrak's New Carrollton station, also part of the DC *Metro* system. Maryland's Mass Transit Administration subsidizes reliable and regular commuter shuttle bus service between New Carrollton and Annapolis. The last bus to Annapolis leaves New Carrollton at 7:50pm. A one-way trip costs $1. Call 1-800-543-9809 or 301-539-5000 for more information.

The Metro subway system, with a stop at Union Station, offers good service throughout Washington's Maryland and Virginia suburbs seven days a week. For information, call 202-637-7000, or 202-638-3780 (hearing-impaired).

GETTING AROUND THE CHESAPEAKE BAY AREA

We've organized the Chesapeake by five geographic regions. At the *Head of the Bay*, on either side of the Susquehanna River, travelers will find historic Havre de Grace and Chesapeake City. The region starts north of Aberdeen, circles the top of the Bay, and ends at the Sassafras River. On the western side of the Bay, we've designated the area south of the Magothy River to the Potomac and west to Rte. 301 as the *Annapolis/West-ern Shore* area. Virginia's *Northern Neck/Middle Peninsula* region is bor-dered by the Potomac and Rte. 301 to the north, Rte. 17 to the west, and the York River to the south. On the eastern side of the Bay, from the Sassafras River south to the Choptank and east to the Delaware line, visitors will be in the *Upper Eastern Shore* area. South of the Choptank to the tip of the Vir-ginia peninsula — with a side trip through Berlin to Assateague Island — is the *Lower Eastern Shore*.

Your best bet for getting around the Chesapeake area is by car — your own, or one you've rented on arrival. You can take the famous Chesapeake ferries at selected points around the Bay, but remember — they're a small-scale tradition not designed for bulk transport.

BY BUS

Visitors will find buses aren't a good option for getting around once you're at the Bay, but here are a few reminders (see also the section on buses in "Getting to the Chesapeake Bay Area" above).

Maryland

Greyhound offers two trips daily from Baltimore (410-752-1393) and one direct from Washington (202-289-5154) to Easton (Rte. 50 at Cordova Rd., 410-822-3333), Cambridge (501 Maryland Ave., 410-228-4626), and Salisbury (350 Cypress St., 410-749-4121).

The *Baltimore Metropolitan Transit Authority* offers express and local bus service between Baltimore and Annapolis. Call 410-539-5000 for schedule and fare information.

For fare and schedule information on public bus service around Annapolis, call the city's Dept. of Transportation, 410-263-7964.

Virginia

Trailways takes three trips a day from Norfolk to Exmore, on Virginia's shore, and back again. In Exmore the bus stops at Lloyd's Drug Store, 804-442-6267. The number for the Greyhound-Trailways terminal in Norfolk is 804-627-7538.

BY CAR

To ease confusion for roadtrippers: U.S. 301 runs north-south from the Potomac River to U.S. 50 at Bowie, Maryland, where it turns east with 50. The northbound road becomes Md. Rte. 3 to Baltimore. South of the Potomac toll bridge, Rte. 301 traverses Virginia's northern Tidewater area to Richmond. Wind southeast along intersecting Va. Rte. 3 or Rte. 17.

U.S. 50, meanwhile, heads east from Washington, picking up a Rte. 50/301 designation at Bowie. Soon after crossing onto the Eastern Shore, the road splits, and Rte. 50 heads south, providing one of the Shore's major north-south arteries, then east again after crossing the Choptank River at Cambridge. North of the split, Rte. 301 goes solo again past the far Upper Eastern Shore. U.S. 13 is the other major north-south highway on the Shore, running all the way up Virginia's Eastern Shore from the Bridge-Tunnel at Kiptopeke, through the middle of Maryland's Lower Shore, and up the Delmarva Peninsula through Delaware.

BY RENTAL CAR

A rrange your rentals before you get to the Northern Neck/Middle Peninsula (see airport rental cars information above). Elsewhere, if you didn't
pick up a car at the airport, try these local offices:

Annapolis/Western Shore

In Annapolis, **Budget**: 2002 West St.; 410-266-5030. **Enterprise**: 1023 Spa Rd.;
410-268-7751. Down in St. Mary's County in California, try **Hertz**: 7978 Three
Notch Rd.; 301-863-0033.

Upper Eastern Shore

At the Easton Airport, **Avis**: 410-822-5040; **Hertz**: Easton Airport; 410-822-1676.
In Trappe, Maryland, try **Old Reliable**: 4041 Ocean Gateway; 410-476-3055.

Lower Eastern Shore

At the Salisbury Airport, **Avis**: 410-742-8566 and **Hertz**: 410-749-2235. In
Pocomoke at 1727 Market St., **U-Save**: 410-957-1414.

Once you've got your wheels, make sure you have a good map. There are
several, including freebies offered by the states of Maryland and Virginia.
Some good bets:

Find the Maryland Dept. of Transportation's excellent state road map, as
well as a map of scenic roads. Call 410-333-6611 or write Maryland State Highway Administration, Map Distribution, 2323 W. Joppa Rd., Brooklandville MD
21022. Virginia's Dept. of Transportation also offers a terrific state map. Call
804-786-2801 or write VDOT Admin. Services Div., 1401 E. Broad St., Richmond VA 23219. For a map of Scenic Roads of Virginia, call 1-800-828-1120.

The Alexandria Drafting Co., aka ADC Maps, sells excellent maps to the
area, available at local convenience stores. Look for their road map of the
Chesapeake region. Order from ADC at 1-800-232-6277 with a credit card, or
with a check to 6440 General Green Way, Alexandria VA 22312.

The ever-helpful American Automobile Association operates throughout the
region, offering emergency service and TripTiks, their famous route recommendations, to members. For Chesapeake region information, call the AAA
Maryland membership offices: 410-821-1458. For emergency roadside help, call
1-800-AAA-HELP. For Triptiks, call 410-631-8748.

AAA Potomac serves the Washington, DC, area. To join, call 703-222-4200.
Emergency service is 703-222-6000. For TripTiks, call 1-800-631-8747 or 410-
821-1458.

For the Tidewater AAA, call 804-622-5634 for membership and TripTiks,
and 804-622-4321 for road service.

BY FERRY

T he 300-year old ferryboat tradition remains in this region of snaking rivers,
creeks, and the you-can't-get-there-from-here roadways that support the

prevailing Bay-influenced terrain. Check your maps for exact locations of these fun, charming ferries for the slow-going, moseying motorist.

Northern Neck/Middle Peninsula

Two small free ferries operate in Virginia's Northern Neck. Near Smith Point at the mouth of the Potomac in Northumberland County, the *Sunnybank Ferry* crosses the Little Wicomico River at Ophelia, Mon.—Sat., year-round. Farther south, in Lancaster County, the *Merry Point Ferry* offers trips across the Corrotoman River.

Upper Eastern Shore

Ready for business at the Oxford crossing, at the Oxford-Bellevue ferry in the early 20th century.

Maryland State Archives

The classic *Oxford-Bellevue Ferry* is the oldest continuously operating private ferry in the country, launched on Nov. 20, 1683. The ferry's longevity can be partially explained by its strategic location. Two of Talbot County's most popular towns, St. Michaels and Oxford, aren't far apart as the crow flies, but they are as the car drives; hence, the ferry (410-745-9023).

Lower Eastern Shore

Tiny *Whitehaven Ferry* crosses the scenic Wicomico River about 18 miles southwest of Salisbury on Rte. 352. Free. Year-round: 6am–7:30pm summer; 7am–5:30pm winter. 410-873-2862.

Several ferries also operate out of Crisfield to Smith and Tangier islands. Check full listings in Chapter Six, *Recreation*, under "Cruises and Excursion Boats." But for year-round service to Smith Island (and this is for adventurers only — tourist amenities are next to nil) contact the *Captain Jason*, at 410-425-4471 or 410-425-5931. Off-season service from the mainland to Tangier Island also is offered sometimes aboard *Steven Thomas*, 410-968-2338.

CHAPTER THREE

Bed & Breakfast & Boat

LODGING

Chesapeake visitors easily discover all range of accommodations, from upscale waterside resorts offering amenities of the good life, to high Victorian inns serving afternoon tea, to small bed and breakfasts operating about like your own home.

Maryland State Archives

Turn-of-the-century vacationers enjoyed the view of the Bay from the spacious porch of "Hotel Love Point" on Kent Island.

Longtime B&B visitors know these unique lodgings are as different as their owners. Some are cute and cozy; others, elegant and highbrow. Some owners are at your disposal; others cook your breakfast, point you toward attractions, then head for a day at work. Decide what you'd like, then keep these considerations in mind when making reservations. Also, be sure to ask about two-night minimum stays. Some hosts require these during high-traffic times, like the October week of boat shows in Annapolis.

Handicapped visitors may already know that many historic accommodations are not well suited to their needs — but some are. Always ask. Also, during our inspections of accommodations, we found that many rooms that push a lodging into the "very expensive" designation tend to be suites, often large enough for at least four people with reasonable add-on prices for more than two guests. After doing the math, you may find they are a very comfortable, economical option for your travel plans.

Most B&Bs require reservations, although a few take walk-ins.

Since the Bay is best visited by automobile, visitors might want to save some money by alternating nights in lodgings with a few nights of camping. See Chapter Six, *Recreation*, for some of the good campsites located in the region's many parks; herein, we offer commercial options.

LODGING NOTES

INFORMATION

Reputable B&B inspection services hold their clients to a high level of service and cleanliness, and can match visitors to B&Bs that suit their tastes. They also can direct folks to very nice, smaller B&B operations not listed here, or newer accommodations, including the occasional boat-and-breakfast operation. Among good services familiar with the region:

Bed & Breakfast of Maryland/Traveller Inn Maryland, Inc. (410-269-6232; fax 410-263-4841; e-mail banb@aol.com) Operated by Annapolis-based B&B owners Greg Page and Robert Zuchelli, who inspect the homes they recommend. 9–5 Mon.–Fri.; 10–3 Sat. PO Box 2277, Annapolis MD 21404-2277.

Amanda's B&B Reservation Service (410-225-0001, 1-800-899-7533) Named for the *Amanda*, a Baltimore ship known for cleanliness, this service handles reservations throughout the mid-Atlantic region. All accommodations inspected. Charges made for cancellations. 1428 Park Ave., Baltimore MD 21217.

RATES

Rates can vary widely according to season. We offer here a rating system generally based on high season — late spring into fall — before taxes. When making reservations, ask about discounts available for senior citizens, business travelers and the like, as well as per-person charges added if a third or fourth person stays in the room or suite.

Inexpensive:	Up to $55
Moderate:	$56 to $85
Expensive:	$86 to $125
Very Expensive:	$126 and above

Credit cards are abbreviated as follows: AE, American Express; CB, Carte Blanch; D, Discover; DC, Diners Club; MC, MasterCard; V, Visa.

INNS AND BED-&-BREAKFAST LODGINGS

HEAD OF THE BAY

Chesapeake City

INN AT THE CANAL
Owners: Mary & Al
   Ioppolo.
410-885-5995.
104 Bohemia Ave./PO Box
   187, Chesapeake City
   MD 21915-0187.
Price: Moderate to Very
   Expensive.
Credit Cards: AE, CB, D,
   DC, MC, V.
Handicap Access: No.

One of the few inns you can reach by water, this 1870 B&B adjoins the anchorage basin in the center of Chesapeake City's historic district. Built by Henry Brady, whose family mules pulled boats through the canal in its early days, the house was a gift to his wife. It retains its original hand-painted ceilings and fine woodwork, and has been nicely furnished with antiques. Six bedrooms and a suite, all with private baths, individual climate control, TV, and good reading lights. Attractive gardens; three rooms overlook the water.

Havre de Grace

**SPENCER-SILVER
MANSION**
Owners: Carol & James
   Nemeth.
410-939-1485.
200 S. Union Ave., Havre
   de Grace MD 21078.
Price: Moderate to Expensive.
Credit Cards: AE, MC, V;
   personal checks
   accepted.
No: Smoking, pets.
Handicap Access: Partial,
   in carriage house.

Carol Nemeth outdid herself when she decorated her stone Victorian, with its high-ceilinged rooms elaborately wallpapered with stunning borders to match. Four gables, a two-story bay window, a tower, and a variety of window shapes offer plenty of opportunities for creativity. Originally built in 1896 for Havre de Grace merchant John Spencer, the house has a slate roof, except out on the veranda, where it's copper. The Nemeths have completely renovated the mansion during their years of ownership, and acquired the stone, two-story former carriage house out back and filled it with antique oak furnishings, a spiral staircase, and a whirlpool bath. Two rooms share a bath; two rooms have their own. Look for lots of architecturally interesting details, such as the fireplace mantels. Full breakfast, great gardens, turndown services.

VANDIVER INN
Innkeepers: Sarah & Robert
   Scardina.
410-939-5200, 1-800-245-
   1655.
301 S. Union Ave., Havre
   de Grace MD 21078.
Price: Moderate to Expensive.

Vivid green tones blanket the outside of this Queen Anne cottage B&B, but the fabulous façade. is nothing compared to what's inside. Ring the doorbell, stand back, and prepare for this century-old treasure, built by a Havre de Grace mayor, Murray Vandiver. Five multi-flued chimneys perform such architectural tricks as splitting above a

Credit Cards: AE, MC, V.
Handicap Access: Partial.

fabulous tiled fireplace framing a stained-glass panel over the mantel. Eight rooms filled with period antiques all have private baths (expect claw-foot tubs); six have fireplaces. Smoking is allowed in rooms but not in common areas. Downstairs, the inn serves dinner on Friday and Saturday nights.

ANNAPOLIS/WESTERN SHORE

B&B owners in the crowded historic district of Annapolis, where parking is notoriously difficult, have worked out a deal with the city. Guests of B&Bs belonging to the Annapolis Association of Licensed Bed & Breakfast owners can park in city-operated parking garages for $4 for 24 hours. Be aware that you cannot come and go during that period without re-paying.

Annapolis

AMERICAN HERITAGE B&B
Owners: Adria & Bob Smith.
410-280-1620.
108 Charles St., Annapolis MD 21401.
Price: Expensive.
Credit Cards: No.
No: Smoking, pets, children.
Handicap Access: No.

This little back street townhouse emphasizes the red, white, and blue — with family military memorabilia, too. The blue and white room, with a nice half-canopy bed, offers an attached bath. The B&B's second room, with pink-floral-canopied bed, supplies terry robes for a quick trip down the hall to the bath. Upstairs is a TV room. A full breakfast is presented, as is tea in the afternoon. There are many delightful guest-oriented details, like decks of cards tucked in dresser drawers, and Adria is a massage therapist who offers therapeutic massage by appointment.

ANNAPOLIS MAR-RIOTT WATERFRONT
General Manager: Colleen Huther.
410-268-7555, 1-800-336-0072.
80 Compromise St., Annapolis MD 21401.
Price: Expensive to Very Expensive.
Credit Cards: AE, CB, D, MC, V.
Handicap Access: Two "city view" rooms, both smoking.

This hotel offers an Annapolis commodity: waterside rooms. Rooms are fairly standard — usually double queen-size beds and a sitting area — but come with niceties like irons and cable TV in each room. Amenities include valet parking (for a fee), boating activities at the wharf, and a fine location for a cold one at Pusser's Landing, a bar right on the waters of Ego Alley, so named for the parade of boaters showing off their craft — or is it their physiques? Room rates are based on full or partial water view, so be sure to specify when making reservations. Suites, king-size beds, a small on-site fitness room, concierge service.

ARK AND DOVE

Owners: Susan Liedlich &
  Sandra Huffer.
410-268-6277.
149 Prince George St.,
  Annapolis MD 21401.
Price: Moderate to Expen-
  sive.
Credit Cards: MC, V.
No: Smoking, pets, children
  under 12.
Handicap Access: No.

Guests sign up for one of two breakfast seatings at this 1820s-vintage B&B backing City Dock's popular Middleton Tavern, where simplicity and practicality carry through the attractive decor. Look for wing chairs in the rooms, and antique or reproduction beds; one room has twins. A second-story suite has a queen-size bed with a lace canopy, a clawfoot tub, and a sitting room. Bath baskets with amenities are a nice touch in the three third-floor rooms that share a bath. Oriental-style runners decorate the pine floors. Reduced rates are offered during the week, when breakfast is not served in this three-story townhouse, operated as a B&B since 1988.

CHESAPEAKE BAY
LIGHTHOUSE B&B

Owners: Janice & Bill
  Costello.
410-757-0248.
1423 Sharps Point Rd.,
  Annapolis MD 21401.
Price: Expensive.
Credit Cards: AE, MC, V.
No: indoor smoking, pets.
Handicap Access: No.

Bill Costello started out building a two-car garage, but ended up creating a unique B&B now highlighted on Bay navigational charts. Definitely not your everyday lodging, this working, Chesapeake-style screw-pile light shines across the Bay at night, and was built based on plans for the famed Thomas Point Light just a few miles down the coast. Guests stay in rooms decorated simply and attractively with colonial-style furniture. The suite offers a private entrance and table and chairs, and a terrific view of the water. A continental breakfast of cereal and such is served. Sweeping, waterside location with dock.

CHEZ AMIS

Owners: Don & Mickie
  Deline.
410-263-6631, 1-800-474-
  6631.
85 East St., Annapolis MD
  21401.
Price: Moderate to Expen-
  sive.
Credit Cards: MC, V .
No: Indoor smoking, pets,
  children under 10.
Handicap Access: No.

Mickie Deline keeps the cellular phone in the pocket of her dusty-rose "Chez Amis" apron, a good sign for those seeking attentive, on-site hosts. This former corner store with four theme rooms is cute and cozy, with such guest-friendly details as the big bowl of peanuts parked on the sitting room table.

Two bedrooms share a nice bath with a lace curtain surrounding a shower-rigged clawfoot tub. The Capital Room salutes both the Maryland Statehouse visible out the window, and the nation's capital, where Mickie was once a tour guide (husband Don was a long-time Army lawyer). Or, choose a red, white, and blue boat-themed room; "the judge's chambers" replete with law books as decoration and its own bath; and a big suite downstairs with trundle beds and prints (and a chunk of the Berlin Wall) picked up during the Delines' overseas travels. Walk-in guests accepted. Full breakfasts. A very comfy place.

THE CORNER CUP-BOARD INN
Owners: Lise & Vic DeLeon.
410-263-4970.
30 Randall St., Annapolis MD 21401.
Price: Moderate to Expensive.
Credit Cards: No; personal checks accepted.
No: Smoking indoors, pets, young children.
Handicap Access: No.

Around the corner from City Dock, the little handpainted sign on the side of this mid-19th century townhouse first signals this inn's comfortable homeyness. Two nicely furnished upstairs rooms and baths are wallpapered or sponge-painted; televisions are hidden in either a cabinet or closet. One room features a matching antique carved oak bed and bureau; the other, a white–eyelet and pink Victorian-style loveseat. The DeLeons are happy to accommodate whatever guests want. They've even invited West Coast folks to their first crab feast in the family backyard.

THE DOLL'S HOUSE BED & BREAKFAST
Owners: Barbara & John Dugan.
410-626-2028.
161 Green St., Annapolis MD 21401.
Price: Moderate to Expensive.
Credit Cards: No.
No: Smoking, pets.
Handicap Access: No.

This tiger-oak-trimmed Victorian, one of the city's longtime B&Bs, recently changed hands and transformed itself into doll devotee heaven. Collector Barbara Dugan displays her favorites throughout the house. Guests are welcome to enjoy them, but this may not be the best option for the frat crowd.

Great fun is the Victoria Room, featuring the queen herself in several bureau-top versions and a print on the wall. A queen-size bed stands amid the soft pink room; next door, yellow walls, wicker furniture, and bright sunflowers on the quilt take over this breezy room. The two rooms share a bath (terry robes available), although arrangements can be made for a private bath. Upstairs is the ultra-eaved Nutcracker Suite, with two double beds in a great big bedroom and a pull-out couch in the sitting room. The comfortable sitting room with TV, and a big bath with its long clawfoot tub and stall shower make this a nice option for families with older children. Full breakfast.

FLAG HOUSE INN
Owners: Connie & Tom Tegen.
410-280-2721 (call before 9pm); 1-800-437-4825 (reservations only).
26 Randall St., Annapolis MD 21401.

This straightforward, no-muss, no-fuss B&B amid the bustle of City Dock and the Naval Academy's main gate is run almost like an inn. Quilts on king-size beds, small cable TVs, and baths in all five rooms allow visitors to the mansard-roofed Victorian to live life as they might

Price: Expensive to Very
Expensive.
Credit Cards: MC, V; prefer
personal checks.
No: Smoking, pets, children
under 12.
Handicap Access: No.

in a hotel — but they are more likely to find themselves chatting with other guests around the breakfast table long after the last muffin is gone. Some rooms have cleverly conceived split bathrooms built around the house's main fireplace, with sink and toilet on one side, and shower on the other. One big two-room suite offers plenty of space for four people. This is a retirement business for the Tegens, who moved into one side of the townhouse, then bought the rental on the other side and expanded. Your hosts, who fly the state or national flags of all their guests, can direct you to nearby attractions, or you can seat yourself on the front porch and watch Annapolis go by. Off-street parking.

Gibson's Lodgings is just around the corner from the City Dock action.

David Trozzo

GIBSON'S LODGINGS
Innkeepers: Claude &
Jeanne Schrift.
410-268-5555.
110 Prince George St.,
Annapolis MD 21401.
Price: Moderate to Expensive.
Credit Cards: MC, V.
No: Smoking, pets.
Handicap Access: One
room.

In the revolving-door world of small tourist accommodations, Gibson's endures. Three buildings at the foot of Prince George Street comprise this inn, around the corner from the thick of the City Dock action. In the parlor downstairs at the three-story **Patterson House**, a white marble fireplace stands across from the Victorian couch. Bedrooms are all different, each with its own touch, such as an antique marble-topped bureau or a walnut bed; botanical prints and floral wallpaper are also featured. A huge mirror frames one end of the formal Chippendale dining room, where a continental breakfast is served every day. Next door is the less formal **Berman House,** which includes a handicapped-accessible room. The newer **Lauer House** features modern amenities and dining and conference areas. Between the three houses is a patio, where breakfast is served on summer mornings. Twenty rooms; off-street parking.

HARBORVIEW BOAT AND BREAKFAST
Owners: Mary Anne & Jeff Stevenson.
410-268-9330, 1-800-877-9330.
980 Awald Dr., Annapolis MD 21403.
Price: Expensive to Very Expensive.
Credit Cards: AE, MC, V.
No: Pets, cooking onboard, smoking in the cabins.

Reach out of your cabin for your day's first cup of coffee, delivered to you in a Thermos and accompanied by fresh croissants when you spend the night in one of Harborview's charter boats. Available boats range from 34 to 50 feet, both sail and power, all with double or queen-size beds and actual bathrooms, and some very luxurious. Boats may even come equipped with TVs, but you'll want to sit out above decks on nice nights. This is the city's most recognized boat-and-breakfast operation, which also offers guests a 3-hour captained sail for an additional cost.

HISTORIC INNS OF ANNAPOLIS
General Manager: Russ Finch
410-263-2641, 1-800-847-8882, fax 410-268-3813.
58 Church Cir., Annapolis MD 21401.
Price: Expensive to Very Expensive.
Credit Cards: AE, DC, MC, V.
No: Pets.
Smoking and non-smoking rooms available.
Handicap Access: Yes, at Calvert & Johnson houses.

This venerable group of four historic district inns has undergone management/ownership shake-ups in recent years, but area director Sharon Fontana offers quality assurances on behalf of the current owners, Remington Hotels. They're new to the historic hotel arena, says Fontana. They've also retained much of the long-term staff.

New curtains are going up and new carpet is going down in the terrific old hotels, led by the flagship **Maryland Inn**. The familiar black-and-white marble lobby, with its crystal chandelier and authentic blue wainscoting, welcomes guests to the 200-year-old inn. Historians guess that many of the Treaty of Paris signers known to have spent time in Revolution-era Annapolis stayed at the Maryland Inn, opened by merchant Thomas Hyde.

Guests will find rooftop views of the city to the harbor, prints hanging on the walls, or marble-topped bureaus in the rooms — all of which are different. The bathrooms are small, and window units cool the rooms. Downstairs is the King of France Tavern, home to noted jazz guitarist Charlie Byrd (see Chapter Four, *Culture*), and the gourmet Treaty of Paris Restaurant (see Chapter Five, *Restaurants*). On adjacent State Circle stands the renovated former home of two Maryland governors, the **Governor Calvert House.** A modern atrium and conference area has been added to the back of the former brick home. (There's even an underground parking garage, a real feat of modern engineering around these narrow streets.) There are also find nine historic, antiques-filled rooms, with wide windows, four-poster beds, TVs ensconced in armoires, and modern baths. One well-appointed, romantic bedroom also has a whirlpool.

Historic Inns also operates the **Robert Johnson House** on State Circle, with a townhouse suite with a four-poster bed and living area downstairs. **The State House Inn** dates from 1820. Guests of the latter two hostelries check in at the Gov. Calvert House, which brings us to a logistical point: guests sometimes are confused about just how to navigate this unique, four-inn operation on two circles. Be sure to specify if you want to stay in a particular lodging (the Maryland Inn is often a sentimental favorite). In all, there are 133 suites and rooms; along with cots, cribs, pull-out couches, valet parking, access to fitness facilities, and all the fine amenities one might expect.

JONAS GREEN HOUSE
Owners: Randy & Dede
  Brown.
410-263-5892.
124 Charles St., Annapolis
  MD 21401.
Price: Moderate to Expensive.
Credit Cards: AE, MC, V.
No: Smoking.
Pets and children allowed
  with prior notice.
Handicap Access: No.

Stand in the 19th-century dining room and look back through the 18th-century hallway that connects to the 17th-century kitchen: this house is the genuine article for visitors seeking colonial accommodations. Widely considered one of the two oldest homes in Annapolis, the Jonas Green house is operated by its namesake's great-great-great-great-great grandson and wife. Green himself was the colony's printer, taught the trade by cousin Ben Franklin. The current owners renovated the old house in the early 1990s, and can offer complete tours to architecture buffs.

The home's decor is carefully reproduced, with white walls and colonial wainscoting. Three rooms offer antique beds with modern, custom-made mattresses and spare, period accents — like a spinning wheel in one room. There are pine floors, and fireplaces in each room. Extended continental breakfasts in the morning. Easygoing, uncluttered atmosphere; off-street parking.

**LOEWS ANNAPOLIS
  HOTEL**
General Manager: Tom
  Negri.
410-263-7777.
126 West St., Annapolis
  MD 21401.
Price: Expensive to Very
  Expensive.
Credit Cards: AE, V, MC.
Pets allowed.
Handicap Access: Yes.

Considered one of the city's finest hotels, Loews provides all the amenities in a brick courtyard-style hotel in Annapolis's former bus station. In all, 217 guest rooms and suites offer irons and ironing boards, hairdryers, remote TVs, and coffee makers in all the rooms; queen or king-size beds. Deluxe accommodations include wet bars, love seats, and access to the living room-style concierge lounge's big TV and microwave. Smoking rooms are available, and some suites offer balconies. For a low fee, guests have access to two nearby pools and a fitness center; a small fitness room is on-site. Children's activities are also provided. The Weather Rail Lounge and the acclaimed Corinthian Restaurant offer plenty of dining options. Valet parking. It may be safest to take the hotel's complimentary van into the nearby historic district at night. Ideal for visitors seeking straightforward luxury.

MAGNOLIA HOUSE
Owners: John & Mary
  Prehn.
410-268-3477.
220 King George St.,
  Annapolis MD 21401.
Price: Moderate.
No: Credit cards, pets.
Handicap Access: Yes, after
  4 steps into house.

Retired Navy captain John Prehn and his wife Mary raised five children in their King George Street home and, when the kids left, there was plenty of unused space. Their B&B, operating for years now, may be the best place in town to take your own kids. A third-floor suite sleeps six. On the second floor, look for the comfortable Peacock Room and Fireside Room, with shelves of good reading. Breakfast is served in the chandelier-lit dining room during winter, and in the townhouse garden by the magnolia come summer. Nearly 60 years old, the house is partially built from bricks from the former McCubben house on Main Street, circa 1740 and long gone. Moderate per-person costs added if families need the trundle beds.

PRINCE GEORGE INN
  B&B
Owners: Bill & Norma
  Grovermann.
410-263-6418.
232 Prince George St.,
  Annapolis MD 21401.
Price: Moderate to Expen-
  sive, depending on day
  of week.
Credit Cards: MC, V.
No: Pets, smoking, children
  under 12.
Handicap Access: No.

Of all the B&Bs that promote themselves as "antiques-filled," this one cannot be accused of exaggeration. In the warm, russet parlor of this high Victorian hostelry are tall ship models under glass — and guests will also enjoy other pieces acquired during the Grovermann's travels. The city's oldest B&B, operating since 1983, the Prince George is almost self-serve. A buffet breakfast is spread out in a side sun room, where canisters of granola or bowls of fruit march down a counter toward the patio breakfast room. In warmer weather, enjoy the garden. Two third-floor rooms share a bath; terry robes are provided. Two others have their own. The rooms are different; one, for example, offers an Arabian motif, complete with a lit wood carving of a mosque-dominated skyline and a brass bed. Then there's the room with a big heavy bed that once belonged to a Marine general who lived over on Cornhill Street. Visually, the Prince George Inn is endlessly interesting — like the moment the second-floor guest looks up to find a cherub beaming down from atop the shower. I like little surprises, says Norma, but that does not include broken antique vases. Not a good place for young children.

REYNOLD'S TAVERN
Owners: Ramsay & Sandy
  Stallman.
410-626-0380.
7 Church Cir./PO Box 748,
  Annapolis MD 21404.
Credit Cards: AE, MC, V.
Price: Expensive to Very
  Expensive.
Handicap Access: No.

Three big suites above this 1747 fine-dining restaurant and tavern offer great views from venerable windows. Restored several years ago when it was still part of the Historic Inns of Annapolis, Reynold's offers one single room with a modern bath, and spacious two-room suites. Accommodations feature antique beds, sitting rooms, fireplaces, colonial wainscoting, and wardrobes (since the tavern was built back when they taxed closets as rooms). Ask to see the fireplace in the conference room, with its colonial-era drawings protected museum-fashion by the Smithsonian Institution itself. Continental breakfasts; parking is included in the price.

**THE WILLIAM PAGE
  INN**
Owners: Robert Zuchelli &
  Greg Page.
410-626-1506, 1-800-364-
  4160.
8 Martin St., Annapolis MD
  21401.
Price: Moderate to Very
  Expensive.
Credit Cards: MC, V.
No: Pets or indoor smok-
  ing.
Handicap Access: No.

Among the city's most dependable accommodations, with knowledgeable on-site hosts, off-street parking, and fresh flowers in each room. Five rooms include the Marilyn Suite, which comprises the top floor and boasts a big sitting area and TV. Two rooms share a bath (terry robes supplied), and two others have their own, including one with a whirlpool bath. While reproductions and antiques add flavor to the turn-of-the-century cedar-shingled home, they don't clutter. Full breakfasts are offered. Your hosts know how to run a classy inn, providing luxury and privacy without a fuss.

Solomons

BACK CREEK INN B&B
Hosts: Carol Pennock & Lin
  Cochran.
410-326-2022.
210 Alexander St. at
  Calvert St./PO Box 520,
  Solomons MD 20688.
Price: Inexpensive to
  Very Expensive.
No: Credit cards, pets,
  smoking.
Deepwater boat slips
  available.
Handicap Access: Partial.

The gardens may be the first thing visitors arriving at this waterside inn in Solomons will notice. There's even a goldfish pond, filled by a small stone waterfall. Inside sliding glass doors is a very comfortable common room, with stereo, TV, and the daily newspaper. The pastel rooms are named for herbs, and the beds are covered with quilts. You'll also find wicker furniture accents. There are a variety of accommodations to choose from among the seven rooms, all with private baths. The stairways and hallways in the 100-year-old section of the former waterman's house tend to slope authentically — certainly no detraction from this comfortable, well-run inn. A full breakfast is

Back Creek Inn B&B in Solomons, a civilized retreat for cruisers who want to dock out back, and have some "land time."

David Trozzo

served. There is also a bungalow built in 1990. Perhaps best of all are the wonderful waterside lawn and dock, with accompanying deep water where a yachtsperson in need of a shower and a bed can appreciatively anchor.

BY-THE-BAY B&B
Hosts: Joan & Tom Hogenson.
410-326-3428.
14374 Calvert St./PO Box 504, Solomons MD 20688.
Price: Moderate to Expensive.
No: Credit cards, children.
Deepwater boat slips available.
Handicap Access: No.

Stencils decorate the walls and hardwood gleams on the floors, while an authentic, five-color Victorian paint job now covers the three-room B&B's façade. There's a downstairs suite, too. A separate refrigerator is available for guests, and a comfortable living room. Also provided are TVs in the rooms, private baths, and a full breakfast with fruit and eggs. At the little boathouse out back, guests can pick crabs and watch the boats go by, or dock if arriving via water. Also relaxing: the fine rope hammock, hanging right next to Solomons' Back Creek.

NORTHERN NECK/MIDDLE PENINSULA

Irvington, Virginia

THE TIDES INN
Owners: The Stephens family.
804-438-5000, 1-800-TIDES-INN.
King Carter Dr./Box 480, Irvington VA 22480.
Price: Expensive to Very Expensive.

One of Virginia's time-honored resorts, where the staff-to-guest ratio is an impressive 1:1. The typical per-person cost may seems pricey at first, but it covers all of the hotel's amenities, including breakfast and dinner — and children can stay free in their parents' room. Swim in the old tiled saltwater pool on the banks of Carter's Creek,

Enjoying the water is easy at the Tides Inn — the resort offers boating, swimming, and sunning along scenic Carter's Creek and the Rappahannock River.

Jean Harper

Credit Cards: AE, D, MC, V.
Closed: New Year's to late Mar.
Pets: Yes.
Handicap Access: Yes.

or send the kids to children's activities or the playground. Room service, lunch aboard the *Miss Ann*, — the tariff covers it all. The 1947 hotel stands amid the newer Windsor and Lancaster houses, where accommodations come with private dressing rooms, sunken tubs, balconies, or living rooms. All 110 rooms have private baths and A/C — and three-fourths of them in each building overlook Carter's Creek. For recreation, there's a 20-slip marina, tennis, boats, and a championship golf course; visitors also have golfing rights at the inn's cousin resort, the Tides Lodge, only a couple of miles away. Dining room dress is informal during the day, but the ladies and gentlemen who repair to the gourmet restaurant for dinner dress in evening wear (see Chapter Five, *Restaurants*). All in all, relaxed but gentrified Tidewater style.

Lancaster, Virginia

THE INN AT LEVELFIELDS
Hosts: Doris & Warren Sadler.
804-435-6887, 1-800-238-5578.
Rte. 3/PO Box 216, Lancaster VA 22503.
Price: Moderate.
Credit Cards: AE, MC, V.
No: smoking inside, pets, children under 12.
Handicap Access: No.

Something about this gracious old place recalls the sultry antebellum south. Maybe it's the boxwood hedge lining the front walk, or a stroll up wide front steps curled oh-so-slightly from 150 years of humidity. Maybe it's your hosts, gracious as their pre-Civil War home. Whatever it is, we see this inn as the ultimate depiction of a time past in time present — in a region that recalls Chesapeake Tidewater the way it used to be. Built in 1857 by a Baptist preacher and lawyer, the house replaced a 1680s version because the good pastor's family was too big for the old place. Civil War troops encamped here, but modern guests can thank 20th-century owners for building bathrooms into each of four rooms that boast a rarity — 7-foot-tall shower heads. Decor is Williamsburg-esque with deep cornflower blues and roses accenting the wainscoting, although, as Doris says, "we jazzed it up a little." Guests get their own pressed wood logs to burn in their fireplaces. The four rooms offer individual color schemes, ceiling fans, sherry decanters, and king- or queen-size beds; one also has an outdoor porch. Eggs benedict or fancy French toast is served in the downstairs, Chippendale-furnished parlor, which was a restaurant until recently. The pool out back is on the site of the former slave quarters. "Stepping back in time" is an overworn tourist-trade slogan, but you'll really find it here.

Mollusk, Virginia

THE GUESTHOUSE ON THE WATER AT GREENVALE
Hosts: Pam & Walt Smith.
804-462-5995.
Rte. 354/Box 70, Mollusk VA 22517.
Price: Expensive to Very Expensive.
Reservations: Yes.
Credit Cards: MC, V.
Handicap Access: No.

A circa-1960s caretaker's cottage offers simple accommodations on 13 waterfront acres along the Rappahannock River, with a small beach, bikes, and a not-quite-kidney-shaped pool. There are two comfortable bedrooms, two baths, galley kitchen (coffee, tea, and orange juice in the fridge), and the occasional bald eagle overhead. This is a real find for folks in search of peace and quiet. Two-night minimum on non-winter weekend.

Reedville, Virginia

CEDAR GROVE
Hosts: Susan & Bob Tipton.
Rte. 1/Box 2535, Reedville VA 22539.
804-453-3915.
Price: Moderate to Expensive.
Credit Cards: No; personal checks accepted.
Handicap Access: No.

Three miles around the point from Reedville, Cedar Grove offers a rare Bay-side B&B. Two guest rooms and one suite replete with bottled water on trays offer their own baths (although only the suite's is attached). Guests in the least expensive room will have to run upstairs to the bath, but those in search of a pampered, nature-oriented retreat won't mind. The Lighthouse Suite offers a queen-size four-poster bed and a private, wicker-furnished balcony with a wonderful view of the Bay. Susan, whose schooling has included New York's Culinary Institute of America, fixes full breakfasts served in the formal dining room, featuring the family silver. There's also a big, airy sun room with a phone. Bikes are available, and call ahead if you're arriving by boat.

Once a sea captain's house, the Gables now welcomes visitors to Reedville, who often arrive by boat at the inn's private dock.

Jean Harper

THE GABLES
Hosts: Dr. & Mrs. Norman Clark.
804-453-5209.
Foot of Main St. (Rte. 360), Reedville VA 22539.
Price: Moderate.
No: Credit cards (personal checks accepted), smoking, children.
Handicap Access: No.

One Capt. Fisher, made rich by the turn-of-the-century menhaden fishery, aligned the roof of this five-story mansion along his compass, erected the wooden mast of his beloved schooner through the top two stories, and stacked the 10-inch walls of brick brought south from Baltimore.

Two rooms are available for guests. The deluxe accommodation offers windows onto Cockrell Creek and a huge, unattached bath of glazed ceramic brick. The floor is built of cypress, the better for the captain to recall his shipboard life while drying his wet feet. Guests in the second room, with its own antique bed, will have to go upstairs to the bath — but it's a good excuse to examine the ship's munitions cabinet, now a bookcase installed just outside the gabled bathroom.

Mrs. Clark has steeped herself in the history of the home, and will happily escort visitors through a detailed tour — from the brass and copper fittings to the Venetian chandelier in the formal dining room beside the fine parlor with its Victorian furnishings. Or relax on one of the second-floor sun rooms or on the screened porch encircling the first floor. Full breakfasts may feature apple fritters — and, if you're lucky, somebody will have set the player grand piano to playing.

White Stone, Virginia

FLOWERING FIELDS BED & BREAKFAST
Hosts: Susan Moenssens & Lloyd Niziol.
804-435-6238.

As the Moenssens children empty the family nest, mother Susan is creating what may be the most homey B&B in the area. There are five rooms in this rambling old house, including a suite

Rte. 2/Box 1600, White
Stone VA 22578;
or PO Box 160, Kilmarnock
VA 22482.
Rte. 795, off Rtes. 3 & 650
bet. Kilmarnock & White
Stone.
Price: Inexpensive to
Expensive.
No: Credit cards (personal
checks accepted), pets,
smoking inside.
Handicap Access: No.

that sleeps five (although some rooms aren't available if the kids are home from college). Big breakfasts always feature crabs or oysters, whichever is in season. Pool and darts are available in the spacious family room, and two amiable dogs, a cat who hangs with the dogs, and two horses reside on the 5 1/2-acre-grounds — along with an easy-living porch. A relaxed accommodation, this is perfect for folks looking for hosts who might gather around the piano along with their guests, or invite visitors along if they're headed out and guests have no plans. As Susan says of her visitors, "So many of them sit on the stool while I'm cooking." You'll certainly feel free to. Call for reservations.

**WINDMILL POINT
RESORT**
Owner: Ron Rickard.
804-435-1166.
End of Va. Rte. 695/PO
Box 368, White Stone
VA 22578.
804-435-1166.
Price: Expensive.
Credit Cards: MC, V.
No: Pets (kennels in nearby
Kilmarnock).
Handicap Access: Yes.

Here is the Northern Neck's bona fide Bay-side hotel, with standard hotel-style rooms on the water, and cement patios or small balconies and big bathrooms. Windmill Point recalls Florida of the '60s, with teal trim and wicker furniture in the bright white lobby, and a Tikki tendency in the bar. Three buildings constructed over several years supply accommodations. Pool, restaurant, tennis courts, and 150 boat slips.

UPPER EASTERN SHORE

Chestertown

BRAMPTON
Hosts: Michael & Danielle
Hanscom.
410-778-1860.
25227 Chestertown Rd.,
Chestertown MD 21620.
1 mi. SW of Chestertown
on Md. 20.
Price: Moderate to Very
Expensive.
Credit Cards: MC, V.
Handicap Access: One
room.

The entrance to this fine, symmetrical Greek Revival manor house is beautifully framed by boxwoods and giant trees. The hospitable, hardworking Hanscoms have furnished Brampton with period reproductions to enhance the wide-plank floors, high ceilings, and varied rooms, which range from the oldest part of the house to brand new bedrooms in the outbuildings. All ten of the meticulously kept guest rooms have private baths and air conditioning, eight have working fireplaces, and two have Jacuzzis. Full breakfast, afternoon tea.

**GREAT OAK MANOR
   B&B**
Innkeepers: Don & Dianne
   Cantor.
410-778-5943.
10568 Cliff Road, Chester-
   town MD 21620.
Price: Moderate to Very
   Expensive.
Credit Cards: AE, D, MC,
   V.
Handicap Access: Yes.

During the 1920s and '30s, a number of mansions were built along the Eastern Shore.
Great Oak Manor is different from many, because
it is a faithful reproduction of a Georgian house,
even to using old brick which probably was
shipped as ballast in Grace Line ships. The detail
and carvings are meticulous, and the Cantors have
preserved the flavor of the original home in their
restoration work; it is formal but not stuffy, classic
but homelike. There are 11 guest rooms, many with
views of the Chesapeake; all are attractively decorated and furnished, and even the smaller ones are
good sized. The public rooms are varied and interesting, and everywhere is an
atmosphere of friendly comfort. Guests have access to the nearby Great Oak
Lodge, with a 9-hole golf course and a marina. There's also an extensive beach
right on the Bay.

**HILL'S INN/
   CHESAPEAKE INNS**
Innkeeper: Janet Thomp-
   son.
410-778-4667, 1-800-787-
   INNS.
114 Washington Ave.,
   Chestertown MD 21620.
Price: Inexpensive to
   Expensive.
Credit Cards: AE, D, DC,
   MC, V.
Handicap Access: No.

There is a lower-cost alternative to the more elegant places downtown. Hill's Inn, at the edge
of the historic district, is an 1877 house that served
as a tourist home for several decades before it was
renovated in 1985 as a B&B. The seven rooms have
private baths (some are across a hallway) and there
are two living rooms, a dining room, and a pleasant side porch for guests. The rambling house is
furnished in a homelike Victorian style. It is comfortable, if not fancy, and in good condition. The
manager is also the agent for two other inns on the
Eastern Shore.

THE IMPERIAL HOTEL
Owners: Robert & Barbara
   Lavelle.
410-778-5000.
208 High St., Chestertown
   MD 21620-1633.
Price: Expensive to Very
   Expensive.
Credit Cards: AE, D, MC,
   V.
Handicap Access: Yes.

The Imperial is a grand hotel on a small scale in
a small town. Its 11 rooms and two suites are
individually decorated in the best Victorian taste
but with modern climate control, wiring, commu-
nications, and plumbing. By any standard, it's luxurious, with heated towel racks, a masseuse, and a
full list of services. The conference center, with its
art exhibit, is modern, but somehow fits with the
rest; perhaps it is the transition through the pretty
courtyard garden that does the trick. The hotel is a
popular place for weddings. Residents recommend
the restaurant for the best fine dining in town, and the Imperial Wine Society
hosts wine tastings and dinners here. A Starbuck's coffee shop is adjacent, and
The Feast of Reason, across the street (see Chapter Five, *Restaurants*), is a great

light lunch spot. The building is right in the historic district, so leave your car and explore the most interesting part of the town on foot.

THE INN AT MITCHELL HOUSE
Innkeepers: Jim & Tracy Stone.
410-778-6500.
8796 Maryland Parkway, Chestertown MD 21620.
On Md. 21 bet. Md. 20 S. & Tolchester.
Price: Moderate to Expensive.
Credit Cards: MC, V.
Handicap Access: No.

Despite the address, Mitchell House is near Tolchester, an old Bay resort town where guests can go oyster dredging on a skipjack, sailing on a bugeye, or fishing on a powered vessel. With tennis courts and the Eastern Neck National Wildlife Refuge nearby, it would be hard for a lover of the outdoors to get bored. The approach to the house is a long, tree-shaded drive. Inside, five guest rooms all have private baths; there are two parlors, a dining room, and a total of five fireplaces. It's all beautifully restored. This is said to be the place where the wounded British commander was brought after the nearby Battle of Caulk's Field in 1814. When surgery on the kitchen table failed to save his life, they pickled Peter Parker in a keg of rum and sent him back to England.

Colonial accommodations at Chestertown's White Swan Tavern include a bedroom in the old John Lovegrove Kitchen.

David Trozzo

THE WHITE SWAN TAVERN
Manager: Mary Susan Maisel.
410-778-2300.
231 High St., Chestertown MD 21620.
Price: Expensive to Very Expensive.

Perhaps the most authentic, meticulous colonial restoration on the Shore, the 1733 White Swan is a time capsule. Check the display cabinet to see artifacts found during the 1978 archeological dig. This handsome, dignified, 18th-century inn needs only a collection of folks in waistcoats and breeches, gathered about the public rooms, to create a perfect time warp. Guest rooms, however,

No: Credit cards.
Handicap Access: Two
   rooms.

have modern comforts, with private baths, fireplaces (not functional), and refrigerators with a
complimentary bottle of wine. Accommodations
range from the old kitchen, with its massive cooking fireplace, to the T.W. Eliason Victorian Suite.
Even if you can't stay here, stop by for afternoon tea from 3 to 5pm daily.

Easton

Dan Wolff

_The Tidewater Inn in
Easton is host to the annual
Waterfowl Festival — and
to a popular Sunday brunch._

THE TIDEWATER INN
Manager: Bill Quinn.
410-822-1300.
Dover & Harrison Sts., Eas-
   ton MD 21601.
Price: Moderate to Very
   Expensive.
Credit Cards: AE, DC, MC,
   V.
Handicap Access: Yes.

The gracious Tidewater Inn became an instant
landmark when it opened in 1949. Renovations
have improved the details without destroying the
Georgian-style ambiance, and the hotel has a reputation for friendly service. Famous folks often stay
here when they visit Talbot County, and the handsome lobby could make a fine movie set. The 114
guest rooms have been cosmetically improved in
recent years and are nicely furnished in period
reproductions, although the bathrooms remain
small. Suites are available. The Gold Room is the
site of the priciest art exhibit of Easton's premier event — the annual Waterfowl Festival — and the restaurant is notable at any time of year, especially
Sunday brunch in the Crystal Room (see Chapter Five, _Restaurants_).

Galena

ROSEHILL FARM B&B
Owners: Marie Jolly.
410-648-5334.
13842 Gregg Neck Rd.,
   Galena MD 21635.
Price: Moderate.
Credit Cards: No; cash &
   personal checks only.
Handicap Access: Yes, after
   4 steps into house.

Here is a place that is reminiscent of a B&B in Ireland or the Canadian Maritimes — it's a private home, without special historical interest, but on a working farm at the edge of a village. Rose fanciers will fibrillate over the big greenhouses full of miniature roses and topiary ivy. The 97-acre farm once operated as a mail-order business, but now concentrates on major flower shows in the Mid-Atlantic region. The fishing pond is being renovated and restocked. Four bedrooms are exceptionally bright, spacious, and homey, with a decor that makes them genuine country. All have color TV and private baths, and there's a living room with a fireplace. Breakfast is deluxe.

Georgetown

**KITTY KNIGHT
   HOUSE**
Owner: Chuck Metzger.
410-648-5777, 410-275-2000.
Rte. 213, Georgetown MD
   21930.
Price: Moderate to Expensive.
Credit Cards: AE, MC, V.
Handicap Access: Yes.

"Miss Kitty" Knight was as determined as she was beautiful, so the story goes. When the British burned the rest of the town in 1813, she was tending an invalid neighbor and refused to move, so Admiral Sir George Cockburn spared the house and the one next door, which are now joined to make the present inn. A newer section expands the dining room to a deck and gazebo overlooking the Sassafras River and its hundreds of boats. The 11 rooms all have private baths, some have (nonfunctioning) fireplaces, and there are 2-room suites especially suited to families. Decor is attractive, with a few pieces dating back to Kitty Knight's time. A 65-foot charter boat is available for cruises.

Oxford

1876 HOUSE
Owners: Eleanor & Jerry
   Clark.
410-226-5496.
PO Box 658, Oxford MD
   21654.
Price: Expensive.
No: Credit Cards.
Handicap Access: No.

The name tells the age, but the Clarks make it friendly. This nicely restored, high-ceilinged, telescope Victorian house is decorated in Queen Anne style, with Oriental carpets on the wide plank floors and lovely period furniture. All three guest rooms have private baths. There's a limo service available to airports, too.

OXFORD INN
Owners: The Schmitt
  family.
410-226-5220.
PO Box 627, Oxford MD
  21654.
Price: Moderate to Very
  Expensive.
Credit Cards: D, MC, V.
Handicap Access: No.

When Oxford was laid out as a town in 1683, the main street had already been there for about 20 years, leading from the site of the Oxford Inn to the Bellevue ferry dock. This building is much newer, but it has a comfortable charm that was not affected by its remodeling a few years ago. At the headwaters of Town Creek, it's friendly, informal place with 11 individually furnished rooms, a nice sitting room, and a fine front porch. The restaurant downstairs that many folks may recall closed in 1995.

ROBERT MORRIS INN
Owners: Wendy & Ken
  Gibson.
410-226-5111.
PO Box 70, Oxford MD
  21654.
Price: Moderate to Very
  Expensive.
Credit Cards: MC, V.

George Washington may or may not have slept here, but one of his pals owned the place. Robert Morris, Jr., helped finance the Revolution and, besides signing checks, he put his John Hancock on the Declaration of Independence, the Articles of Confederation, and the Constitution. There are lovely rooms in nearby waterfront buildings as well as in the original section, and all are authentic, romantic, and oozing with historical atmosphere. Interesting art is displayed all around, and the restaurant is noted for its seafood (see Chapter Five, *Restaurants*).

Rock Hall

THE INN AT OSPREY
Manager: Robyn Wendt.
410-639-2194.
20786 Rock Hall Ave.,
  Rock Hall MD 21661.
Price: Expensive to Very
  Expensive.
Credit Cards: MC, V.
No: Pets, smoking.
Handicap Access: No.

If the building looks familiar, that's because it is modeled after the Coke-Garrett house in Williamsburg, but it was all built new in 1994. Seven very pretty rooms with colonial-style furnishings and decor all have private baths, air conditioning, and other pleasantries of the late 20th century. The house overlooks a fine, new marina complex which has a swimming pool, volleyball, horseshoes, nature trails, and complimentary bicycles for the guests; it is more like a small resort than an inn. The management can arrange sailing, fishing, or horseback riding nearby, and the restaurant downstairs serves dinner Thurs.–Mon.

St. Michaels

**HARBORTOWNE
GOLF RESORT
AND CONFERENCE
CENTER**
Manager: Harold Klinger.
410-745-9066.
PO Box 126, St. Michaels
MD 21663.
On Martingham Dr., just
W. of St. Michaels off
Md. 33.
Price: Very Expensive.
Credit Cards: AE, DC, MC,
V.
Handicap Access: Yes.

It looks like you are driving through a golf-course community to get to Harbortowne, and you are. The 18-hole Pete Dye–designed course is maintained well, the public areas are especially attractive, and the 111 rooms all have water views and terraces. There is a beach on a shallow little inlet from the Miles River, lawn games, and the management can arrange horseback riding nearby. The water view from most of the resort, including the restaurant, is spectacular.

**THE INN AT PERRY
CABIN**
Manager: Stephen Creese.
410-745-2200,
1-800-722-2949.
308 Watkins Lane, St.
Michaels MD 21663.
Price: Very Expensive.
Credit Cards: AE, DC, MC,
V.
Handicap Access: Yes.

The 1820 house was a landmark for years, then Sir Bernard Ashley, of the Laura Ashley fabric and fashion empire, bought it in 1988. Several million dollars later, it was a showplace for the company's products and a lovely, idealized English country inn. Management strives for perfection here; service is at the highest level, and anything you want, your hosts will surely provide. While Americans talk about class differences, the English actually believe in them — this is upper crust. If you are aiming to impress for either business or personal reasons, here is the place — perhaps with one of the special package deals that won't extract so much from the wallet. The restaurant is as good as the inn, and that's very good, indeed.

KEMP HOUSE INN
Owners: Diane & Steve
Cooper.
410-745-2243.
412 S. Talbot St./PO Box
638, St. Michaels MD
21663.
Price: Moderate to Expensive.
Credit Cards: D, MC, V.
Handicap Access: Yes. (first
floor).

If you are following your southern heritage, suh, you can stay where Robert E. Lee did in St. Michaels, in the Yellow Room of the Kemp House. Five guest rooms have private baths, two are shared, and there's a separate cottage. All are furnished in Queen Anne reproductions, and four have working fireplaces. Trundle beds allow flexibility when accommodating families. The innkeepers do not reside here, so breakfast is normally served in the rooms or on the patio in the summer.

THE PARSONAGE INN
Owner: Will Workman.
410-745-5519, 1-800-394-5519.
210 N. Talbot St., St. Michaels MD 21663.
Price: Expensive to Very Expensive.
Credit Cards: MC, V.
Handicap Access: One room.

Easily the most distinctive house on the main street of town, it is easy to see that the builder owned a brickyard. The 1985 restoration was skillful, and the inn now has air conditioning and eight guest rooms with private baths, all decorated in attractive Victorian style. You can take one of the touring bicycles and tour the town to work off the big breakfast.

ST. MICHAELS HARBOR INN AND MARINA
Manager: Cindy Long.
101 North Harbor Road, St. Michaels MD 21663
410-745-9001, 1-800-955-9001.
Price: Expensive to Very Expensive
Credit Cards: All major accepted.
Handicap Access: Yes.

By far the largest hotel in town, this waterfront resort has its own 60-slip marina; you can't miss seeing it from anywhere around the harbor. Of 46 guest rooms, 38 are suites, while large windows and decks throughout the hotel and the restaurant maximize the view. There's a nice pool, a workout room, a Jacuzzi, and pedal-boat and bike rentals, all run by a friendly staff. The hotel is not adjacent to the historic sites and the Maritime Museum, but St. Michaels is small enough to walk around, and a ferry operates on the harbor during the summer.

VICTORIANA INN
Owner: Janet Bernstein.
410-745-3368.
PO Box 449/205 Cherry St., St. Michaels MD 21663.
Price: Expensive to Very Expensive.
Credit Cards: MC, V.
Handicap Access: No

You can't get closer to the attractions of St. Michaels than this. The 1883 Italianate house overlooks the Maritime Museum, the harbor, and a boatyard specializing in wooden craft, and it is just a block from downtown shops. The wide lawn and handsome proportions of the house always catch the eye of passersby, and the interior is equally attractive in its period furnishings. Only one of the five guest rooms has a private bath, but all are individually air conditioned.

WADES POINT INN ON THE BAY
Owners: Betsy & John Feiler.
410-745-2500.
PO Box 7, St. Michaels MD 21663.
At the end of Wades Point Rd., 5 mi. W. of St. Michaels off Md. 33.

Go home to Grandma's. This quiet 120-acre waterfront complex has an 1819 house and a 1990 guest building, with a total of 23 water-view rooms available. The house, with its small guest rooms (some with shared baths), was built by Thomas Kemp, whose clipper ship *Chasseur* was called "The Pride of Baltimore" during the War of 1812. The new building's accommodations are

Price: Moderate to Very
  Expensive.
Credit Cards: MC, V.
Handicap Access: One
  room.

more spacious and the baths are private; from any, you can walk along the beach, explore the nature trail, or go fishing or crabbing from the pier. Breakfast is served in the main house.

Stevensville

Dan Wolff

Kent Island farmland is the setting for the plantation-style Kent Manor Inn, and for strolling and bicycling along Thompson's Creek.

KENT MANOR INN
Owner: David Meloy.
410-643-5757.
500 Kent Manor Dr.,
  Stevensville MD 21666.
On Kent Island; U.S. 50 to
  Md. 8 S.
Price: Moderate to Very
  Expensive.
Credit Cards: AE, MC, V.
Handicap Access: Yes.

Kent Manor is a faithful restoration of a large plantation house. There's a lovely garden house, a pier on the shallow headwaters of Thompson Creek, and a 1 1/2-mile trail winding through the extensive property. All 24 rooms are tastefully furnished in period style, some with porches and French marble fireplaces; Chesapeake waterfowl and workboat prints decorate the walls. The restaurant seems a bit expensive for what it serves, but the setting is romantic. The new owner of the property does not plan to make major changes to this quiet, dignified getaway.

The view from the porch at the Black Walnut Point Inn on Tilghman Island takes in a 57-acre wildlife refuge and a panorama of the Choptank River and the Bay.

Tom Curley

Tilghman Island

BLACK WALNUT POINT INN
Innkeepers: Tom & Brenda Ward.
410-886-2452.
PO Box 308, Tilghman Island MD 21671.
Price: Expensive to Very Expensive.
Credit Cards: MC, V.
Handicap Access: Limited.

At the southern tip of Tilghman Island, Black Walnut Point was washing away at an astonishing rate. So the previous owner of this farm convinced the state of Maryland to buy and preserve it as a wildlife sanctuary, bulkheading it against further erosion. Nobody knew what to do with the farmhouse until the Wards proposed a B&B here, which the state happily accepted. The result is a truly remote getaway on 57 acres, with a swimming pool, hot tub, tennis court, nature trail, and a perfectly placed hammock overlooking the Bay. Seven rooms all have private baths, and one is in a separate cottage with its own kitchen.

**THE TILGHMAN
ISLAND INN**
Owners: Jack Redmon &
David McCallum.
410-886-2141, 1-800-866-
2141.
PO Box B, Tilghman Island
MD 21671.
At the eastern end of Coop-
ertown Rd.
Price: Expensive to Very
Expensive.
Credit Cards: AE, MC, V.
Handicap Access: Yes.

Blanche DuBois may greet you as you go
through the art exhibit in the lobby, while one
of that beautiful cockatoo's cousins, an osprey, is
rearing a family on the nesting platform outside.
This is basically a 20-room motel with an attractive
restaurant (see Chapter Five, *Restaurants*) but the
location on the boating thoroughfare of Knapps
Narrows, the surrounding marshes with their
wildlife, and the pleasant hosts make it more than
that. There are 62 dock slips, so you can arrive in
your own boat or charter one for fishing, and the
management can arrange bicycling, swimming,
tennis, golf, volleyball, and croquet. There are
weekend singalongs, and the deck is a sociable
place — boredom is an unlikely option.

LOWER EASTERN SHORE

Berlin

THE ATLANTIC HOTEL
Manager: Beverly
Meadows.
410-641-3589.
2 N. Main St., Berlin MD
21811.
Price: Moderate to Very
Expensive.
Credit Cards: AE, MC,
V.
Handicap Access: Yes.

It was the renovation of this 1895 hotel that began
the revival of the town of Berlin — residents
gained a new pride in their unique surroundings
and undertook the restoration of many other local
buildings. The 16 lovely guest rooms and the common areas create a 19th-century feeling with their
rich color schemes and antique furnishings. All
rooms are non-smoking. The restaurant no longer
has the chef who established its reputation, but still
offers an interesting (if expensive) menu and an
excellent wine list.

Cambridge

GLASGOW INN B&B
Owners: Louiselee Roche &
Martha Ann Rayne.
410-228-0575.
1500 Hambrooks Dr.,
Cambridge MD 21613.
Price: Expensive to Very
Expensive.
Credit Cards: MC, V; prefer
personal checks.
Handicap Access: Yes, after
3 steps into house.

This lovely 1760 plantation house, across the
street from the Choptank River on the west
side of Cambridge, is listed on the National Register of Historic Places. Besides the seven rooms (four
with private baths) in the main building, three
more are in an adjacent smaller building, arranged
around a central fireplace in authentic colonial
form. All are comfortably furnished in antiques
and period reproductions, and all are air conditioned in defense against the Maryland summer.

Knowledgeable proprietor Louiselee Roche can refer visitors to other historic lodgings around the Eastern Shore.

SARKE PLANTATION
Owner: Genevieve Finley.
410-228-7020, 1-800-814-7020.
6033 Todd Point Rd., Cambridge MD 21613.
Price: Moderate to Expensive.
Credit Cards: AE, MC, V.
Handicap Access: No.

You'll drive ten miles beyond Cambridge to get here, and find nothing else around but the quiet, shallow waterfront of Todd Creek and 27 acres of space. The house has three bedrooms, one suite, fireplaces, a "great room" with a grand piano, a billiards room, and a display of works by local artists. It's all an antidote to the busyness of what most of us call "real life."

Cape Charles, Virginia

NOTTINGHAM RIDGE B&B
Owner: Bonnie Nottingham.
804-331-1010.
28184 Nottingham Ridge Ln., Cape Charles VA 23310.
Price: Moderate to Expensive.
No: Credit cards, children under 8.
Handicap Access: No.

If you grew up in an old house, this place will feel like home; the surprise is that it was built in 1974 on an old family farm. While the address says "Cape Charles," Nottingham Ridge is nowhere near the town. It's on one of the rare hills that overlooks the water in this otherwise flat part of the Shore. There are four rooms with private baths and a swimming beach; the woods are quiet except for the tunes of nature.

SEAGATE B&B
Innkeeper: Chris Bannon.
804-331-2206.
9 Tazewell Ave., Cape Charles VA 23310.
Price: Moderate
No: Credit cards.
Handicap Access: No.

"There's no cha-cha, no excitement. It's a place you come to take your girdle off," says owner Chris Bannon. Less than a block from the waterfront of this little town with the most period homes in Virginia — 90% of the town is a Historic District — this 1910 Victorian has been nicely restored. There are four rooms; two have full baths, and two have half-baths with a shared shower. The extensive, full breakfast should fuel you for the rest of the day — at least until afternoon tea.

Chincoteague, Virginia

CHANNEL BASS INN
Owners: David & Barbara
　Wiedenheft.
804-336-6148.
6228 Church St.,
　Chincoteague VA 23336.
Price: Expensive to Very
　Expensive.
No: Credit cards; not
　suitable for children.
Handicap Access: No.

Now under the same ownership as Miss Molly's, but more formal in atmosphere, this simple frame building conceals an elegant, quiet decor. There are five rooms, all with private baths and air conditioning, and most have queen- or king-size beds. The attractive dining room is used as the island's only tea room.

**ISLAND MANOR
HOUSE**
Innkeepers: Charles
　Kalmykow & Carol
　Rogers.
804-336-5436, 1-800-852-
　1505.
4160 Main St., Chin-
　coteague VA 23336.
Price: Moderate to Expen-
　sive.
Credit Cards: MC, V.
No: Children under 12.
Handicap Access: No

Not the usual story: two brothers built a house in 1848, married two sisters, split the house and moved half of it next door. Today, the two sections have been connected with a large, bright garden room and redecorated in the Federal style to make a most attractive place to stay. There are eight rooms, six of them with private baths and some with water views. Breakfast is large, and there is an afternoon tea with homemade desserts.

MISS MOLLY'S INN
Owners: David & Barbara
　Wiedenheft.
804-336-6686.
4141 Main St., Chin-
　coteague VA 23336.
Price: Moderate to Very
　Expensive
No: Credit cards, children
　under 8.
Handicap Access: No.

Miss Molly, daughter of J.T. Rowley, "The Clam King of the World," lived here until age 84, and this 1886 inn has a long-standing reputation of pleasant accommodation. Marguerite Henry wrote the children's classic Misty of Chincoteague while staying here and it is still a home-like, friendly place. Barbara's scones are a local legend, breakfast is substantial, and you'll find a really good pot of tea, too.

New Church, Virginia

**GARDEN AND THE SEA
INN**
Innkeepers: Tom & Sara
　Baker.
804-824-0672.
PO Box 275, New Church
　VA 23415.

Just south of the Maryland line on Rte. 710, this beautifully decorated pair of Victorian houses offers five luxurious rooms in a garden setting. The Bakers are continuing the tradition of personal service and fine continental dining set by the original

Elegance at an outpost: the Garden and the Sea Inn near Chincoteague, on the Lower Shore in Virginia.

David Trozzo

Price: Moderate to Very Expensive.
Credit Cards: AE, D, MC, V.
Handicap Access: No.

owners. The original inn was built in 1802 as Bloxom's Tavern and later expanded, while the Garden House is a separate, restored farmhouse recently moved to the site. The inn's restaurant draws rave reviews (see Chapter Five, *Restaurants*).

Onancock, Virginia

COLONIAL MANOR INN
Owners: May & Ed Oswald.
804-787-3521.
84 Market Street, Onancock VA 23417.
Price: Inexpensive to Moderate.
No: Credit cards.
Handicap Access: No.

This 1882 farmhouse — after 1936 run as a boarding house — has been converted into a very pleasant inn. May Oswald makes it friendly, the grounds make it quiet, the rooms make it comfortable, and the location makes it convenient. There's attractive new decor in appropriate Victorian style, and the nine rooms all have air conditioning and cable TV. All rooms are non-smoking. This is a perfect base for exploring the area, including a day trip by ferry to Tangier Island.

Princess Anne

HAYMAN HOUSE
Owners: Edna Mae & Charles Nittel.
410-651-2753.
30491 Prince William St., Princess Anne MD 21853.
Price: Moderate to Expensive.
No: Credit cards.
Handicap Access: No.

This 1898 Georgian Revival house, named after lumber tycoon Charles H. Hayman, is on a quiet, shaded street. The curving stairway, the balustrades ringing the porch, the double-mantled fireplaces in both parlor and dining room, and the restored original cooking fireplace are architectural highlights of the building. Guest rooms are attractively furnished. Continental breakfast.

THE WASHINGTON HOTEL AND INN
Owner: Mary A. Murphey.
410-651-2525.
11784 Somerset Ave./Rte. 675, Princess Anne MD 21853.
Price: Inexpensive.
Credit Cards: MC, V.
Handicap Access: No.

The Murphey family bought this 1744 building at auction in 1936 and they have run it as a hotel ever since. You can spend a lot of time just looking: there's a double staircase (one for ladies with their hoop skirts, one for gentlemen); a wonderful collection of varied furniture, Confederate money, and pictures of notables; and simple, clean, neat accommodations at a very fair price. This is genuine Eastern Shore without nouveau gentrification. (See Chapter Five for a restaurant review.)

Snow Hill

Peaceful Lower Shore living at the Greek Revival Chanceford Hall B&B Inn.

David Trozzo

CHANCEFORD HALL B&B INN
Hosts: Thelma & Michael Driscoll.
410-632-2231.
209 W. Federal St., Snow Hill MD 21863.
Price: Expensive to Very Expensive.
No: Credit cards, pets, children under 12.
Handicap Access: No.

Anybody who wants to see how a restoration should be done needs to visit the Driscolls. This splendid Greek Revival mansion in the center of town is structurally and cosmetically excellent, and Michael stays busy making reproduction furniture for the rooms when he's not fixing big breakfasts. The five rooms have private baths and there's central air conditioning. There's even a nice lap pool for exercise. Thelma is a most gracious hostess; everything is first class.

SNOW HILL INN
Innkeepers: Jim & Kathy Washington.

This inn is especially popular as a restaurant, but there are three rooms with private baths (one with a working fireplace), decorated with period

David Trozzo

Is it haunted? This room at the Snow Hill Inn may be home to a resident ghost.

410-632-2102.
104 E. Market St., Snow Hill
  MD 21863.
Price: Moderate.
Credit Cards: AE, D, MC,
  V.
Handicap Access: No.

furnishings. After the continental-plus breakfast, you are in a perfect location to explore the historic town of Snow Hill, with its exceptional collection of restored houses.

Vienna

THE TAVERN HOUSE
Hosts: Harvey & Elise
  Altergott.
410-376-3347.
111 Water St./PO Box 98,
  Vienna MD 21869.
Price: Moderate.
Credit Cards: MC, V; per-
  sonal checks preferred.
Handicap Access: No.

It was an inn two hundred years ago and it is an inn today. This tavern on the north bank of the Nanticoke River has been carefully restored to its 1730s form, right down to analysis of the original paint to duplicate the colors. Several of its rooms have fine views of the water and the marshes on the other side. Breakfasts are exceptional (try the "fruit flakes") and there is wine and cheese in the evening. You'll learn all about the interesting little town of Vienna and its surroundings by the time you leave, courtesy of your knowledgeable and gregarious hosts.

MOTELS

HEAD OF THE BAY

Havre de Grace

SUPER 8 (Manager: Michael Heife; 410-939-1880; 929 Pulaski Hwy., Havre de Grace MD 21078) Price: Inexpensive to Moderate. AE, CB, D, DC, MC, V. 63 rooms; one handicap access. Small pets allowed with permission.

Perryville

COMFORT INN (Manager: Gloria Holsopple; 410-642-2866; 61 Heather Ln., Perryville MD 21903) Price: Inexpensive. AE, D, MC, V. 104 rooms; 4 handicap access. Pets allowed.

ANNAPOLIS/WESTERN SHORE

Annapolis

COURTYARD BY MARRIOTT (General Manager: Shelly Saunders; 410-266-1555, 1-800-321-2211; 2559 Riva Rd., Annapolis MD 21401) Price: Moderate to Expensive. AE, CB, D, DC, MC, V. Handicap access. 149 rooms and suites, indoor pool, exercise room, whirlpool. Restaurant open for breakfast and lunch.

HOLIDAY INN (Manager: Camille Dean; 410-224-3150, 1-800-HOL-IDAY; 210 Holiday Court, Annapolis MD 21401) Price: Moderate to Expensive. AE, DC, D, MC, V. Handicap access. 220 rooms, sports bar, outdoor pool, Traditions restaurant. Free parking. At the edge of town off Rte. 50.

HOWARD JOHNSON'S LODGE (General Manager: Lou Steele; 410-757-1600, 1-800-213-7432; 69 Old Mill Bottom Rd. N., Annapolis MD 21401) Price: Inexpensive to Moderate. AE, CB, DC, D, MC. Handicap access. 70 rooms, outdoor pool. Continental breakfast. Pets allowed with deposit.

RESIDENCE INN BY MARRIOTT (General Manager: Roger Kruse; 410-573-0300; 170 Admiral Cochrane Dr., Annapolis MD 21401) Price: 102 suites priced according to length of stay. AE, D, DC, MC, V. Handicap access. Breakfast, evening social hour Mon.–Thurs. Cable, exercise rooms, microwaves. Outdoor pool and whirlpool. Pets allowed.

WYNDHAM GARDEN HOTEL (Manager: Scott Mounier; 410-266-3131, 1-800-351-9209; 173 Jennifer Rd., Annapolis MD 21401) Price: Expensive to Very Expensive. AE, CB, D, DC, V, MC. Handicap access. 197 rooms, conference facilities, suites. The Cafe restaurant, indoor pool, fitness room, sauna, whirlpool. At the edge of town off Rte. 50.

Lexington Park

DAYS INN (General Manager: Hans Weisstanner; 1-800-428-2871 (reservations only); 60 Main St., Lexington Park MD 20653) Next to Patuxent Naval Air Station. Price: Inexpensive. AE, D, DC, MC, V. 165 rooms, cable TV. Closest motel to Point Lookout.

Patuxent Inn (General Manager: Cheryl Ahearn; 301-862-4100; Rte. 235/PO Box 778, Lexington Park MD 20653) Price: Inexpensive to Moderate. AE, DC, MC, V. Convenient to the Patuxent Naval Air Station and Solomons.

Solomons

COMFORT INN (General Manager: Katherine Gooch; 410-326-6303; Rte. 2-4/Lore St., Solomons MD 20688) Price: Moderate to Expensive. AE, D, DC, MC, V. 60 rooms, marina. Handicap access. Non-smoking rooms available.

HOLIDAY INN (Manager: Jeff Shepherd; 410-326-6311; 155 Holiday Dr., Solomons MD 20688) Price: Moderate to Expensive. AE, D, DC, MC, V. 326 rooms. Handicap access. Whirlpool suites, gift shop, waterfront dining in the Maryland Way restaurant. Overlooking the water; one marina next door and another behind.

NORTHERN NECK/MIDDLE PENINSULA

Deltaville, Virginia

DOCKSIDE INN (Co-Manager: Jane Deagle; 804-776-9224; PO Box 710, Deltaville VA 23043) Price: Inexpensive to Moderate. MC, V. 23 rooms, handicap access. Most efficiencies with small fridges and microwave, in clean accommodations. The only motel around this part of the Middle Peninsula.

Gwynn's Island, Virginia

THE ISLANDER (General Manager: Lester Graham; 804-725-2151; at Gwynn's Island; write Grimstead VA 23064) Price: Moderate to Expensive. MC, V. From Potomac River Bridge and Rte. 301, go E. on Rte. 3 to Rte. 198 in Mathews County, E. to Hudgins, left on Rte. 223 to Gwynn's Island. Just off the Chesapeake Bay in a sheltered harbor, with easy maneuverability for boats.

36 waterfront rooms and 3-room suite. Handicap access. Swimming pool, sand beach, and tennis. No pets (kennel available). One hour to Williamsburg.

Reedville, Virginia

BAY MOTEL (Manager: Debbie French; 804-453-5171; Rte. 360, bet. Burgess and Reedville. RR 1, Box 210, Reedville VA 22539) Price: Inexpensive to Moderate. D, MC, V. Close to Island cruises and the best of the Chesapeake Bay charter boat fishing area. All 20 rooms are ground level, handicap access. Cable TV and direct dial phones. Swimming pool, gift shop. Reservations recommended, especially during fishing season.

White Stone, Virginia

WHISPERING PINES MOTEL (Owners: Mr. & Mrs. Howard Schillinger; 804-435-1101; PO Box 156, White Stone VA 22578) Price: Inexpensive. AE, MC, V. This quiet country motel, nestled in a pleasant wooded setting in Lancaster County, is .5 mi. N. of White Stone on Rte. 3. 29 rooms, all on one floor, each with TV and phone. No pets. Reservations recommended in summer.

UPPER EASTERN SHORE

Chestertown

FOXLEY MANOR MOTEL (Manager: Reba Postles; 410-778-3200; 609 Washington Ave., Chestertown MD 21612) Price: Inexpensive to Moderate. AE, D, MC, V. 29 units, A/C, cable TV, swimming pool.

GREAT OAK LODGE (Manager: Marie Barbato; 410-778-2100, 1-800-526-3464; Great Oak Landing Rd., Chestertown MD 21620) Price: Moderate to Expensive. Major credit cards. An older motel on a nice marina, with a 9-hole golf course and a pool. Restaurant overlooks the water.

Easton

COMFORT INN (Manager: Tammy Green; 410-820-8333; 8523 Ocean Gateway, Easton MD 21601) Price: Inexpensive to Expensive. AE, D, DC, MC, V. Handicap access. 84 rooms, A/C, cable TV, swimming pool, conference rooms, complimentary continental breakfast.

DAYS INN (Manager: Wade Barnhart; 410-822-4600; 7018 Ocean Gateway, Easton MD 21601) Price: Inexpensive to Moderate. AE, D, DC, MC, V. 50 rooms, cable TV, swimming pool. Recent remodeling.

ECONO LODGE (Manager: Diane Dodge; 410-820-5555; 8175 Ocean Gateway, Easton MD 21601) Price: Inexpensive to Moderate; weekly & monthly rates in winter. AE, D, MC, V. Recently renovated, AAA-approved. Some rooms non-smoking. Refrigerators, microwaves in some rooms. Cable TV. Senior citizen rates. Pets accepted.

HOLIDAY INN EXPRESS (Manager: Brandee Diggs; 410-819-6500; 8561 Ocean Gateway, Easton MD 21601) Price: Moderate to Expensive. Major credit cards. 73 rooms, cable TV, HBO, exercise room, conference rooms, indoor pool, hot tub, continental breakfast. Handicap access.

Grasonville

COMFORT INN KENT NARROWS (Manager: Cindy Grout; 410-827-6767, 1-800-828-3361; 3101 Main St., Grasonville MD 21638) Price: Moderate to Very Expensive. Major credit cards. 86 rooms. Water-view location next to the Kent Narrows boating area; numerous restaurants and marinas nearby. Indoor pool, hot tub, sauna, exercise room. Refrigerators, microwaves, coffee makers in all rooms. Continental breakfast.

FRIENDSHIP INN (Manager: Ursula Ferguson; 410-827-7272, 1-800-424-4777; 107 Hissey Rd., Grasonville MD 21638) 42 rooms. Price: Inexpensive to Moderate. Major credit cards. An older motel next to a restaurant locally known for good breakfasts.

HOLLY'S MOTEL (Managers: Gary Reamy, Ward Ewing, Justin Ewing; 410-827-8711; Exit 43B off Rte. 50, 108 Jackson Creek Rd., Grasonville MD 21638) Price: Inexpensive. MC, V, personal checks. Venerable gateway motel to the Shore for 40-odd years. 22 rooms.

SLEEP INN (Manager: Arlyn Banks; 410-827-5555, 1-800-627-5337; 101 VFW Ave., Grasonville MD 21638) Price: Moderate. Major credit cards. New and attractive, with 51 bright, pleasant rooms. Two miles from Kent Narrows, near Queenstown outlets .

LOWER EASTERN SHORE

Cambridge

KNIGHT'S INN (Manager: Jennifer Jones; 410-221-0800, 1-800-843-5644, fax 410-221-0357; 2831 Ocean Gateway, Cambridge MD 21613; formerly Econo Lodge) Price: Inexpensive. AE, D, MC, V. Indoor pool. Children under 18 free. RV/truck parking. Pets OK; $15 fee. Restaurant closed Mon.

QUALITY INN (Manager: Charlene Burton; 410-228-6900, 1-800-221-2222; U.S. 50 & Crusader Rd./PO Box 311, Cambridge MD 21613) Price: Inexpensive. AE, CB, D, MC, V. Handicap access, AARP & AAA discounts, 60 units, A/C, cable TV, restaurant, lounge, off-track betting. No pool.

Crisfield

SOMERS COVE MOTEL (Manager: Jackie Ward; 410-968-1900, 1-800-827-6637; PO Box 387, Crisfield MD 21817) Price: Inexpensive to Moderate. 40 rooms. Basic, simple, and clean, its location on the municipal marina is the attraction.

Pocomoke City

DAYS INN (Manager: Donna Byrd; 410-957-3000, 1-800-325-2525; 15 Ocean Highway, Pocomoke City MD 21851) Price: Moderate. Steam baths in all rooms.

QUALITY INN (Manager: Jacqueline Upshaw; 410-957-1300, 1-800-221-2222, fax 410-957-9329; 825 Ocean Highway/PO Box 480, Pocomoke City MD 21851) 64 rooms. Cable TV, some Jacuzzis and refrigerators. Swimming pool.

Princess Anne

ECONO LODGE (Manager: Georgianne Schade; 410-651-9400, 1-800-424-4777; 10936 Market Lane, Princess Anne MD 21853) Price: Inexpensive to Moderate. Major credit cards. 50 rooms. Cable TV, fax, morning coffee, continental breakfast.

Salisbury

ECONO LODGE, STATESMAN (Owner: Edward Baker; 410-749-7155, 1-800-424-4777; 712 N. Salisbury Blvd., Salisbury MD 21801; formerly Best Western) Price: Inexpensive to Expensive. AE, D, DC, MC, V. Handicap access. AAA-recommended. 92 rooms, cable TV. Complimentary continental breakfast. Swimming pool.

COMFORT INN (Manager: David Douglas; 410-543-4666; U.S. 13 N., Salisbury MD 21801) Price: Inexpensive to Expensive. AE, D, DC, MC, V. Handicap access. 96 rooms, cable TV. Complimentary continental breakfast, lobby coffee.

DAYS INN (Manager: Robert Jones; 410-749-6200; 2525 N. Salisbury Blvd., Salisbury MD 21801-9091) Price: Inexpensive to Expensive. AE, D, DC, MC, V. Handicap access. 99 rooms, cable TV. Conference rooms. Swimming pool. Pets allowed.

HAMPTON INN (Manager: Stephanie Spoul; 410-546-1300; 1735 N. Salisbury Blvd., Salisbury MD 21801) Price: Moderate. AE, D, DC, MC, V. Handicap access. AAA-approved. AARP, group rates available. 101 rooms, cable TV. 75% of rooms non-smoking. Complimentary continental breakfast. Free local calls, fax available. Fitness room, swimming pool.

HOLIDAY INN (Manager: Pat Disharoon; 410-742-7194; 2625 N. Salisbury Blvd., Salisbury MD 21801) Price: Moderate to Expensive. AE, CB, D, DC, MC, V. Handicap access. 123 rooms, cable TV, pay-per movies. Restaurant, lounge. Swimming pool.

SHERATON INN (Manager: Shaahab Taj; 410-546-4400; 300 S. Salisbury Blvd., Salisbury MD 21801) Price: Expensive to Very Expensive. AE, CB, D, DC, MC, V. Handicap access. AAA, AARP discounts. 156 rooms, cable TV, room service. Restaurant, lounge. Heated indoor pool. Adjacent to riverside park.

Chincoteague, Virginia

ASSATEAGUE INN (Manager: Graham Dill; 804-336-3738, fax 804-336-1179; 6570 Chicken City Rd./PO Box 1038, Chincoteague VA 23336) Price: Inexpensive to Expensive. Major credit cards. 26 rooms and efficiencies. This is a condominium complex at the edge of a marsh.

BIRCHWOOD MOTEL (Manager: Mary Lou Birch; 804-336-6133; 3650 Main St., Chincoteague VA 23336) Price: Moderate. Major credit cards. 41 rooms, including two family rooms.

DRIFTWOOD MOTOR LODGE (Manager: Scott Chesson; 804-336-6557, 1-800-553-6117; 7105 Maddox Blvd., PO Box 575, Chincoteague VA 23336) Price: Inexpensive to Expensive. Major credit cards. 52 rooms. Closest motel to the national wildlife refuge.

ISLAND MOTOR INN (Manager: Anna C. Stubbs; 804-336-3141; 4391 Main St., Chincoteague VA 23336) Price: Expensive. AE, CB, DC, D, V, MC. Probably the best motel in Chincoteague, boasting a splendid sunset view. 60 waterfront rooms with private balconies, indoor and outdoor pool, hot tub, workout rooms and cable TV. Handicap access.

THE REFUGE MOTOR INN (Manager: Jane Stewart; 1-800-544-8469; 7058 Maddox Blvd./PO Box 378, Chincoteague VA 23336) Price: Inexpensive to Very Expensive. AE, DC, D, MC V. At the entrance to Chincoteague National Wildlife Refuge. Handicap access. Whirlpool, sauna, exercise room, suites, bike rentals. 72 rooms with patios or balconies look out into loblolly pine trees. Guest laundry, sun deck, gift shop, pony corral, and little cook-out areas. Fifteen deluxe rooms include sitting areas. Meeting rooms for groups up to 75.

SEA SHELL MOTEL (Manager: Chris Conklin; 804-336-6589; 3720 Willow St., Chincoteague VA 23336) Price: Moderate. Major credit cards. 40 rooms and efficiencies plus six cottages.

SUNRISE MOTOR INN (Manager: Valerie Tolbert; 804-336-6671, fax 804-336-1226; 4491 Chicken City Rd./PO Box 185, Chincoteague VA 23336) Price: Inexpensive to Moderate. Major credit cards. 24 rooms and efficiencies. Efficiencies rent by the week only.

WATERSIDE MOTOR INN (Owners: Donna & Tommy Mason; 804-336-3434; 3761 S. Main St., Chincoteague VA 23336) Price: Inexpensive to Very Expensive. AE, CB, D, DC, MC, V. Private balconies overlook Chincoteague Channel. A/C, direct-dial phones, in-room coffee, double to king-size beds, refrigerators, waterfront swimming pool, and a fishing/crabbing pier with boat slips. Pretty, glass-enclosed Jacuzzi room. The only private tennis courts among Island motels.

Onley, Virginia

COMFORT INN (Manager: Jay Bundick; 804-787-7787, 1-800-228-5150; Four Corner Plaza, U.S. 13/PO Box 205, Onley VA 23418) Price: Inexpensive to Moderate. 80 rooms. New and nice, with boat models in lobby. Complimentary continental breakfast. Close to Onancock, "the gateway to Tangier Island."

CAMPGROUNDS

HEAD OF THE BAY

Havre de Grace

SUSQUEHANNA STATE PARK (410-836-6735, 410-557-7994; 801 Stafford Rd., Havre de Grace MD 21078) Seasonal. Tents, picnic tables, laundry tubs, showers, flush toilets. Has merged with Rocks State Park. Administrative offices: 3318 Rocks, Chrome Hill Rd., Jarretsville MD 21084.

ANNAPOLIS/WESTERN SHORE

Millersville

CAPITOL KOA CAMPGROUND (410-923-2771; 768 Cecil Ave., Millersville MD 21108) Just over 10 mi. from Annapolis, featuring hiking trails and pool.

POINT LOOKOUT STATE PARK (301-872-5688; Rte. 5/Box 48, Scotland MD 20687) 143 improved sites, handicap access, boat access, great location. Reservations required. (See Chapter Six, *Recreation*.)

St. Leonard

MATOAKA BEACH CABINS (410-586-0269; PO Box 124, St. Leonard MD 20685) Chesapeake Bay front, sandy beach, fishing, crabbing, fossil hunting, walking. Eight cabins, each with kitchen, bath, and screened porch, on 40 acres. $315 or $355 for the week.

NORTHERN NECK/MIDDLE PENINSULA

New Point, Virginia

NEW POINT CAMPGROUND (Owners: Buck, Gay, & Benita Webster; 804-725-5120; 7 mi. S. of Mathews Court House on Rte. 14 E, New Point VA 23125.) Open Apr.–Oct. Right on the Bay, with a beach, fishing, crabbing, clamming, boating, trailer rentals, boat and motor rentals, boat slips, marina, adult and kiddie pools, recreation hall, mini-golf; 300 full-hookup sites.

Oak Grove, Virginia

SOUTHFORK RANCH RV PARK (804-224-7093; off Rte. 3, Oak Grove; PO Box 1116, Colonial Beach VA 22443) Open Apr. 15–Oct. 15. Reservations recommended. Wooded sites with full hookups, seasonal, overnight, and yearly. Near Colonial Beach, Washington's Birthplace, and Stratford.

Reedville, Virginia

CHESAPEAKE BAY/SMITH ISLAND KOA (804-453-3430; Reedville VA 22539) 90 shaded sites on scenic creek, boat ramp, dockage .5 mi. from Bay, pool, mini-golf; also air conditioned cabins, and camp store. Point of departure for one of the Smith Island excursion boats.

Warsaw, Virginia

NAYLOR'S BEACH CAMPGROUND, INC. (804-333-3951; off Rte. 360 to Rte. 624; RR 1, Box 569, Warsaw VA 22572) Family camping on the Rappahannock River. Sand beach, grass-covered picnic grounds and 100 campsites. Boat ramp, electric and water hookups, small camp store.

UPPER EASTERN SHORE

Chestertown

DUCK NECK CAMPGROUND (410-778-3070; 500 Double Creek Point Rd., Chestertown MD 21620) Open Apr.–mid-Oct. Full hookups, partial hookups and dump stations, tent camping, bath house, laundry, camp store, leashed pets allowed.

Delmar

WOODLAWN CAMPGROUND (410-896-2979; 1209 Walnut St., Delmar MD 21875) Partial hookups and dump stations, new bath house, leashed pets allowed.

Denton

CAMP MARDELA (410-479-2861, 1-800-MARDELA; PO Box 460, Denton MD 21629) Pond, retreat house, partial hookups, tent camping, bath house, picnic pavilion.

Goldsboro

LAKE BONNIE (410-482-8479; PO Box 142/Rte. 313, Goldsboro MD 21636) Open Apr.–Nov. Partial hookups and dump stations, tent camping, boating, swimming, camp store, leashed pets allowed.

Greensboro

HOLIDAY PARK (410-482-6797; PO Box 277, Greensboro MD 21639) Open Apr.–mid-Nov. MC, V. Partial hookups and dump stations, tent camping, bath house, laundry, swimming pool, camp store, cable TV, miniature golf, tennis, rental trailers on-site, picnicking, four playgrounds, indoor room for groups and concerts to 400, handicap access.

Rock Hall

ELLENDALE CAMPSITES (410-639-7485; 4084 Ellendale, Rock Hall MD 21661) Partial hookups and dump stations, tent camping, bath house, boat ramp, camp store, game room, leashed pets allowed.

LOWER EASTERN SHORE

Chincoteague, Virginia

TOM'S COVE CAMPGROUND (804-336-6498; PO Box 122, Chincoteague VA 23336) Boat docks, clubhouse, country store. The site of the annual Chincoteague Seafood Festival each May.

Madison

MADISON BAY CAMPGROUND (410-228-4111; Rte. 16, PO Box 33, Madison MD 21648) Open year-round. Partial hookups and dump stations, tent camping, bath house, barn restaurant, boat fuel, leashed pets allowed.

Nanticoke

ROARING POINT WATERFRONT CAMPGROUND (410-873-2553; PO Box 104, Nanticoke MD 21840) MC, V. Full hookups, partial hookups and dump stations, tent camping, bath house, laundry, camp store, propane, ice, leashed pets allowed.

Princess Anne

PRINCESS ANNE CAMPGROUND (410-651-1520; 12388 Brittingham Lane, Princess Anne MD 21853) Open Apr.–Nov. Partial hookups and dump stations, tent camping, bath house, leashed pets allowed.

Quantico

SANDY HILL FAMILY CAMP (410-873-2471; 5752 Sandy Hill Rd., Quantico MD 21856) Open Mar.–Nov. Partial hookups and dump stations, bath house, laundry, camp store, leashed pets allowed

Snow Hill

POCOMOKE RIVER FOREST AND STATE PARK (410-632-2566; 3461 Worcester Hwy., Snow Hill MD 21863) Open year-round. 250 sites (30 with electricity), dump stations. MC, V. Reservations needed for summer campsites. Great location near the Blackwater River.

Taylor's Island

TAYLOR'S ISLAND FAMILY CAMPGROUNDS (410-397-3275; PO Box 156, Taylor's Island MD 21669) Open year-round. Partial hookups and dump stations, tent camping, bath house, laundry, camp store, leashed pets allowed.

TIDELAND PARK CAMPGROUND (410-397-3473; 525 Taylor's Island Rd./PO Box 64, Taylor's Island MD 21669) Open Apr.–Nov. Partial hookups and dump stations, tent camping, bath house, log cabins.

Westover

LAKE SOMERSET CAMPGROUND (410-957-1866; 8658 Lake Somerset Ln., Westover MD 21871) Open year-round. AE, D, MC, V. Full hookups, bath house, laundry, camp store, swimming pool, fishing pond, small boats, leashed pets allowed.

CHAPTER FOUR
The Best of the Bay
CULTURE

Chesapeake culture is a combination of Southern graciousness and pieces of city living imported by refugees from nearby metropolitan centers. Add to that the traditions and influence of the Bay itself, and you get a varied mix that includes band concerts by the Naval Academy, tours of colonial-era homes, and folk festivals celebrating duck decoys and oysters. Whatever the medium, the emphasis is on the Bay and the region's abundant heritage.

David Trozzo

Examining the sweep of a Bay-built boat's hand-laid curves at the Chesapeake Bay Maritime Museum in St. Michaels.

The performing arts scene in the smaller cities and towns is a miniature replica of that found in the big city, but with an emphasis on classics appropriate to the cradle of U.S. history. That means, for example, that you'll easily find classical symphonic or chamber music; if you're in the mood for, say, improvisational jazz, you'll find it too, but not as readily.

Visually, expect to see what the locals jokingly refer to as "art ducko." The grand duck hunting tradition here is depicted in small galleries scattered from Havre de Grace to Cape Charles, with concentrations in Annapolis and Easton. Hanging alongside are lots of maritime watercolors and prints. Stop by the Academy for the Arts in Easton or Maryland Hall for the Creative Arts in Annapolis for the exhibitions of more experimental work.

Here is your guide to what to see and do around the Bay. For details on events, schedules, or seasonal offerings, check area newspapers and magazines (see Chapter Eight, *Information*, for a list of publications).

Decoy carver David Wallace of Havre de Grace keeps alive the old art.

David Trozzo

ARCHITECTURE

Architecture buffs make beelines to the Chesapeake region, where old manor houses are looked after as a matter of civic duty. Plantations have been long settled on country waterways, while Federal townhouses line village streets. Many of these homes passed out of families and into the non-profit sector; others have spent time as places of business. Sooner or later, the value of the past is recognized and the homes duly marked for preservation and posterity.

Construction of elegant Tidewater buildings began in the 18th century, particularly in Annapolis, with what truly were "town houses" owned by wealthy plantation owners. They moved to town for the social season, launched by sessions of the General Assembly or House of Burgesses. In the country remain some fine Georgian mansions such as **Mount Harmon Plantation** on the Sassafras River in _Cecilton_, as well as the house that reportedly inspired Mount Vernon, **Sotterley Mansion** on the Patuxent, in _Hollywood_.

Among the more famous building designs indigenous to the Chesapeake is the five-part Georgian mansion, exemplified by the **William Paca House** in _Annapolis_. Two hyphens, or hallways, connect the main house to two wings. Another example of this distinctly Maryland form of Palladian architecture is the **Hammond-Harwood House**, also in Annapolis. The intricately carved doorway is considered to be one of the country's loveliest from this era. There are also the workers' houses: Maryland's first printer, Jonas Green, cousin to Ben Franklin, owned a journeyman's home now operated as the **Jonas Green House B&B** by his great-great-great-great-great grandson. The original 1690 kitchen still stands — as does the 1720s family living room and 1740 addition built by Green for his growing family.

In just about any single town, say, _Chestertown_, visitors will find examples of several eras, bespeaking the region's longevity. Georgian, Federal, and Victorian houses sit nearly side by side, and historical societies are dominant forces. And in *Havre de Grace*, look for a fine example of high Victorian architecture, the B&B called the **Vandiver Inn**. Originally built as a private home in the 19th century, it has five chimneys and a wealth of interior detail.

Historic preservationist groups in the Bay have done their jobs well. With the bricks re-pointed and the docents well trained, three centuries of mansions and estates — and warehouses and cottages — are still here to connect present-day Bay visitors and residents to the life of the past.

CINEMA

A vant-garde cinema is not a great strength here, probably for the same reasons that only so many other forms of experimental culture thrive — booming Washington and Baltimore are just up the Maryland road, while Virginia's cities screen classics of their own.

Still, local institutions of higher learning always can be counted on to fill the cultural void. For example, if you're in search of non-commercial films in the *Annapolis* area, **St. John's College** offers the gem. For $3, the school's Saturday film series is a great find during the school year. Movies start at 8:15pm in the Francis Scott Key Auditorium; it's rarely overcrowded (410-263-2371). On the Easter Shore in *Chestertown*, **Washington College** fills in where the commercial movie business does not. Free weekly films in this otherwise cinema-less town include high-quality movies like *Eat, Drink, Man, Woman* or *Pulp Fiction* soon after they've left the cineplexes. At the Norman James Theatre on campus, on Fri., Sun., and Mon. at 7:30pm during the school year. Call 410-778-2800.

For commercial movie houses in and around *Annapolis*, try the old Eastport Cinemas, officially known now as the Apex Eastport Cinemas. You'll pay 99 cents for recent feature films. Multi-screen **Apex Harbour Center 9** has become the local favorite. It's spacious, and provides plenty of parking (although bumper-to-bumper when the movies let out). Also, the **Apex Annapolis Mall**, with five screens. Information for all three theatres: 410-224-1145. Also on the Western Shore, in *Prince Frederick*, first-run films are shown at **Apex Cinemas** at the Calvert Village Shopping Center; 410-535-0776.

On the Upper Easter Shore, look for first-run commercial fare at the **RC Easton Movies 4** (410-822-5566), in the Tred Avon Square shopping center on Marlboro Road in *Easton*.

Down *Salisbury* way on the Lower Eastern Shore, movies play at **Hoyts Cinema 10** (410-543-0902) in the Centre At Salisbury and **Hoyts Cinema 6** (410-546-4700) at 317 E. Main St. Call the Hoyts box office at 410-546-1776.

DANCE

ANNAPOLIS/WESTERN SHORE

Annapolis

BALLET THEATRE OF ANNAPOLIS
410-263-2909.
Maryland Hall for the Creative Arts, 801 Chase St.
Season: Oct., Dec., Apr.
Tickets: $10–$16.

The Western Shore's proximity to Baltimore and Washington means most denizens head there for their dance fixes. One notable exception is the Ballet Theatre of Annapolis, with its own principal dancers and school. Three major performances each year at Maryland Hall usually include one original by long-time artistic director Edward Stewart, a former principal dancer with the Pittsburgh Ballet Theatre. The annual *Nutcracker* is a holiday sellout. Matinee tickets go first.

UPPER EASTERN SHORE

Easton

TIDEWATER PERFORM-ING ARTS SOCIETY
410-476-9002.
PO Box 455.
Season: Sept.–Mar.
Tickets: prices vary with concert; season tickets available.

Musical artists dominate the annual performance schedule; one international dance troupe a year is usually invited. Performers have included Jose Greco, the Shanghai Acrobats, and the London Ballet; the annual *Nutcracker* is given by the Ballet Theatre of Philadelphia.

LOWER EASTERN SHORE

Salisbury

SALISBURY STATE UNIVERSITY DANCE COMPANY
410-543-6353.
1101 Camden Ave.
Season: Sept.–May; free.

Two major productions are held each year at the university's Holloway Hall Auditorium. Student choreography is featured during the annual Fall Showcase; the Spring Concert highlights faculty and student works, or nationally noted guest artists.

GALLERIES

ANNAPOLIS/WESTERN SHORE

The visual arts scene in Annapolis revolves around Maryland Hall and the historic district's commercial galleries. Watercolors of local scenes and marine prints are more likely to hang than cutting-edge abstracts, although efforts to boost the latter seem to be on the upswing. Locally, look at non-commercial art in a handful of places. (See Chapter Seven, *Shopping*, for commercial galleries).

ELIZABETH MYERS MITCHELL GALLERY
410-626-2556.
Mellon Hall, St. John's College.
Tues.–Sun. 12–5; Fri. 7–8 during school year.

Your best chance in Annapolis to see major works by major artists. Visiting shows here often were curated elsewhere by groups like the Smithsonian Institution's Traveling Exhibition Service or the Trust for Museum Exhibitions in Washington, D.C. Recent exhibitions: "Henry Moore: The Last Portfolio," including the sculptor's etchings; "Masterpieces of Renaissance and Baroque Printmaking"; and "Rembrandt Etchings: Selections from the Carnegie Museum of Art." Accompanying lectures.

Relish the fine arts at the Maryland Federation of Art gallery, across from the Statehouse in Annapolis.

David Trozzo

MARYLAND FEDERATION OF ART GALLERY ON THE CIRCLE
410-268-4566.
18 State Circle.
Tues.–Sun. 11–5.

A fun space. Originally built in the mid-1800s as a storage loft for the Jones and Franklin General Store, the building's exposed brick walls serve as backdrop for changing shows. Paintings, sculpture, wearable art, and photographs by artists in the 350-member roster.

MARYLAND HALL FOR THE CREATIVE ARTS
410-263-5544.
801 Chase St.
Mon.–Fri. 9–5.

A range of regional artists with a range of styles rotate shows. Expect multimedia installations, sculpture, or paintings. You'll also find the **AIR Gallery**, showing the work of Maryland Hall's 12 artists-in-residence, as well as students. While you're in the building, wander upstairs and see if any of the artists are working in their studios scattered throughout the old schoolhouse.

NORTHERN NECK/MIDDLE PENINSULA

Warsaw, Virginia

THE GALLERY
804-333-6700.
Justice Joseph W. Chinn
   Community Center,
   Rappahannock
   Community College.

Virginia's Tidewater artists hang three or four exhibitions a year. Check local papers or call for current information.

UPPER EASTERN SHORE

Chestertown

CHESTERTOWN ARTS LEAGUE
410-778-5789.
PO Box 656, 204 Cannon St.
Call for hours.

Chestertown's promoters of the local arts scene offer a variety of classes and gallery exhibits year-round featuring works by members and guests. The Arts League hosts an annual juried art show in spring, and an Art in the Park Festival.

CONSTANCE STUART LARRABEE ARTS CENTER
410-778-2800.
Gibson Fine Arts Center,
   Washington College, 300
   Washington Ave.
Tues.–Sun. 1–5 during
   school year.

This large studio-and-exhibitions space was once the school's boiler plant. Thanks to the building's rebirth, the college's fine arts department has expanded studio space for painting, drawing, pottery, sculpture, printmaking, and photography.

Chestertonian Larrabee was one of the first women photojournalists in World War II, and has had several exhibitions at the Smithsonian. The center premiered with an exhibition of her work, and continues with displays of student artwork. Washington College also hangs exhibits in the multi-purpose **Gibson Fine Arts Center**.

Easton

ACADEMY OF THE ARTS
410-822-0455.

Long the gathering place for the area's artists, the academy, a white clapboard former school-

Once a schoolhouse, the Easton Academy of the Arts is now home to art exhibits and performances.

R. Doster, *Star Democrat*

106 South St.
Mon.–Sat. 10–4; Weds. until 9pm.

house, provides 20,000 square feet of studios and gallery space.

Looking like what you'd expect to find in the middle of a cosmopolitan city, the academy supports a growing membership, changing exhibits, popular classes, growing permanent collection, and periodic performances and lectures. The spirit is democratic, with exhibited artworks ranging from small, traditional still lifes to the large, vibrant seascapes of the late Herman Maril.

Stevensville

KENT ISLAND FEDERA-
TION OF ART
410-643-7424.
405 Main St.
Tues.–Fri. 1–4, Sat. noon–4.

Easily overlooked by those who rush by on nearby U.S. 50, the Kent Island Federation of Art is located in a fine Victorian house in a historic town. Local and regional artists in various media, including oils, watercolors, pastels, and acrylics. Look for strong photography exhibitions.

LOWER EASTERN SHORE

Cambridge

DORCHESTER ARTS
CENTER
410-228-7782.
120 High St.
Mon.–Fri. 10–2.

Headquartered in one of historic High Street's great homes, the center showcases area artists and offers classes, weekend workshops, and musical performances. The center stages the Dorchester Showcase every fall, a street party devoted to arts, crafts, music, and food. Everybody parties the full length of High Street.

Salisbury

**ART INSTITUTE
AND GALLERY OF
SALISBURY**
410-546-4748.
PO Box 193/Rte. 50 &
   Lemmon Hill Ln.
Mon.–Sat. 12–4.

In a former police headquarters, the Art Institute and Gallery exhibits works by area artists in all media, including juried and one-artist shows. The Institute offers a variety of classes, a fine gift shop, and an extensive outreach program to area schools.

UNIVERSITY GALLERY
410-543-6271.
Fulton Hall, Salisbury State
   University.
School year, Tues.–Thurs.
   10–5, Fri. 10–8, Sat. &
   Sun. noon–4; summer,
   Mon.–Fri. 10–4.

This gallery in the new $16-million Fulton Hall complex for liberal and fine arts is a fine venue for group, national, and international exhibitions. Also presented are works by regional folk crafters, local one-artist shows, and pieces produced by university students and faculty. Another gallery at the university is the **Atrium**, at the Guerrieri Center.

HISTORIC BUILDINGS AND SITES

HEAD OF THE BAY

Cecilton

**MOUNT HARMON
PLANTATION**
410-275-8819.
Grove Neck Rd.; off Rte.
   282; about 1 mi. S.W. of
   Rtes. 282 & 213 intersection at Cecilton.

In colonial days, when "King Tobacco" was the main moneymaker in these parts, Tidewater gentry set themselves up in sprawling plantations. Mount Harmon now represents these shoreside fiefdoms that ruled the river-laced frontier. The restored Georgian manor house, built in 1730, has, alas, been closed to the public, but all are welcome to tour the more than 200 acres of gardens along the Sassafras River until the gates close at dusk. Owned and operated by the non-profit Natural Lands Trust, the site is a nature preserve featuring rare and endangered plant species like the American lotus.

Havre de Grace

**CONCORD POINT
LIGHTHOUSE**
410-939-3303.
Foot of Lafayette St.
Sat. & Sun 1–5, Apr.–Oct.

The Susquehanna River, prehistoric precursor to the Chesapeake, flows into the Bay at Havre de Grace. Perhaps the best view — though only during weekends from spring to fall — is from the Concord Point Lighthouse. The 1827 light opened about the same time the 14-mile Chesapeake and Delaware Canal opened, linking the Chesapeake to the Atlantic.

The Concord Point Light-house in Havre de Grace overlooks the head of the Chesapeake Bay.

Dan Wolff

Visitors to the lighthouse also will notice the spiffy new boardwalk that ends here. One-half mile long, the promenade rounds the point along the Susquehanna, affording an exhilarating view. Lots of locals stroll the boardwalk, or take in the view from one of many benches placed alongside.

ANNAPOLIS/WESTERN SHORE

Annapolis

CHARLES CARROLL HOUSE
410-269-1737.
107 Duke of Gloucester St.
Fri. & Sun. noon–4, Sat.
10–2, or by appt.
Handicap Access: Yes.
Admission: $6 for adults;
$5 for seniors; $2 for
students. Children
under 12 free.

Four Marylanders signed the Declaration of Independence; all of them, at least for a time, owned homes in Annapolis. This was the birthplace and boyhood home of Charles Carroll of Annapolis, the only Roman Catholic to sign the Declaration. His home, on the grounds of St. Mary's Church, housed a chapel in which Catholics worshiped during the mid-18th century, when the religion was forced underground.

The home has undergone extensive renovations, beginning with archaeological digs in the formal gardens outside that turned up artifacts likely from a tavern that once operated on the property.

Construction of the original house began in 1721; Carroll himself added a story, an A-frame room, and a three-story wing in 1770. His chapel was the precursor of **St. Mary's Church** (410-263-2396), which stands in front on the same property. It's worth a peek inside the century-old church to see the magnificent altar.

CHASE-LLOYD HOUSE
410-263-2723.

Samuel Chase, yet another Annapolitan to sign the Declaration, started this house in 1769 —

22 Maryland Ave.
Tues.–Sat. 2–4; Jan. & Feb.,
Tues., Fri., & Sat. 2–4
only.
Admission: $2.

before he became one of the new nation's first Supreme Court justices. Later, Chase sold the home, unfinished, to Edward Lloyd IV, member of a prominent Maryland political dynasty. Inside, the brick mansion is most noted for the spectacular "flying" stairway, which has no visible means of support.

GOVERNMENT HOUSE
410-974-3531.
State & Church Circles.
Tues.–Thurs. 10–2, by appt.
only.

Maryland's latest governor came to town and promptly restored the old name — "Government House" — to what the previous administration had called the "Governor's Mansion." Built in 1868, the Georgian-style home is filled with Maryland arts and antiques. Arrange tours by appointment only.

A fine example of 18th-century architecture, the Hammond-Harwood House in Annapolis.

David Trozzo

HAMMOND-HARWOOD HOUSE
410-269-1714.
19 Maryland Ave.
Mon.–Sat. 10–4, Sun.
noon–4.
Gift shop; small admission
fee.

Widely considered one of the nation's finest remaining examples of Georgian architecture, this 1770s center-block house boasts two wings connected by two hyphens, a style known as a five-point Maryland house (a Palladian varietal that turned up only in colonial Maryland). The symmetry is meticulous : false doors balance actual entrances. Intricately carved ribbons and roses mark the front entrance. Inside hang portraits by one-time Annapolitan Charles Willson Peale and furniture by noted Annapolis coffinmaker-turned-cabinetmaker John Shaw. Discount tour tickets for those who also visit the nearby William Paca House.

**MARYLAND STATE-
HOUSE**
410-974-3400.
State Circle.
Mon.–Fri., 9–5; Sat. & Sun.
10–4; tours at 11 & 3
daily.

The first statehouse was built on this hill in 1699; the present building is the third. Fire, the scourge of so many colonial-era buildings, destroyed the first building, replaced in 1705. The second statehouse lasted until 1766, when the government decided to build a more architecturally distinguished capitol building. Marylanders now boast that theirs is the country's oldest state capitol building in continuous use. And, from Nov. 26, 1783, to Aug. 13, 1784, the building served as the capitol to a new nation.

The Old Senate Chamber where George Washington resigned his commission to the Continental Army in 1783 remains, the legislators' chairs lined up in rows. The Treaty of Paris officially ending the Revolution was ratified here in 1784. Visitors will also see Charles Willson Peale's portrait of Gen. Washington with Marylander Tench Tilghman and the Marquis de Lafayette. Maryland's annual, 90-day legislative session still draws the General Assembly here. Abundant state travel information is available in the visitor center.

**SAINT ANNE'S EPISCO-
PAL CHURCH**
410-267-9333.
Church Circle.
Daily. Call Parish House
for tours.

This church was first built in the late 18th century. Fire destroyed much of the building several decades later, but parts of the old building were incorporated when the new church went up in 1859. Many graves in the old churchyard were moved when Church Circle was widened years ago, but the graves of Annapolis's first mayor, Amos Garret, and Maryland's last colonial governor, Sir Robert Eden, remain. Inside is a silver communion service given by King William III dating from the 1690s.

SHIPLAP HOUSE
410-626-1033.
18 Pinkney St.
Mon.–Fri., when volunteers
available.

Rumored to be haunted by a friendly female ghost, this historic site features an exhibit, such as a depiction of colonial taverns (also known as "ordinaries"), on its first floor. Upstairs houses the administrative offices of Historic Annapolis, Inc., long the guiding light of the city's historic preservation and reconstruction efforts.

**WILLIAM PACA HOUSE
AND GARDEN**
House: 410-263-5553.
Garden: 410-267-6656.
186 Prince George St.
Mon.–Sat. 10–4, Sun. 12–4.
Winter hours: Fri. & Sat.
10–4; Sun. noon–4.
Gift shop; admission.

William Paca, three-time colonial governor of Maryland and signer of the Declaration of Independence, built his magnificent Georgian mansion between 1763 and 1765. Here he entertained during the era known as Annapolis's golden age.

Preservationists always say they've meticulously restored their buildings, but what they've done here really is amazing. During renovations in the 1960s and '70s, X-rays revealed that two architectural styles found in the main staircase dated to the same era, a mixing and matching apparently chosen by Mr. Paca himself. First-floor antiques date to Paca's residency here, with a few more liberties taken on the second floor — like a 19th-century spinet.

Early in the 20th century, the house became the Carvel Hall Hotel. In 1965, high rise apartments were slated to replace the building. Historic Annapolis, Inc., bought the house, and in six weeks' time, convinced the Maryland General Assembly to buy the two-acre garden site in back. Archaeologists set about reconstructing the gardens, and knew they had hit pay dirt when they uncovered an original pond — it promptly refilled from a spring beneath. A must-see for any gardener, the formal, terraced Paca Gardens now boast a reconstructed pavilion and Chinese-style bridge. A discount package is available to those touring the Hammond-Harwood House, too.

Edgewater

LONDON TOWN HOUSE AND GARDENS
410-222-1919.
839 Londontown Rd.
S. on Rte. 2 from Annapolis; 1 mi. past South River Bridge, left on Mayo Rd. (Md. 253),1 mi. to left on Londontown Rd.
Mar.–Nov.; Tues.–Sat. 10–4, Sun. 12–4.
Admission: Adults $5, seniors $3.50, children $2.50.

Take time to cross the South River Bridge south of Annapolis to visit this old ordinary, or pub, on the banks of the South River. Knowledgeable docents in colonial garb give complete tours of traveling-class life in the 18th century. Men of limited means shared beds upstairs. Traveling gentleman professionals — an itinerant dentist, say — had their own rooms while they stayed in town to do business. Notice the clay pipes stored in a box by the hearth in the main drinking room. A pipe was communal property; the smoker merely broke off the end and returned pipe to box at the end of the evening. Special events for adults and children are also presented.

Hollywood

SOTTERLEY MANSION
301-373-2280.
9 mi. E. of Leonardtown on Rte. 245.
June–Sept., Tues.–Sun. 11–4; Oct.–Nov. by appt. only.
Admission: $5 adults, $4 seniors, $2 children under 12.

Gaslights flicker at night at this private working plantation on the Patuxent River. An orchard, smokehouse, and slave's cabin stand near the magnificent mansion. Begun as a manorial grant issued in 1650 by Lord Baltimore, Sotterley's first house was built in 1717 by a wealthy Englishman named James Bowles. The sixth governor of Maryland made the home into the mansion it is today. Legend says the house may have inspired George Washington's Mount Vernon. Annual public events include Family Heritage Day in spring, a celebration of African-American life.

St. Marys City

ST. MARYS CITY
301-862-0990.
PO Box 39; Rte. 5.
Late Mar.–Nov.;
Weds.–Sun. 10–5.
Admission: Adults $6.50,
seniors & students $6,
children 6–12 $3.25.
Take-out restaurant in living-history park; visitor
center gift shop; special
events and programs.

In 1634, newly arrived settlers created Maryland's first capital here. By 1720, the city was gone. Now, as researchers unearth more about 17th-century colonial life, this living museum has become one of the nation's important archaeological sites.

A tantalizing discovery came a few years back when archaeologists exhumed three lead coffins, which, given their cost in the late 1600s, surely belonged to a family of means. Historians theorized they had discovered the remains of Maryland's founding family, the Calverts. In came experts from all disciplines, including NASA scientists who tested to see if 17th-century air was trapped inside. Alas, it was not. In the end, the team concluded — "99.9%" as one insider said — that the bodies were those of Philip Calvert, the colony's first chancellor; his first wife, Anne Wolsey Calvert; and a six-month-old child whose identity remains unknown — but might have been Philip's child from a second marriage.

There are also costumed interpreters. "Hey!" shouts the man in knee-breeches. "Have you seen the piglets?" It's Godiah Spray himself, master of the re-created 17th-century tobacco plantation here, gathering young visitors to take them to the field to find the Ossabaw pigs, a 300-year-old species the colonists likely brought to early Maryland. Just as they would have during the early years, the pigs are wild and wander in the nearby woods.

Also at St. Marys City, or "St. Maries Citty," the 100-acre **Governor's Field** serves as a rustic town green; and there's **Farthing's Ordinary**, where you can

Costumed interpreters prepare food at Farthing's Ordinary and Garden, St. Marys City.

David Trozzo

grab a sandwich; the reconstructed **1676 State House;** and the *Maryland Dove*, a replica of the type of square-rigged boat that brought the first colonists. A new and popular addition is the **Woodland Indian Hamlet**, with a longhouse, field, and work areas. St. Marys City is wrapped around portions of the **St. Mary's College** campus (see "Historic Schools").

NORTHERN NECK/MIDDLE PENINSULA

Westmoreland County, Virginia

George Washington's birthplace in Westmoreland County, Virginia, gives visitors a taste of life on an 18th-century plantation.

Ben Barnhart

GEORGE WASHINGTON BIRTHPLACE NATIONAL MONUMENT
804-224-1732.
Rte. 3 to Rte. 204, 38 mi. E. of Fredericksburg.
Daily 9–5.
Admission: $2.

It didn't all start at Mount Vernon, as visitors here will soon discover. Colonial history and the Washington family headline this mansion-park complex on Pope's Creek off the Potomac River. The home where Washington was born burned to the ground in 1779, but archaeologists have outlined the footprint of the U-shaped house in oyster shells. The brick Memorial House here was built in the early 1930s. Costumed docents tell of early life on the colonial plantation. The park also includes a visitor center, a burying ground, hiking trails, and a picnic area. Look for special holiday events and programs such as Colonial Medicine Days.

STRATFORD HALL PLANTATION
804-493-8038.
45 mi. E. of Fredericksburg, Rte. 214.

"Light Horse Harry" begat Robert E., the best-known members of the illustrious Lee family. Their historic home features a 1,600-acre working plantation and Great House (circa 1738) and is considered one of the finest museum houses in Amer-

Museum daily 9–4:30; dining room 11:30–3. Admission: Adults $7, children $3.50.

ica. It was built in 1738 by another Lee named Thomas, one-time acting governor of the colony and father to six sons, almost all of whom went on to distinguished careers. Two, Richard Henry Lee and Francis Lightfoot Lee, were the only brothers to sign the Declaration of Independence. Gen. Robert E. Lee's birthday is celebrated every Jan. 19.

Built of brick made on-site and timber hewn nearby, the H-shaped manor house features the 29-square-foot Great Hall, renowned as one of the finest colonial rooms still in existence. Visitors can see the crib in which the Confederate general slept as an infant in 1808. Trails lead through the working farm — which includes 1,600 original acres.

UPPER EASTERN SHORE

Centreville

QUEEN ANNE'S COUNTY COURT-HOUSE
410-758-1773.
100 Courthouse Sq.
Mon.–Fri. 8:30–4:30.

This town of 18th-century and Victorian structures is home to the oldest courthouse (1791) in continuous use in Maryland. Queen Anne's County is named after the English monarch who reigned from 1702 to 1714. A bronze of her seated upon (what else?) a Queen Anne chair was erected in 1977 on the Queen Anne's County Courthouse green. Princess Anne herself came for the unveiling.

David Trozzo

The old Concord Light shines on a mural in Havre de Grace every day (the real thing is open on weekends).

Chestertown

GEDDES-PIPER HOUSE
410-778-3499.
101 Church Alley.
May–Oct.; Sat.–Sun. 1–4.
Admission: $2.

This three-and-a-half story brick townhouse designed in the "Philadelphia style" was built in the early 1700s. Now the museum headquarters of the Kent County Historical Society, the home was owned by a series of 18th-century merchants, including William Geddes, customs collector for the Port of Chestertown. Geddes claims a notorious local fame — his was the brigantine ravaged during the 1774 Chestertown Tea Party, which is still celebrated (see "Seasonal Events and Festivals"). Geddes sold the house to merchant James Piper. It now features 18th- and 19th-century furnishings, maps, and china, and a library. Private tours can be arranged.

Easton

HISTORICAL SOCIETY OF TALBOT COUNTY
410-822-0773.
125 S. Washington St.
Tues.–Sat. 10–4, Sun. 1–4 (closed Sun. Jan.–Feb.).
Gift shop (same weekday hours as museum, but closed Sun.).
Admission: $2.

Flagship of the eight buildings of the Historical Society of Talbot County is the **Neall House**, circa 1810. This Federal-era townhouse is home to the society's permanent exhibit of furnishings and artifacts. Adjacent is the society's research library and changing historical exhibitions. A colonial-style garden is maintained outside, and the auditorium, in an old church sanctuary, is now the location for a film retrospective, lectures, and workshops. **Tharpe House**, another early 19th-century Federal townhouse, serves as a regional history museum, with changing exhibitions. Check the Museum Shop for books of regional interest.

Out back stand a couple of small and interesting buildings well worth a look: the shop of an 18th-century cabinetmaker and "The Ending of Controversie," a 17th-century dwelling that now houses the artifacts and folk art collection of H. Chandlee Forman, the scientist who helped discover St. Marys City early this century. The Historical Society also can arrange tours of Easton's **Historic District**.

THIRD HAVEN FRIENDS MEETING HOUSE
410-822-0293.
405 S. Washington St.
Daily 9–5; services Sun. 10, Weds. 5:30.

Built in 1682, this Quaker Meeting House is believed to be the oldest frame building in the country continuously used for religious purposes. The town of Easton grew up around it. It's local lore that William Penn preached here and Lord Baltimore visited, but that actually occurred at a nearby site.

WYE GRIST MILL
410-827-6909.
Rte. 662.
Apr.–Oct.; Sat.–Sun. 11–4 &
by appt.
Donations accepted.
Gift shop.

Back in 1671, when a grist mill first lumbered into activity here, it's doubtful the miller expected it still to be working in the 21st century. Visitors generally take home a bag or two of its ground flour and yellow cornmeal, perhaps with a copy of *Wye Millers Grind*, a 100-recipe cookbook. They grind by water on the third Saturday of each month, Apr.–Oct. Non-profit Preservation Maryland and Friends of Wye Mill operate the mill.

Elsewhere around Wye Mills, look for the restored Old Wye Church, circa 1721, an early Episcopal church. Nearby stands Maryland's official State Tree, the Wye Oak, now more than 400 years old. It is massive — over 95 feet high, with a 165-foot leaf canopy — and comprises its own state park.

Maryland's official State Tree, the Wye Oak, is 95 feet high with a trunk 21 feet around.

Ben Barnhart

Stevensville

**KENT ISLAND HER-
ITAGE SOCIETY**
410-643-5969.
PO Box 321.
May–Oct.; Sat. 1–4.

Colonial and Victorian buildings fill the center of this small town north of the first exit east of the Bay Bridge. The Cray House is a simple dwelling from 1823; a costumed guide describes the way of life in that era. The railroad station, built in 1902, was moved to the site recently and is being restored by Gil Dunn, the island's tireless pharmacist. Both are operated by the Heritage Society.

Tilghman Island

The skipjack fleet at Tilghman Island is worth seeing, especially since the days are numbered for these beautiful anachronisms. Famed because they're the country's last workboats that operate under sail, several even date back a century — and few have been built since World War II. They periodically sink and are resurrected, and some go on to lives in museums or as tour boats for eco-groups. But most of the remaining boats on the Bay winter at the harbor just south of Knapps Narrows and offer a splendid photo opportunity when the sun is low in the afternoon sky. Follow Rte. 33 beyond St. Michaels, cross the drawbridge and turn left to the harbor.

LOWER EASTERN SHORE

Cambridge

**MEREDITH
HOUSE/DORCHESTER
COUNTY HISTORICAL
SOCIETY**
410-228-7953.
902 LaGrange Ave.
3 blocks E. of U.S. 50.
Thurs.–Sat. 10–4, & by appt.
Free to individuals; large
groups and bus trips $2
per person.

This circa 1760 Georgian house is noted both for Flemish bond brickwork and its memorial to Dorchester's contributions to the governor's mansion. Six state governors came from the county's lowlands, including Thomas Holiday Hicks, who managed to suppress the state's strong secessionist element to maintain Maryland's Union status; one-time U.S. senator Phillips Lee Goldsborough; Emerson C. Harrington, founder of the state's Conservation Commission; and Henry Lloyd, yet another member of this prominent family, and one-time owner of this house. The **Neild Farm Museum** stands on the grounds, displaying the sickles, scythes, yokes, and boats of the Lower Shore's yeoman class. Look also — believe it or not — for memorabilia from one-time Cambridge resident Annie Oakley. The **Goldsborough Stable** (circa 1790), moved from a nearby site, houses a transportation exhibit.

Created by boatbuilder "Mr. Jim" Richardson, the Spocott windmill in Cambridge is the only post windmill in Maryland.

Star Democrat

SPOCOTT WINDMILL
410-228-7090.
Rte. 343, 7 mi. W. of Cambridge.
Daily 10–5.
Free; donations accepted.

One of the region's most enduring residents, the great boatbuilder James B. "Mr. Jim" Richardson took it upon himself to build this reproduction of a windmill destroyed here during the blizzard of 1888. "Mr. Jim," who passed away in 1989, kept his master builder's wooden boat workshop at his LeCompte Creek boatyard. His windmill, the only post windmill in Maryland, boasts a 52-foot span. Also open to the public here are the colonial tenant house, the former home of Adaline Wheatley (ca. 1800), and the **Castle Haven** one-room schoolhouse from 1870. A new addition is **Lloyd's Country Store Museum**.

Princess Anne

TEACKLE MANSION
410-651-3020.
Mansion St.
Weds., Sat., & Sun. 1–3 Mar.–mid-Dec.; other times by appt.
Admission $3, children under 12 free.

Back before the Manokin (pronounced Ma-NO-kin) River got so shallow, its deep water encouraged ships to travel upriver. Plantations and ports thrived along its banks, and Teackle Mansion is a well-preserved holdover from that era. Modeled after a Scottish manor house and dating from 1801, the 200-foot-long pink-brick mansion was built with stylish symmetry. Built by Littleton Dennis Teackle, expatriate Virginian and apparently also an occasional confidant of Jefferson, Madison, and Monroe, the house boasts a great room with high ceilings, multiple stairways, and both river and land entrances. Outside are beautiful gardens. Teackle seems to have lost his shipping fortune after Barbary pirates plundered much of his merchant fleet.

Salisbury

PEMBERTON HISTORI-CAL PARK:
Pemberton Hall:
410-742-1741.
Wicomico Heritage Centre:
410-546-0314 or 749-7361.
Pemberton Dr.; about 2 mi.
S.W. of Rte. 349 & U.S. 50.
Pemberton Hall:
Apr.–Sept.; Sun. 2–4 & by appt.
Wicomico Heritage Centre:
May.–Sept., Sun. 2–4 & by appt.
Admission: Donations accepted.

One of the oldest brick gambrel-roofed houses in Maryland, **Pemberton Hall** was built in 1741 for Col. Isaac Handy, a plantation owner and shipping magnate who helped found what would become the city of Salisbury. Col. Handy's home is the centerpiece of a museum complex that includes nearby **Wicomico Heritage Centre**, designed to resemble a colonial tobacco barn. It's headquarters for the Wicomico Historical Society, with a permanent collection of local history memorabilia and rotating exhibits. Nature trails; picnic area.

HISTORIC SCHOOLS

ANNAPOLIS/WESTERN SHORE

Annapolis

The "Johnnies," as students at **St. John's College** are called, study only the Great Books during their years here, where intellect is greatly valued and humor tends toward plays on Greek or Latin phrases. The college, descended

The yin and yang of Annapolitan collegiality, at the annual croquet match between St. John's College and the U.S. Naval Academy.

David Trozzo

from King William's School, claims to be the nation's third oldest. On campus, look for the centuries-old Liberty Tree, where the Sons of Liberty met to dispel any hint of closed-door politics. The oldest building on campus, McDowell Hall, houses the venerable Great Hall, where contemporary college kids hold waltz parties (and the students really do waltz), and also where a banquet was tossed for the aging General Lafayette in 1824 and a hospital was set up during the Civil War. Visitors interested in looking around the college should stop by the news and information office in the building named after famed alumnus Francis Scott Key. For more information, call 410-263-2371, or write 60 College Ave., Annapolis MD 21401.

Graduation ceremonies at the U.S. Naval Academy, Annapolis, in 1939.

Maryland State Archives

For many in the U.S.A., "Annapolis" and "U.S. Naval Academy" are synonyms. Although the locals would beg to differ, none would disagree that the **U.S. Naval Academy** has had great influence on the city. Founded in 1845 at old Fort Severn, the Academy's long history includes its notable move from Annapolis to Newport, R.I., during the Civil War, prompted by the Maryland city's overwhelming Southern sympathies. During the war, both the Academy and St. John's College up the street became military hospitals. Upon their return, naval officers found the campus in great need of military spit-shine. "It was quite a mess," says Academy museum curator Jim Cheevers. "The cavalry horses had eaten the leaves off the willow trees and in the superintendent's quarters were beer bottles and pool tables."

So commenced plans for a "new Academy," the collection of Beaux Arts buildings designed by architect Ernest Flagg and constructed between 1899 and 1908. Inside the Academy chapel, begun in 1904, is the final resting place of "Father of the U.S. Navy," John Paul Jones. Jones was finally entombed in 1913 after a fantastic journey. He was buried in Paris in 1792, but his grave was lost in the turmoil of the French Revolution as the cemetery, owned by the House of Bourbon, was seized, sold by the Revolutionary government, and later developed. After a concerted search, Jones's tomb was rediscovered 100 years later. Following much politicking, it was determined that the admiral should be laid to rest in the **Academy Chapel** — then still under construction. The casket arrived at the Academy in 1905-06.

"The midshipmen carried the casket into the newly finished Bancroft Hall, put it under the grand staircase that leads to Memorial Hall, and there the casket sat . . . for seven years," says Cheever. Finally, the chapel was completed.

Visitors today enter the grounds at Gate 1, at the foot of King George Street, then head to the Armel-Leftwich Visitor Center, next to the Halsey Field House.

Tour guides escort visitors to the nation's largest college dormitory, **Bancroft Hall**, where the rotunda features one of the best views of the Bay in Annapolis, or the **Academy Museum** in Preble Hall. Notable is the Henry Huddleston Rogers Ship Model Collection, 108 models of British and French sailing ships built from 1650 to 1850. Also, the Beverly Robinson Collection of naval prints includes 5,000 images of every naval engagement from the 13th century to the Spanish-American War. For information about tours: 410-293-3363. To reach the Academy Museum, open from 9–5 Mon.–Sat. & 11–5 on Sun., call 410-293-2108.

St. Marys City

St. Mary's College was established at St. Marys City in 1840 to commemorate the legacy of the colonial achievements of Maryland's first settlers. A small public liberal arts institution, the college is set on a beautiful riverside campus on the grounds of Maryland's first settlement and capital. Its reputation as a well-kept secret may be out, however: *Money* magazine recently named it one of the country's top liberal arts education values. The campus includes a number of historic buildings, and gardens. For more information, call 301-862-0380, or write to the college at St. Marys City MD 20686-9990.

UPPER EASTERN SHORE
Chestertown

The father of our country gave express permission for use of his name to the founders of **Washington College**. The nation's president was a close friend of The Rev. Dr. William Smith, founder and first president of the college, chartered in 1782. Visitors to the tree-lined liberal arts college may want to take note of the Washington Elm, a "grandchild" of the Washington Elm in Cambridge, Massachusetts, under which Washington stood as commander of the armed forces in 1775. This is an elegant, small liberal arts college known, among other things, as an integral neighbor to the Chestertown community, which habitually consults the college's schedule of events. For more information, call 410-778-2800, or write to the college at Washington Avenue, Chestertown MD 21620.

LECTURES

Annapolis

U.S. Naval Academy offers several lectures or lecture series, focusing on a variety of topics such as history or oceanography. For information and dates, check local papers or call 410-293-1000.

St. John's College students attend Friday lectures at the Francis Scott Key Auditorium, and those of classically like minds are invited to join the 8:15pm sessions. Here one can learn about "The Wrath of Achilles," or "Storytelling with Pictures: A Greek Invention." Free. For more information: 410-263-2371.

Chestertown

Among **Washington College**'s offerings is the year-long Sophie Kerr Lecture Series, featuring a range of writers and editors; it culminates in March, when such noted figures as Toni Morrison or William Warner come to speak. Also check out the series on environmental science and public policy. Free. Call 410-778-7849, or e-mail college_relations@washcoll.edu.

St. Marys City

Prominent scholars are guest lecturers at **St. Mary's College**, sponsored by the college's Woodrow Wilson, Margaret Brent, and Carter G. Woodson lecture series. For more information: 301-862-0380.

LIBRARIES

Libraries here focus on resources for Chesapeake historical, archival, and genealogical information. Bridging the magic of old, yellowing documents is the new and ever-growing number of virtual libraries serving on-line readers and researchers. The Maryland public libraries have gone on-line with their catalogs, and more services will become available as the **Sailor** network, an on-line connection to the state libraries, government, and related information, gets up and running. Telnet address: sailor.lib.md.us. Or, pick up an old-fashioned phone and call their help desk, at 410-396-INFO (4636). Finally, you can e-mail helpdesk@epfl1.epflbalto.org.

Meanwhile, **Chesapeake Free-Net** in Easton provides a free community forum on-line and low-priced access to the Net and World Wide Web. The nonprofit operation serves Kent, Queen Anne's, Talbot, Dorchester, and Caroline counties. Set your modem to 8N1 and call 410-819-6860 or talk to a human at 410-819-0303. Telnet to cfn.bluecrab.org.

HEAD OF THE BAY

Havre de Grace

HARFORD COUNTY LIBRARY
410-939-6700.
120 N. Union Ave.
Closed Sun. & Mon.; call for hours.

Harford County Library is in the middle of old Havre de Grace. Ask for the Maryland Collection. To access the public stacks through Sailor, modem 410-638-KNOW.

ANNAPOLIS/WESTERN SHORE

Annapolis

ANNE ARUNDEL COUNTY PUBLIC LIBRARY
410-222-1750.
1410 West St.
Mon.–Thurs. 9–9, Fri.–Sat. 9–5, Sun. 1–5.

The Annapolis branch of the county public library, better known as the West Street Library, is the most comprehensive in the system. It offers an excellent selection of Maryland and Chesapeake area history, as well as works by local writers and a good reference section. To access Sailor, modem in through 410-222-7100.

MARYLAND STATE ARCHIVES
410-974-3914.
350 Rowe Blvd.
Mon.–Sat. 8:30–4:30.

Archivists here seem to go above and beyond to help researchers. A full 115,000 cubic feet of space hold 7,509 different series of records, from vital statistics to church registers, including many from the Roman Catholic Archdiocese in Baltimore. Here author Alex Haley of *Roots* fame found his African ancestor, the slave Kunta Kinte. Noted local historian and long-time archivist Phebe Jacobsen figured out how to use manumissions and other documents of slave-holders to help African-Americans trace their pasts. A wealth of other interesting documents turn up true gems from time to time. In 1990, a researcher unearthed the first eyewitness account of John Brown's historic raid on the federal arsenal at Harper's Ferry, West Virginia.

Researchers must register, and first-timers are encouraged to write ahead for registration packets. A small but well-selected inventory of Maryland and Chesapeake-region books is for sale in the lobby. For selected reference information through the Internet, try http://www.mdarchives.state.md.us.

NORTHERN NECK/MIDDLE PENINSULA

Heathville, Virginia

NORTHUMBERLAND COUNTY HISTORICAL SOCIETY
804-580-8581 or
804-453-5691.
Rte. 360.
Tues.–Thurs. 9–4; every
2nd & 4th Sat. 9–1.

Behind the courthouse in Heathsville, this is a collection of genealogical and historical documents. The well-trained staff is very helpful.

Lancaster, Virginia

MARY BALL WASHINGTON MUSEUM
804-462-7280.
Rte. 3/PO Box 97.
Tues.–Fri. 9–5, Sat. 10–3 or
by appt.

A valuable resource for genealogists, this museum and library combined offers a historical lending collection, genealogical sources, research facilities, museum exhibitions, programs for the general public, workshops, film series, and information on archaeology, archives, and oral history. The genealogical department and library contain an extensive collection of original research material. Lancaster County records from its 1651 founding are virtually complete.

Montross, Virginia

WESTMORELAND COUNTY MUSEUM AND INFORMATION CENTER
804-493-8440.
Off Rte. 3 across from
Courthouse Square.
PO Box 716 for Northern
Neck of Virginia Historical Society Library.
Apr.–Oct.: Mon.–Sat. 10–5,
Sun. 1–5. Nov.–Mar.:
Tues.–Sat. 10:30–4.

While you'll find the usual tourist brochures, you'll also find the Northern Neck of Virginia Historical Society Library and a small museum. The curator there will be able to help you with any questions.

UPPER EASTERN SHORE

The **Kent County Public Library**, with a main branch in *Chestertown* (410-778-3636), also has a branch in *Rock Hall* (410-639-7162). The **Historical Society of Kent County** headquarters are at the Geddes-Piper House (410-778-3499), also in *Chestertown*, with a library that contains historic site surveys, genealogical records, and documents, as well as books; call ahead.

The **Queen Anne County Libraries** in *Centreville* (410-758-0980) and *Kent Island* (410-643-8161) were tops in a recent statewide survey when it comes to helping users with research questions.

The **Talbot County Free Library** in _Easton_, at 100 W. Dover St. (410-822-1626), houses the Maryland Room, a research facility filled with books and periodicals (some on microfiche) about the area. Talbot also has a library branch in _St. Michaels_ (410-745-5877).

The **Chesapeake Bay Maritime Museum** in _St. Michaels_ maintains the **Howard I. Chappelle Memorial Library**, devoted to maritime and Chesapeake writings and named for the famed boatbuilder (410-745-2916; call ahead).

LOWER EASTERN SHORE

The **Dorchester County Library**'s Maryland Room, in its main branch in _Cambridge_, offers reference works on regional and state history (410-228-7331).

In _Salisbury_, the **Salisbury State University Research Center for Delmarva History and Culture**, in Room 190 of the Powers Professional Building, is a gold mine of documents, maps, and archives going way back. Here also is the Dryden Collection of genealogical records of the Eastern Shore. Call ahead (410-543-6312).

The main branch of the **Somerset County Library** in the charming little town of _Princess Anne_ has a genealogy room (410-651-0852).

Maryland and regional history, as well as genealogical data, can be researched in the Worcester Room of the **Worcester Free Library** in _Snow Hill_ (410-632-2600). The **Eastern Shore Public Library** in _Accomack, Virginia_ (on old U.S. 13; 804-787-3400) has a genealogy room with historical materials. Mon.–Weds. 9–6, Thurs. 9–9, Sat. 9–1.

MUSEUMS

See also "Historic Buildings and Sites."

HEAD OF THE BAY

Havre de Grace

HAVRE DE GRACE DECOY MUSEUM
410-939-3739.
Giles & Market Sts.
Daily 11–4.
$2, $1 seniors, children under 8 free.
Handicap Access: Yes.

So you want to know about decoy carving? You've come to the right place, where you'll immediately discover a proud piece of the past of this growing little tourist/sailing town. Recently expanded to include an upstairs gallery with an expansive view of the Susquehanna River, the museum is dedicated to preserving the Bay's old "gunning" tradition, the art of hunting with

Famed decoy carver Capt. Harry R. Jobes lives on at Havre de Grace's Decoy Museum.

David Trozzo

decoys. Works by noted carvers R. Madison Mitchell, Bob McGaw, Paul Gibson, and Charlies Joiner and Bryant are exhibited here, as well as tools of the trade and displays recalling the days earlier this century when they gathered round the stove. Perhaps most intriguing is a peek into why conservation measures have become so important: the sinkbox. This clever contraption was outlawed in the mid-1930s "because it was too effective," chuckled a long-time Chesapeake outdoor enthusiast. Shaped like a bathtub with square wings weighted down with flat-bottomed decoys, the sinkbox held a hunter who climbed inside and took to the duck hunt at the Susquehanna Flats. The flats were famous in the first half of this century, drawing the rich and famous from Baltimore, Washington, and Philly. But in the '40s, the river's wild rice and wild celery disappeared — and so did the Flats. Volunteer decoy carvers work every weekend in the museum vestibule, where the curious can learn a little more about the modern evolution of this old tradition. Nice book/giftshop features duck and decoy books.

South Chesapeake City

C&D CANAL MUSEUM
410-885-5621.
Second St. & Bethel Rd.
Mon.–Sat. 8–4:15, year-round; Sun. 10–6
Easter–mid–Oct. only.

The 14-mile-long Chesapeake and Delaware Canal severs the top of the Delmarva Peninsula from the mainland, linking the Upper Chesapeake Bay with the Delaware River. In so doing, the grand old C&D shaves 300 miles off an otherwise roundabout journey from Philadelphia to Baltimore by way of Norfolk and the Virginia capes.

The tiny museum, in the pumphouse for the old locks, is a neat little place to learn more about this engineering feat. The canal was discussed for 150 years before it finally opened in 1829. Photos, models, maps, and a 38-foot 19th-century waterwheel, at the time considered a marvel of engineering, are on display. Run by the U.S. Army Corps of Engineers, the same outfit that runs the canal.

ANNAPOLIS/WESTERN SHORE

Annapolis

BANNEKER-DOUGLASS MUSEUM OF AFRICAN-AMERICAN LIFE AND HISTORY
410-974-2893.
84 Franklin St.
Tues.–Fri. 10–3, Sat. 12–4.

Victorian Mount Moriah African Methodist Episcopal Church, built in 1874, stood amid what was the historic district's black neighborhood going back to the mid-19th century. Now named for two prominent black Marylanders, Frederick Douglass and Benjamin Banneker, it's Maryland's African-American museum. There is an eclectic range of exhibitions; permanent collections include the Arctic artifacts brought home by explorer Herbert M. Frisby. Lectures, films, and educational programs.

Chesapeake Beach

CHESAPEAKE BEACH RAILWAY MUSEUM
410-257-3892.
PO Box 783; Mears Ave. & C St.
May–Sept. daily 1–4, Apr. & Oct. weekends 1–4; open by appt. year-round.
Handicap Access: Yes.
Free.

Near the turn of the century, a group of Colorado businessmen working in Washington, D.C., decided to open a resort. Visitors from the capital city took the railway to tiny Chesapeake Beach, while Baltimoreans rode the steamer south. The former railway station is now a museum, featuring photographs and artifacts from the old resort, including a kangaroo that once rode the boardwalk carousel. Extensive collection of early 20th-century photographs of the area.

Lexington Park

NAVAL AIR TEST AND EVALUATION MUSEUM
301-863-7418.
Patuxent Naval Air Station, Rte. 235 & Shangri-la Dr.
July–Sept.; Weds.–Fri. 11–4, Sun. 12–5. Oct.–June; Fri. & Sat. 11–4, Sun. 12–5.

At Patuxent River Naval Air Station, home to the Navy's Test Pilot School, is most likely the only museum you'll find with this specialty — they'll show you how naval aircraft are tested.

Solomons Island

CALVERT MARINE MUSEUM

A recent renovation brings visitors an updated look at life in the Bay — down to the river

410-326-2042.
Rte. 2.
10–5 daily.
Admission: Adults $4,
  seniors $3, children 5–12
  $2.
Gift shop; library for use by
  appt.; docking.
Handicap Access: Yes.

otters swimming merrily in a large tank out back. Overall, the museum presents Chesapeake marine life from prehistoric to recently historic, including crocodile jaws and the teeth of mastodons and other creatures dating to the Miocene era, dug from nearby Calvert Cliffs. There's also the tale of the Patuxent River, drawn from the post-war years of the recreational boating boom. Everything from a red metal "Drink Coca-Cola" cooler to a Maryland Charter Boat Association Rockfish Tournament plaque pays tribute to the days when even Lucy and Desi Arnaz owned a Solomons-built boat from the M.M. Davis & Sons Shipyard. Out back stands the **Drum Point Lighthouse**, one of only three remaining screw-pile lighthouses. Forty-three of these distinctly Chesapeake-designed sentinels once stood in the soft bottom of the Bay, warning mariners off dangerous shoals. Once electricity came along, a 100-watt bulb beamed 15 miles to sea, dimming forever laborious oil lights. When threatened by wreckers in 1975, the lighthouse was moved to the museum from Drum Point, a few miles north. But Drum Point Light was manned for 79 years, and visitors can see the cozily re-created lighthouse keeper's home during tours given several times a day. Or go aboard the bugeye *William B. Tennison*, the oldest U.S. Coast Guard–approved vessel to carry passengers on the Bay (Weds.–Sun.). During weekends, look for interpreters to tell of the fishing techniques of the area, including crabbing with crab pots and oyster tonging. There's also a boatbuilding shed featuring such craft as a 1936 draketail workboat. The museum's holdings also include the 1934 **J.C. Lore Oyster House** down the street, where visitors can see how oysters moved from tongers' boats to gourmets' plates. Lots of family events.

NORTHERN NECK/MIDDLE PENINSULA

Reedville, Virginia

**REEDVILLE FISHER-
  MEN'S MUSEUM**
804-453-6529.
Main St.
Mon.–Fri. 3–5, Sun. 1–5.
  Hours are subject to
  change in winter.
No admission; donations
  accepted.
Gift shop.

Reedville is still a little fishing village, where an old deadrise sits alongside the marine railway and the menhaden plant emits what old-timers call "the smell of money." Stop in at this little museum culled from neighborhood attics and homesteads to view a photographic explanation of purse-seining for menhaden, or visit the little fisherman's home called the Walker House, constructed in one day for $25 a century ago. Appropriately enough, visitors have been known to arrive here by water, rowing or motoring in by dinghy to the museum dock.

UPPER EASTERN SHORE

St. Michaels

Preserving the past: Richard Scofield, the Chesapeake Bay Maritime Museum's assistant boat-shop manager, applies a coat of varnish to the mast of the classic log-hull bugeye Edna E. Lockwood, *built in 1889. The Hoopers Straight Lighthouse, an 1879 screw-pile light, stands sentinel in the background.*

David Trozzo

CHESAPEAKE BAY MARITIME MUSEUM
410-745-2916.
Off Md. 33 at Mill St., Navy Point.
Daily in summer 9–7; Jan.–early Mar. 10–4 weekends only.
Admission: $7.50, seniors $6.50, children 6–17, $3.
Gift shop.

The small fleet of indigenous Bay workboats here tells the story of the watermen's history — and indeed of the Bay itself. There's the *Rosie Parks*, a famous skipjack; the *Edna E. Lockwood*, the last log-built bugeye still plying the Bay; and the *Old Point*, a crab dredger from Virginia. Inside the Small Boat Shed is everything from an old Indian dugout to a five-log oyster tonger. Craftsmen demonstrate the traditional art of wooden boat-building in the Boat Shop.

The 16-acre complex on the shores of Navy Point includes the **Hooper Strait Lighthouse**, moved to the museum grounds in 1966. Inside, the lighthouse keeper's late 19th-century life is re-created, and everyone stops for the prime view of the Miles River.

Also displayed are the massive punt guns used by the market gunners, as well as a huge collection of the decoys used by all waterfowl hunters. The museum gift shop offers a range of items with nautical themes, as well as maritime and Chesapeake books. At its **Tolchester Beach Bandstand**, the museum hosts summer concerts by sea chanteymen, bluegrass bands, folksingers, bagpipers, gospel singers, and brass bands. Look for boat-related festivals (see "Seasonal Events and Festivals" below in this chapter).

LOWER EASTERN SHORE

Hudson's Corner

EARLY AMERICANA MUSEUM
410-623-8324.
30195 Rehobeth Rd.,
  Marion Station.
1pm to dark, year-round.
  Call for appt.

The ultimate attic exploration, all in a collection of ex-chicken houses. Look for farm equipment and household junque. Southbound on U.S. 13 out of Salisbury, go right on Md. 413 and then left on Old Westover Road to Hudson's Corner. Call ahead to be sure Lawrence Burgess is available to open the unheated buildings for you.

Salisbury

WARD MUSEUM OF WILDFOWL ART
410-742-4988.
909 S. Schumaker Dr.
Mon.–Sat. 10–5, Sun. 12–5.
Admission: $4, students &
  seniors $3, K–12 $2.
Gift shop.

The legendary Ward Brothers, Lem and Steve, elevated the pragmatic craft of decoy-carving to artistry, and their name symbolizes the decoy-as-artform around here. This is probably the region's most extensive public collection of antique decoys. The evolution of decoys is traced from the American Indians' functional twisted-reed renderings to the latest lifelike wooden sculpture. Shown here is the personal collection of the Ward Brothers, including their own favorites among their earliest and latest efforts. The Ward Foundation was established in 1968, and holds the annual World Championship Carving Competition and a wildlife art exhibition and sale. The building is on a 4-acre site overlooking a pond.

MUSIC

From chamber concert series to opera musicales to jazz, any music-lover will find fine performances. Also check the Performing Arts and Theater section for information about additional happenings.

HEAD OF THE BAY

Forest Hill

**SUSQUEHANNA SYM-
PHONY ORCHESTRA**
PO Box 485, Forest Hill.
Program information: 410-
838-6465.

This well-established semi-professional organization is still performing under founding director Sheldon Bair. They offer four performances during the fall to spring season, and two more in summer, including one at the historic Liriodendron mansion. Their Christmas concert features several local church choirs; they also recently performed Bach's *St. John Passion* with the Penn State chorus. And there's a summertime patriotic concert in the park.

ANNAPOLIS/WESTERN SHORE

Annapolis

ANNAPOLIS CHORALE
410-263-1906.
Maryland Hall for the Creative Arts, 801 Chase St.
Tickets: $12–$20.

Conductor J. Ernest Green has built this group into a veritable cottage industry of chamber music. The 150-voice chorale, which has performed at Carnegie Hall, includes the smaller Chamber Chorus, the Annapolis Chamber Orchestra, and an all-youth chorus. Several performances are given each year of baroque, renaissance, and contemporary music. A local favorite: the annual Christmas performance, in which a high-profile celebrity (they even got local thriller author Tom Clancy not too long ago) narrates a performance. Concerts are held at Maryland Hall for the Creative Arts and occasionally at St. Anne's Episcopal Church.

ANNAPOLIS OPERA
410-267-8135.
PO Box 24.
Tickets: $12.50–$20 for
musicales; $25 for major
production.

Annapolis Opera now offers a highly popular new form of entertainment: the monthly musicale, often held in local parks or historic homes. Four or five singers and an accompanist perform. The opera still stages its annual vocal competition, and one major production per year, such as *Madame Butterfly*. Housed at Maryland Hall.

**ANNAPOLIS SYM-
PHONY ORCHESTRA**
410-263-0907 (tickets); 410-
269-1132 (administra-
tion).
Maryland Hall for the Creative Arts, 801 Chase St.
Season: Oct.–Apr.

A sophisticated five- to six-performance season under the direction of Gisele Ben-Dor, also musical director for Boston's Pro-Arte Chamber Orchestra, the Santa Barbara Symphony, and a cover conductor for the New York Philharmonic. Saturday concert tickets usually go to subscription holders, so call a week in advance if you hope to

Michael P. Majer

The Annapolis Symphony Orchestra delights audiences at the Maryland Hall for the Creative Arts.

Tickets: $18–$26; $8 for children attending family concerts.

attend that night; Friday night tickets are easier to obtain. The annual children's concerts are also quite popular, and school-based educational efforts — demystifying the orchestra to youth — have been stepped up in recent years.

NAVAL ACADEMY MUSICAL PERFORMANCES
410-268-6060 or 1-800-US-4-NAVY (tickets); 410-293-2439 (information).
Music Department, Mitscher Hall, U.S. Naval Academy.
Ticket prices vary; usually range from $12–$25.

The Naval Academy's **Distinguished Artist Series** brings in about four productions a year offered by traveling groups such as the New York City Opera or the Kirov Orchestra, plus a choral concert by the academy's glee club. Performances are held in the Bob Hope Performing Arts Center in Alumni Hall, in which an acoustic shell is lowered into the basketball arena. Acoustics are admittedly less than perfect, but it works for large orchestras and boasts a powerful sound system.

Whatever you do, don't pass up a chance to hear a performance in the exquisite Naval Academy chapel. Long-time chapel organist Jim Dale offers four free performances, and a major choral performance featuring the academy men's and women's glee club. Ticket prices for choral performances are low, and seats for the Christmas *Messiah*, performed now for 50 years, sell out fast.

The Naval Academy also provides another very popular offering: the **Summer Serenade Concert Series**. It's fun and casual. Folks bring chairs and blankets to the City Dock, settle in, and listen to the USNA band perform everything from Broadway to the blues. Tuesdays at 8 in the summer. Free.

NORTHERN NECK/MIDDLE PENINSULA

Gloucester, Virginia

CONCERTS ON THE GREEN
804-693-2355.
Gloucester County Recreation Dept.

Summer evenings in Gloucester bring Concerts on the Green at the Courthouse Green. Bring a chair or blanket and enjoy the music.

Kilmarnock, Virginia

CENTER FOR THE ARTS
804-435-2400.
PO Box 790.
Tickets: $10 adults, $4 children.

Eight events are held each winter, including four plays or puppet shows for children, and opera, musicals, and other concerts. Both professional and community musicians are featured.

Mathews, Virginia

DONK'S THEATER
804-725-7760.
PO Box 284; intersection of Rtes. 198 & 223.
Tickets: $7.99; $2 children under 12.

Home of Virginia's "Li'l Ole Opry," this is Tidewater's capital of country music. Hometown musicians and stars alike show up on stage. "We've had the big ones," says Harriet Smith Farmer, one of the abundant Smith family who own the place. "We had Dolly. She was here in 1977." The former movie theater is an appropriate venue for families, who may want to check out the Smith Family Christmas Concert the first week of December. Number of musical Smiths? "It's a bunch," says Harriet. Shows every other Saturday night.

UPPER EASTERN SHORE

Centreville/Kent Island

QUEEN ANNE'S COUNTY ARTS COUNCIL
410-758-2520.
PO Box 218; 206 S. Commerce St., Centreville.
Concerts at various locations, all year.
Tickets: Prices vary with concert; many are free.

The Arts Council always presents a number of events, including performances by the well-regarded Queen Anne Chorale (a 50-voice classical/popular chorus) and summer Concerts in the Park at several locations featuring top-grade regional talent. The Baltimore Symphony always performs a winter concert series.

Chestertown

WASHINGTON COLLEGE CONCERT SERIES

This ever-popular offering is pushing toward the half-century mark. The annual five-concert

410-778-2800 ext. 7849
800 Washington Ave.
Season: Sept.–Apr.
Tickets: $15; 18 and
  under $5; series tickets
  $40.

series features the likes of the Juilliard String Quartet, the Peabody Trio, and the madrigal group Chanticleer, performing at Tawes Theatre.

Easton

**TIDEWATER
PERFORMING ARTS
SOCIETY**
410-476-9002.
PO Box 455 (Box Office).
Concerts held at various
  locations.
Season: Sept.–Mar.
Tickets: Prices vary with
  concert; season tickets
  available.

Every year from fall through spring, this varied series brings high-quality performing arts to the Eastern Shore. The series emphasizes music, but usually features some dance as well. In recent years, the TPAS has brought flutist Eugenia Zuckerman, blues and folk artist Tom Chapin, jazz by the Billy Taylor Trio, and many others. Smaller events, such as fundraisers for the Wye Mill, feature excellent regional talent.

St. Michaels

**EASTERN SHORE
CHAMBER MUSIC
FESTIVAL**
410-819-0380.
PO Box 1048.
Season: Second & third
  weekends in June.
Tickets: $12–$22;
  subscription packages
  available.

Since 1986, J. Lawrie Bloom, principal clarinetist with the Chicago Symphony Orchestra, has brought in a host of top young names on the international concert circuit for a week of performances at various Talbot County locations. For audiences, it's a week of chamber music at its finest. For the musicians, including Bloom, whose parents live here, it's a busman's holiday of sorts.

The Mendelssohn String Quartet are regulars, and the rest of the talent roster is always equally impressive. Performances are usually held at the Avalon, Wye Plantation, and a private estate on the Miles.

LOWER EASTERN SHORE

Salisbury

**SALISBURY SYMPHONY
ORCHESTRA**
410-543-ARTS.
Salisbury State University
  Dept. of Music.
Season: Winter and spring
  concerts.
Tickets: Prices vary.

Based at Salisbury State University and supported by the Salisbury Wicomico Arts Council, this community orchestra puts on two major concerts a year at Holloway Hall Auditorium. It's composed of faculty, students, and townspeople, and enjoys enthusiastic community support.

NIGHTLIFE

HEAD OF THE BAY

hesapeake City has always enjoyed an interesting paradox. It's small and remote, but ships from all corners of the globe pass by on the bustling C&D Canal. Applaud the Caribbean flavor brought by calypso combos that play from June through Aug. at the dockside terrace of **Schaefer's Canal House** (410-85-2200; off Rte. 213 on the north side of the canal). The owner of Schaefer's, we're told, travels to the Islands to book talent for his popular summertime Caribbean fiestas.

ANNAPOLIS/WESTERN SHORE

Nighttime in 'Naptown (better known as Annapolis) means folks head for City Dock, where places that are quaint colonial taverns by lunchtime open their doors to the music and tourist scene by night. Summer weekends can be mobbed, but even locals try to slip in one night down there to soak up the warm breezes off the water. Over the Spa Creek Bridge is Eastport, a hotbed of sailors and some good places to grab a drink.

Downtown *Annapolis* is on the regional circuit for many bands playing the mid-Atlantic states. To find out who's playing where, check out the reliable *Alive!* magazine, available free at many locations around town; *The Publick Enterprise*, a good free bimonthly that keeps up with local happenings; and Friday's Entertainment section in *The Capital*, Annapolis's daily. *Inside Annapolis*, another free, about-town publication, offers complete listings. Many taverns listed here also serve good food (see Chapter Five, *Restaurants*).

The best rock and roll is at **Armadillos** (410-268-6680; 132 Dock St.), a southwestern-style bistro that recently was sold, but reportedly won't change its style. Regional bands on the bar circuit play. Next door at **Mums** (410-263-3353; 136 Dock St.), with a similarly cozy downstairs with brick walls and a bar tucked nicely into a corner, the music also plays.

Move up the block to **McGarvey's Saloon** (410-263-5700; 8 Market Space) if you're up for a mixed crowd in a good mood. The place is uptown saloon-style, with mirrors and polished dark wood, although its popularity means that what looks like ample space diminishes as a Friday or Saturday night wears on — and tableside conversation becomes nearly impossible.

Next door is **Middleton Tavern** (410-263-3323; 2 Market Space), an 18th-century watering hole that apparently drew 'em in then the way it does now. Middleton's has a great patio overlooking the City Dock scene, waiters who appear to be in perennially good moods (actually, most City Dock pubs can boast excellent service), and acoustic music just about every night. There's a piano bar upstairs, or catch the "Sunday Blues" with local musicians about 8pm each week. Both McGarvey's and Middleton's serve their own house lagers, which are excellent.

Also in the vicinity is **Riordan's Saloon** (410-263-5449; 26 Market Space), one of the hometown pubs where you'll run into local folks. It serves food late, and everyone loves the burgers. Next door is **Griffins Restaurant** (410-268-2576; 22 Market Space), which draws a youngish crowd (avoid at all costs during college breaks). Nearby is **O'Brien's Oyster Bar & Restaurant** (410-268-6288; 113 Main St.), where the local politicos hang out.

One of the nicest places in town is up Main Street at Church Circle, at the **Maryland Inn** (410-263-2641). Tucked back in what seems like a tiny space is a great jazz club at the **King of France Tavern**, where national figures like Mose Allison, or local favorites like Charlie Byrd, play solo or with their well-known buddies. Often two shows on weekend nights. Highly recommended.

The ever-popular **Ram's Head Tavern** (33 West St.; see *Restaurants*) adds to the city's nightlife with its new microbrewery, the **Fordham Brewing Co.** The only drawback may be the crowd; this place is packed on Saturday nights.

And the coffeehouse **The Moon Café** (410-280-1956; 137 Prince George St.) has picked up on the poetry craze. To an SRO crowd every Tuesday night, "You can write your own poetry, you can do a skit. You can make a literary observation," says a regular there.

Over in *Eastport*, every sailor in town shows up at **Marmaduke's** (410-269-5420; 3rd St. & Severn Ave.) after a day on the Bay. This is *the* hangout for the yachting crowd. Also in this neck of the woods is **Chart House** (410-268-7166; 300 2nd St.), where the waterside bar has the best view in town. The expansive former Trumpy Boat Yard warehouse has been taken over by the national chain, and the picture windows mean you'll have the best view in town of Annapolis Harbor. The best table in the house is right behind the stove, where, in winter, you can watch the occasional flakes fall. Also in Eastport is the much-beloved **Carrol's Creek Café** (410-263-8102; 410 Severn Ave.). Go for drinks on the café's patio in summer, and a friend or two always shows up.

There's also **Jillian's**, an upscale billiards hall — with parking! — that packs them in. Sixteen pool tables, two pingpong tables, an arcade/game area, and a huge bar mid-room with big televisions showing all the current sporting events. They charge by the hour ($10 for two players on weekends) and the place really gets crowded Thurs.–Sat. nights. Look for specials like Beat the Pro night. Located in *Parole*, right off Rte. 50 (410-841-5599; 2072 Somerville Rd.).

And in the summertime, the waterside bar scene down South County way heats up, with jazz or reggae at **Herrington on the Bay** in *Friendship* (410-741-5101; 7149 Lakeshore Dr.) or, in *Galesville*, **Big Mary's Dock Bar** outside the Inn at Pirate's Cove (410-867-2300; on the West River) where acoustic musicians serenade.

UPPER EASTERN SHORE

A round *Chestertown*, you'll find 50-cent-draft establishments for the college crowd as well as rough-and-tumble roadside saloons. The best destination for the discerning nightlifer is **Andy's** (410-778-6779; 337 1/2 W. High

Kick back on the weekends and dig bands like Croom Station, performing jazz at Herrington on the Bay in South County, south of Annapolis.

David Trozzo

St.), a small, friendly, popular club that regularly hosts live music — jazz, blue-grass, folk, rock, blues, country, you name it.

Kent Narrows, where Kent Island and the Queen Anne's County mainland meet, has undergone a real growth spurt in recent years that's spawned its own dock-bar night scene, particularly on summer nights when the boating set ties up here. **Redeye's Dock Bar** (410-827-3937; at Mears Point Marina) brings in rock bands and DJs and generally gets wild and crazy on the weekends — and some weeknights — during the busy season. Serves own house beer. The **Jetty** (410-827-8225), on the south side of the Narrows, joins the decibel competition. By comparison, the hometown waterfront bar at **Angler's** (410-827-6717) seems tame. If the watermen (look for white boots) there are wearing T-shirts with a beer logo, the summer crabs are in. If they're wearing plaid flannel, it's oyster season.

Meanwhile, in *Easton* you'll find a fair number of night spots. The **Washington Street Pub** (410-822-9011; 20 N. Washington St.) can get pretty packed, especially Thurs.–Sat. nights, and even more especially when a DJ or local band plays. At the **Avalon Theatre** (410-820-0345; 42 E. Dover St.) you've got **Legal Spirits** (410-820-0033), a small bar done up in cozy lawyer's-office green and dark polished wood. Prohibition-era iconography adorns the walls: framed photos of Al Capone and Pretty Boy Floyd, or a tommy gun in a violin case. Check out the beautiful woodwork framing the massive mirror behind the bar.

If you feel like dancing, **Yesteryear's** (410-822-2433; Easton Plaza) is one place for you. There's a DJ every Friday, and the dance floor is usually busy. The crowd is a bit on the young side, and a singles-bar atmosphere pervades on Fridays.

In *St. Michaels* there's **Top of the Dock** (410-745-5577; 125 Mulberry St.), the upstairs nightclub at the Town Dock Restaurant (see *Restaurants*). On weekends, find some of the best rock bands in the area. The dance floor responds accordingly.

If you're overnighting in *Oxford*, visit the **Masthead** (410-226-5303; 101 Mill St.). It's got a devoted corps of regulars who make the place sort of a boatyard-abutting "Cheers." It's most fun in summer, when the crowd spills out onto the outdoor deck. But other Oxford bars have their adherents as well, in particular **Schooners Llanding** (410-226-0160; 318 Tilghman St. — see *Restaurants*) on Town Creek. Ask the bartender about the annual cardboard boat races held in Oxford by the local chapter of Boat Bums International.

PERFORMING ARTS AND THEATER

A lso refer to the sections on "Music" and "Nightlife" for other performances and events.

HEAD OF THE BAY

Bel Air

PHOENIX FESTIVAL THEATER
410-836-4211; 410-879-8920, ext. 211; TDD 410-836-4199.
Harford Community College, 410 Thomas Run Rd.
Tickets individually or by subscription; under $15 for adults.

This community-college-based theater group presents three performances during what is usually a dark time for theaters — summer through fall; recent shows included *The Glass Menagerie* and *Little Shop of Horrors*.

ANNAPOLIS/WESTERN SHORE

Annapolis

ANNAPOLIS SUMMER GARDEN THEATRE
410-268-0809.
143 Compromise St.
Memorial to Labor Day season.
Tickets: Generally $10 or less.

This blacksmith shop near City Dock dates from 1696 and may even have housed George Washington's horses out back — right where the audience sits today. The Annapolis Summer Garden Theatre, established in 1966, offers light musicals or comedies under the stars.

COLONIAL PLAYERS
410-268-7373.

This venerable community theater is the oldest in town, and performs five productions each

108 East St.
Performances Thurs.–Sun.
Tickets: generally $10 or
  less.
Handicap Access: Yes.

season. Count on them to present interesting work outside the usual Broadway moneymakers. Tickets are less than $10 for some of the best theater around. Performances include everything from drama to comedy.

**MARYLAND HALL FOR
THE CREATIVE ARTS,
INC.**
410-263-5544, 410-269-1087,
  301-261-1553.
801 Chase St.

The old brick Annapolis High School is now the center for the arts in town; it's headquarters for the major performing arts groups, and a school offering everything from children's theater to music classes by teachers from Baltimore's Peabody Conservatory. The symphony and ballet alike perform in the hall, although the acoustics are known to be less than the best. Also home to a jazz/world music performance season, featuring such artists as Stanley Jordan. Also here are the Cardinal Gallery and the AIR Gallery, showcasing local artists (see "Galleries").

UPPER EASTERN SHORE

Church Hill

**CHURCH HILL
THEATRE**
410-758-1331.
PO Box 91.
Md. 19/Walnut St. off Md.
  213 bet. Centreville &
  Chestertown.
Tickets: Prices vary.

This 1929 building has gone full circle, from town hall to movie theater to decline and, finally, rescue. Now restored with its 1944 Art Deco theater interior, it maintains a lively performance schedule. Home to the enthusiastic Church Hill Players, it offers community theater showcasing a repertoire that has included *Steel Magnolias*, *The Foreigner*, and *Move Over, Mrs. Markham*. A range of touring performers and an active Young People's Series offer theater, magic, and puppetry.

Easton

AVALON THEATRE
410-822-0345.
40 E. Dover St.

This beautifully restored and renovated 1920s movie house is now the showplace for all the performing arts here. There's a concert series that recently included the Navy Band "Country Current" and the bluegrass group "Chesapeake" (formerly of the "Seldom Scene"). Also offered are classic films on Sunday afternoons, traveling theater groups, and three music festivals each year featuring jazz, blues, and contemporary and popular music. The film *Silent Fall* premiered at the Avalon. Seating is only adequate, but acoustics are perfect.

LOWER EASTERN SHORE

Salisbury

COMMUNITY PLAYERS OF SALISBURY
410-543-ARTS.
c/o Salisbury Wicomico Arts Council, PO Box 884.
Tickets: Prices vary.

Noteworthy among the Eastern Shore's community troupes, the Players, at over 50 years, is the oldest continually running community theater organization in the state. They perform at various locations in and around Salisbury, and they usually do a musical, one drama, and one comedy a year.

SEASONAL EVENTS AND FESTIVALS

A couple of easy rules: oysters in the "R" months, and crabs all summer long. Keep an eye peeled for the many festivals, church suppers, and volunteer firemen's association events that include a chance to chow down on these Chesapeake delicacies. For current information about such food-theme festivities and other happenings, pick up a copy of *Maryland Celebrates*, an annual calendar of festivals and events. Contact the Maryland Office of Tourism Development, 410-333-6611.

ANNAPOLIS/WESTERN SHORE

Annapolis

If you're up for an all-you-can-eat, you've met your match at the **Annapolis Rotary Club Crabfeast**. Always held the last Friday in July, at the Navy-Marine Corps Memorial Stadium. Call 410-841-2841. Admission.

Thousands show up for the annual **Chesapeake Bay Bridge Walk**, an early May event that goes hand-in-hand with the early morning **Governor's Bay Bridge Run** that fills up far in advance. Shuttles take bridge walkers from the U.S. Naval Academy–Marine Corps Stadium, as well as other locations; 410-288-8405.

The beauty of distinctly Bay-oriented festivals is the good crowd — from the common-sense watermen to the environmentalists and scientists. **Chesapeake Appreciation Days** is one of the best, featuring great local seafood, environmental discussions, oyster-shucking contests, entertainment, and the main event — skipjack races. The Maryland Watermen's Association has hosted the races for more than 30 years, picking up where old tradition left off. Some of the oystering workhorse-boats date to the 19th century, but the watermen's association will hold the races "as long as there are skipjacks," says their administrative mainstay, Betty Duty. At Sandy Point State Park every October; 410-269-6622.

Celebrate Maryland's African-American history every September at the **Kunta Kinte Festival**, named for author Alex Haley's African forebear in *Roots*, who stepped off a slave ship at Annapolis City Dock. Entertainment, African dancers, crafts, food and more; 410-349-0338.

The Maryland Seafood Festi-val at Sandy Point State Park always draws a crowd.

David Trozzo

The **Maryland Seafood Festival** features big-name entertainment and lots of crabs. Held in September at Sandy Point State Park. For details, call 410-268-7682 or 410-268-7676. Handicap access.

U.S. Sailboat Show, Annapolis City Dock, is on Columbus Day weekend. Every mariner for miles arrives for this. The very latest in sailboat designs, from racing to cruising vessels, can be found in the water along with every imaginable service or sailing gimmick. Parking will be a nightmare, but expect bargains, deals, and celebrations among the restaurants and bars at City Dock. 410-268-8828. Admission.

U.S. Powerboat Show, Annapolis City Dock. The weekend after the Columbus Day weekend sailboat show. Here's your chance to see the newest work-boats and playboats, from yachts to inflatables, also in the water. 410-268-8828. Admission.

Crownsville

The **Maryland Renaissance Festival**, held just west of Annapolis in Crownsville, is a much-anticipated event, and it's convenient, too, because you haven't missed it if you had other plans one weekend. From the last week in August through mid-October, 16th-century England is the order of every weekend. The scene is wild, with bearded men wrestling in the mud, and lovelie ladies working the crowd. A roving band of jesters, crafters, jugglers, magicians, and minstrels. 410-266-7304. Admission.

Two-fisted swordsman "Barcon" (Greg Cantor) performs at the Maryland Renaissance Festival.

Tom Curley

Davidsonville

Spectators bring family crystal to their picnics at the **Marlborough Hunt Races**, also known as the Roedown. Held since 1975 at the private Roedown

David Trozzo

Equestrians run for the Roedown Cup every spring at Davidsonville, Maryland.

Farm in Davidsonville, south of Annapolis, the event draws hundreds to watch the thoroughbred fox hunt. The only caution is that the hunt is held on private property. Contact the Annapolis & Anne Arundel Co. Conference and Visitors Bureau, 410-280-0445, if you are in town at the beginning of April and wish to attend.

Port Republic

Maryland's official state sport, believe it or not, is jousting. The savvy visitor may want to find Port Republic, in Calvert County south of Annapolis, for the **Calvert County Jousting Tournament**, now well into its second century. Knights engage in mock battle, and a bazaar is set up. Held at the end of August at Christ Episcopal Church, which you can call for information at 410-586-0565. Admission; handicap access.

NORTHERN NECK/MIDDLE PENINSULA

Gloucester County, Virginia

The **Daffodil Festival and Show** celebrates the annual daffodil harvest with tours of the many daffodil plantations in Gloucester County, and includes a parade, arts and crafts show, 5K- and 1-mile run, historical exhibits, live entertainment, food, children's games, and rides. First Saturday in April. Contact the Gloucester County Parks and Recreation Dept., 804-693-2355.

Mathews, Virginia

Mathews Market Days hosts the **Governor's Cup Blue Crab Derby**, a crab race. The big event takes place on the Saturday of the Thursday-through-Saturday festival held the weekend after Labor Day. The Courthouse Green is filled with the goods of local craftsmen and artists, and there's local seafood, music, and other entertainment. A Saturday night street dance caps festivities. Contact the Mathews Extension Office, 804-725-7196.

Urbanna, Virginia

Middlesex County's biggest claim to fame is the annual **Urbanna Oyster Festival**. People come by road and water to attend this event, which essentially is an excuse to eat oysters served in every way possible, be they frittered or on the half shell. But there are also crafts, live music, and tall ships that you can board. One note: parking will not be easy. You can get into town by way of Rte. 227 off Rte. 33, or Rte. 602 off Rte. 17. Either way, expect to walk. Held each year on the first Friday and Saturday in November. Call the Urbanna Oyster Festival Foundation at 804-758-0368 for information.

The Tench Tilghman Fife and Drum Corps marches in the Chestertown Tea Party parade.

Kent County Chamber / A. Walmsley

UPPER EASTERN SHORE

Chestertown

Chestertown's contribution to pre-Revolutionary War radical politics is commemorated the last Saturday in May in the **Chestertown Tea Party Festival**. The townwide celebration features parades, music, festivities, and food recalling the 1774 Chestertown Tea Party, wherein the townspeople rose up against Port Collector William Geddes (see "Historic Buildings and Sites"), whose brigantine *Geddes* was plundered, Boston-style, by the locals. (Maybe it's apocryphal, but some say they saved the same shipment's rum.) Handicap access. 410-778-0416.

Grasonville

The **Waterman's Festival** at Kent Narrows is unique. Where else can you see an anchor-throwing contest, a rowing race, and a docking competition for Bay workboats while listening to country music and munching food? An easygoing, friendly event that's growing. Admission is only $3. Held on the first Sunday in June from 11am–6pm at Wells Cove Public Landing. Contact Queen Anne's County Visitors Service at 410-827-4810; 3100 Main St. Handicap access.

Easton

The Mid-Atlantic Maritime Festival in Easton is Talbot County's rite of spring, a long weekend festival with maritime paintings, prints, photography, waterfowl and fish carvings, ship models, and seafood, which spills out of the buildings and into the street. This is a fun event that is held downtown on the third Friday, Saturday, and Sunday of April; 410-822-4606.

Easton undergoes a transformation on the second weekend in November — and what small town wouldn't, if 20,000 visitors showed up? — during the **Waterfowl Festival**. This three-day event features more than 500 of the world's finest decoy carvers and wildlife painters, and has become internationally known. Since its founding in 1971, the Waterfowl Festival has raised more than $4 million for conservation organizations devoted to preserving waterfowl.

Exhibits spread across town. The most prestigious display space is at the Tidewater Inn's Gold Room, with art generally priced above $700. The Blue Room, now at the Elk's Lodge, showcases art priced below $1000. The exquisite decoy art, housed in two areas, ranges from classic traditional pieces to uncannily lifelike decoratives. Antique decoys are vied for at the Saturday afternoon auction. It's lively — and not for the shallow-pocketed. Other Festival events include retriever demonstrations, the Federal Duck Stamp exhibit, and, always a hit, the World Championship Goose Calling Contest. More than 1,000 local volunteers pitch in, and a fleet of shuttle buses provide free transportation from the parking areas to the exhibit locations around town. Handicap access; 410-822-4567; admission fee.

St. Michaels

Two terrific events at the Chesapeake Bay Maritime Museum shouldn't be missed. In mid-June, look for the **Antique and Classic Boat Show,** with lovely old boats and fine old cars judged for perfection, and seminars and food, too. Early October brings the **Mid-Atlantic Small Craft Festival**, a favorite for folks who enjoy little boats. Home workshops and professional builders turn out canoes, kayaks, dinghies, and dories, powered by oars, engines, or innovative sailing rigs. Have you ever seen a geodesic-patterned transparent canoe or a schooner-rigged kayak? Great for kids. Call 410-745-2916.

Tilghman Island

The annual **Tilghman Island Day** celebration combines demonstrations of the watermen's way of life with a heaping helping of what that way of life yields: seafood. Crab and oyster aficionados come from afar on the third Saturday of October. Watermen's tricks like boat-maneuvering and oyster-tonging are shown off in folklife demonstrations and high-spirited contests. But the big event is the skipjack races — it's great to see them under sail. The celebration benefits the Tilghman Volunteer Fire Company. Call Harrison's Country Inn, 410-886-2121, for details.

LOWER EASTERN SHORE

Chincoteague, Virginia

According to legend, the wild ponies of Assateague Island, on the Maryland-Virginia border, descended from Spanish horses who swam ashore following a long-forgotten shipwreck. Scientists, always ready to dispel a good story, suggest they descended from the ponies grazed on the outpost island in centuries past. Whatever the case, the annual **Pony-Penning** in Chincoteague, Virginia, is an event to see. Always held the last Wednesday and Thursday of July, it starts when members of the sponsoring Chincoteague Volunteer Fire Co. corral the ponies and send them swimming across the channel from Chincoteague National Wildlife Refuge to town. The pony sale, held on Thursday, is a long tradition to raise funds for the fire company, who officially own the ponies in Virginia. For information, call 804-336-6161 or write Chincoteague Chamber of Commerce, Box 258, Chincoteague VA 23336.

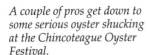
A couple of pros get down to some serious oyster shucking at the Chincoteague Oyster Festival.

Dan Wolff

The Chincoteague Oyster Festival, held annually on the Saturday of Columbus Day Weekend, is sponsored by the island's Chamber of Commerce. There are lots of oyster festivals around the Bay, but this one is designed for those who are very serious about sitting down and eating a pile of famous Chincoteague oysters, slightly salty and considered by many to be the best around. The event, held at Maddox Family Campground, is sometimes sold out by mid-summer. For information, call or write the Chincoteague Chamber listed above.

Crisfield

In the late 1800s, Crisfield was a noisy strip of brothels and saloons and street-brawl recklessness. The harbor was thick with watermen's vessels and people were getting rich on oysters. The oyster boom faded a century ago, but Crisfield remains an active working watermen's port. These days, the town calls itself "Crab Capital of the World" and, for nearly 50 years, has hosted the **National Hard Crab Derby & Fair**. The highlight of the Labor Day Weekend bash is the annual Governor's Cup Race — a crab race, mind you, with entrants from as far away as Hawaii. There's also a crab-picking contest, a crab-cooking contest, the "Miss Crustacean" beauty contest, a boat-docking contest, a 10K race, a parade, a fishing tournament, fireworks, live entertainment, and, of course, plenty of excellent eating. Handicap access. Call 410-968-682 or 1-800-782-3913.

Deal Island

Of all the sailing-vessel designs indigenous to the Chesapeake, the skipjack is the most familiar — and most evocative of a passing age. Hundreds of these sloop-rigged oyster dredgers began working the Bay in the 1890s. They are the last commercial sailing fleet in America, and in honor of these graceful veterans, each Labor Day the annual **Skipjack Races** are held in Tangier Sound off Deal Island, Maryland, a watermen's community that is home to many of the remaining skipjacks. The races begin in Deal Island Harbor, and on-shore spectators can take part in the land festival that accompanies the racing. Food, crafts and a "Little Miss Skipjack" contest are part of the festivities; 410-651-9110.

TOURS

For historic or cultural tours in addition to those listed below, contact the local historical society or visitor center. For boat tours, see "Boating" in Chapter 6, *Recreation*.

HEAD OF THE BAY

Chesapeake Horse Country Tours offers a private, narrated walking tour of _Chesapeake City_, a little town with a historic district featuring early 19th-century homes that prospered accordingly with the nearby C&D Canal. A van takes visitors on to see private horse farms nearby. Three hours, $15; reservations necessary. Call for other tours, too. Uniglobe Hill Travel, 103 Bohemia Ave., Chesapeake City MD 21915; 410-885-2797.

ANNAPOLIS/WESTERN SHORE

Tour _Annapolis_ with Walter Cronkite. A few years back, the **Historic Annapolis Foundation** convinced the avid Chesapeake sailor to narrate a 45-

minute walking tour of the 300-year-old city. Toting your rented "Acousti-guide" recording, you'll hear the familiar newsman tell of historic homes and times past. Pick up the guide at the Historic Annapolis Foundation's Welcome Center and Museum Store, right at City Dock; 410-268-5576. $7 adults, $2.50 children.

Anyone who's walked around Annapolis can't help but notice those lovely gardens tucked down alleys and into tiny backyards, English-style. Now's your chance to have a closer look, with **Gardens of Annapolis**. Start at Government House — viewing from the outside — then on to the Reynold's Tavern kitchen garden and more. The tours are led by a trained horticulturist. $7 adults, $3 children under 12. PO Box 4577, Annapolis MD 21403; 410-263-6041.

From **Three Centuries Tours**, docents in colonial dress lead groups through the streets of Annapolis, show you the highlights, and disclose insider stories you'd otherwise miss. Included are the City Dock and Statehouse areas. Besides the standard historic district tour, they will arrange group looks at historic houses, or will take children for a specially tailored stroll. Leave at 9:30am and 1:30pm from Apr. 1 to Oct. 31. The early tour leaves the Annapolis Marriott lobby at City Dock; the afternoon tour leaves from the Visitor Center, 26 West St. From Nov.–Mar., leave from the Visitor Center at 10:30 daily, and on Sat. at 2:30 from Gibson's Lodging at 110 Prince George St. $7 adults, $3 children 6–18. PO Box 29; 48 Maryland Ave., Annapolis MD 21404; 410-263-5401/5357.

Discover Annapolis tours take visitors for one-hour bus rides through the city's sights, leaving from the Visitor Center. Contact 410-626-6000, 31 Decatur Ave. for schedules and information. $7 adults, $3 children 12 and under.

Visitors to Annapolis can't help but notice the pedicabs, wherein young people inevitably clad in crisp white shirts pedal passengers in bicycle-rickshaw-style contraptions known as "pedicabs." **R&R Pedicabs, Inc.** has trained its pedalers to show their passengers the historic sights. A good choice for disabled visitors who want to see the city in style. 11am to midnight, except Fri. and Sat. until 2am. Based in front of the Annapolis Marriott at City Dock; call 410-841-6235.

UPPER EASTERN SHORE

In *Chestertown*, follow the **Walking Tour of Old Chester Town**, a 28-stop self-guided tour, stretching from the entrancing riverfront through this picture-book colonial maritime town. The brochure is available at the Kent County Chamber of Commerce, 400 S. Cross Street, or at many of the town's shops and restaurants. Buildings on the tour are marked by numbered plaques. Bear in mind that, with the exception of the Geddes-Piper House, these are largely private residences, and closed to the public. Guided group tours, too, include the annual **Candlelight Walking Tour** in September and a **Christmas House Tour**. For more information, call 410-778-0416.

Historic Chestertown & Kent County Tours on Sunday mornings are led by a knowledgeable area historian. Learn a blend of architectural, local, regional, and national history. Meet at the fountain in Fountain Park, High & Cross Sts., at 11am. $5. About 1 ¹/₂ hours; call to check in the off-season. Other tours can be arranged. Call 410-778-2829.

Pick up the brochure at the **_St. Michaels_** Chamber of Commerce or in one of the shops and do the **self-guided walking tour** of the "Town That Fooled The British." Takes about an hour.

LOWER EASTERN SHORE

Don't overlook the historic area of **_Cambridge_**, hidden well behind the dull strip of modern businesses along U.S. 50. See the remarkable collection of fine old buildings in this town with the help of Dorchester County Tourism's walking-tour brochure. There's plenty of history along this beautiful waterfront.

The **_Snow Hill_** **self-guided walking tour** lists more than 50 points of interest in this peaceful town of brick sidewalks on the banks of the Pocomoke River. The town is known for its numerous historic houses; none is open to the public, but you can admire the architecture from the street. A brochure is available, complete with map and numbered descriptions of sites. Call the Julia A. Purnell Museum at 410-632-0515.

CHAPTER FIVE

Catch of the Bay

RESTAURANTS AND FOOD PURVEYORS

Seafood dominates Chesapeake cuisine; the word crab, for instance, appears more than 100 times in this chapter. That truly is an accurate reflection of this beloved crustacean's dominance hereabouts. Chesapeake blue crabs are in season during the summer and grown to a tasty size by mid-July, although picking meat from the hardshells may be a bit of a problem for the uninitiated. The safest course through the formidable task is simple: ask somebody. Seafood festivals here feature fierce crab-picking and oyster-shucking contests, proof that one's knowledge of the quickest route to the meat of these creatures is indeed a matter of Chesapeake pride — unless you're seated on a waterside deck on a languid afternoon, in which case an unhurried pace is the point entirely.

David Trozzo

Chesapeake crabbers check their pots daily in season, the better to meet the demand for the Bay's beloved blue crabs.

We'll discuss various crab recipes in a moment; first, let's look at native seafood. Oysters are available in the months with R in the name. Prime oyster season runs up to about Christmas, if the vastly declined Bay population lasts that long. Better to eat up by Thanksgiving. Rockfish is a finfish readers will find us referring to lovingly. Called striped bass elsewhere, the sweet-tasting but endangered rockfish were protected from fishing in Maryland for nearly five years up to 1990. Even though the fishing season has been extended since (and aquaculturists ensure availability), recovering rockfish lovers still can't believe their good luck. You'll find preparations ranging from French to Vietnamese to savvy New American.

Choice Chesapeake eating: striped bass, known hereabouts as the rockfish.

David Trozzo

Clams — cherrystones (also called hardshell clams or little necks) and the thin-shelled manoes or mananoes (also called softshells, longnecks, or steamers) — may or may not be available (softshells are best in spring), but if you're dining in a good old seafood house, chances are fairly good they'll tell you if you're eating native shellfish. Any native lobster comes from the Atlantic offshore from Ocean City. Bluefish, one of the Bay's 200 species of finfish, shows up in the summer, and tastes great smoked. But, like learning to pick crabs, the secret to finding out what's native and what's not is the same: ask your server or fishmarket proprietor. Most reputable seafood houses, of which there are gloriously many, are pleased to pass along details about their offerings.

Now, back to the crabs. Males are called jimmies, and are easier to pick than the female sooks, whose eggs tend to make the eating a bit messy. People tired of fooling with mallets and knives and all the accoutrements of picking will likely order crab cakes. Crab cakes may well be a version of the ubiquitous crab imperial, which binds crabmeat with a filler of bread or cracker crumbs mixed with egg or mayonnaise and a bit of Worcestershire sauce. The artful chef adds a subtle flair that enhances the delectable crabmeat and overcomes what otherwise sounds like a rather ordinary dish. The following reviews that rave about lump or backfin crabmeat are passing along a valuable tip — those cuts come from the choicest part of the crab.

Other tips: fried seafood items on a menu, such as crab cakes, often can be broiled by request. Softshell crabs have just molted and are extremely tender, if crunchy. Chincoteague oysters are generally the cream of the crop; find them on the half shell if you can. They may have spent years in the Chesapeake or its estuaries growing to prime size, but after harvesting they are taken to the saltier bays behind the Atlantic barrier islands for a quick dip: even a single change of the tide gives them the extra salty flavor associated with oysters that have spent their whole lives there. And non-seafood Chesapeake dishes do indeed exist. South of Virginia's Middle Peninsula lies Smithfield, home of the famed Smithfield ham. In southern Maryland, there's kale-stuffed fresh ham. All around the region, the revered fried chicken (and fried oysters) tell you you're south of the Mason-Dixon Line. Native produce from nearby farms and orchards adds a great deal to the local diet from mid-summer on — most notably, Silver Queen corn (a must with hardshell crabs), knock-out tomatoes and Eastern Shore cantaloupes, and peaches. Finally, one truly native foodstuff is the decidedly Eastern Shore beaten biscuit. They're hard little floury biscuits, and, frankly, they're real good.

While Chesapeake seafood dominates, fine dining offered by creative chefs has made significant inroads to the region, particularly in Baltimore and around Annapolis. An infusion of international talent and top cuisine trends arrived in the early '90s, and seems to be here to stay.

More restaurants than we could ever count lie around the Chesapeake Bay. Nine of us, advised by spouses, partners, and others who heartily joined our dining adventure, sought to review a sampling of the best. We tried to consider a range of tastes and prices throughout the region so folks in search of a simple café or crab deck would look no further than those planning to dine at the region's most renowned restaurants.

We arranged the reviews geographically by region, then alphabetically, first by town and then by the name of the restaurant. For instance, on the Lower Eastern Shore diners will reach New Church, Virginia, before Whitehaven, Maryland.

Price descriptions in the restaurant reviews are based on the average cost of an appetizer, entrée, and dessert for one person (not including cocktails, wine, tax, or tip), and are as follows:

Inexpensive:	up to $15
Moderate:	$16 to $22
Expensive:	$23 to $32
Very Expensive:	$33 or more

Abbreviations are as follows:

AE:	American Express
C:	Choice
CB:	Carte Blanche
D:	Discover Card
DC:	Diner's Club
MC:	MasterCard
V:	Visa

B:	Breakfast
L:	Lunch
D:	Dinner
SB:	Sunday Brunch

If you're picnicking, planning to be out on the water, or eating in, you'll need to know where to buy your own provisions. This chapter also lists a selection of farm and fish markets, bakeries, and gourmet shops.

RESTAURANTS

HEAD OF THE BAY

Havre de Grace

The Tidewater Grille in Havre de Grace looks out on the Susquehanna River.

Tom Curley

TIDEWATER GRILLE
410-939-3313.
300 Foot of Franklin St.
Open: Daily.
Price: Moderate to Expensive.
Cuisine: American, seafood.
Serving: L, D, SB.
Credit Cards: AE, MC, V.
Handicap Access: Yes.

Travelers on Interstate 95 have made this restaurant more popular than your usual fast food & fuel pit stop along this particularly endless highway. The Tidewater Grille is way out of that league. Wide windows open onto the Susquehanna River, topped with stained-glass icons of things Chesapeake. The menu offers classic seafood, poultry, pasta, and beef dishes. The kitchen also tries its hand at Chesapeake adaptations like the successful veal Chesapeake, with smoked ham and lump crab in a brandied cream sauce. For Sunday brunch, sample eggs-Benedict-style crab Tidewater. Your iced-tea glass will be attentively refilled, although midday-weekend diners shouldn't be surprised if the traveling kids at the next table are ready for naptime. Lovely restaurant; lots of parking.

ANNAPOLIS/WESTERN SHORE

Annapolis

CAFÉ LA MOUFFE
909 Bay Ridge Ave., East-
  port
410-263-CAFE.
Open: Daily except Mon.
Price: Inexpensive to Mod-
  erate.
Cuisine: Provençal, new
  American.
Serving: B, L, D.
Credit Cards: V, MC, DC.
Handicap Access: Yes.

Single black-eyed Susans in cobalt-blue sparkling water bottles, cane-backed chairs, and local artists' work on the walls set this little eatery's airy tone, which carries through to the exquisite food on your plate. We really can't say enough about La Mouffe's food, and consider this perhaps the city's lunch spot of choice. Lightly grilled, fat shrimp on a croissant, or equally well-grilled eggplant brushed with pesto on crunchy French bread are favorites. Enjoy a good choice of coffees and non-alcoholic drinks, and a small but well-considered wine and beer list (imports and microbrews only). Tarts, tortes, and derby pies tempt from their perch in the bakery case. Dinners revolve around the specials board, rotisserie meats, and grilled veggies, and the occasional prix fixe. Breads are baked on premises; an unpretentious little market out back ("Le March") offers squash or corn, displayed in baskets.

CAFÉ NORMANDIE
410-263-3382.
185 Main St.
Open: Daily.
Price: Moderate to Expen-
  sive.
Cuisine: French, American.
Serving: B, L, D.
Credit Cards: AE, MC, V.
Reservations: Advised on
  weekends.
Handicap Access: Yes.

Two of us always dine at Café Normandie together, and always, we order the same. He goes for the specials, like rockfish, or a $19.75 red snapper with crabmeat. We always snitch a succulent bite, but order Caesar salad if it's warm, apple and cheddar crêpes if it's cold, and fill up on crunchy French rolls if we're starved. We drink a Shore-brewed Wild Goose amber lager in summer and tell ourselves we can afford the calories since we're eating salad. Late Saturday afternoons in January, we sip a nice glass of French burgundy with our crêpes, and decide winter can be cozy, after all. A small upstairs dining balcony peers over windows onto Main Street; a bustling dining room below offers Impressionist prints on the wall and matching cloths on closely-set tables. A big fireplace dominates center stage. It does seem that service at Café Normandie has grown a tad indifferent compared to what it used to be, but we still like to eat here.

**CANTLER'S RIVERSIDE
  INN**
410-757-1467.
458 Forest Beach Rd.

We no longer need a map to find Cantler's, one-time waterman's bar turned major-league seafood house, but you might. Tucked back on Mill Creek northeast of Annapolis, the rangy

Open: Daily.
Price: Inexpensive to Expensive.
Cuisine: Seafood.
Serving: L, D.
Credit Cards:AE, D, DC, MC, V.
Reservations: No.
Special Features: Boat access, waterside.
Handicap Access: Yes (not bathrooms).

dining room opens on to a waterside patio offering both covered and open-air seating, straightforward beer offerings, and the biggest crabs around — even when supplies are low. Non-crab-eaters will discover buckets of clams, platters of properly broiled rockfish, ears of corn (still in the husks), and a selection of pies ranging from Key lime to Reese's Pieces. After dinner, ask if you can take the kids down by the water to see the tanks of peeler crabs. A fun, bustling place with maps imbedded in tables and wood-paneled walls. Operated by former waterman Jimmy Cantler and a handful of his many siblings, this restaurant never seems to suffer from its overwhelming popularity. Cars line up early along the winding road in summer; call for directions.

CARROL'S CREEK
410-263-8102.
410 Severn Ave.
Open: Daily.
Price: Moderate to Expensive.
Cuisine: New American.
Serving: L, D, SB.
Credit Cards: AE, D, DC, MC, V.
Handicap Access: Yes.

Whenever we can't decide where to dine in Annapolis, we go to neighborly Carrol's Creek. Parking is handy, the Spa Creek view is great, and diners comfortably order anything from the Caesar salad made right before your very eyes to a fine entrée. The classy blond-wood-and-windows decor sets a breezy tone that extends outside to the deck, the city's numero uno onshore place to see the summer's Wednesday night sailboat races finish. Menu options focus on seafood, although the kitchen has produced some originals. Among the best is a mushroom salad, featuring six types of fungi brushed with walnut oil. We direct diners to the specials, which often tend toward fresh seasonal seafood. The restaurant also carries its own wine label, and serves an enormous Sunday brunch — but get there early.

CHICK AND RUTH'S DELLY
410-269-6737.
165 Main St.
Open: 24 hours daily.
Price: Inexpensive.
Cuisine: Simple American, kosher.
Serving: B, L, D.
Credit Cards: None.
Reservations: None.
Handicap Access: Limited.

The patriarch of this restaurant, Chick Levitt, died recently but the spirit of his local institution lives on through son, Ted. People crowd behind the orange formica tables not for the food, which can be marginal, but for the atmosphere, which is as Americana as the apple pie. The Pledge of Allegiance is recited every morning and Ted entertains the children with magic tricks and jokes. The corn beef is lean and the coffee is always plentiful, even if it is served in plastic cups with disposable liners. A table is permanently reserved for Marvin Mandel, a former governor and frequent patron, while sandwiches are named after local

They pledge allegiance to the U.S. flag every morning at Chick and Ruth's Delly, an Annapolis institution.

David Trozzo

attorneys, lawmakers, and politicians who subsist on the deli's stock. The atmosphere can turn extraterrestrial in the wee hours, but mornings are always civilized and great for local gossip.

Dining at Harry Browne's in Annapolis offers a fine view of Maryland's historic statehouse.

David Trozzo

HARRY BROWNE'S
410-263-4332.
66 State Circle.
Open: Daily.
Price: Expensive.
Cuisine: New American.
Serving: L, D, SB.
Credit Cards: MC, V.
Reservations: Suggested on
weekends.
Handicap Access: Yes.

Asked to scan the mental Rolodex for the best restaurant in town, many Annapolitans compile a short list that includes Harry Browne's. With its dusky mauve TV bar upstairs and bronze globe chandeliers down, the State Circle-side restaurant offers perhaps the city's highest style.

We always like the touches at Harry Browne's, like raspberry sorbet served after the salad course. Recorded string music wafts amid the chatter at white linen-covered tables. We order simple, sophisticated food: filet mignon, cooked to our specified, medium perfection; salmon Werthman, in which our favorite, endangered fish is respectfully prepared and served on a bed of greens du decade — arugula for the '90s, and wilted spinach for the '80s (or was that the '70s?). Those of us who can't bear to pass up Cajun BBQ shrimp perhaps made a misstep — it was way too hot. But by now we should have known better, since it's never too good outside Louisiana. Considering Harry Browne's relatively moderate prices and its abundant style, we always consider this a good night-out option.

JOSS CAFÉ AND SUSHI BAR
410-263-4688.
195 Main St.
Open: Daily.
Price: Inexpensive to Expensive.
Cuisine: Japanese.
Serving: L, D.
Credit Cards: AE, DC, MC, V.
Reservations: No.
Handicap Access: Yes.

Patrons willingly stand in line for a seat at one of eight tables at this tiny sushi bar, which tells you something about the food. They never scrimp on the wasabi and ginger that go with the extensive sushi and sashimi menu. Order something familiar-sounding, like Maryland crab roll with lump meat, scallions, and cucumber, or go for the exotic — like smoked eel maki rolls. The regular menu includes dishes like mahi mahi or salmon with teriyaki served with grilled veggies, and a choice of miso soup or salad to start. We're never disappointed. White and blue linens add a classy air to the tiny space, which also has five seats at the sushi bar. If you're seated next to the door, you may find yourself crushed by folks coming and going to leave their names on the waiting list, but your hosts have hung a curtain there in an effort to create space. Plans to double the restaurant shouldn't threaten the intimate tea-room feel. Get here by 5:30 on weekends or plan to place your name on the list and head to a nearby watering hole for the wait.

LA PICCOLA ROMA
410-268-7898.
200 Main St.
Open: Daily.
Price: Expensive.
Cuisine: Italian.
Serving: L, D.
Credit Cards: AE, MC, V.
Reservations: Recommended on weekends.
Handicap Access: Yes, into café; steps into restaurant.

Downtown Annapolis has sprouted new Italian restaurants, but none so fine as Piccola Roma, firstborn of the talented local restaurateur Gino Giolitti. Although Gino and his wife Mary are often there to ensure service, the real star is Mario, an Italian with bushy eyebrows and a deep voice who makes diners feel they are in Italy. A plate of appetizers includes antipasto or carpaccio, while a steady array of entrées ranges from several pastas, which can be ordered as side dishes, to fish with Mediterrean seasoning. Dress tends to be casual in the summers, but changes to coat and tie in the winter when the locals reclaim their town. Bas reliefs accent the simple, elegant dining room.

Wonderfully situated, here diners can watch the world pass by their tables and stroll down to the City Dock to burn off the calories after dinner.

THE LITTLE CAMPUS INN
410-263-9250.
63 Maryland Ave.
Open: Daily.
Price: Moderate.
Cuisine: American, Greek, seafood.
Serving: L, D.
Credit Cards: AE, MC, V.
Handicap Access: Yes.

Settle into a Naugahyde booth in the back of the bar, order some shepherd's pie, and consider yourself lucky that you can still eat in a restaurant that existed back before Annapolis got so darn gentrified. The Nichols family opened the two-sided restaurant in 1924, and they're still serving the locals, including students from nearby St. John's College and the Naval Academy. On the other side of the neighborhood bar is a typical dining room, served by Miss Peggy, who's waited tables here since 1957. Although the menu offers the usual crab dishes, we say try the specials. Where else are you going to find Limerick Stew, replete with corned beef and potatoes, the week after St. Paddy's Day?

David Trozzo

McGarvey's Saloon in Annapolis, all decked out for the Fourth.

MCGARVEY'S SALOON
410-263-5700.
8 Market Space.
Open: Daily.
Price: Moderate.
Cuisine: Saloon fare.
Serving: L, D, SB.
Credit Cards: AE, MC, V.
Reservations: "Preferred seating" only.
Special Features: Raw bar.
Handicap Access: Yes (restrooms are downstairs).

The Annapolis version of Boston's "Cheers" saloon, everyone here knows your name — even if it isn't Walter Cronkite, an occasional visitor and friend of owner Mike Ashford. Mike holds court at the foot of the long bar where people belly up for a Maryland-brewed Aviator beer, named after Ashford's hobby of flying antique places, or an Old Hydraulic, the locally made root beer. Tables alongside the bar offer quick seating but expect to be jostled by the standing bar crowd. More relaxing is the adjacent dining room which offers the same food without the madding crowd.

Food here is devoted to plump oysters and clams from the raw bar and a host of hamburgers grilled to perfection. Try the meaty backfin crab cakes, a local delicacy, or the crab balls, an appetizer version of the cakes. On weekends, the line to get inside can wind down the street but it's worth the wait if you want to be part of the young, and often in search of, crowd.

MIDDLETON TAVERN
410-263-3323.
2 Market Space.
Open: Daily.
Price: Moderate to Expensive.
Cuisine: Seafood, American.
Serving: L, D; B weekends.
Credit Cards: AE, D, MC, V.
Handicap Access: No.

Drawn to the porch of this colonial-era tavern, casual people-watchers end up returning to Middleton's to check out the cuisine inside. Pastas, seafood, and meat dishes include the classics: fettuccine gorgonzola, simply broiled rockfish, or Chateaubriand for two. Anything on the menu will be good, but try the seafood, because the kitchen shows off how well it understands Chesapeake food. The dining room evokes its origins; the tavern in back is more contemporary but very friendly. Always-dependable Middleton's also serves its own bottled microbrew.

While you're here, ask about the building's history. Originally constructed as a home for seafaring men in 1740, Samuel Middleton took it over in 1750. He operated an inn and a ferry from Philadelphia, which is why so many Revolutionary War-era names, like Washington, Jefferson, and Franklin, have been tied to the tavern. Co-owner Jan Hardesty tells us that back then, the basinlike waterfront came right up to the front of the building, and boats docked right here.

The Chesapeake's many rivers and creeks mean you often can't get there from here by road, so waterside restaurants like Mike's draw the boating crowd come summer.

David Trozzo

MIKE'S RESTAURANT AND CRAB HOUSE
410-956-2784/269-6628.

Mike's startled us the last time we visited, inasmuch as we'd just nixed the notion of our own wedding celebration amid a restaurant's typical public throng. And here we found a group

3030 Old Riva Rd., Riva.
Open: Daily.
Price: Moderate to Expensive.
Cuisine: Seafood.
Serving: L, D.
Credit Cards: AE, MC, V.
Special Features: Outdoor waterside deck.
Handicap Access: Yes.

equipped with a videotape recounting the life of the groom. They took up one-half of the barn-like back dining room one Friday night, and frankly, we were fascinated. The groom dispensed pewter beer mugs to ushers; try as we might, however, we could not discern what the bride gave her bridesmaids in those small white boxes.

No matter. It's the food that counts, and Mike's is a take-it-as-it-comes seafood house that seems to stay filled year-round. We always recommend the porchside picnic tables on the South River for a crab feast, but any of the house seafood dishes will be good. The salad bar is basic, the waitresses are nice, and they serve drinks in little juice glasses. Boats tie up out back, and the crowds always come summer weekends.

THE MOON CAFÉ
410-280-1956.
137 Prince George St.
Open: Daily until midnight.
Price: Inexpensive to Moderate.
Cuisine: New American.
Serving: B, L, D; kitchen closes 11:15pm.
Credit Cards: MC, V.
Handicap Access: Yes, to indoor café.

Pretty much the most visibly hip place in town, with music ranging from jazz to the outer limits, Oscar Wilde's wisdom on the wall, and Xeroxed guidelines for how long you can hang out — if you promise to spend some money. We always go there for double lattes and the $3.95 fresh fruit sundae, but others drop in for healthy bowls of veggie chili, quiches, or big fresh salads. Great outdoor patio through the back, full coffee menu, lots of magazines if you're alone in this latter-day Bohemian enclave.

NORTHWOODS
410-268-2609.
609 Melvin Ave.
Open: Daily (evenings).
Price: Expensive.
Cuisine: Continental, Italian.
Serving: D.
Credit Cards: AE, CB, D, DC, MC, V.
Handicap Access: Yes.

Because of its location off the beaten track, this jewel of a restaurant is known mostly to the locals. It may not have a view of the water, but the nicely appointed dining room still makes for an intimate setting. The fact that it has outlasted a number of other restaurants over the years indicates its success in delivering quality food.

Every day but Saturday, Northwoods offers an exceptional $22.95 fixed price dinner that allows diners to pick from anything on the menu. And what a choice. The menu is more continental than it used to be, and there is plenty of Italian/Mediterranean influences in the pasta and veal. The classic entrées include beef Wellington, duck eslov, and a tilapia fish. Appetizers feature escargots bugatti, seviche, and artichoke Milano. The emphasis here is on the intense sauces.

Fresh herb bread, locally made desserts, and attentive service make this an excellent choice if atmosphere is secondary to innovative cuisine.

Smart diners arrive when O'Leary's Seafood Restaurant opens in Eastport, Annapolis's waterman's district.

David Trozzo

O'LEARY'S SEAFOOD RESTAURANT
410-263-0884.
310 3rd St., Eastport.
Open: Daily.
Price: Moderate to Expensive.
Cuisine: Seafood.
Serving: D.
Credit cards : AE, MC, V.
Reservations: Preferred seating only.
Special Features: Exotic seafood.
Handicap Access: Yes.

O'Leary's continues to maintain its lock on its reputation as the best seafood house in Annapolis. In the Eastport area, within a pleasant walk of downtown, O'Leary's is the place locals go for a good seafood dinner. Diners can choose from a school of perfectly done, fresh fish that ranges from copia to wahoo and have it prepared in any of several ways: poached, baked, sautéed, steamed, or blackened. The white-walled, gallery-esque dining room is small and there is no bar to wait for a table, so the trick is to put your name on the waiting list early, hit an adjacent bar for at least 45 minutes, and designate a representative to check occasionally on your table. Because the restaurant doesn't take reservations, it is best either to eat early or avoid the weekends. A knowledgeable wait staff will point you to the best choices on the menu.

THE RAM'S HEAD
410-268-4545.
33 West St.
Open: Daily.
Price: Inexpensive to Moderate.
Cuisine: New American, tavern fare.
Serving: L, D, SB (kitchen open until midnight; drinks served until 2am).
Credit Cards: AE, MC, V.

Like REM playing college-town pubs, the Ram's Head outgrew its tavern-food-with-great-ale gig a few years back. It expanded into a two-floor restaurant with a new brewpub, Fordham Brewing Co., next door. The kitchen has adopted a sophisticated take on traditional tavern fare, keeping prices restrained in the process. In other words, you'll order a catfish po' boy with sun-dried tomato pesto, not a fried fish sandwich. The menu also adopted a fun, even sassy tone, serving "voodoo relish" with the crab cakes and "Round the World Benedicts" at

Reservations: No.
Handicap Access: Yes.

Sunday brunch (smoked salmon in the Russian version; pâté and coarse mustard for the French). We also like the specials, such as veggie lasagna, or apple chutney added to the chicken salad. Folks in town are enthusiastic about this expanded addition at the gateway to the historic district, and we are, too. A huge selection of brews is offered on a separate, four-page menu.

RED, HOT & BLUE
201 Revell Hwy.
410-626-7427.
Open: Daily.
Price: Inexpensive to Moderate.
Cuisine: Memphis pit barbecue; Southern.
Serving: L, D.
Credit Cards: AE, MC, V.
Reservations: No.
Handicap Access: Yes.

Of course we were aware of RH&B's major-league rib reputation around Washington, but not being much for ribs and/or barbeque, we just let the chain's opening out on Rte. 50 pass us by. Then one day we stopped in to make a phone call. The busy signal at the other end of the line bleeped endlessly, but the down-home Memphis blues boogeying through the restaurant's speakers chased our frustration away. As we waited for the line to clear, we examined posters for happenings like the King Biscuit Blues Festival that slather the walls. Tried again; still no answer. We decided to stay for lunch. Our waitress suggested the pulled pork sandwich. We haven't eaten pork in years, but devoured the barbeque sandwich (just enough cole slaw), made quick work of the warm, full-red-potato salad, listened to the end of "Baby, Meet Me With Your Black Drawers On," got through to our party, and danced on out the door.

Chesapeake's proximity to urbia brings international cuisine to the Bay, including the Vietnamese fare at Saigon Palace in Annapolis.

David Trozzo

SAIGON PALACE
410-268-4463.
609B Taylor Ave.
Open: Daily.

They say good things come in small packages — or occur in unexpected places — and so it goes for Saigon Palace. Easily a leading contender for

Price: Moderate.
Cuisine: Vietnamese.
Serving: L, D.
Credit Cards: AE, DC, MC,
   V.
Reservations: Recom-
   mended on weekends.
Handicap Access: Yes.

our favorite restaurant in town, this little eatery owned by long-time local restaurateur Toi Van Tran and his wife Xuan Phung offers the exquisite blends of French and Chinese cooking that create Vietnamese cuisine. Swoon over the cinnamon beef or rockfish with lemon grass, always prepared with fresh herbs. Anything you order will be excellent; ask your host for his nightly menu suggestions. The low-key dining room of linen table cloths and attentive service is sandwiched into a shopping center at the edge of West Annapolis, not far from the historic district. Moderately priced, including the wine list, but recommended.

**SCIRROCCO MEDITER-
RANEAN GRILL**
410-573-0970.
2552 Riva Rd.
Open: Daily.
Price: Moderate.
Cuisine: Mediterranean.
Serving: L, D.
Credit Cards: AE, MC, V.
Reservations: Recom-
   mended on weekends.
Special Features: Open
   grill, good wine list.
Handicap Access: Yes.

Located just outside of the city, this is the hottest new restaurant in Annapolis. There's no view from the windows (in fact, there are no windows) but the food is healthy and creatively Mediterranean with an emphasis on fresh produce and seafood. Inside, the duct work is exposed à la New York but tables are neatly tucked into corners and the atmosphere is lively. Although the paella is a good choice, your best bet are the specials which generally focus on seafood and pasta. Entrées are consistently well packaged with unique seasoning and great presentation. The highlights here are the wine list, a collection of more than 50 wines all priced at $18, and the three choices of bread baked daily from Giolitti's, the owners' nearby deli.

**TREATY OF PARIS AT
THE MARYLAND INN**
410-263-2641.
16 Church Circle.
Open: Daily.
Price: Expensive.
Cuisine: Continental.
Serving: B, L, D, SB.
Credit Cards: AE, DC, MC,
   V.
Reservations: Recom-
   mended.
Handicap Access: Yes;
   prior notice requested.
Special Features: Historic
   setting; fireplaces.

This historic restaurant with brick walls, pewter plates, exposed beams, and a candlelight atmosphere has been long recognized as the most intimate dining room in Annapolis, but over the years the quality of the food has become inconsistent. A frequent change of staff and chefs makes a visit dicey even though traditional dishes like the crown-and-crab appetizer and the Treaty of Paris sampler entrée make a stop worth the gamble. The seafood is tantalizing but the beef and the lamb chops can be mouthwatering when the chef du jour is at his peak. Perhaps most popular among regulars is the bread basket of popovers and cornbread sticks, but the real attractions are the intense sauces that are not for the cholesterol-conscious. The challenge here is to avoid the tempting dessert tray. Adjacent to the dining room is a great jazz lounge with top artists but a high tariff. Down the hall is the Drummer's Lot, a wonderful bar that offers waiting diners a respite from the crowded dining room entrance.

Broome's Island

Steamers at Stoney's: a Chesapeake treat off the beaten path.

David Trozzo

STONEY'S SEAFOOD HOUSE
410-586-1888.
Oyster House Rd.
Open: Daily in season.
Price: Moderate.
Cuisine: Seafood.
Serving: L, D.
Credit Cards: MC, V.
Handicap Access: Yes.

Smart diners go where the locals go, and the Calvert County locals go to Stoney's. In fact, they tend to be downright pleased to hear you know about the place, especially the location at Broome's Island. (A second branch is open year-round in Prince Frederick.) Owner Phillip Stone has renovated the tiny old place and invested in one of the more expansive waterside crab decks encountered in our travels. It's a good place to knock crabs come July. But in the "R" months during Stoney's open three seasons, stand back. Now's the time for oysters. Fried oysters in March, imported from Cobb Island, were nearly the size of waffles. We'd neither seen nor tasted much like them in our substantially oyster-fueled lives. And who's complaining when seafood menus advise not just a fried fish sandwich, but a rockfish sandwich? We couldn't believe our good luck, and heartily endorse Stoney's as a day-trip luncheon destination. Head west down Broome's Island Road from Rte. 2/4.

Deale

FISHER'S WHARF
410-867-0511.
477 Deale Rd.
Open: Daily.

Like a fisherman who guards his prized fishing hole, we considered leaving Fisher's Wharf out of our restaurant reviews. Last time we visited, it

Price: Inexpensive to Moderate.
Cusine: Seafood.
Serving: L, D.
Credit Cards: MC, V.
Handicap Access: Yes.

was busier than ever — and all of us on the deck must have double-tipped the single waitress who kept the beers flowing and the best, and we mean best, crabs in the world coming. Amid a season where stocks were low and dire predictions high, we feasted on local crabs caught by trot-line, which means they're the fat, good ones. The corn was sweet, the breeze off Rockhold Creek brisk, and the laughs were even better. As it happened, we'd arrived during Deale's annual "Christmas in July," when local yachts and fishing boats dress up and hold a zany parade of lights after dark. Crack a crab; wave to Santa.

HAPPY HARBOR INN
410-867-0949.
533 Deale Rd.
Open: Daily.
Price: Inexpensive to Moderate.
Cuisine: Seafood.
Serving, B, L, D.
Credit Cards: D, MC, V.
Handicap Access: Yes.

We hate to be unadventurous, but we can't see why anyone would eat in a little seafood joint in a waterman's town like this and order anything but seasonal seafood. We come here for oysters on the half shell in winter, and we often order crab soup — spitting small crab shells out as we go. This is the kind of place where the guy at the next table buys beers for his buddy after he wins at Keno. A regional favorite, right on Rockhold Creek. No hardshell crabs, though.

Galesville

THE INN AT PIRATE'S COVE
410-867-2300.
4817 Riverside Dr.
Open: Year-round.
Price: Moderate.
Cuisine: Seafood, American.
Serving: L, D, SB.
Credit Cards: AE, DC, MC, V.
Handicap Access: Partial, with assistance

A table at the far side of the bar at Pirate's Cove is one of our favorites around, where the view is wide onto the West River and service is attentive. Nautical prints mix with your perfect plates of half-shell oysters or crab cakes. The lunch menu attends to those arriving late for brunch, offering egg dishes as well as the usual sandwiches. Dinner is more upscale, but keep in mind that you're in seafood country. Crab shows up in imperials and seafood mixes, and flounder is even served two ways. In nice weather, Big Mary's Dock Bar boogies; folks who don't feel like listening to a latter-day Jimmy Buffet can move around to the back of the restaurant and still enjoy al fresco dining on the West River.

Lusby

VERA'S WHITE SANDS RESTAURANT
410-586-1182.
Rte. 4.

We still can't get over Vera's, which we describe as John Waters meets Trader Vic's. That's still so, but the shock that registered when we first encountered this incongruous Chesapeake-

Open: May–Sept. (closed
  Mon.).
Price: Expensive.
Cuisine: Southern Mary-
  land, American, seafood.
Serving: D.
Credit Cards: MC, V.
Reservations: Recom-
  mended.
Special Features: Outdoor
  patio, boatslips.
Handicap Access: Partial.

side Far East extravaganza has subsided with time
and familiarity. As Vera herself told us, "We're just
different than anyplace." It's true. The menu is
pretty basic, serving upscale standards of old such
as osso buco, or Maryland crab cakes. But the
meandering restaurant offers treasures collected
during owner Vera Freeman's world travels,
ensconced in rooms with names like "The Palm
Palm Room." As the keyboardist plays, swill a
drink with an umbrella in it from your perch on a
leopard-covered barstool, and behold the magnificent portrait of Vera, who wears Cleopatra-style
headgear and caftans. During one visit, we were asked to photograph an
apparent spiritual stepchild, a woman dressed Vera-style, who posed before
the portrait. We also once watched a river otter — or was it just a muskrat? —
from our table at a wide window onto St. John's Creek. Take Rte. 2/4 to Lusby,
and follow the airbrushed signs west from the highway.

Solomons

**SEA HORSES RESTAU-
  RANT AND NIGHT-
  CLUB**
410-326-1412.
Solomons Island Rd. S.
Open: Daily; closed
  Mon.–Tues. in winter.
Price: Inexpensive to Mod-
  erate.
Cuisine: Tavern fare.
Serving: L (Sat.–Sun); D.
Credit Cards: AE, MC, V.
Handicap Access: Yes.

If you're in Solomons at lunchtime, stop by. The
amiable staff offers a good place to watch a game
at the bar's TV, or serves up a variety of sandwiches and simple seafood (spiced shrimp; fish of
the day) in the upstairs dining room with spectacular views of the Patuxent and the bridge to St.
Mary's. Pool tables downstairs; crabs in season.

NORTHERN NECK/MIDDLE PENINSULA

Deltaville, Virginia

RED SKY
804-776-6913.
Rtes. 102 & 33.
Open: Tues.–Sun.
Price: Moderate to Expen-
  sive.
Cuisine: New American.
Serving: L, D, SB.
Credit Cards: MC, V.

The little bayfront town of Deltaville is home to
many boats whose owners live around Richmond, and it's a popular stop for Chesapeake cruisers, too. Red Sky opened here to give these folks
something more elegant than standard local fare.
With its creative sauces, fresh ingredients, and skillful use of herbs and seasonings, it was instantly successful. The menu changes, but after an appetizer of
beer-battered Vidalia onions with a Creole honey
mustard sauce, our group enjoyed a perfectly

cooked peppered and pan-seared New York strip steak with a bourbon, garlic, and horseradish demi-glace, a delicate shrimp and scallops Diane with shallots, garlic, and mushrooms in a brandy butter sauce served over angel hair pasta, and a very nice sautéed chicken, shrimp, and Bay scallops combination served in a tomato basil cream sauce over linguine pasta. You get the idea; the chef is having fun in the kitchen. The service was a bit inexperienced but enthusiastic, and the young staff really wants to make the place work. The chef is talented, the informality matches the town, and a regular clientele is developing. Acoustic guitar music some evenings.

Irvington, Virginia

THE TIDES INN
804-438-5000.
King Carter Dr.
Open: Daily.
Price: Expensive.
Cuisine: Continental,
  seafood.
Serving: B, L, D, SB (L at
  main restaurant Sun.
  only; L at pool and golf
  course daily).
Credit Cards: AE, D, MC, V.
Reservations: Highly rec-
  ommended.
Special Features: Resort
  atmosphere, water view,
  boat access.
Handicap Access: Yes.

We knew were in for a treat the moment we stepped into The Tides Inn dining room. Here is subdued elegance — a glowing candle among the blue and gold place settings, two carnations in each bud vase, an army of staff at the ready.

We were immediately escorted to a table next to the huge window with a panoramic view of the manicured lawn, Carter Creek, the resort's 126-foot yacht *Miss Ann*, and a gorgeous sunset over the Rappahannock River.

The service was attentive, yet unobtrusive. When the lady in our party started to remove her jacket, assistance appeared suddenly and silently at her side.

The four dining rooms are airy, bright, and huge — yet intimate; busy, yet relaxing. Every table commands a water view, even the upper level of the main room.

The prix fixe menu changes daily, but always includes five appetizers, two soups, three salads, seven entrées, several vegetables al dente, and six or seven deserts. The wine list is extensive.

For openers, we chose the shrimp and scallop seafood terrine. Our companion had the Chesapeake crabmeat cocktail, which she pronounced too yummy to share a taste. We also chose the Maine lobster bisque (exquisite!), and the spinach leaves with hot bacon dressing.

Selecting an entrée was difficult. They all sounded so tempting: fried soft-shell crabs with seafood sauce; poached salmon with tarragon cream sauce; grilled lamb chop, calf's liver and bacon; sliced beef tenderloin with wild mushroom compote.

The stuffed Cornish game hen supreme was scrumptious, with barely an intrusive bone to be found. Our companion tried seafood medley en croute, featuring pastry so light it seemed to drift away. The subtle sauces were deliciously underwhelming. She did allow us a taste.

It was worth wearing a tie for.

Kilmarnock, Virginia

**THE CRAB SHACK
RESTAURANT AND
SEAFOOD SHOP**
804-435-2700.
Follow the signs from
Rte. 200.
Open: Tues.–Sun.,
mid-Apr.–mid-Oct.
Price: Moderate.
Cuisine: Seafood.
Serving: L, D.
Credit Cards: AE, D,
DC, MC, V.
Reservations: No.
Special Features: Views
of Indian Creek and
Chesapeake Bay; quick
boat access from Bay,
dock.
Handicap Access: Yes.

Don't let the Crab Shack's name fool you. Instead of picnic tables, paper plates, plastic forks, and crab mallets, this is tablecloths, fresh flowers, and water glasses with lemon wedges. The menu features seafood, seafood, and seafood, with a smattering of beef and chicken for landlubbers. For openers, we couldn't resist the seafood bisque, which turned out to be great. The most expensive item on the menu, an $18 seafood sampler, proved to be tender and tasty, especially the flaky fish. Only a few drops of lemon required. The sautéed shrimp could have gone lighter on the spices. But the main attraction here is the location — right on beautiful Indian Creek with a view of the Bay through floor-to-ceiling windows. In pleasant weather, full service is available at umbrella-topped tables on a waterside deck, or picnic tables on the lawn. Cruisers can berth in 15 slips for their meal, then anchor in the creek overnight. Prefer to cook aboard? Pick up fresh crabmeat, shrimp, scallops, and fish at the shack's Seafood Shop. Then drop the hook nearby and fire up the barbe.

LEE'S RESTAURANT
804-435-1255.
Main St.
Open: Mon.–Sat.,
7am–8:30pm.
Price: Inexpensive.
Cuisine: Seafood,
steaks, burgers.
Serving: B, L, D.
Credit Cards: No
(checks accepted).
Reservations: No.
Special Features: Friendly,
home-town
atmosphere.
Handicap Access: Yes.

Every town's main drag has a favorite local downtown eatery where you know you can't go wrong. In Kilmarnock, it's Lee's Restaurant, a favorite among locals and regular visitors for decades. The food is good, the prices are right, and the service is friendly.

Decor is knotty-pine nautical, with pictures and models of sailing and team boats. A few years ago, Lee's broke through a wall next door and more than doubled its size, upgrading and enlarging the restrooms in the bargain.

The New York strip steak and the seafood platter, each under $10, are among the most expensive items on the menu, so you really can't miss. The crab cakes are great. We usually drop in for lunch when we're in town, and have crab cake sandwiches, served with French fries and cole slaw. But one dinner, we splurged on the seafood platter (a tasty assortment) and the softshell crabs. The crabs were running small, the waitress said, explaining why she brought four instead of two. Tossed salad is extra (under $1) — but try the cornbread. It's light, smooth and sweet, not dry and crumbly. If Forrest Gump showed up at

Lee's to savor a chunk, he just might say, "Life is like a platter of cornbread. You never know what you're gonna get."

THE NORTHSIDE GRILLE
804-435-3100.
Rte. 3/Main St.
Open: Weds.–Mon.
Price: Moderate.
Cuisine: American.
Serving: L, D.
Credit Cards: D, MC, V.
Handicap Access: Yes.

Blonde wood, green booths, daisies on the tables, and lemon slices on water glass's edge — here's a nice little café that would blend right in on any city street. But at the end of the Northern Neck, perhaps it's reassuring. The food matches the dining room. Look for grilled crab cakes ($12.95), veggie stir-fry, or basic salmon filet in dill sauce. Altogether, food and atmosphere are pleasant, clean, and efficient, and not overly fancy — but not overly funky, either. Foster's on tap, William Wycliff house wines by the glass. Kids' menu, too.

Lancaster, Virginia

LANCASTER TAVERN
804-462-5941.
Rte 3, Lancaster Courthouse.
Open: Thurs.–Sun., 11–2, 5–8.
Price: Inexpensive.
Cuisine: Grandma's home cooking.
Serving: L, D.
Credit Cards: No (checks accepted).

If you're lucky enough to be near Lancaster Courthouse when the tavern is open, drop in for all the good food you can eat for little more than the price of a movie. It's like dining at Grandma's house — homey, rustic, and old. Like Grandma's, choices are limited, but good and plentiful.

Except for the small, painted sign hanging over the front door (Lancaster Tavern 1790), the weathered brown building could be mistaken for the private home it once was. We had to make sure it was really open for business. We walked in and heard history creak beneath our feet; the pine-plank floors and much of the building, we were told, are original.

Casual and friendly, the tavern seats 20 at four traditional dining room tables surrounded by assorted pine and mahogany chairs. A Singer treadle sewing machine serves as cash drawer.

There is no menu — you just take your chances. We haven't been disappointed yet. Have a seat, and the ladies start bringing in the food du jour.

Our first visit, homemade vegetable soup was hot and tasty. A parade of platters and serving bowls followed, featuring chicken and dumplings every Thursday ("They're delicious! Just like Grandma used to make!" a guest at the next table exclaimed to her companions), and slices of sugar-cured ham. Vegetarians could make do on the side dishes alone: boiled buttered potatoes, green beans, corn, beets, and the best homemade applesauce we've ever tasted, along with dinner rolls and coffee or tea (hot or iced). Alcohol is not served. They kept the plates and bowls coming until we said stop. Then came the homemade spice cake with raisins.

On a second visit, the kitchen issued sliced turkey and roast beef (each in their own gravy), and peas, broccoli, glazed carrots, and that wonderful apple-sauce, all topped off with white cake and chocolate icing.

It's impossible to walk out of Grandma's tavern hungry.

Mollusk, Virginia

CONRAD'S UPPER DECK
804-462-7400.
End of Va. Rte. 624.
Open: Mar.–Nov., Fri.–Sat.,
    5–9pm.
Price: Inexpensive to Moderate.
Cuisine: Seafood.
Serving: D.
Credit Cards: No (cash or checks).
Special Features: Water view, powerboat access.
Handicap Access: Yes.

Local residents and regular visitors to the Northern Neck know that Conrad's Upper Deck is the place to find fresh seafood, prepared to perfection. After all, the restaurant sits atop Conrad's wholesale seafood business overlooking the Rappahannock River.

We have been dining at Conrad's for nearly a decade and have never been disappointed. The clam chowder, piping hot in a salad-bar tureen, is a special treat.

The all-you-can-eat seafood buffet, which includes the soup and salad bar, is a tasty variety of steamed shrimp, fried scallops, oysters, clams, and crab balls, baked fish, fried chicken, hush puppies, corn on the cob, and several other vegetables.

Alas, the ever-popular Alaskan king crab legs have priced themselves off the buffet, much to owner Milt Conrad's dismay. But they are available on the menu by the pound.

The buffet, Conrad's most expensive item, is recommended only if you are starved. We have a friend with a hollow leg who can devour his weight in oysters — what a deal for him. Selections from the menu are very generous.

The "Pick 3" allows a choice of any three seafood delights. Try more than enough flounder stuffed with crabmeat, or shrimp, scallops, and oysters. They were delicious, but we took half home. We never have room for dessert, but usually we can't resist a slice of Gale Conrad's yummy homemade German chocolate pie — with two forks.

White Stone, Virginia

ANNABEL LEE & MENHADEN LOUNGE
804-435-2123.
Old Ferry Rd.
Open: Daily, 4–10pm (lounge until 2am).
Price: Moderate to Expensive.
Cuisine: Seafood, prime rib.
Serving: D.
Credit Cards: D, MC, V.
Reservations: Optional.

Annabel Lee is one of our favorite restaurants when we feel like dining instead of merely eating. The menu is varied, and prices are, too. Service is friendly and the sunset over the Rappahannock River is fantastic. These days, there's even a flock of cranes in sight on the river — not the birds, but the machines they're using to redeck the Robert O. Norris, Jr., Memorial Bridge.

Prime rib pot roast, Virginia sugar-cured ham, and frog legs in the rough are among selections in

Special Features: Water view.
Handicap Access: Yes.

the moderate range, but you can splurge on surf-and-turf (lobster and prime rib).

Seafood bisque is our appetizer of choice. It's extra yummy, spicy, creamy where it should be creamy and lumpy where it should be lumpy.

Prime rib is an Annabel Lee special, and it's always just right. There's a $3/4$-inch-thick "lady's cut" (they really call it that on the menu) and a regular cut almost twice as thick — enough for two. We're never disappointed in the seafood dishes. Just about everything comes with a great salad and a choice of many dressings; we love the Vidalia onion vinaigrette.

Owner Billy Ancarrow, known as Capt. Billy, says everything on the menu is also available upstairs in the Menhaden Lounge until 2am. Early-bird breakfast is from midnight till 2.

Not bad for the Northern Neck, where they usually roll up the sidewalks at sundown.

UPPER EASTERN SHORE

Chester

CHESTER RIVER INN
410-643-3886.
205 Tackle Circle.
Open: Weds.–Mon.
Price: Moderate.
Cuisine: New American, Continental.
Serving: L, D.
Credit Cards: AE, D, MC, V
Reservations: On weekends.
Handicap Access: Yes.

Chef Mark Henry must be immune to the resident ghost which seems to have chased away many other restaurateurs from this location. He built a reputation at the Milton Inn, north of Baltimore, and many of his regular customers from there now make the trek across the Bay. Add those who have recently discovered him in this somewhat out-of-the-way location, and you now call for Saturday reservations. The dining room is not in the original 1860 brick farmhouse but in a windowed addition which offers nice views out to a marina and the Chester River. The menu is well balanced, with seafood, beef, lamb, and pork, most served with creative sauces. A roast loin of pork was memorable. Served with succotash, fried grit cakes and sautéed apples, it sounds like a southern home-cooked dinner — but only the ingredients are related. A melon soup was wonderfully cool on a summer day. You can also get here by water. Castle Harbor Marina is three miles south of Love Point Light.

Chestertown

THE FEAST OF REASON
410-778-3828.
203 High St.
Open: Mon.–Fri. 10–6, Sat. 10–4.
Price: Inexpensive.

The only complaint ever expressed about The Feast of Reason is that it isn't open 24 hours. Freshly made salads, soups, and an ever-changing variety of sandwiches make this New Age delicatessen a local favorite. Two entrées are listed on

Cuisine: Light fare.
Serving: L; D to go.
Credit Cards: None.

the chalkboard every day that are also available for carry-out.

The Feast of Reason offers specialty coffees and teas as well as a good selection of bottled soft drinks. The café also will pack a picnic and the staff is accommodating for special orders. Boaters, it's just a short walk from the public landing on the Chester River.

What makes the sandwiches so good here? It might be the fresh honey-wheat bread or sunflower-seed bread baked in the shop. Most patrons say, though, that it's the variety of flavored and herbed mayonnaise toppings made on the premises. The sun-dried tomato mayonnaise is inspiring. And the vegetable-topped flatbread pizza is worth writing home about. Daily vegetarian choices and luscious home-baked desserts round out the menu.

GIARDINO'S
410-778-9420.
Washington Square
    Shopping Center,
    Rte. 213 N.
Open: Daily.
Price: Moderate.
Cuisine: Italian.
Serving: L, D.
Credit Cards: D, MC, V.
Reservations: Recom-
    mended on weekends.
Handicap Access: Yes.

Don't be fooled by the pizza shop in the front of this restaurant. Turn to the right and enter a comfortable dining room where restaurateur Ron DelNaja treats you like family. Here is pasta paradise.

Linger over appetizers like hot bruschetta or sliced fresh tomatoes with baby mozzarella drizzled in olive oil and sprinkled with fresh basil. Spaghetti and meatballs are on the menu, to be sure, but so are fresh gnocchi, linguine, and fettuccine topped with divine chicken, veal, seafood, and vegetable sauces. The tortellini in a prosciutto cream sauce is worth mentioning by name.

The portions are large, but be sure to leave room for a traditional Italian dessert of spumoni or cannoli.

Open for only a relatively short time, Giardino's is quickly becoming a local favorite. On Thursday nights, Giardino's offers a prix fixe meal with a choice of five entrées. But for the smaller appetite — or for the kids — pizzas, calzones, and Italian-style sandwiches are available.

HARBOR HOUSE ✓
410-778-0669.
23145 Buck Neck Rd.
Open: Daily (closed Tues.).
Price: Moderate to Expen-
    sive.
Cuisine: Seafood, Ameri-
    can, pasta.
Serving: L (Sat. only); D, SB.
Credit Cards: D, MC, V.
Special Features: Water
    view.

Looking out over peaceful Worton Creek, Harbor House Restaurant caters not only to the boaters who tie up at the marina next door but also to those who venture off the beaten track for some surprisingly interesting dishes. With delightful, friendly service and generous, well-executed dishes, Harbor House surpasses its modest first impression.

The crab quesadilla appetizer — definitely meant to be shared — could be a meal unto itself. The quesadillas come floating on a lake of black beans and offer a tasty diversion from the more traditional crab cakes and imperial, also on the menu.

Even the tried-and-true steaks, seafood, and surf-and-turf offerings are given a nice touch. This restaurant excels in sauces, and steaks can come adorned with portabella mushroom, Zinfandel, Stilton cheese, or French mustard sauces. Better still, several pasta dishes round out the menu. The penne al Trieste with beef tips in an artichoke and tomato sauce was unexpectedly savory.

The restaurant has been closing seasonally, but manager Carlo Fernandes said that the months of operation could be expanded in the future. Call first, though, if you're planning to visit in the late fall and winter.

Attention to detail marks Chestertown's Imperial Hotel dining room.

David Trozzo

IMPERIAL HOTEL & RESTAURANT
410-778-5000.
208 High St.
Open: Weds.–Sun.
Price: Expensive.
Cuisine: Creative Chesapeake.
Serving: D (Weds.–Sat.), SB.
Credit Cards: AE, D, MC, V.
Reservations: Recommended, especially on weekends.
Handicap Access: Limited.

For an elegant dining experience, the Imperial is the place to go in Chestertown. This hotel turned bed-&-breakfast inn (see Chapter Three, *Lodging*) has one of the most creative menus on the Shore.

The menu changes seasonally, but always expect to see choice meats, fresh seafood, and waterfowl prepared in interesting ways. Dinner at the Imperial is an experience, not merely a meal. Sumptuous Victorian surroundings enhance every meal prepared here. It is a place where memories are made.

Superb chilled soups and salads highlight the summer menu. Hearty duck dishes are featured when the weather turns cold.

The Imperial has added a Starbucks coffee café in its lower level, accessed by steps from the street.

In a region known for steamed crabs and fried seafood, the Imperial stands out as an innovator. Skilled preparation and presentation, exciting combinations of tastes and textures, and artful service all add up to make the Imperial a Chesapeake treasure.

IRONSTONE CAFÉ
410-778-0188.
236 Cannon St.
Open: Tues.–Sat.
Price: Expensive.
Cuisine: Creative American.
Serving: L, D.
Credit Cards: MC, V.
Reservations: Recommended.

The Ironstone comes up with some incredible combinations of tastes and textures on what must be one of the most original menus in the region. The dishes are constantly changing, so give this light, airy café extra points for providing handwritten menus each day for lunch and dinner.

Typical appetizers include smoked salmon and herb cream cheese tortilla rolls with coriander-lime white bean salad. That's one dish. Another is baked crab, celery, and mushrooms on flatbread.

Entrées are robust — filet of beef in a bourbon sauce, sautéed veal sweetbreads, breast of duck in a red wine sauce roasted with garlic and garnished with juniper berries, as well as garlic-roasted shrimp.

Desserts are fresh, made on the premises, and feature fresh fruits in season. Out of season, the dessert list weighs in with a double chocolate torte that's worth a special trip.

Lunch comes in under $10. Folks rave over the Tidewater sandwich: turkey salad, swiss cheese, and Smithfield ham on marbled rye bread. Salads come with creative dressings — lemon thyme parmesan or spicy coriander-cumin vinaigrette, for example.

The Ironstone is only a couple of blocks from the Chester River and near some of the most elegant homes in Chestertown. For traditional Eastern Shore fare, look elsewhere. But for a meal worth lingering over, few restaurants do any better.

THE OLD WHARF
410-778-3566.
Cannon St. , next to Kibler's Marina.
Open: Daily.
Price: Moderate.
Cuisine: American, Chesapeake.
Serving: L, D, SB.
Credit Cards: AE, MC, V.
Reservations: Recommended on weekends.
Handicap Access: Yes.

If one of your travel goals is to rub elbows with local folks, go no further than the Old Wharf. Perhaps the restaurant can be forgiven for jamming its tables so close together, though, because it serves the best crab omelet in three states for Sunday brunch.

The dining room is dominated on one side by windows overlooking the Chester River and on the other by a huge salad bar supplemented with freshly baked bread. Eastern Shore oyster and crab dishes get equal time on the standard American menu with steaks, scallops, and pork chops. Nothing fancy here — plates come garnished with a spiced apple ring. The dishes are prepared well, especially the seafood.

Until only recently, this was *the* family restaurant in Chestertown, and the place still packs a crowd, especially during special occasions on the Washington College calendar.

Easton

LEGAL SPIRITS
410-820-0033.
Dover & Harrison Sts.
Open: Mon.–Sat.
Price: Moderate.
Cuisine: Chesapeake,
   American.
Serving: L, D.
Credit Cards: AE, MC, V.
Reservations: Accepted.
Handicap Access: Yes.

This classic pub evoking the Roaring Twenties is the only surviving eatery in the theater that once housed the three popular restaurants known as Trio at the Avalon. Elegant Cecille's and Chambers under the skylight, alas, have departed, leaving Legal Spirits and its busy bar and booths in its front room. In the back, seven tables comprise the small dining room where reservations for dinner are advisable.

Both the bar area and the dining room share the same menu, a tempting range of pub to dinner fare. The atmosphere is informal with a livelier crowd out front in the bar. The tiny dining room is attractive, with dark green wainscoting below white walls, festooned with such speakeasy icons as matched guns in a violin case and photos of Pretty Boy Floyd.

Among appetizers and light fare, the crab dip is a standout. As a starter for a more ambitious dinner, try the escargots on angel hair pasta or the curried crab in crêpes Madras. Entrées include the usual chicken and beef dishes, plus veal in a silky marsala sauce and two styles of lamb. Edible flowers on some entrées are a nice touch. A word of warning on the boneless duck breast in berry sauce: the fried pasta bows kill it.

For dessert, the amaretto cheesecake is likely to provoke a daze of pleasure and the spun sugar garnishes on the other selections are festive.

RUSTIC INN
410-820-8212.
Talbottown Shopping
   Center.
Open: Daily.
Price: Moderate to
   Expensive.
Cuisine: American,
   Chesapeake.
Serving: D daily, L
   Tues.–Fri.
Credit Cards: AE, MC, V.
Handicap Access: Yes.

This gem of a restaurant is hidden in a corner of a shopping center near downtown Easton. It's sign is inconspicuous so you have to look hard to find it. The search is well worth the effort. The interior is a space that could have been plunked down right out of the Norman countryside: rough-textured walls that look as if they've been whitewashed; farm implements on the walls, as well as hunting prints, nautical scenes, and hanging lanterns; a ceiling of stakes on beams that could hold a haymow. The bar/lounge features a four-sided fireplace and cozy seating.

The excellence of the food is on a par with the charm of the decor. The seafood section of the menu alone lists five crab entrées and three of lobster, some in combination with finfish, shrimp, and scallops. A word of advice: in season, the kitchen uses only backfin lump in its crab dishes. When the delicious lump is unavailable, the chef uses plain backfin. Ask to be sure.

A happy alternative is one of three beef entrées. The prime rib may well be the best on the Shore, cooked to perfection. Three veal and three fowl complete the choices. Service is prompt and professional, and the bartender has perfected an almost-lost art, that of creating the perfect martini.

THE TIDEWATER INN
410-822-1300.
Dover & Harrison Sts.
Open: Daily.
Price: Moderate to Expensive.
Cuisine: American, Chesapeake.
Serving: B, L, D.
Credit Cards: AE, DC, MC, V.
Handicap Access: Yes.

Just as we always try to be agreeable to people we admire, the temptation is to praise the places that we like. So it is with the venerable Tidewater Inn, an Easton landmark that looks as if it had been there since colonial times, but dates only to 1949 (See Chapter Three, *Lodging*). The truth is, the ambiance rates way above the kitchen. Any night's dinner may be Lucullan; a month later, it's quite possibly a big disappointment.

The Sunday brunch, however, always rates as one of the best in the area. It's served in the beautiful Crystal Room, which is closed the rest of the week. (Alas, the lovely Gold Room is reserved only for banquets and receptions, so it's off limits most of the time.) The day-to-day dining room is the Hunter's Tavern, a two-level space with big murals of colonial life in the upper tier and beamed ceilings and carved waterfowl dominating the lower level. A cozy cavelike Decoy Bar at the rear also seats the lunch crowd.

Having damned with faint praise the dinner experience, one must give credit where it's due. Breakfasts are excellent. The eggs Benedict are superb and the menu always lists that comfort-food staple of the South, grits swimming in butter.

The lunch menu is fairly standard, featuring first-rate crab cakes and an open-face concoction that is to die for: English muffins under tomato slices, backfin lump crab, and hollandaise sauce. Off-menu, a businessperson's buffet offers a big selection of hot dishes and salads for $6.95.

At lunch or dinner, the star of the show is the snapper soup, not made, as strangers sometimes assume, from red snapper fish but from the humble snapping turtle. Served with a little dollop of sherry to stir into the dark, rich broth, it makes up for any other sins in the kitchen.

YESTERYEARS
410-822-2433.
Easton Plaza Shopping Center, Marlboro Rd.
Open: Mon.–Sat.
Price: Moderate.
Cuisine: Chesapeake, American.

Informality is the code word in this popular bar and restaurant tucked into a corner of a shopping center. The theme is turn-of-the-century Eastern Shore. Renovations are responsible for the removal of a handsome sleigh that used to be suspended above the bar, as well as the disappearance

Serving: L, D.
Credit Cards: AE, MC, V.
Handicap Access: Yes.

of framed early advertisements from the local newspapers. Still, the replacement decor harks back to the images of the locale's seafood and farming heritage.

The bar is big and busy; its companion dining room has booths and tables for regulars who come for the thick, juicy burgers and Hawaiian taco salad, a great crispy cup filled with greens, crab, shrimp, and zesty dressing. The dense cream of crab and classic vegetable crab soups can't be beat.

An adjacent dining room festooned with hanging ferns handles the overflow crowds at lunch and dinner. Beef and seafood — from prime rib to stuffed flounder — dominate the dinner menu, with a smaller selection of chicken and pork dishes. Plus, there's a rousing rendition of Italian food, notably a house recipe for lasagna. Early bird diners (from 4 to 6pm) get a break with as much as $4 off entrées.

If you're not turned off by some men eating with their hats on, this is a pleasant place to relax and feed the inner person.

Grasonville/Kent Narrows

ANGLER'S
410-827-6717.
3015 S. Kent Narrows
   Way.
Open: Daily.
Price: Inexpensive to
   Moderate.
Cuisine: Seafood.
Serving: B, L, D.
Credit Cards: D, MC, V.
Handicap Access: Yes.

Crab in your eggs for breakfast, a plastic dispenser filled with sherry to squirt into your lunch's crab soup. This place is authentic Chesapeake all the way around, whether you've stopped in for a dozen half-shell oysters at the bar, or you intend to dig into an extensive seafood dinner — broiled or fried. The dining room is the kind of place where you expect to hear a screen door slam any minute, and you might catch some local gossip in winter if you keep your ears open. The kitchen serves until 1am on weekends; midnight during the week.

**ANNIE'S PARAMOUNT
   STEAK HOUSE**
410-827-7103.
500 Kent Narrows Way N.,
   Grasonville.
Open: Daily.
Price: Moderate to
   Expensive.
Cuisine: Steak, seafood.
Serving: L, D, SB.
Credit Cards: AE, MC, V.
Handicap Access: Yes.

The sign says Annie's is long established, but that was in Washington, not Kent Narrows, where the company took over the former Poseidon restaurant a few years ago. It was an instant success as a place where one could take the family for a good, traditional dinner. The standout is the prime rib. Not that the seafood isn't good — it is — but most folks come here for the beef. In either case, the servings are large, the atmosphere is casual and friendly, and the view over the water is always interesting. After a meal, stroll around the Narrows and look at the boats.

FISHERMAN'S INN
410-827-8807.
Rte. 18 S., Kent Narrows.
Open: Daily.
Price: Moderate.
Cuisine: Seafood.
Serving: L, D
Credit Cards: AE, D, MC, V.
Reservations: No.
Handicap Access: Yes.

An institution on the Eastern Shore, this classic family restaurant offers local fish and such culinary throwbacks as applesauce and coleslaw on the side. Inside the lobby is one of the best collection of antique oyster plates in Maryland and the signatures of a handful of Hollywood stars who have stopped by. If basic food with local seasoning is your choice, this is your place for value. Seafood is the specialty, but there's passable beef and pasta alternatives. The dining room is a cavernous hall with kitschy nautical tables and homespun service. Next door, try the Shultz family's next generation of restaurants — the informal Crab Deck. Have a pile of steamed jimmies and a beer, or a crab-cake sandwich made with very little filler and lots of lump meat. At intervals, an unmuffled "Vice Boat" drowns out conversation as a migrating, gold-chained chick-hunter crows for attention, but that's part of the Narrows scene, too.

Crabs, corn, and beer: the Harris Crab House stocks it all for a classic Chesapeake crab feast.

David Trozzo

HARRIS CRAB HOUSE
410-827-9500.
Exit 42 off Rte. 50, Kent Narrows Way.
Open: Daily.
Price: Moderate.
Cuisine: Seafood.
Serving: L, D.
Credit Cards: V, MC, Most.
Reservations: No.
Special Features: Deck in season; transient boating slips.
Handicap Access: Yes.

Long gone is the era when Harris's Crab House was a shack lined with picnic tables piled with crab shells. Today the Kent Island landmark within view of Rte. 50 sports an upstairs deck overlooking the busy Kent Narrows waterway. But the long, paper-covered picnic tables, party atmosphere, seasoned crabs, and loyal customers remain. Maintaining its hold on the best crab house on the island, Harris's offers diners a fun experience plus great crabs, oysters, and clams. Barbecued ribs and chicken offer alternatives, but your best choice is the seafood. Budweiser is spoken here. Placemats include instructions on eating crab but the wait staff is more than willing to tutor novices. While you're waiting for a table, which is common on summer weekends, you can stroll on the outside deck to check out a few shops or gaze at the yachts just passing through. Not a place for romance or intimate conversation.

THE NARROWS
410-827-8113.
3023 Kent Narrows Way S.,
    Grasonville.
Open: Daily.
Price: Inexpensive to
    Expensive.
Cuisine: New American.
Serving: L, D.
Credit Cards: D, DC, MC,
    V.
Handicap Access: Yes.

A rarity in the volatile restaurant business; this is a stable, attractive, fine-dining establishment. The pretty dining room overlooking busy Kent Narrows gained convenience and space but lost beauty and charm with a recent remodeling, but it's still a nice spot. The menu is as varied as ever, with a nice range of seafood and land food, prepared in the New American style. The sauces are interesting and the presentation is attractive. Crabmeat, tuna, and grouper are regional and fresh, and if there are no New Yorkers in your party to object, you might check out the catfish Reuben at lunch. There is also a good selection of light suppers and a children's menu. The wine list is extensive, with an emphasis on California products, with no inflated prices. We have been coming here for years, with never a bad experience.

Oxford

PIER STREET MARINA &
    RESTAURANT
410-226-5171.
Pier St.
Open: Apr.–mid-Nov.
Price: Moderate to Expen-
    sive.
Cuisine: Regional seafood.
Serving: L, D.
Credit Cards: MC, V.
Handicap Access: Yes.

L unch or dinner at Pier Street calls for your best bib and tucker — not fancy duds, but a layer of something to keep the juices off your T-shirt and shorts. Paradoxically, the hands-on dining style is the epitome of informality, while the view of the Tred Avon River lapping up on the covered deck is the stuff of elegant travel brochures. A late afternoon sun drops into the water while racing and cruising sailboats duck into shelter from the big Choptank downriver. It's breathtaking.

This is seafood country, and the day's catch is unloaded right next to the kitchen's steamers. Hard crabs cooked in the shell, or course, with enough spicy seasoning to make your eyes water. Steamed clams to extract from their shells and slosh in melted butter. Ditto for mussels, tiny and fragrant. Don't worry about messing up the tablecloth; it's most likely a slab of brown paper. Napkins come disguised as a roll of paper towels.

Standard tableware is a wooden mallet and a knife (eating steamed crabs is probably the only occasion in post-medieval etiquette where it's permissible to eat off a knife). For the misguided aesthetes who resist eating caveman style, forks are provided for orders of crab cakes, crab imperial, and fish stuffed with crab. There's also roast beef and chicken on the menu, but who in his right mind would order it where seafood is almost a religion?

ROBERT MORRIS INN
410-226-5111.
Morris St. at the Strand.
Open: Daily exc. Tues.;
    closed Jan. 14–Mar. 30.
Price: Expensive.
Cuisine: Regional seafood,
    Continental.
Serving: B, L, D.
Credit Cards: MC, V.
Handicap Access: Yes.

Eating at the Robert Morris Inn is a lot like eating in Williamsburg; along with the food comes a heady whiff of authentic history. This wonderful grande dame of an inn originally was a pre-Revolutionary private home (*way* pre-Revolutionary — the main section was built in 1710) built for the father of Robert Morris, Jr., known as "the Financier of the Revolution." Never mind that Sonny was accused of making a bundle as a war profiteer but still spent time in debtors' prison. He spent some of his life in a truly handsome house and you can too (see Chapter Three, *Lodging*).

Ladies who wear hats and gloves (and Oxford still has them) will choose the Main Dining Room with its crystal chandeliers, painted murals on the walls, rose-colored table linens, and flowers. The Tavern and the Tap Room both have big open fireplaces and less formal seating. Cruising sailors are perfectly comfortable in either of the latter rooms wearing shorts, short-sleeve shirts, and sneakers. In recent years, bicyclists have come in droves wearing, alas, lots of Spandex in day-glo hues.

Many of the Inn's regular patrons never get further on the menu than the famous crab cakes, either broiled or fried. They are without peer; poems should be written about them. In season, the chef's way with flounder is also celebrated, either with or without a topping of crab imperial. Lamb, beef, and chicken are on the menu, and an early summer treat is strawberry pie made with local berries. By all means, allow time for admiring the view from the porch with its vista of sailboats on the river.

SCHOONER'S LLAND-
ING
410-226-0160.
318 Tilghman St.
Open: Bar and deck, daily;
    dining room, daily in
    season; Thurs.–Sun. off
    season.
Price: Moderate.
Cuisine: Seafood.
Serving: L, D.
Credit Cards: MC, V.
Reservations: Accepted for
    5 or more.
Handicap Access: Yes.

Casual waterside drinking and dining is the theme of this bar/restaurant on Town Creek in Oxford. Boat traffic provides the show from big windows or the outdoor deck with tables and its own separate bar. Food service is offered al fresco from indoors. The menu changes with the seasons to reflect the availability of fresh catches. Summer's emphasis is on crabs, clams, and finfish; in winter expect oysters to be prominently featured. All desserts are made on the premises and the Key lime pie is a luscious finale to seafood — although you might be torn between the pies and the homemade pound cake with fresh fruit and whipped cream.

For the convenience of cruising sailors, there's a little store on the parking lot. Beer and ice are also available for the boating crowd (or any other thirsty soul) and there's overnight dockage with showers for a fee. The kitchen is open until 10pm; last call at the bar is 1:30am.

TAPPO'S TRATTORIA
410-226-0134.
26342 Oxford Rd.
Open: Daily exc. Tues. &
 Weds.
Price: Moderate.
Cuisine: Italian.
Serving, L, D.
Credit: AE, MC, V.
Special Features: Secluded
 garden for outdoor
 drinks and dining.
Handicap Access: Yes.

Don't be put off by the gas pumps and the deli sign in front of Tappo's Trattoria. This is no truck stop, but a jewel of a restaurant in addition to its convenience services. And in good weather, there's a bonus: a handsome walled garden with brick patio, tables and umbrellas, flowers, and a pond with a fountain.

Indoors, the spacious dining room is separated from the bar where murals depict the Oxford boatyards and harbor. Artwork on the walls continues in the dining room, with trailing grapevines and climbing flowers ascending to the ceiling above the colors of the Italian flag: deep green in the wainscoting and striped curtains, Venetian red on the painted chairs with cane seats.

The house performs small miracles with veal prepared five different ways — con funghi, piccatina, alla Romano, marsala, and alla salvia. There's a passing swipe at pork, chicken, and lamb, and specials of the day list the fish menu. The house-made bread is a dense focaccia served with a little bowl of extra virgin olive oil for dipping. But, ah! The pastas! Ten styles and flavors make choices difficult with toppings of Alfredo, carbonara, cream sauce and prosciutto, salsicce, and on and on. Or choose from seven pizzas. On a summer evening, linger in the garden over a mélange of flavors in the antipasto and a glass of the house chianti under the stars.

Rock Hall

BAYWOLF
410-639-2000.
21270 Rock Hall Ave.
Open: Daily.
Price: Moderate to Expen-
 sive.
Cuisine: American, Ger-
 man.
Serving: L, D.
Credit Cards: AE, MC, V.
Reservations: Recom-
 mended in summer.

It's evident by the stained glass in the large dining room that this restaurant had a past life as a church. But it's more evident by the creative seasonal dishes and beautifully presented salads that the chefs in the kitchen are answering another noble calling, and doing so reverently.

Baywolf is the only restaurant in the region to specialize in authentic German dishes. Depending on the time of year — or the whim of the chef — the menu carries Weiner schnitzel, pork roulade, sauerbraten, or various wurst dishes. But there's room on the menu, too, for unexpected combinations: deviled crab and steak or Cajun swordfish, for example. For those who can't choose, Baywolf obliges with a sampler of pork, beef, and crab prepared different ways on different occasions.

And for dessert, Black Forest cake tops a changing list of German sweets prepared on the premises. Reservations are a good idea in summer, but more importantly, call ahead to find out just what the Baywolf's creative kitchen has in mind for you.

David Trozzo

Need we say more? Durding's Store in Rock Hall offers ageless treats.

DURDING'S STORE
410-778-7957.
5742 Main St.
Open: Daily until 9pm.
Price: Inexpensive.
Cuisine: Soda fountain.
Credit Cards: MC, V.
Handicap Access: Yes.

Step through the door of Durding's Store and step back in time. Durding's is a real, 1935 soda fountain. Clamber up on one of the red leather stools to the marble bar and watch as your frozen treat is deftly made the old-fashioned way. Shakes, malteds, floats, soda syrup pumped by hand and topped with fizzling water, hand-scooped ice cream — all under a pressed tin ceiling complete with lazily turning fans. The soda fountain is original, as are some of the creations on the menu: Durding's Delight, a slice of warm apple pie topped with cinnamon ice cream; and a Decadent Brownie Delight, a brownie that carries a delicious burden of ice cream, peanuts, and whipped cream. Many of the treats are crowned with a maraschino cherry.

True to its name, Durding's remains a store, carrying greeting cards, candy, and over-the-counter health products.

WATERMAN'S CRAB-HOUSE
410-639-2261.
Sharp St.
Open: Daily.
Price: Moderate.

Follow your nose to Waterman's, where the aroma of barbecuing baby back ribs wafts up Sharp Street from dockside. The restaurant gives diners a tremendous view of the Bay and the Bay Bridge, which is well over an hour away by land but only a few miles by water. The place is a local

Cuisine: American, Chesa-
  peake.
Serving: L, D.
Credit Cards: MC, V.
Special Features: Water
  view, waterside bar.

institution and offers everything one could look for in a traditional Chesapeake Bay crab house, right down to the rolls of brown paper at every table for cracking crabs.

Waterman's advertises hot crabs, cold beer, and free dockage. It's a great place to soak in some local color and enjoy crabs or a steak, fried chicken, steamed shrimp, raw oysters or clams, or one of a list of sandwiches. The crab cakes and crab soup are the stuff of local lore. But don't forget your sunglasses if you plan to eat dinner at one of the dockside picnic tables. The bar hosts live bands on summer weekends, and the restaurant has all-you-can-eat crab feasts on summer Tuesdays and Thursdays.

St. Michaels

THE CRAB CLAW
410-745-2900.
Navy Point.
Open: Daily, mid-
  Mar.–early Nov.
Price: Moderate to Expen-
  sive.
Cuisine: Seafood.
Serving: L, D.
Credit Cards: None.

Hordes of day-trippers on bus tours to the adjacent Chesapeake Bay Maritime Museum often make this popular restaurant crowded and noisy, but nobody seems to mind. The young staff is friendly and hustling, so pick a picnic table on the first-floor deck on the water (you might have to share with strangers), or in the upstairs room overlooking the harbor.

Steamed crabs in mounds are universal favorites here, with pitchers of beer to cool down the seasoning. No matter if opening crabs is a mystery; placemats are illustrated with drawings of the technique for those who are baffled. For the faint of heart, or aesthetes who can't stand to get their hands dirty, there are plenty of other choices, but it isn't called the Crab Claw for nothing. Delicate crab fluffs are like miniature crabcakes married to soufflés, the crab imperial is perfectly seasoned, and soft crabs in season have crispy legs, not the limp appendages that dangle from the aberration listed elsewhere as "soft-shell crabs sautéed in butter with lemon."

Shrimp, lobster, blackened fish, steamed mussels, and clams all tempt the seafood lover. The noise level is high, and so are the prices, but the location and the food are good.

**THE INN AT PERRY
  CABIN**
410-745-2200.
308 Watkins Lane.
Open: Daily.
Price: Very Expensive.
Cuisine: Continental.
Serving: L, D.
Credit Cards: AE, MC, V.

One doesn't "grab a bite to eat" at the Inn at Perry Cabin. One dines, and dines splendidly in the dining rooms or outdoors on the terrace of this elegant inn owned by Sir Bernard Ashley. It's gussied up in English grand country house style with Laura Ashley fabrics and wallpapers, its lawns slope down to Fogg Cove in St. Michaels harbor, and its brick terrace looks like a movie set

Reservations: Necessary.
Special Features: Prix fix
$57.50 for 5-course din-
ner. Prix fix lunch $25.
Handicap Access. Yes.

for *The Great Gatsby*. One would expect that the resident guests would be dressed to the nines to go
with the ambiance. Alas, many of them look as
tacky as thee and me.

The food and service, on the other hand, are as
outstanding as you'd expect from a place where
lunch or dinner, without a cocktail or sip of wine, costs such a bundle. The
menu changes daily, but at lunch we chose (from five appetizers) cold cucumber soup with shrimp and crab, and a duck spring roll with spiced pears and
plum chutney. We moved on to medallion of salmon and breast of chicken
with toasted pine nuts. Our desserts were a tartlet of rhubarb and strawberries
under a golden meringue, and dense carrot cake with lemon sorbet.

We loved the waitress's uniforms. Except for the skirt length, they were
right out of the Edwardian era: no-nonsense black shoes and stockings, white
collars and cuffs on a little black dress, and an apron starched to within an inch
of its life.

Add a cocktail before, a glass of wine with, and a tip, and you have a $100
lunch. It's more than a meal, it's total submersion in the Grand Style.

**TOWN DOCK
RESTAURANT**
410-745-5577.
125 Mulberry St.
Open: Daily.
Price: Expensive.
Cuisine: Creative regional
   seafood.
Serving: L, D.
Credit Cards: All major.

There's hardly a spot in St. Michaels better
designed for the hungry, foot-weary visitor to
pause and still bask in the beauty of the boat-clot-
ted harbor. The dining room and open-air deck
descend in tiers, so any table has a great view. Man
does not live by picturesque vistas alone, however,
and chef-owner Michael Rork brings his highly
praised talent from Baltimore's Harbor Court to
this lovely, lively small town. He took over the
business, formerly called Longfellow's, in June
1994.

Rork's vision for Town Dock is filtered through his firm belief that the
region has "the best produce and seafood in the world," and the menu reflects
it. The fish selections change every day, so ask about the specials. The soups
are legendary. In winter there's an oyster stew as voluptuous as sin; summer
favorites are New-England-style clam chowder, crab bisque, and a classic
bouillabaisse that's a meal in itself.

Service can be slow on a weekend lunch hour, so it's a good idea to ask for
an appetizer when you place a drink order. In hot weather, bypass the soup
and go straight to crab Monterey, great lumps of backfin baked in cheese and
fresh tomatoes served as a dip with crisp tortilla chips. One order serves two
or three people, so judge accordingly. Then sip and munch at leisure while the
sun sparkles on the water and swans petition anchored boats for handouts. It's
so pleasant you may never stroll another step in town.

At dinner time, the menu lists 20 entrées with all the usual suspects. Our choice is flounder, with or without a crab imperial topping, but there are plenty of other options for fans of beef, lamb, pork, chicken, and duck. Save room for the Black Russian cake.

208 TALBOT
410-745-3838.
208 North Talbot St.
Open: Tues.–Sun.; L
  Tues.–Fri. only.
Price: Expensive.
Cuisine: Innovative Ameri-
  can.
Serving: L, D, SB.
Credit Cards: DC, MC, V.
Reservations: Suggested.

Since its opening in 1990, this jewel of a restaurant has been quietly developing a cult following for food exquisitely prepared and beautifully served. The four dining rooms seat 60 in the atmosphere of a charming country inn setting, despite its location in a tourist mecca. There's curb parking and a back lot; look for the side entrance tucked into attractive landscaping.

The menu is selective rather than expansive, with six or seven choices each of appetizers and entrées, each a work of art. Rack of lamb is a permanent fixture, with seafood in several forms as staple offerings, depending on what's in season. Spring brings shad roe and soft crabs, followed by summer's bounty of other crab dishes and finfish. Autumn and winter usher in oysters. There's always a beef and a chicken entrée and the menu changes at the whim of the chef. Trust him and expect the unexpected, like sautéed sweet breads with asparagus, chestnuts, and Dijon mustard.

Appetizers are equally inventive; where else could you have a structure like the Napoleon of smoked salmon inside layers of crispy wontons in a puddle of pale green wasabi sauce embellished with a rim of hearts drawn with beet juice? It looks like a construction made by Pennsylvania cooks gone worldly. Or grilled quail with a glaze of basalmic vinegar and rum on a salad sparked with grapes, almonds, and bacon?

A modest but choice wine list has four reds and six whites by the glass.

It's no exaggeration to say that this may be *the* restaurant on the mid-Shore. Expensive, but not wildly so, and worth every penny.

Stevensville

CAFÉ SOPHIE
410-643-8811.
401 Love Point Rd.
Open: Weds.–Sun.
Price: Inexpensive to Mod-
  erate.
Cuisine: Provincial French.
Serving: L Weds.–Sun., D
  Fri.–Sat.
Credit cards: No.
Reservations: Yes.
Handicap Access: Yes.

Chef/singer/weaver Suzanne Peach (her daughter is Sophie) works amazing things singlehandedly with a very limited kitchen in this turn-of-the century ex-hardware store. The lunch menu, on a blackboard, usually includes a ramekin, a quiche, and a couple of excellent salads, while the prix fixe dinner varies according to what is available fresh — often duck. The wine list is short, French, moderately priced, and high quality. The style is provincial, not haute, cuisine, and the meals are elegantly simple. Make dinner reservations; this place is being discovered.

Tilghman

BAY HUNDRED RESTAURANT

410-886-2622.
Rte. 33 & Knapp's Narrows.
Open: Daily.
Price: Moderate to Expensive.
Cuisine: Seafood, ethnic.
Serving: L, D.
Credit Cards: All major.
Reservations: Recommended on weekends.
Handicap Access: Yes.

The glass-walled dining room overlooks the busiest drawbridge in Maryland, a yawning behemoth that opens every few minutes for workboats and pleasure craft taking the shortcut between the Choptank River and the Chesapeake Bay. The view and the food are superb. The lunch menu features "sandwiches from the sea" plus Cajun dishes and Zuni stew. Dinners also include the ethnic dishes, as well as entrées of crab, salmon, tuna, duck breast, and New York strip steak, the highest priced item at $18.95. The flounder is almost overwhelmed by a batter crust, so be forewarned if you prefer it sautéed in butter. Some of the spelling on the menu is quixotic, but don't be put off by it. The chef is excellent and the service is pleasant.

HARRISON'S CHESAPEAKE HOUSE

410-886-2121.
Rte. 33.
Open: Daily.
Price: Moderate.
Cuisine: Seafood, American.
Serving: B, L, D.
Credit Cards: MC, V.
Special Features: Outdoor dining and live music on weekends, kid's menu.
Handicap Access: Yes.

A generations-old, family-run operation, Harrison's never seems to change (except for a recent renovation to a dining room), offering that all-too-rare combination of reasonable prices, generous portions, and a kitchen that knows what it's doing. On the waterfront, next to Harrison's country inn and charter-fishing fleet, the unpretentious dining area exudes warmth. Paintings and prints of Eastern Shore maritime scenes adorn the rooms, alongside model skipjacks and mounted trophy fishes. The waitresses are pros — consistently helpful, never harried. Along with the standard Shore seafood — crab cakes, crab imperial, fried oysters — the menu includes variations such as sautéed lump crabmeat au gratin and crab-and-shrimp Norfolk sautéed in butter and wine. The specialty of the house is that classic Eastern Shore combination, fried chicken and crab cakes. French onion soup, covered with a blanket of melted cheese, makes for a hearty appetizer. But best of all are the crab balls. They are truly excellent: heavenly, mouthwatering orbs of flaky, all-backfin crabmeat chunks. The crust is perfect and golden brown, with just the right amount of seasoning. The same enthusiastic thumbs-up applies to the crab cakes. Rockfish stuffed with crab imperial, an occasionally offered special, is also four-star. With all the side dishes, presented home-style in serving bowls, it's enough to feed an army. If by some chance you're still hungry, there's a staggeringly long, varied dessert menu.

TILGHMAN ISLAND INN
410-886-2141.
21384 Coopertown Rd.
Open: Daily exc. Tues.
Price: Moderate to Expen-
sive.
Cuisine: Seafood, Continen-
tal.
Serving: L, D.
Credit Cards: All major.
Special Features: Live
piano music in the bar
Fri.–Sat. 6pm, Sun. 8pm,
weeknights 10pm.
Handicap Access: Yes.

Anyone who thinks the fishing village of Tilghman hasn't gone upscale should dine at Tilghman Island Inn, a surprise that starts at the gardens
at the entrance and continues to the outdoor deck
on the side facing the waters of Knapps Narrows.

Inside is a bar with seating for lunch and light
fare and a formal dining room with an art exhibit
that changes monthly.

Menus change weekly, but there's always the
house specialty appetizer, black-eyed-pea cakes
served with salsa. Good crabs, and, in season, soft-
shell crabs deep-fried in beer batter until they're
swollen with pride, a pouf of pure flavor. At dinner
there's the choice of more seafood, duck breast,
chicken supreme on a haystack of crispy noodles,
beef filets stuffed with shiitake mushrooms, crab with bourbon sauce, and
lamb chops with braised beans and artichokes. Homemade house desserts
include cheesecake and chocolate in beguiling forms. Highly recommended.

LOWER EASTERN SHORE

Berlin

THE GLOBE THEATRE
410-641-0784.
12 Broad St.
Open: Daily.
Price: Inexpensive.
Cuisine: Café.
Serving: L all day; closes at
6.
Credit Cards: D, MC, V.
Handicap Access: Yes, 1st
floor; no, restrooms.

The Globe is one of those rare places where
charm, art, coffee, and quiche converge to create an atmosphere both eclectic and welcoming.
With its earthy suburban appeal, the Globe isn't
the sort of spot one would expect to find on the
Lower Shore, but one that is nonetheless a favor-
able sight. Just around the corner from the turn-of-
the-century Atlantic Hotel, the Globe, once a
bustling cinema, sits quietly awaiting both the
locals and tourists who stroll the quaint little
streets of historic Berlin. But there's more to the
Globe than just quiche and latte. In addition to an
impressive art gallery upstairs, the Globe has a colorful selection of cookbooks,
gardening books, and books for regional interest. There are also wind chimes,
CDs and cassettes, spices, greeting cards, jams and jellies . . . it's a virtual New-
Age smorgasbord. After a good bit of browsing, tuck in to the Globe Café &
Deli's tasty lunch selections. Though the menu is decidedly vegetarian, many
of their excellent sandwiches are made with enough turkey, chicken, and
shrimp to please even the most carnivorous. So sit back, relax, maybe take in a
Globe concert, have an espresso, cappuccino, double cap, or latte because if
you're on your way to Ocean City, you'll need the caffeine to survive.

Cambridge

MCGUIGAN'S PUB AND RESTAURANT
410-228-7110.
411 Muse St.
Open: Daily.
Price: Moderate.
Cuisine: Pub food, gourmet dinners, local beers.
Serving: L, D; Sun. D only.
Credit Cards: AE, DC, MC, V.
Reservations: Recommended for upstairs dining room.
Special Features: Live music every other Friday.
Handicap Access: Difficult.

Grab a seat at the bar for a pint of the local brew or climb the stairs to the fine-dining room for a more intimate dinner setting. This cozy local in the heart of Cambridge draws everyone from grandparents to young adults to families. The pub is named for the owner's dog, but that's as gimmicky as it gets. Unlike many Irish- or Scottish-themed restaurants, this one forgoes quaint decor in favor of a nice dartboard, a jukebox, and an unforced, homey atmosphere. The pub's building was once a Victorian home, and guests in the main dining room may find themselves eating in what used to be a porch. It's a good spot to visit for any of four kinds of Wild Goose beer, brewed in a warehouse several blocks away. For a casual dinner, try one of McGuigan's pub pies or a cheese-stuffed burger. Dinner entrées are a little fancier and cost a bit more.

Crisfield

SIDE STREET SEAFOOD RESTAURANT
410-968-2442.
204 S. Tenth St.
Open: Daily in season, Oct. Sat. & Sun. only, closed winter.
Price: Moderate.
Cuisine: Seafood.
Serving: L, D.
Credit Cards: D, MC, V.
Reservations: Weekends.
Handicap Access: No.

London has its bridge, Sydney its opera house, New York its statue, and Crisfield its crab. And what better place in all the world to eat steamed crabs than the indisputable "Crab Capital of the World." This once-mighty fishing port, still home to a sturdy group of watermen, is also home to a number of restaurants, all of which boast the best crab "something" in town. A best bet is an exemplary place called Side Street; a formidable contender in the battle of the crabs. Perched high above the street and just a short stroll from the Tangier and Smith Island ferries, Side Street offers a towering second-story deck with both screened-in and open-air seating. It's a wonderful place to watch the evening sun duck behind the Bay, or just to glance down upon the maze of colorful tin roofs that dot this little fishing village. The tables, immense picnic benches, come set up for the most furious of crab feasts. Thick brown paper is clamped to the table tops and on them sits a tray full of tongs, mallets, margarine, paper towels, and other implements of necessity. The crabs are superb, as are many other items on their full menu. The staff is well versed in the art of crab-eating protocol and can be quite helpful if you've yet to wrangle a Maryland Blue. So go ahead, don't be shy. It's a wonderful place to have good fun, eat a great meal, and make a huge mess all at the same time.

Fruitland

CAFÉ PORTOFINO
410-749-8082.
213 N. Fruitland
  Blvd./Business Rte. 13.
Open: Weds.–Sat; Fri.–Sat.
  only, in summer (call to
  check).
Price: Moderate to
  Expensive.
Cuisine: Northern Italian.
Serving: D.
Credit Cards: MC, V.
Reservations: Recom-
  mended fall to spring.
Handicap Access: Yes.

Tucked between a launderette and a rib joint on Business Rte. 13, there's nothing to indicate to the passing motorist that there's anything special under the faded sign for Café Portofino. Even the inside is unprepossessing — a plethora of green plants, dim light, and only 16 tables in a square room. But the restaurant doesn't have to make points with decor, because it's what comes from the kitchen that counts. In a time when chain restaurants have helped make Italian food taste the same from Atlanta to Alaska, Café Portofino will bowl over your taste buds with meltingly tender beef dishes cooked in wine, pasta made a few steps away in the kitchen, and seafood in rich, flavorful sauces. Veal paradise, one of several veal dishes on the menu, delights with its combination of mild veal stuffed with crab imperial and topped with a lemon and wine sauce. Come hungry and leave your calorie counter in the car. This is real, rich food.

Hooper's Island

A Hooper's Island oysterman hoists the Bay's treasures toward market.

David Trozzo

**OLD SALTY'S
  RESTAURANT**
410-397-3752.
2560 Hoopersville Road,
  Fishing Creek.
Open: Mon., Weds.–Sun.
Price: Inexpensive to
  Moderate.

Sit on one side of Old Salty's Restaurant and look out on the Chesapeake Bay or, from the other, watch egrets in the marsh or watermen on lunch break headed up the sidewalk in rubber workboots. Location is everything for this eatery, which benefits from being the only sit-down spot to eat within 30 miles. People touring Blackwater

Cuisine: Seafood, American.
Serving: L, D.
Credit Cards: None. Checks accepted.
Reservations: Recommended on weekends.
Special Features: Gift shop with local crafts.
Handicap Access: Yes.

National Wildlife Refuge in search of deer or bald eagles, or just driving through the vast marshes of southern Dorchester County, regularly trek to Old Salty's because it's the ideal place to have a hearty meal and take in some of the local color. The hulking gray building used to be a schoolhouse; special functions are held in the old gym. Locals stop in at the lunch counter for take-out sandwiches. In two separate dining rooms sparsely decorated with nautical oils, feast in summer on fried soft crabs caught by the island's watermen, on oyster puffs in the winter, and sweet homemade yeast rolls in any season. Seafood and fish — most of it fried, though there are a couple of broiled selections — are Old Salty's specialties. Save room for dessert — there are several meringue pies with a dense, sweet filling topped off with inches of light meringue. Smoking and nonsmoking dining areas.

New Church, Virginia

THE GARDEN AND THE SEA INN
804-824-0672.
Rte 710, off Rte. 13.
Serving: D.
Open: Tues.–Sun 6–9, in season.
Price: Expensive to Very Expensive.
Cuisine: Chesapeake, Continental.
Serving: D.
Credit Cards: AE, D, MC, V.
Reservations: Required Tues. & Weds., strongly suggested Thurs.–Sun.

Just when you thought it was all fast food and fireworks, there looming on the horizon is a magnificent place; a virtual oasis rising from the vastness of the Lower Eastern Shore. Just a mile south of the Maryland-Virginia border and a block from Rte. 13, the Garden and the Sea Inn soars proudly above the smooth landscape. It is a sterling bed & breakfast (see Chapter Three, *Lodging*) which is a convenient stopover for the Chincoteague crowd, a midpoint for north-south travelers, and, for many, a destination in and of itself. Nearly 200 years old, the inn is a beautiful early Victorian showpiece which has been lovingly restored to what appears to be its original splendor. The grounds are equally impressive, and an adjacent converted farmhouse offers guests three large, well-appointed rooms and a lazy afternoon porch. The meals alone are worth a visit. Chef-owned and operated, its elegant entrées are prepared from local produce and fresh seafood from the farms and waters of the Eastern Shore: roast duck in a cranberry-apricot chutney, or pecan-crusted Allegheny mountain trout pan-fried with famed Chincoteague oysters. Desserts are impossibly delicious and their wine list is extensive. The place has an unmistakable romantic spirit much in the same fashion as some of the extraordinary inns from France's Provence region. But you and yours don't have to be starry-eyed with one another to appreciated the Garden and the Sea experience; the food is superb, prices are good, and so is the service. Delight in it while you can; France is a long drive.

Pocomoke City

BEAVER DAM
410-957-1621.
3 mi. S. of Pocomoke on
    Rte. 13.
Open: Daily until 2am.
Price: Inexpensive.
Cuisine: American.
Credit Cards: Cash only.

You can't get much more "Eastern Shore" than Pocomoke, and you can't get much more "Pocomoke" than Beaver Dam, a jewel in the Nile of honkytonk. Forty years ago you pulled up to this fillin' station on the outskirts of Pocomoke City, serviced your Chevy, went inside for a cold Schlitz and a counter lunch, rambled on, and then rambled home. That was pretty much the daily routine for quite a few locals until about eight years ago when Beaver Dam fell into disrepair and ceased. A few unsuccessful attempts at reopening yielded little for the various operators, until now. Proprietor Ronnie Lewis has resurrected this almost mythic watering hole complete with pool tables, dart boards, and a bar that nearly extends out the doors. The menu presently consists of only four microwaveable items, all of which are of the convenience store, reach-in cooler variety, although Mr. Lewis claims he is in the process of expanding his menu by building a kitchen. However, it is the place's complete lack of pretense and unabashed authenticity that eclipse any need to go there for food. What the places misses in inventory, it more than makes up for in local appeal. The prices are great, the beer's chilly, and happy hour lasts seven days a week. Trendy it ain't, so if you're looking for a Sam Adams and a veggie burger, motor on. Otherwise, if you want to stare Eastern Shore philosophy in the face, pull in and belly up while you still have the chance.

Princess Anne

**THE WASHINGTON
    HOTEL INN**
410-651-2526.
11782 Somerset Ave.
Open: Mon.–Sat.
Price: Inexpensive.
Cuisine: Eastern Shore,
    seafood, American.
Serving: B, L, D.
Credit Cards: C, MC, V.
Handicap Access: Yes.

You haven't tasted Eastern Shore cuisine until you've worked your way through a plateful of the Washington Hotel's spicy muskrat, one of many seasonal delicacies offered in the restaurant (the trick is to feel out the muskrat bones with your tongue so you won't swallow them). If muskrat on a cold winter day isn't to your liking, try the chicken and dumplings, another Shore favorite, or fried trout or flounder. Portions are big, side dishes (including local favorites turnip greens, cucumbers and onions, and macaroni cheese) are tasty, and the prices are low, making this a favorite hangout for everyone from judges to chicken farmers to senior citizens. Tune your ears to the local scuttlebutt in the dark, paneled front eating area, where those who do business in the county seat come to talk. You can also eat in the dining room, a comfortable room decorated with floral wallpaper, antique furniture, and china plates. There's also a small bar. And if you get too full of good food and drink to continue your journey, you can walk one door down and check into the Washington Hotel, a 12-

room accommodation dating all the way back to 1744 (see Chapter Three, *Lodging*).

Wattsville, Virginia

RAY'S SHANTY
804-824-3429.
Rte. 175.
Open: Daily in season; closed Dec. & Jan.; open Thurs.–Sun. only, rest of the year.
Price: Inexpensive to Moderate.
Cuisine: Seafood.
Serving: L, D.
Credit Cards: MC, V.
Handicap Access: Yes.

Of the zillion or so places along the Eastern Shore in which to park oneself in front of a plate of freshly steamed shrimp, Ray's Shanty is, quite frankly, among the best. Despite its windowless exterior and nondescript location, it has been a virtual gastronomic gold mine for the locals as well as for the throngs of tourists who pass by on their way to Chincoteague every summer. It hasn't been such a bad deal for owner Ray Twilford, either, who started out in 1986 with nothing more than a rundown shack and a few loyal customers. But he also happened to have a direct pipeline to some of the freshest, most sought-after shrimp on the East Coast — a resource which was, and still is, the lifeblood of his thriving business. The menu is quite standard with its omnipresent crab cakes, scallops, and fried fish platters. However, the combination of value, quality, and friendly service differentiates Ray's from the flock of comparable regional restaurants. Although now more than ever designed for summer volume, the interior is still homey and comfortable with a classic spread of waterman memorabilia scattered about the walls. There is even a small bar off to one side which has managed to retain some of the Shanty's original charm. From this vantage point you might even catch a glimpse of Ray, or one of his family, hauling, loading, peeling, or steaming the mountains of shrimp that roll through this restaurant on any given day. This shrimp is extraordinary, the hushpuppies divine, and the French fries exquisite — a high achiever in the world of the seafood shack.

Whitehaven

THE RED ROOST
410-546-5443.
2670 Clara Rd.
Open: Daily Apr.–Nov.
Price: Inexpensive to Moderate.
Cuisine: Seafood.
Serving: L, D.
Credit Cards: AE, D, MC, V.
Handicap Access: Yes.

Driving here is half the fun because you are absolutely in the middle of nowhere and the notion of a hugely popular restaurant nestled within the buggy back roads of Wicomico County is beyond reason. For 20 years this converted chicken house has been home to one of the true restaurant phenomenons in the history of the world. Yes, a weighty claim, but one that speaks more for its conceptual, not culinary, brilliance, the tour-de-force here being the ubiquitous "all-you-can-eat" menu, the most compelling of Americanisms. Though there exists with this menu a theoretical stream of never-ending food, the Red Roost pads the menu (and your stomach) with enough introductory munchies in the form of clam strips, corn on the cob, fried shrimp, hushpuppies, and even fried chicken, that by the time your meal comes you are already well into your food coma. Nonetheless, the Roost is an intriguing, almost cult-like place where patrons keep coming back to sing songs, beat their crab mallets down, devour mountains of fried food, and worry of nothing, save finding their way back home.

FOOD PURVEYORS

BREWERIES AND WINERIES

Ingleside Plantation and Winery (804-224-8687; 2 $^{1}/_{2}$ mi. S. of Oak Grove, on Rte. 638, Oak Grove, Virginia) Owned by the Flemer family since the 1890s, this 2500-acre plantation dates from 1832. It's been the site of a boys' school, a Civil War garrison for Union troops, a courthouse, and a dairy farm. In 1969, Carl Flemer planted the first grapevine. Today, Ingleside produces award-winning wines from a variety of vines, including American, grafted European, and French-American hybrids. Try their Virginia champagne, too. Free tours and wine tastings. Open Mon.–Sat. 10–5, Sun. noon–5.

Wild Goose Brewery (410-221-1122; 20 Washington St., Cambridge) Wild Goose Amber Beer, its label boasting both a flying goose and a blue crab, is finding its way out of the Chesapeake and onto shelves throughout the mid-Atlantic region. Brewed in Cambridge, along with five other Goose microbrews, these beers owe their start to founder Alan Pugsley, an expatriate Englishman who is now brewmaster. Alan Lutz, who hails from Milwaukee itself, has moved in as a partner. Among their brews: Samuel Middleton's Pale Ale (house brew at Middleton Tavern in Annapolis), Oliver's Ale (ditto for Baltimore's popular Wharf Rat pub), Pride of Maryland, and Blue Dog, issuing forth from this brewery capable of putting out 20,000 barrels a year — and that includes their summer and winter brews. They call the winter ale Snow Goose. No on-premises sales. Open daily; tours Mon.–Sat. 10–3.

CITY MARKETS

Market House (Market Space, Annapolis City Dock, Annapolis) One of the more venerable phoenixes in Annapolis, the Market House at Market Space is heir to a long line of city markets that started back in the 18th century when shops and markets were first set up near the State House. A market has stood near City Dock since 1788. This particular city-owned market was reopened in 1971 following a two-year renovation. Inside are nine separate shops, each selling varied wares. The oldest is Mann's Sandwiches, which moved here from the start after the original owner sold sandwiches in town on consignment for 22 years. Kaufman's Fancy Fruits and Vegetables arrived a year later; we recommend their salad bar. And we'd also note that the fish market has the city's only belly-up-to-the-bar raw bar outside a restaurant. All nice places. **Annapolis Fish Market**, 410-269-0490; **The Big Cheese**, 410-263-6915; **Chutney's Gourmet**, 410-280-1974; **International Delicatessen**, 410-280-2504; **City Dock Bakery**, 410-269-6361; **I Can't Believe It's Yogurt**, 410-267-0363; **Kaufman's Fancy Fruits and Vegetables**, 410-269-0941; **Machoian Poultry**, 410-263-5979; **Mann's Sandwiches**, 410-263-0644. Open daily. Vendors open at 7 or 9am; some close early on Tues.

COFFEEHOUSES AND SHOPS

Some good coffee shops are also listed in the restaurant reviews above; check out The Moon in Annapolis and the Globe Theatre in Berlin. Or have a latte at one of the following:

City Dock Café (410-269-0969; Market Space, Annapolis) Bright, clean, and always packed. Sit down and read the newspaper, or pick up an espresso to go. Flavored coffees, too. Mon.–Thurs. 7am–10pm, Fri. & Sat. 7am–12am, Sun. 7am–10 pm.

Java by the Bay (410-939-0227; 118 N. Washington St., Havre de Grace) Nice little café-style coffeehouse that also sells teas and specialty foods, right next to a few nice shops. Open daily; closes by 6pm except Fri.; open till 7pm.

The Pony Espresso (410-280-6160; 33 $^1/_2$ West St. Annapolis) Catchy name for the place that keeps West Street workers wired. Fruit and lemon juices, and varietals such as espresso Americano — hearty coffee shot with steamy, and calorie-free, water. Muffins, quiches, and other on-the-run eats. Mon.–Fri. 7–5, Sat. 8–4; closed Sun.

Starbucks Coffee Co. (410-573-0076; 2500 Solomons Island Rd./Annapolis Harbour Center, Annapolis) The famed Seattle firm that started the coffee craze operates from the bustling shopping mall. Terrific range of high-voltage or decaf coffees for sale. Open daily, Fri. & Sat. to 11.

GOURMET SHOPS

Blue Crab Bay Co. (804-787-3602; 108 Market St/PO Box 180; Onancock, Virginia) A small storefront for growing mail-order retail firm that ships clam sauces for pasta, "Stingray" Bloody Mary mix, dried herb blends, and more, in packages hand-labeled on the premises. Fortnam & Mason recently placed an order. Gift baskets, some other Virginia products. Open Mon.–Fri. 9–5, Sat. 10–4.

The Bread Place Bakery (410-268-6677; 1410 Forest Dr., Clock Tower Plaza, Annapolis) There are those who will forever mourn the passing a few years back of the Bread Place's funky little shop, but back then, you couldn't get curried chicken salad with grapes from the deli case. This great bakery has expanded to include fancy cheeses, deli, more baked goods, and the Café du Vin, a stylish eatery offering a 40-wine tasting. Beer and wine on-premises only — and it's still open early for those fancy cups of commuting coffee. Open daily.

Chesapeake Gourmet (410-827-8686; 189 Chesapeake Village Road, Queenstown) At one end of the big outlet store complex near the junction of U.S. 50 and U.S. 301, this well-supplied shop has an extensive collection of coffees, teas (including leaf teas for those who dislike the omnipresent bags), wines, and microbrewery beers. There's kitchen gear, and the good deli makes for a pleasant lunch stop. Open Mon.–Sat. 10–8, Sun. 11–7.

Giolitti Delicatessen (410-266-8600; 2068 Somerville Rd., Annapolis) Very fine Italian bakery and gourmet shop brought joy to local hearts when it opened at the edge of town in Parole, offering sandwiches and focaccia, lots of wines, tiramisu. Small café, catering. Open Mon.–Fri., 10–8, Sat. 9–6, Sun. noon–5.

Pennsylvania Dutch Farmers' Market (410-573-0770; 2472 Solomons Island Rd./Annapolis Harbour Center, Annapolis) Operating weekends in its huge space. Stalls filled with *everything*: subs, salads, doughnuts, fresh produce, funnel cakes. Quilt shop next door, restaurant. Open Thurs.–Sat.

The Railway Market (410-822-4852; 108 Marlboro Rd, Easton) Where healthy gourmets on the Shore shop. Originally located in Easton's old-time railway depot, the store moved several years back and is bigger than ever. Cinnamon-tinged string cheese, powerful sandwiches, carry-out, café. And, get this: they stopped selling beer and started selling books — holistically feeding body *and* mind. Open Mon.–Fri. 9–7, Sat. 9–6, Sun. 10–6.

White Stone Wine and Cheese Co. (804-435-2000; Rte. 3, White Stone, Virginia) Smart market in upscale Northern Neck town stocks imported cheeses, tasty good meats, imported wines, fresh breads and cookies. Open Mon.–Sat. 10–5.

HEALTH FOOD

Country Sunshine Market (410-268-6996, fax 410-268-4060; 115 Annapolis St., Annapolis) Bright veggie-oriented grocery charges a wee tad on the pricey side, but their take-out sandwiches and soups (try the chilled cucumber with dill on a hot day) are worth it. Friendly staff. Parking, too. Mon.–Sat. 10–7.

Fresh Fields Market (410-573-1800; 2504 Solomons Island Rd./Annapolis Harbour Center, Annapolis) Grocery-style whole foods market where everybody in town goes for exotic melons, fruit juice sodas, fresh flowers, breads, seafood, and more. Great place, where you can even buy grilled veggie burgers out front on warm days.

Sun and Earth Natural Foods (410-266-6862; 1933 West St., Annapolis) Funky old beloved whole foods market moves to new location up the street, taking with it hydroponically grown tomatoes and bargain-priced Green Goddess sandwiches. Open Mon.–Sat. 9:30–6:30, Sun. noon–4.

ICE CREAM

Emack and Bolios (410-626-1046; 71 Maryland Ave., Annapolis) We were slumming on Cape Cod when this sensational ice cream shop opened there several years back, and we couldn't believe our eyes when we found it ensconced in our new home, right on Maryland Avenue. Some of the best ice cream anywhere. Open Sun.–Thurs. 8–10, Fri.–Sat. 8–11.

Storm Brothers Ice Cream Factory (410-263-3376; 130 Dock St., Annapolis) The shop of choice for ice cream devotees who find themselves around City Dock, and they've got the line out the door to prove it. In all, 42 ice cream flavors, 5 sherbets, 3 yogurts. Open year-round.

PRODUCE MARKETS

Summer means stands full of beautiful Chesapeake produce almost everywhere. Visit a farmer selling from the back of his pickup, or a well-oiled business operating beneath a canopy. Some move from year to year, so it's difficult to tell you exactly where to go. But keep your eyes peeled; you won't have to travel far down most country roads to find fresh corn (even Silver Queen), 'lopes, peaches, squash, and more. Here are a couple of our favorites:

Anne Arundel County Farmers' Market, Inc. (410-280-0751; Harry S. Truman Pkwy., off Riva Rd., Annapolis) Upwards of 50 local farmers and vendors spread their wares, from county-grown produce to canned goods, at the former county-run farmers' market, now operated by the farmers' cooperative. Open mid-Apr.–mid-Dec., Tues. & Thurs.–Sat. 7am–2pm.

Lowery's Produce (410-643-4557; 1912 Main St., Chester. Exit 39-B from U.S. 50, then left on Md. 18/Main St., just past shopping center) The family farm across the road is the source for much of the fresh produce here, supplemented by others in the region. Stop in May for strawberries and August for Silver Queen corn. Closed in winter.

The Bay's famed bounty extends to her shore, which means shoppers pick up the best in local produce at stands like Lowery's.

David Trozzo

SEAFOOD AND FISH MARKETS

Annapolis Seafood Market (410-269-5380; Forest Dr. & Tyler Ave., Annapolis) The local kingpin seafood dealer, where the very efficient staff cuts up your tuna steak, steams your crabs, or grills your fish sandwich while you wait. Fresh corn in the summer, and all kinds of good seafood spices and accoutrements for sale. Parking lot can get chaotic on summer (read *crab*) weekends. Open daily until 8pm, sometimes later.

Cap'n Tom's Seafood (804-462-5507; Rte. 2, Box 539, Lancaster, Virginia) Some of the fanciest restaurants from Richmond, D.C., and beyond have discovered Cap'n Tom's, and now you can, too. If you're in the area, drop by and pick up a pound tub of some of the best fat lump crab anywhere. Picked on premises, there's hardly a shell in sight. It's .3 miles before the road to the community of Bertrand dead-ends.

Captain's Ketch Seafood Market and Carry-Out (410-820-7177; 316 Glebe Rd., Easton) Picked crabmeat, lobster, fish, catfish, smoked bluefish, and orange roughy are at this thriving place, along with a good take-out business.

Chesapeake Landing Seafood Market and Restaurant (410-745-9600; Rte. 33, 2 ½ mi. W. of St. Michaels, McDaniel) People drive all the way from Easton to find the Chesapeake Landing Seafood Market and Restaurant, which has its own picking plant, softshell crab shedding tanks, and oysters, crabs, and all the other Bay natives. Run by the Spurry family, long-time wholesale crab dealers who opened this place in the fall of 1990. Good deals, too.

Cockrell's Creek Seafood (804-453-6326; Fleeton Rd., Reedville, Virginia) Crab cakes to go, scallops, shrimp, and more here at the edge of Virginia where the whole Northern Neck falls into the Bay. Open daily; closed Sun. off-season.

Chincoteague shrimp boats, dockside.

Dan Wolff

E.J. Conrad and Sons Deli (804-462-7400; Mollusk, Virginia) Downstairs from Conrad's (see review in *Restaurants*, above), buy great deli sandwiches and the fresh seafood served weekends upstairs. Open Mon.–Sat. 7–3.

J&W Seafood (804-776-6400; Rte. 33 E./Box 549, Deltaville, Virginia) Stop here for fresh seafood in this little outpost town, where everybody fishes or sails. Peeler tanks in back.

Kool Ice and Seafood Co. (410-228-2300; 110 Washington St., Cambridge) Crabs caught by Dorchester watermen find their way here. Fine selection of oysters, clams, lobster, and crabs, both soft- and hardshell. The ice selection is varied, too, and includes big party-sized blocks.

McNasby's Seafood (410-280-1823;723 2nd St., Eastport) McNasby's is back under new management, taking over from the Maryland Watermen's Cooperative that operated from the waterside site for several years. Watch the boats unload the catch. Open Tues.–Sun. 11–8.

David W. Wehrs Seafood (410-643-5778; P.O. Box 425, Chester. Exit 39-B (Dominion Road) from U.S. 50; 2 miles to right at T onto Little Creek Rd., then go to end) Wehrs is the place on Kent Island to get fresh crabmeat, live or steamed crabs, and clams right at the boats. A high deck over the water offers dining out with a view, in the best Bay tradition. Great crab cakes and steamed crabs — this is the real thing.

Winter Harbor Seafood (804-224-7779; Rte. 3, Oak Grove, Virginia) Stop in for your crabs, locally caught fish, and while you're at it, pick up fishing or hunting licenses, too. Open daily.

CHAPTER SIX

Water, Water Everywhere
RECREATION

The Chesapeake is a huge playground, where those who are so inclined can sail out onto her waters, drop fishing or crabbing lines deep, or sit on the shore and admire the view. Trails wander through the surrounding woods and shoreline, drawing hunters in season and bird watchers and hikers year-round.

David Trozzo

Spinnakers up on a Bay sail race.

Boating enthusiasts will be duly impressed not only by the wide variety of watery worlds available for exploring, but also by the tremendous recreational industry that has grown up around the pursuit. No one should have any problem figuring out how to get on the Bay. Most folks take rod and reel onboard, and enjoy some of the best fishing anywhere. For those interested in the famed Maryland blue crab, fishing and hardware stores around the area can show you how to drop a line or net in the Bay.

This is also the kind of place that encourages meandering and exploration. Be sure to set aside time to explore state and federal parks. There are woodlands and marshes and all their diversity of creatures who are drawn to water's edge just like the rest of us.

This chapter covers everything from Baseball to Zoos, arranged alphabetically by subject, then geographically by region and alphabetically by town, as in the rest of the book. Because so many partake of so much inside parks and wildlife refuges, we also offer a quick-glance reference to some of the best (see the "Parks and Wildlife Areas" section later on in this chapter).

Besides the information provided here, more details, maps, and advice are available through the Maryland Dept. of Natural Resources, 1-800-688-FINS (Tawes State Office Bldg., Annapolis MD 21401). In Virginia, contact the Dept. of Conservation and Recreation, 203 Governor St., Suite 302, Richmond VA

23219; 804-786-1712. Sportspersons should contact the Dept. of Game and Inland Fisheries, 4010 W. Broad St., PO Box 11104, Richmond VA 23230; 804-367-1000.

BASEBALL

The Bowie Baysox are recently arrived on the scene, offering the pleasures of the national pastime to those who don't want to fight traffic to visit Baltimore's Oriole Park at Camden Yards. (Although there is much to recommend the vaunted ballpark — for more information, see Chapter Nine, *Baltimore and Nearby Attractions*.) The Baysox play at the Prince George's Stadium, south of the intersection of Rtes. 50 and 301; 301-805-6000, tickets 301-805-2233.

BICYCLING

Bicycling is one good way to see the Chincoteague Island salt marshes.

Ben Barnhart

Low-lying coastal plains meet rolling farmland along the Bay and tributaries, where wide shoulders stretch alongside many main roads. The most famous local route sends cyclists out across the Eastern Shore road from St. Michaels to Oxford, across the Tred Avon River on the Oxford-Bellevue Ferry, and back. (By the way, all Bay-area ferries allow bicycles — some for a fee.) Cyclists should remember that many roads are heavily traveled by motorists, but nearby, designated bike paths are safe and enjoyable for casual cyclists. You can't cross the William Preston Lane Jr. Memorial Bridge (aka the Bay

Bridge) and a few other major bridges in the region, but you can stop in at the administrative offices based at each bridge to request a ride. Maryland's Department of Transportation offers a **Bicycle Information Hotline**, 1-800-252-8776. Or, write the **Bicycle and Pedestrian Coordinator's Office**, 707 N. Calvert St., Baltimore MD 21203. In Virginia, call 804-786-2964. Bike shops that serve as local cycling centrals are also listed here.

ANNAPOLIS/WESTERN SHORE

A *nnapolis* offers some good in-town riding, but remember that streets are narrow, weekend motorists plentiful, and helmets required on Naval Academy grounds. (Helmets are required by Maryland state law on all roads for cyclists under age 16.) Try these routes:

From downtown, take King George St.; pass the **Naval Academy**, right, and **St. John's College**, left. Cross College Creek, bear right on Md. 450 N. across the U.S. Naval Academy Bridge, aka the "new" or "high" bridge. If you can, stop at the pier fashioned from the "old" or "low" bridge that was just replaced, and drink in a terrific view of the Severn, a nationally designated Scenic River. Downriver, the academy grounds stretch along the banks to Spa Creek, the town's central harbor. Upriver, mansions and the former Catholic retreat house, Manresa, nest on the high banks of the Severn. When you get to the far side of the bridge, go straight to the 13.3-mile-long **Baltimore-Annapolis Trail** on your left, built for cyclists along the old railroad bed. The trail goes from Annapolis to Glen Burnie, and you'll share it with bladers and walkers, too. Some complain that the trail has become overcrowded, but judge for yourself. Information or maps: 410-222-6244.

Quiet Waters Park is a favorite destination for family cyclists and in-line skaters. Paved trails wind through woods and open parkland, and end at an overlook on the banks of the South River. Seasonal bike rentals start in April. South of town on Hillsmere Dr.; call 410-267-5976 for rentals; 410-222-1777 for park management. Closed Tues.

A couple of major popular Maryland-based organized rides and centuries — 100-mile trips — often route through the Bay region. Check **Cycle Across Maryland** (410-653-8288) and the series sponsored by the **Multiple Sclerosis Society** (1-800-FIGHTMS). You'll often find the latest about these and other events at this local cycling shop:

Bike Doctor (150 Jennifer Rd.; 410-266-7383) Also in Arnold, just north of the city on Md. Rte. 2; 410-544-3532. Good place to find out what's happening on the cycle front. Ask about rentals.

Down toward *Solomons*, the main highway, Rte. 2/4, has a wide shoulder. Off the beaten path are rolling or flat coastal farm roads that take riders to the Chesapeake Bay to the east, or Patuxent River to the west. Cross the Thomas

Johnson Bridge to reach rural St. Mary's County. This area is one of the great uncrowded corners of Chesapeake. Get off Rte. 4 at Md. 5, Indian Bridge Rd., a lightly traveled highway with a wide shoulder. It's a 14-mile ride south to waterside St. Mary's College and historic St. Marys City. A little more than 12 miles farther south on Rte. 5, you'll reach Point Lookout State Park. A nice day trip.

Sea Dive & Cycle (Rte. 2/4, S&W Shopping Center; 410-326-4386) The local cycling shop.

UPPER EASTERN SHORE

The Shore's user-friendly topography moves from pleasantly rolling hills at its upper extreme to sprawling flatland further south, giving cyclists a mix of riding conditions through great coastal scenery. In *Kent County*, the Chamber of Commerce offers a booklet detailing bike-tour options. Distance and difficulty levels range from the 11-mile "Pomona Warm-Up" to 81-mile "Pump House Primer." The Baltimore Bicycling Club developed the routes. For a copy of *The Kent County Bicycle Tour*, contact the Kent County Chamber of Commerce, 118 N. Cross St., Chestertown MD 21620; 410-778-0416. In *Talbot County*, the 31-mile Easton-to-St. Michaels and 10-mile Easton-to-Oxford runs are popular bicycling jaunts. Many cyclists make a point of riding the Oxford-Bellevue Ferry (see "Ferries" in Chapter Two, *Transportation*). For a map of the best cycling routes, contact the Talbot County Chamber of Commerce, 805 Goldsborough St., Easton MD 21601; 410-822-4606. For other ideas, check:

Bikework (208 S. Cross St., Chestertown; 410-778-6940)
Easton Cycle & Sport (723 Goldsboro St., Easton; 410-822-7433)
Oxford Mews Bike Boutique (105 S. Morris St., Oxford; 410-820-8222)
St. Michaels Town Dock Marina (305 Mulberry St., St. Michaels; 410-745-2400; 1-800-678-8980)

LOWER EASTERN SHORE

Dorchester County offers **Blackwater National Wildlife Refuge**, a favored cyclists' destination. For a map of the region's recommended cycling trails, write the Dorchester County Chamber of Commerce, 203 Sunburst Hwy., Cambridge MD 21613; 410-228-3575. In *Worcester County*, relatively light traffic makes for some good riding on the main roads. (Beware the overcast day, however. Heavy traffic often heads inland from the Atlantic beaches.) A good ride starts in *Berlin*, a historic town with some interesting shops and a couple of worthy cafés, then heads down Evans Rd. Wander off to the west along Bethards Rd. to Patey Woods Rd., then pedal down Basket Switch Rd. to Taylor Rd. This route is about 19 miles, and brings you to a good choice of destinations: go left and head to Chincoteague Bay, or travel another 4 miles west to little **_Snow Hill_**, a pretty, historic town that's undergone recent renovation. Local shops:

The Bikesmith (1053 N. Salisbury Blvd., Salisbury; 410-749-2453)
Salisbury Schwinn Cyclery & Fitness Center (1404 S. Salisbury Blvd.,
  Salisbury; 410-546-4747)

BILLIARDS

The upscale pool hall trend has made a spotty appearance in the area. One note: here's one PG-rated activity for unchaperoned teens, which means the rooms can get crowded on weekends.

ANNAPOLIS/WESTERN SHORE

Bill and Billie's Q Club (1244 Ritchie Hwy./Rte. 2; 410-544-8185) Just north of Annapolis. The place is huge and open 24 hrs. No alcohol.

UPPER EASTERN SHORE

Chestertown Pool & Games (932 Washington Ave., Chestertown;
  410-778-9015)
Easton Billiards (Easton Plaza, Easton; 410-822-5794)

BIRD WATCHING

Avian enthusiasts will find no shortage of hotspots to visit in the Chesapeake, whether you tote a worn and crumpled "life list," or you've just learned to distinguish a robin from an osprey. Among the treats: an ever-growing population of bald eagles.

But there are always surprises. When a whiskered tern appeared on the Eastern Shore, folks came from all over the world to see. Not long ago, an Australian swan paddled up Kirwan Creek on Kent Island just to say "G'day mate." Also spotted on the Shore: an Asian mandarin duck. Purists say these exotics probably escaped from aviaries, but it's still fun to see them alongside the profusion of local birds.

Wintering birds come from the north, and include species ranging from common loons to charming black-and-white bufflehead ducks. Blue herons

Binoculars up at Kent Island's Horsehead Wetlands Center, a popular bird watcher's destination.

David Trozzo

can be claimed as Chesapeake mascots, and the gawky glossy ibis also lives here. Train your binoculars on the Bay's many channel markers, and you'll quite likely discover an osprey nest, constructed with kindling-sized sticks.

The usual coterie of common shorebirds pop up, including various species of sandpipers scuttling near the water. If you're in a wooded area, maybe you'll get lucky and see a barred owl.

Blackwater Wildlife Refuge in Maryland's Dorchester County carries the Chesapeake's blue-ribbon birding reputation, especially if you want to see eagles. Over by the ocean is Assateague Island, home of **Assateague Island National Seashore**. The location draws abundant shorebirds and waterfowl, including nesting species like black skimmers. The island straddles the state border, becoming **Chincoteague National Wildlife Refuge** in Virginia. The "Virginia end" of the island generally is considered to be the superior birding spot. Piping plovers scratch their near-invisible nests in the sand, and man-made lagoons offer a natural stop-off on the Mid-Atlantic Flyway for skimmers and coots. At the very tip of the Shore peninsula is the 651-acre **Eastern Shore of Virginia National Wildlife Refuge**, where you may see endangered peregrine falcons and bald eagles. At the intersection of Bay and ocean, it's a terrific fall migration staging spot for many avian species.

For information about these sites, we refer you to "Parks and Wildlife Areas" in this chapter. Any of the parks listed should offer excellent birding opportunities.

Got your binoculars? You might also want to pick up these publications:

Finding Birds in the National Capital Area: Just about the best field guide to birding around the Bay. Smithsonian Institution Press. Herndon, Virginia. $14.95.

Birds and Marshes of the Chesapeake Bay Country: With its black-and-white photos, it's a better home reference than a field guide. Tidewater Publishers. Centreville, Maryland. $8.95.

Your final stop before heading out may include the local bird store, where folks can always let you in on recent spottings. There are **Wild Bird Centers** just north of Annapolis in Severna Park at 5 Riggs Ave., or further south in Calvert County, at the Dunkirk Country Plaza; 410-257-4435.

ANNAPOLIS/WESTERN SHORE

For neophyte birders, especially families with children, we suggest a stop at **Merkle Wildlife Sanctuary**. It's a few miles west of the area covered by this book, in *Upper Marlboro*, Maryland, but well worth a detour. The 1,600-acre sanctuary on the Patuxent River offers limited access to the river in deference to the fantastic number of Canada geese who rule their grassy winter roosts here — up to 5,000 some years. In warm weather, there's a humming-bird garden.

The visitor center is set up for learning. Downstairs, a glass wall looks out to two ponds and the fields; a counter runs alongside. A couple of telescopes are set up for viewing, and photo albums filled with pictures and descriptions of birds are available for identification. Specimens of birds native to the area, such as cedar waxwings, Eastern bluebirds, or the Eastern screech owl, are behind glass. But best of all for the kids is the Nature Discovery Room, where they can color a picture of a bluebird to the soothing sounds of water filling two aquaria — which contain neat natives like diamondback turtles. After your "discovery," hike trails of a half to three miles. Ask directions to the blue heron rookery, and be sure to stay on the trail. 11704 Fenno Road, Upper Marlboro MD 20772; 410-888-1410.

Like Assateague Island, **Jug Bay** is a single ecosystem with a few bureaucratic boundaries tossed in. The former colonial deepwater harbor offers the range of marsh species. On the Anne Arundel County side, in *Lothian*, the **Jug Bay Wetlands Sanctuary** offers trails, including a nice one overlooking the water. 1361 Wrighton Rd.; 410-741-9330. Across the river in Prince George's County, and also in *Upper Marlboro*, **Jug Bay Natural Area** offers 2,000 acres. There's also a nice observation platform near the parking lot. It's part of the Patuxent River Park. 16000 Croom Airport Rd.; 301-627-6074.

A quarter-mile boardwalk runs through the spookily beautiful, 100-acre sanctuary **Battle Creek Cypress Swamp** in *Prince Frederick*. Go in the offseason, where you may well find yourself alone to look for birds. The excellent nature center offers programs. Grays Road, off Rte. 506 in Calvert County; 410-535-5327.

Jefferson Patterson Park in *St. Leonard* has easy trails through fields and along rivers, and a farm museum, too. A good place to take the kids; about 500 acres. 410-586-8500.

NORTHERN NECK/MIDDLE PENINSULA

Belle Isle State Park, right on the Rappahannock River, is under development — a good sign for those seeking undisturbed possibilities. Call for hours: 804-462-5030; Rte. 3 to Rte. 354; Rte. 683 near Litwalton to the park.

UPPER EASTERN SHORE

On *Kent Island*, **Terrapin Park** includes the Terrapin Beach Nature Shore, which offers a new nature trail with excellent bird watching for birds of prey, migratory birds, and waterfowl. There's a pond with blinds, and beach access. Take the first exit east of the Bay Bridge, go north on Md. 18 and turn left into the industrial park. Continue until you reach the natural area. 410-643-8170.

Millington Wildlife Management Area in upper *Queen Anne's County* has lots of nature trails and ponds. Operated by the Md. Dept. of Natural Resources; 410-928-3650.

To reach *Wye Island* take Carmichael Road west from U.S. 50 near Wye Mills and cross the little wooden bridge to the island. The Eastern Shore Nature Conservancy occasionally sponsors bird walks here, like their sunset "Owl Prowl" on the spring equinox; 410-827-7577. It's operated by the Wildfowl Trust of North America, which also brings you another good spot — especially for beginners — with a useful nature center: **Horsehead Wetlands Center** in *Grasonville*; off Rte. 18 E. of Kent Narrows; 800-CANVASBACK.

In *Rock Hall*, the **Eastern Neck Wildlife Refuge** is a favorite spot in the Upper Bay, nestled at the end of the peninsula where the Chester River meets the Bay. Past Rock Hall; 410-639-7056.

LOWER EASTERN SHORE

In *Dorchester County*, the **Blackwater National Wildlife Refuge** hosts all manner of species on its almost 21,000 acres of lowland and forest; 2145 Key Wallace Dr., Cambridge; 410-228-2677.

The **Fishing Bay Wildlife Management Area** is 14 miles south of Cambridge, next to the better known Blackwater refuge; 410-376-3236.

Deal Island and the vast *Somerset County* marshes nearby are wild space. Go to Princess Anne, then take Md. 363 through Monie and Chance to Deal Island. The **Chesapeake Bay Natural Estuarine Research Reserve** and the **Deal Island Wildlife Management Area** are here. Take the nifty little Whitehaven Ferry across the Wicomico River to the **Ellis Bay Management Area**.

In Virginia's *Accomack County* is the **Saxis Waterfowl Management Area**, just south of the state line. Turn west off U.S. 13 at Temperanceville.

In *Northampton County*, Virginia, **Kiptopeke State Park** is three miles from the Bay Bridge Tunnel on the Eastern Shore. Prime flyway viewing; Eastern Shore Birding Festival each fall. U.S. Rte. 13; west on Rte. 704 to the park.

BOARDSAILING/WINDSURFING

You'd expect the Bay's vast shoreline to breed lots of boardsailing, and that's true, with a caveat: public access to the water is famously limited. Many folks make friends in the windsurfing community who, in turn, then lead them to sailing spots. **Sandy Point State Park** (see "Parks and Wildlife Areas") on the Bay near Annapolis is a mecca. Windsurfing Unlimited in Annapolis (410-573-9463) offers public windsurfing; call for info.

BOATING

Sailors say you can spend a lifetime exploring the Chesapeake coastline and never see it all. The nation's largest estuary stretches 200 miles and is fed by some 150 rivers. The surface of the Bay spans nearly 2,500 square miles, and its tributaries add as much again. Cross the Bay Bridge on a breezy, clear day between April and November, and you'll see schools of sails heading both north and south — as well as the white wakes of power boats.

In addition to the sheer volume of water and coastline available to explorers, the Bay offers a soft bottom more forgiving than that along the Atlantic coast. Sailors are out year-round, the most hardy joining the January frostbite races. High summer brings flat calm, but the water is still filled with boaters seeking refuge from the humidity onshore. That leaves some of the year's best sailing to April, May, September, and October, when predictable breezes blow.

Annapolis calls itself America's Sailing Capital, a claim up for some dispute. Still, there's no doubting the huge number of pleasure boats per capita in this gateway town to the Bay. Deck shoes are *de rigueur*, masts fill Spa Creek in the middle of town, and everybody can talk a little boat talk. Wednesday nights in summer, the business suits do a mad dash from their Washington or Baltimore offices to make the 6 o'clock starting gun for the Annapolis Yacht Club races on Spa Creek. These are about the only sailboat races in Annapolis easily watched from land. Stake out a spot at the Eastport Bridge, or the Naval Academy seawall, and cheer the spinnakers pounding to the finish, usually by 7:30. For a close-up view, consider Chesapeake Marine Tours' regularly scheduled evening cruise aboard *Miss Anne*, which sails right past the races (see "Cruises and Excursion Boats" below).

Elsewhere, the snaking Bay coastline offers endless opportunity for "gunkholing," a pastime that might be defined as the leisurely sport of moseying around a body of water. On Maryland's Eastern Shore, Talbot County lays claim to more than 600 miles of shoreline — said to be the most of any county

Catch the finish line of the Wednesday night sailboat races in Annapolis at the Eastport Bridge.

David Trozzo

in the continental U.S. Around the Chesapeake, boating is as natural to the natives as knowing how to spice steamed crabs.

Sailors rave about the Bay but it is also ideal for power boating, especially during the summer calms. While the coves and creeks were once the domain of sailing vessels, more cruising power boats are showing up at anchor there as their owners discover how fine the boating life is. With leisure time short and working hours long, many people find that the only practical way they can enjoy the water is with a motorboat; they can zip across to St. Michaels or Kent Narrows for dinner and be certain that they will get home on schedule.

BOATING OPTIONS

Excursion or cruise boats are good get-acquainted options. Boats offer half-day or evening trips, often with narration about the history of the passing shoreline. **Charter boats** are what you want if you plan to sail for a day or longer, but keep in mind that the term "charter" can mean different things. You can charter the 50-ft. yacht you're thinking of buying and take yourself all the way to the Caribbean, or you can charter a sailboat with a skipper to navigate while you occasionally lend a hand or relax on deck all weekend. "Bare-boat" chartering means you'll be fully in charge. Charter agencies will want to see your sailing resume, and they will check references. Some offer courses for experienced sailors who'd like to be certified to bare-boat.

Chartering isn't cheap. Most places prefer to set a two-day minimum, which runs from a low of about $250 for the smallest cruising sailboat in the fleet. Add about $125 per day for a captain.

For those who bring their own boats along, volumes have been written about Chesapeake Bay sailing. Recommended marinas are listed below.

INFORMATION ABOUT CHESAPEAKE WATERS

Public Boat Access Areas: Virginia Game Commission, PO Box 11104, Richmond VA 23230; 804-367-9369.

Guide to Cruising Chesapeake Bay, published by *Chesapeake Bay Magazine*, is comprehensive, down to suggested cruises to fill a week. Write 1819 Bay Ridge Ave., Annapolis MD 21403; 410-263-2662. $34.50. They also publish a very good chartbook of the entire Bay, a bargain at $24.95.

Guide for Cruising Maryland Waters is a popular chartbook that takes care of the upper part of the Chesapeake. Dept. of Natural Resources, Consumer Services, PO Box 1869, Tawes State Office Bldg., 580 Taylor Ave., B-1, Annapolis MD 21401; 410-974-3211. $20.

Cruising the Chesapeake: A Gunkholer's Guide. The Bay is known as gunkholing paradise, where sailors can meander among secluded anchorages. International Marine/McGraw-Hill; 1-800-822-8158. $34.95.

Also, check the bibliography in Chapter Eight, *Information*, for those all-important field guides. One we recommend: *Life in the Chesapeake Bay*, an illustrated guide to fishes, invertebrates, and plants of bays and inlets from Cape Cod to Cape Hatteras, by Alice Jane Lippson and Robert L. Lippson, Johns Hopkins University Press, 1984. $16. The title says it all.

Also, check the free *PortBook*, published twice a year, for its wealth of information about boating services. Available at marine stores or newsstands.

CRUISES AND EXCURSION BOATS

Listings reflect the main interest of the business noted, but many are multi-service. For example, marinas and sailing schools often offer charters. A sailing

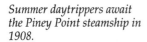

Summer daytrippers await the Piney Point steamship in 1908.

charter outfit may offer fishing trips, and vice versa. Check with the boat owners, and remember that weather may dictate your day.

ANNAPOLIS/WESTERN SHORE

Bay Cruising Adventures (601 Sixth St., Annapolis; 410-269-5140) This is a new cruise from an old company — Annapolis Sailing School — but it's not an instructional course. Travel from one fine hotel or B&B to another on either a sail- or a power boat (your choice) during the day, dining and staying ashore at night. Depart on Monday and return on Friday. Weekend trips available, too.

Beginagain (Annapolis City Dock; 410-626-1422, 1-800-295-1422) This 36-ft. schooner operates three-hour trips three times a day. May 1–Sept. 30. $40 per person plus tax.

Chesapeake Marine Tours (Annapolis City Dock; 410-268-7600) Long-time operators offer tours out of Annapolis Harbor and Severn River or excursions across the Bay to St. Michaels aboard 11 vessels including the *Harbor Queen*. Look also for their water taxis for a quick ride across Spa Creek, or the only eco-tour in town, offered by the associated Chesapeake Bay Boat Tours. These naturalist-led trips offer boatloads of up to 48; tickets are under $10. Contact the Annapolis Gardening School for eco-tour schedules at 410-263-6041.

Schooner Woodwind (Waterfront Marriot dock, Annapolis; 410-263-7837) Take a 2-hour tour of Annapolis Harbor aboard a classic 74-ft. wooden schooner. Sails daily; call for schedule. They can also arrange other water sports, such as parasailing.

Stanley Norman (162 Prince George St., Annapolis; 410-268-8816) The famed skipjack belongs to the Chesapeake Bay Foundation, and stays busy. If it's not running trips for Maryland's junior high school students, maybe you can spend three nights at Smith Island on a foundation-sponsored Bay Discovery Trip. A waiting list is likely, but the trip will be a long-remembered treat. Sign up through the foundation (410-268-8816).

Wm. B. Tennison (Calvert Marine Museum, Solomons; 410-326-2042) Restored 1899 bugeye sloop offers seasonal cruises around Solomons Harbor.

Captain Tyler I (Tyler Cruises, Rhodes Point; 410-425-2771) Sails from Point Lookout State Park, St. Mary's County. From Memorial Day to Labor Day, the *Tyler I* offers cruises to Smith Island and back. Weds.–Sun., Memorial to Labor Day, 10am–4pm. Smith Island, often mentioned in the same breath as Tangier Island, is an outpost of the Chesapeake waterman's life. Tickets, $20 per person; with lunch, $32 per person.

NORTHERN NECK/MIDDLE PENINSULA

Smith Island and Chesapeake Bay Cruises (Reedville, Virginia; 804-453-3430) Capt. Gordon Evans knows his way through the inland waterways, creeks, and canals that lace the cluster of islands known collectively as Smith Island, about 13 miles off the Virginia shore. Boats sail from the KOA Campground in Reedville and dock at Ewell, the largest of Smith Island's three fishing villages. Island tours are offered. Visitors can bring picnics, but most go for the ultimate Chesapeake experience: the family-style, all-you-can-eat meals at two of the island's three restaurants. Reservations required, and remember that weather conditions may dictate your trip. Departs at 10am and return by 3:45pm. $18.50; youngsters 3-13 $9.25. May 1–Oct. 31.

Tangier and Rappahannock Cruises (Rte 1, Box 1332, Reedville, Virginia; 804-453-2628, 1-800-598-2628) Daytrips to windswept Tangier Island. To some extent, mass communication has eroded the Elizabethan accents long identified with remote Tangier. But, as in Louisiana's Cajun Country, old lifestyles have a way of withstanding intrusion, and the distinctive accent still can be heard. Leaves 10am, returns at 3:30. $18.50 round-trip. Operates May–Oct.

Rappahannock River Cruise (Operated by Tangier and Rappahannock River Cruises; 804-453-2628) A good day-long cruise along one of the Bay's major tributaries. Bald eagles and a mix of waterfowl are among the sights of this cruise from the town of Tappahannock to Ingleside Winery where tours and tastings are offered (see Chapter Five, "Food Purveyors" section), and a buffet lunch is available. Reservations. May–Nov., except Mon. Leave 10am, return 5pm.

UPPER EASTERN SHORE

Patriot Cruises Inc. (St. Michaels; 410-745-3100) Perennially popular cruise of the Miles River, with narration on local history. The 180-capacity *Patriot* departs daily at 11am, 12:30pm, and 2:30pm. During the peak summer tourist months, prepare to wait in line. Special lunch cruises and evening charters available.

LOWER EASTERN SHORE

The Maryland Lady (Salisbury; 410-543-2466) This 85-ft. riverboat with a Victorian-style interior offers sightseeing cruises along the Wicomico River. Special luncheon and moonlight cruises. Reservations required 48 hrs. in advance.

Tangier Island Cruises (1001 W. Main St., Crisfield; 410-968-2338) The cruise boat *Steven Thomas* takes tourists across Tangier Sound to Tangier Island, the classic waterman's community. One of the more venerable of the island boat businesses. Runs May 15–Oct., 12:30 daily (returns about 5:15pm). Reservations on weekends.

Tangier-Onancock Cruises (16458 W. Ridge Rd., Tangier, Virginia; 804-891-2240) Leave from Onancock's historic Hopkins & Bro. General Store, aboard the *Capt. Eulice* at 10am. After a narrated, 1 hr. 45 min. cruise, passengers are met at

Smith Island Impressions

The land doesn't really rise out of the water here, nine miles off the Eastern Shore. The low lumps on the horizon are clumps of trees rather than elevations of land. As the boat gets closer to Smith Island, the marsh stretches out flat, a green and tan shag rug spread out on the water with a few lumpy spots, hummocks of slightly higher ground with a tree cover. Great egrets on this early summer day, their bills orange and their breeding plumage like Edwardian ladies' hats, wade in the shallows or stalk the marsh edges. Gulls patrol the air, swallows dip and chatter. The scene looks as pristine as the first day of creation, altered only by channel markers that jut from the shallow water of guts, swales, and thoroughfares to unravel the twisting maze of the marsh.

By the time the first town houses come into view, hunkered down in the middle of the Chesapeake Bay, signs of human imprint appear; rotting skeletons of boats pushed into the marsh to die, their naked ribs disintegrating in the relentless tide. Then come pilings over the water with long, unpainted shacks where peeling crabs are held to molt. Then, finally, the village of Ewell, population about 300 sturdy souls, with the Methodist Church spire dominating the town, these pious people would agree, as the church dominates their lives.

Ewell, reached only by the island's mail boat, is the largest of three villages on the collection of land known as Smith Island, settled inside the muscular force of the Chesapeake Bay, a body both threatening and nurturing. Rhodes Point is the smallest community, joined to Ewell by a thread of road one and a half miles over the marsh. Before it was a settled village, it was known as Rogue's Point, the hiding place for pirates and raiding picaroons. When enough God-fearing people put down roots and were numerous enough to justify having a post office, they were a little bit embarrassed by being identified with rogues and changed the name to Rhodes Point. Tylerton, separated from the other two settlements by a broad gut of water, has no roads, no cars except a few ancient trucks, a golf cart or two, and a whole fleet of bicycles. In this world where roads are liquid, boats are the major transportation.

It's been more or less like this for more than 200 years. The terrain has changed only as the vagaries of storm and tide rearrange the contours of the fragile land. Wave erosion has gnawed away several miles of land that once held large plantations and cattle farms. In recent times, the pace of erosion has speeded, and the islands shrink by about eight feet a year on the western side.

What also has been constant, at least until recently, has been the human occupants, descendants of the original English settlers who reputedly were mostly Cornishmen and women arriving at the turn of the 18th century. Five major families remain the most common names on the islands: Evans, Tyler, Marsh, Marshall, and Bradshaw.

Some linguists describe their accent as Elizabethan; to the untutored ear, it sounds more like an extreme form of Lower Eastern Shore dialect. It is beguiling, if slightly incomprehensible. And there's no mistaking the genuine friendliness with which it's delivered. Total strangers are greeted with a smile and a pleasant "Good Morning" or "Good Evening."

We suggest touring the island with one of the organized tour boats that departs the Eastern Shore or the Northern Neck; accommodations for the lone traveler arriving aboard the mail boat can be unpredictable.

— From an essay by Anne Stinson

the Tangier dock by a guide, who takes them through the narrow streets of this tiny fishing village. Gift shops feature locally made crafts, such as dolls; dining features family-style dinner at the well-liked Chesapeake House, or picnic lunches. Reservations required for groups only. June 1–Sept. 15.

Tillie the Tug (Snow Hill; 1-800-345-6754, 410-632-0680) History buffs will enjoy this hour-long narrated cruise on the Pocomoke River aboard a canopied passenger tug. Mid-June–Labor Day.

Captain Tyler II (Tyler Cruises, Rhodes Point; 410-425-2771) Sails from Somers Cove Marina, Crisfield, Somerset County. Like the *Tyler I*, the *Tyler II* taxis tourists to Smith Island for lunch and sightseeing. Memorial Day–Oct., daily 12:30pm to 5:15pm. Tickets: $18.

CHARTERS AND BOAT RENTALS

Charters can come and go, so be sure to ask around at the local marinas if you have any questions. Most of the sailing schools also offer rentals, and are a good, dependable bet — see their listings, too. For a free roster of sailboat and power boat charters on the Bay, contact the Chesapeake Bay Yacht Charter Association, c/o C&C Charters, 506 Kent Narrows Way North, Grasonville MD 21638. And remember to be careful out there.

ANNAPOLIS/WESTERN SHORE

Annapolis

Annapolis Bay Charters (7310 Edgewood Rd.; 301-261-1815, 410-269-1776) Charter one of 30 yachts up to 55 ft., captained or bare-boat. Also delivers to Zahniser's in Solomons. Since 1980.

AYS Charters & Sailing School (7416 Edgewood Rd.; 410-267-8181) All-sail fleet of 28- to 46-ft. vessels, and three catamarans. Offers three charter certification courses, including one week-long class on bare-boat chartering. Long-time business.

Chessie Cat Charters (309 Third St.; 410-268-3664) Bare-boat and captained catamaran charters for long-term charters. Try them for a weekend, or a week.

Paradise Bay Yacht Charters (980 Awald Rd., Annapolis Landing Marina; 410-268-9330, 1-800-877-9330) Specializing in crewed charters and group events. Boats from 27-ft. daysailers to larger yachts, including catamarans and power boats.

Quiet Waters Park (410-267-5976) Sail-, pedal-, and rowboat rentals, as well as canoe rentals, through Chesapeake Sailing School. Although the park is on the busy South River, rentals are out of protected Harness Creek, a quarter-mile from the river. Canoeists, pedalboaters, and rowboaters will want to stay in the creek, since the South is known as "the power-boat river." Powerful engines kick up mighty wakes.

Southern Anne Arundel County

Hartge Chesapeake Charters (Church Lane, Galesville; 410-867-7240) Charter fleet of 14 sailing vessels, 28- to 44-ft., all bare-boat.

Suntime Boat Rentals (2820 Solomons Island Rd., Edgewater; 410-266-6020) Good place to find seasonal rentals and waverunners; wide range of craft.

Solomons

Baileywick Sailboat Leasing (PO Box 710, Solomons; 410-326-3115)

Bluewater Yacht Charter & Delivery (2110 Herring Way, St. Leonard; 410-586-1076) Long-time charter delivery captain offers daysails aboard an Endeavour 35.

Solomons Boat Rental (Rte. 2 & "A" St., Solomons; 410-326-4060) Waverunners and power boats.

Solomons Island Yacht Sales (Solomons; 410-326-4700) One 30-ft. Saber available for week or weekend use.

NORTHERN NECK/MIDDLE PENINSULA

Deltaville, Virginia

Gratitude Yachting Center (Dozier Marine Center, Rte. 33; 804-776-7056) Sailboat rentals.

UPPER EASTERN SHORE

Grasonville

C&C Charters (506 Kent Narrows Way N.; 410-827-7888,1-800-733-SAIL) Bare-boat or captained cruises; choice of 15 to 20 power and sailing vessels ranging in size from 17 to 53 ft. One of the area's better-known companies.

Greensboro

All Aboard Charters Out of Tilghman Island (McDaniel; 410-745-6022) A "Bay boat" for fishing, nature tours, and the like.

Oxford

Eastern Shore Yacht Charters (202 Bank St.; 410-226-5000) Sailboats from 30 to 45 ft. plus trawlers and daysailers. Bare-boat or captained charters, with 15 boats.

St. Michaels

St. Michaels Town Dock Marina (305 Mulberry Street; 1-800-678-8980, 410-745-2400) 15-ft. runabouts with 40-horsepower outboards.

Wye Mills

Schnaitman's Boat Rentals (12518 Wye Landing Lane; 410-827-7663) 16-ft. rowboats without motors.

SAILING AND POWER BOAT SCHOOLS

Taking a few sailing lessons is a good way to spend a Chesapeake-area vacation, especially with kids. Like chartering, learning to handle a boat is not an inexpensive proposition, but the money is well-spent for those who really want to know how, and you'll learn proper, safe technique.

HEAD OF THE BAY

Havre de Grace

Havre de Grace Sailing Services (Tidewater Marina; 410-939-2869, 1-800-526-1528) This long-time business just got its third owner, who plans to offer a range of courses, for everyone from the neophyte to experienced. Look for classes spring through fall (weather depending, of course), with 85 percent of the course onboard the boat. Most folks learn to sail aboard 19-ft. Flying Scots, which are stable boats for beginners.

ANNAPOLIS/WESTERN SHORE

Annapolis

American Powerboat Schools (222 Severn Ave.; 410-721-7517) Also, excursion and destination charters. From 20- to 55-footers.

Annapolis Sailing School (601 6th St.; 410-267-7205, 1-800-638-9192) Classes offered by venerable, reputable school. Experienced instructors teach classes from "Become a Sailor in One Weekend" to "Celestial Navigation." Sail the waters off Annapolis, between the Chesapeake Bay Bridge and Tolly Point, and up the Severn River, popular with local sailors. Rentals of 24-ft. Rainbow daysailers available.

Chesapeake Sailing School (7074 Bembe Beach Rd.; 410-269-1594, 1-800-966-0032, 301-261-2810) A good school offering a wide range of sailing courses, as well as half-day to week-long charters on a range of different vessels. Also offers classes in piloting, navigation, and other aspects of sailing. Children's program, boat rentals. Look for them also at the Annapolis City Dock, where sailing instruction is offered out of the Marriot Waterfront.

Womanship (410 Severn Ave., aka The Boathouse, beneath the Carrol's Creek Café deck; 410-267-6661, 1-800-342-9295) Womanship sailors wear T-shirts that say, "Nobody Yells," and any woman who has ever been one half of a boating couple can appreciate the laugh. This reputable school was started by women for women, and now has spread to four other locations, including the Pacific Northwest and the Virgin Islands. A range of classes, including some for families and couples.

MARINAS

There are many Bay marinas; they vary in quality, and we do our best to list those that are reported back to us as reliable. Unless otherwise indicated, these marinas offer "full service," meaning electrical hookups, holding tank pump-out facilities, fresh water, and, sometimes, other amenities such as laundry, showers, and groceries. For specifics, call ahead. In high season, reservations may be necessary for "transient" slips.

HEAD OF THE BAY

Chesapeake City

Bohemia Bay Yacht Harbor (1026 Town Point Rd.; 410-885-2601) Full service, 290 slips. 9am–5pm daily.

Havre de Grace

Penn's Beach Marina (Foot of Lewis St.; 410-939-2060) 146 slips.
Tidewater Marina (Foot of Bourbon St.; 410-939-0950) Nice facility.

ANNAPOLIS/WESTERN SHORE

Annapolis

Annapolis City Marina (410 Severn Ave.; 410-268-0660) Right in the midst of the bustle. Transient dockage for boats drawing up to ten feet. Groceries, laundry, showers, fuel, and pump-out.
Annapolis Landing Marina (980 Awald Dr.; 410-263-0090) Transients, fuel, showers, laundry, café, pump-out. Swimming pool.
Annapolis Yacht Basin (2 Compromise St.; 410- 263-3544) Transients, fuel, ice, showers, laundry.
Arnold C. Gay Yacht Yard (1 Shipwright St.; 410-263-9277) Full service for boats up to 80 ft.
Bert Jabin's Yacht Yard, Inc. (7310 Edgewood Rd.; 410-268-9667) One of the biggest marinas in the area, including a huge yard with all services. Transients. Also in Eastport section of Annapolis at 410-268-6812.
Chesapeake Harbour Marina (2030 Chesapeake Harbour Dr.; 410-268-1969) Transients, water taxi to City Dock area.
Mears Marina (519 Chester Ave.; 410-268-8282) Transient slips. Headquarters of Severn River Yacht Club. Pool, continental breakfast on weekends during high season.

Petrini Yachtyard & Marina (1 Walton Ln.; 410-263-4278) Huge range of services, transient slips. On Spa Creek. Biggest Travelift in Annapolis. Since 1946.

Chesapeake Beach

Breezy Point Marina (5230 Breezy Point Rd.; 410-535-6911, 1-800-235-6101) South of Annapolis, on the Bay. Used to be Halle Marina. 225 slips, transients.

Galesville

Hartge Yacht Yard (4880 Church Ln.; 410-867-2188; 301-261-5141) A favored area marina that's been there forever — since 1865. All services.

Ridge

Point Lookout Marina (32 Millers Wharf Rd.; 301-872-5145) Transient dockage for years.

Severna Park

Magothy Marina (360 Magothy Rd.; 410-647-2356) On the Magothy River, just N. of the Bay Bridge; deep draft slips. Marina services, swimming pool.

Solomons

Hospitality Harbor (Next to Holiday Inn; 410-326-1052) Popular transient dockage.

Spring Cove Marina (410-326-2161) Popular dockage for transients. Fuel, laundry.

Zahniser's Sailing Center (245 C St.; 410-326-2166) Where the Patuxent meets the Bay. Over 300 slips, pump-out station, pool, restaurant, sail loft, yacht brokerage.

Tall Timbers

Tall Timbers Marina (12 mi. from Point Lookout; 301-994-1508) On N. shore of the Potomac. About 20 transient slips; call ahead.

NORTHERN NECK/MIDDLE PENINSULA

Callao, Virginia

Olverson's Lodge Creek Marina (Off the Yeocomico and Potomac rivers; contact Frederick Olverson, 804-529-6868) 168 open and covered slips, fuel dock, showers, open year-round.

Cobbs Creek, Virginia

Ginney Point Marina (At end of Rte. 628; 804-725-7407)

Coles Point, Virginia

Coles Point Plantation (804-472-3955) Near prime Chesapeake Bay fishing grounds, up the Potomac River. 115 deepwater slips. Transients welcome. Fuel dock with long hours, and boat ramp. Beach, 575-ft. fishing pier available to the public for a nominal fee. Seafood restaurant and 105-site campground.

Deltaville, Virginia

Dozier's Yachting Center (Broad Creek & Rte. 33; 804-776-6711) Power boat and sailboat slips and storage, ship's store, marine and clothing supplies. Yacht club, pool.

J&M Marina (Rte. 33 through Deltaville to Dockside Inn; left on Rte. 1112; at end of road; 804-776-9860) Complete ship's store, slips for both power boats and sailboats. Transients welcome; they'll even arrange your trip to the grocery.

Marina Resorts Group (804-776-6463) Managers of the four "The Club" marinas on Broad Creek, Fishing Bay, Jackson Creek, and Porpoise Cove, which cover the waterfront at this popular sailing town.

Kinsale, Virginia

Kinsale Harbour Marina (804-472-2514) On the Yeocomico River, a tributary of the Potomac. Fuel and fresh water, pool, tennis courts, showers, laundry, launching ramp, boat rentals, ship's store, and restaurant.

Lancaster, Virginia

Yankee Point Marina (Rte. 2; 804-462-7018) On the Corrotoman River, with 95 slips, charters, a sailing school and a good reputation for repairs and restoration.

Lewisetta, Virginia

Lewisetta Marina (804-529-7299) Deep water fuel dock, covered and uncovered slips, winter dry storage, boat rentals, general store. Where the Coan and Potomac rivers meet.

Urbanna, Virginia

Southside Marine (804-758-2331) Transients welcome in this popular, small-town port. Yacht repair and custom work. Been there for 50 years.

White Stone, Virginia

Windmill Point Marine Resort (Rte. 695, 7 mi. E. of Rte. 3.; 804-435-1166) Protected harbor, deepwater slips on the Chesapeake Bay. Lodging and restaurant also on site.

UPPER EASTERN SHORE

Chester

Castle Harbour Marina (410-643-5599) 314 open and covered slips. Restaurant nearby. On the Chester River.
Piney Narrows Yacht Haven (500 Piney Narrows Rd.; 410-643-6600) 278 slips. On Kent Narrows.

Chestertown

Kibler's Marina (Cannon St.; 410-778-3616) On Chester River. 54 slips.

Georgetown

Georgetown Yacht Basin (410-648-5112) Here, 276 slips; 156 more at Granary Marina directly across river.
Skipjack Cove Yachting Resort (410-275-2122) 360 slips, 33 moorings.

Grasonville

Lippincott Sailing Yachts (410-827-9300) 200 slips.
Mears Point Marina Kent Narrows (410-827-8888) An impressive 600 slips; many power boats live here. Restaurants adjacent.

Lankford Creek

Lankford Bay Marina (23002 McKinleyville Rd., Rock Hall; 410-778-1414) On a tributary of the Chester River. 100 slips, 23 moorings. Open weekends mid-Mar.–Nov.

Oxford

Crockett Brothers Boatyard (Bank St.; 410-226-5113) 74 slips.
Oxford Boatyard (410-226-5101) 76 slips.

Rock Hall

Gratitude Marina (Lawton Ave.; 410-639-7011)
Rock Hall Landing (Sharp St.; 410-639-2224)
Sailing Emporium (Green Ln.; 410-778-1342) 150 slips.

St. Michaels

St. Michaels Harbour Inn & Marina (101 N. Harbor Rd.; 410-945-9001) 60 slips. Long hours — 8–8, daily; 7–8 weekends. Hotel adjacent.
St. Michaels Town Dock Marina (305 Mulberry St.; 1-800-678-8980, 410-745-2400) 40 slips.

Stevensville

Pier 1 Marina (Pier One Rd.; 410-643-3162) Next to Bay Bridge on Kent Island. Restaurant and small airport adjacent. Shopping nearby.

Tilghman

Knapps Narrows Marina (Rte. 33; 410-886-2720) 128 slips.

LOWER EASTERN SHORE

Cambridge

Cambridge Municipal Yacht Basin (410-228-4031) City-run docks at Port of Cambridge. Next to historic district.

Crisfield

Somers Cove Marina (Broadway & Water St.; 1- 800-967-3474 or 410-968-0925) Municipal marina with 500 slips, right in the town.

Salisbury

Port of Salisbury Marina 506 W. Main St., Salisbury MD 21801; 410-548-3176. Downtown, on Wicomico River. 112 slips.

BOWLING

If you feel like knocking down some pins, there are a few bowling alleys around. In the *Annapolis/Western Shore* area, check out the **Annapolis Bowl**, 2057 Generals Hwy., Annapolis (410-266-0700). Farther south, in Calvert County, is the **Lord Calvert Bowl** in Huntingtown (410-535-3560). And if you're south of Virginia's *Middle Peninsula*, drop by the **Village Lanes** in Gloucester (804-693-3720). On the *Eastern Shore*, the offerings include **Queen Anne's Bowling Centre**, 6401 Church Hill Road/Rte. 213, Chestertown (410-778-5800); **Chesapeake Bowl 2000**, in the Easton Plaza, Easton (410-822-3426); **Cherokee Bowling Lanes**, 5 Salisbury Blvd., Salisbury (410-742-3030); **Eastern Shore Lanes**, Market St. Extension, Pocomoke City (410-957-0775).

CAMPING

BACKCOUNTRY CAMPING

The only true backcountry camping in Chesapeake territory is at **Assateague Island National Seashore** (Rte. 611, 7206 National Seashore Lane, Berlin MD 21811; 410-641-3030). This worthwhile experience may include waking up in the night to the sound of the Assateague wild ponies' hoofs. The seashore gov-

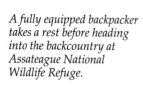

A fully equipped backpacker takes a rest before heading into the backcountry at Assateague National Wildlife Refuge.

David Trozzo

erns for 13 miles, protecting a spectacularly wild beach where you can see bottlenose dolphin offshore during the summer. Shellfishing and crabbing are allowed in island waters, as is canoeing. Hike down the beach (stay off those coastal dunes) or move slightly to the interior along miles of hiking trails to explore each aspect of the barrier-island ecosystem. Inland from the dunes grow myrtle brush, loblolly pine, and some hardwoods. Or, look out on salt meadows.

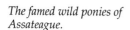

The famed wild ponies of Assateague.

David Trozzo

A word about the ponies: expect to run into them, especially in the less-crowded spring or fall seasons. They're mild-tempered and will leave you alone if you leave them alone. Explanations of their origin are mixed (and your belief therein seems to depend on whether you're a romantic or pragmatist).

They may have descended from Spanish mustangs that swam ashore after a shipwreck, or from the animals owned by 17th-century settlers who grazed them here. At the Maryland-Virginia line, you'll run into the fence that separates the two herds of 150 ponies each. This also is where management changes again, to the **Chincoteague National Wildlife Refuge** — and you're not allowed to camp. But you might spot the intriguing Sika deer, an animal that's actually part of the elk family, and no larger than a big ol' dog.

If you camp at Assateague (or even visit, for that matter) be forewarned that the mosquitoes are world-class. As one park ranger here put it: "I've had friends visit from Maine; I've had friends visit from Alaska. They've *never* seen 'em quite like this."

CAMPGROUNDS

Experienced folks know the best campgrounds are often found at federal parks, but in the ecologically aware Chesapeake, you'll find the same true of state parks — especially in Maryland. Budget cuts in these lean-government times may affect dates, costs, or even closures, so be sure to check ahead. For full listings that include commercial spots, see "Campgrounds" in Chapter Three, *Lodging*. The temperate Chesapeake climate means camping can be quite comfortable for six months a year, but during summer, remember: never forget your mosquito repellent.

HEAD OF THE BAY

Susquehanna State Park (410-836-6735, 410-557-7994; 801 Stafford Rd., Havre de Grace) Seasonal. Tents, picnic tables, laundry tubs, showers, flush toilets; has merged with Rocks State Park. Administrative offices: 3318 Rocks, Chrome Hill Rd., Jarretsville MD 21084.

ANNAPOLIS/WESTERN SHORE

Point Lookout State Park (Rte. 5, Point Lookout, St. Mary's County; 301-872-5688) Hookups available at this 143-site area at the tip of Southern Maryland where the Potomac meets the Bay. A great, out-of-the way park with plenty of activities, including pier and beach fishing. Small Civil War museum, for this was once the site of a Union holding prison for Confederate soldiers.

NORTHERN NECK/MIDDLE PENINSULA

Westmoreland State Park (RR1, Box 600, Montross, Virginia; 804-493-8821) On the southern shore of the Potomac River, known for its fossil cliffs. Sharks' teeth of the Mesozoic era are found on the beaches here, as at Maryland's Calvert Cliffs. The geologic history of the Coastal Plain is told at the visitor center, set near miles of hiking trails. Along the river beaches and at the foot of Horsehead Cliffs, explorers also turn up whale bones and other fossilized remains of ancient marine animals from the Miocene Sea. Beachfront picnic areas; wooded campsites and cabins; boat rentals; plus a complex including a restaurant, swimming pool, and camp store. Cabins rented on a nightly or weekly basis, limit two weeks, minimum stay two nights. 1-800-933-PARK for reservations.

LOWER EASTERN SHORE

Assateague State Park (7307 Stephen Decatur Hwy., Berlin; 410-641-2120) Ocean beaches, a huge parking lot, bathhouse, and a nature center. Campsites are more developed than those on the more natural federal seashore next door; water toilets available. First-come, first-served, Apr. 1–Nov. 1, unless you want a week-long site (Sat.–Sat. only). In that case, make reservations at least two weeks in advance. There's a waiting list for July and August. $20 a night.

Assateague Island National Seashore (Rte. 611; 7206 National Seashore Ln., Berlin; 410-641-3030, 410-641-1441) If you're not interested in backpacking, the seashore offers some of the best campgrounds around. Both oceanside and Bay-side sites are offered, for RVs and tents. There's lots to do: good nature trails; canoe and bike rentals. Reservations are required during the summer; 1-800-365-2267 — and you might want to plan well in advance. $8 during the off-season, and $10 from May 15–Oct. 31. Check in with the campground registration office at the Maryland end of the island, or at the Tom's Cove Visitor Center in Virginia, 15 miles south of the closest camping area.

Janes Island State Park (Rte. 2, Alfred Lawson Dr., Crisfield; 410-968-1565) Also rents four cabins, with screened-in porches. Reserve well in advance.

Pocomoke River State Park (Rte. 12, Snow Hill; 410-632-2566) A neat place that offers camping along the shores of the intriguing, peat-filled waters of the Pocomoke River, where escaping slaves hid en route north along the Underground Railroad. Two areas: Milburn Landing, open seasonally, and Shad Landing, 4 mi. S.W. of Snow Hill, off Rte. 113.

CANOEING AND KAYAKING

The Bay's many creeks and rivers offer quiet canoeing for paddlers of all ages and abilities. The greatest variety of Chesapeake canoeing is on the Eastern Shore. We explore the options in that region for you here. Addresses and phone numbers for these locations are offered in the "Parks and Wildlife Areas" section in this chapter.

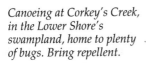

Canoeing at Corkey's Creek, in the Lower Shore's swampland, home to plenty of bugs. Bring repellent.

David Trozzo

There is plenty of wildlife to enjoy. Canoeists will discover the great blue herons living in nearby marshes or will see barn owls flying from nearby woods. The exception to typical Bay area flatwater is Tuckahoe Creek, south of the dam at the lower end of Crouse Mill Lake, which, after heavy spring rains, is roughly equivalent to Class 3 whitewater.

GENERAL INFORMATION

The Chesapeake Bay Foundation: 162 Prince George St., Annapolis MD 21401; 410-268-8816.

The Nature Conservancy: 2 Wisconsin Circle, Suite 600, Chevy Chase MD 20815; 301-656-8673.

ANNAPOLIS/WESTERN SHORE

A placid canoeing spot that tends to be uncrowded — and rents canoes — is the **Jug Bay Natural Area** of Patuxent River Park in *Prince George's County*. Jug Bay, a former deepwater harbor, was formed after the old Chesapeake Beach Railway was built to carry vacationers from the city to the Bay, and the treeline still marks the old railroad bed. (The railroad was dismantled in the '30s). Paddlers should keep in mind this is a tidal river, which means you don't want to be caught downstream on a windy day with the tide running out and the sun sinking low. In the marsh itself, water hyacinths grow dense by mid- to late summer, and they're filled with bugs. Fish for largemouth bass, or perch when they're running. You can get your fishing license at the park office. 16000 Croom Airport Rd., Upper Marlboro MD 20772; 301-627-6074; 301-699-2544 (TDD).

Across the river, in *Anne Arundel County*, is the **Jug Bay Wetlands Sanctu-**

ary (410-741-9300), which offers guided canoe trips from time to time. Together, the two areas are part of a research cooperative known as the **Chesapeake Bay National Estuarine Research Reserve**.

In *Annapolis,* at **Quiet Waters Park**, explore Harness Creek. Avoid the South River, where fast boats kick up rocky wakes. To rent canoes, call 410-267-5976.

NORTHERN NECK/MIDDLE PENINSULA

Belle Isle State Park is a new park still under development; open Thurs.–Sun. and holidays only. Offers guided canoe trips into the river every weekend. Watch for osprey, and learn about the Rappahanock River. Nominal fee. Call in advance. Off Rte. 354 on Rte. 683; 804-462-5030.

UPPER EASTERN SHORE

The **Choptank River**, the largest of the Shore's 20-odd rivers, is fed into by King's Creek, worthwhile canoeing territory. Put in at Kingston Landing, accessible via Rte. 328 and Kingston Landing Rd. A meandering tidal waterway, King's Creek runs past the Nature Conservancy's **Choptank Wetlands Preserve** and some of the most pristine marshes on the East Coast. Plenty of wildlife and blessedly few boats. Watch out during duck-hunting season, though.

Tuckahoe Creek, which runs through **Tuckahoe State Park** in *Caroline County* before reaching the Choptank, is one of the Shore's more popular canoeing spots. At the park, Tuckahoe Creek runs into Crouse Mill Lake, which has a dam at its lower end, after which the Tuckahoe continues its journey to the Choptank. The lake and the section of the creek north of it are freshwater; it's a good area for less experienced canoeists. Below the dam, the Tuckahoe is tidal, with different vegetation from the freshwater upper reaches. From the dam to the landing in Hillsboro are six miles of pleasurable canoeing, with great fishing for bass, pickerel, and bluegill. Warning: Do NOT run the dam.

Watts Creek, entering the Choptank at **Martinak State Park** near *Denton,* makes for a pleasant two-hour paddle up and back. Go at high tide; it's a bit muddy at low tide.

In *Queen Anne's County,* put in to the **Corsica River** at Centreville and poke around up- or downstream on a pretty stretch of water. **Turner's Creek**, which flows northwest into the Sassafras River in Kent County, affords some scenic canoeing past stunning 60- to 70-foot-high bluffs. While development has crept in on the north side, the south side remains unspoiled.

The **Nanticoke River** (which defies our neat Upper/Lower Shore boundary) is too broad and busy for canoeing; its tributaries, though fine for paddling, are generally hard to get to. The exception is **Marshyhope Creek**; put in at

Federalsburg and canoe downstream for some sunny open tripping, or upstream, brush-ducking your way toward **Idylwild Wildlife Management Area**.

LOWER EASTERN SHORE

Grab a canoe from the dock and go fishin' at Pocomoke River State Park, way down on the Eastern Shore.

David Trozzo

Near _Snow Hill_, deep in Worcester and Dorcester counties, is **Pocomoke River State Park**. This is where you'll hear about "blackwater." Indeed, the water is tea-dark. Rich peat soil spawns swamps and stands of loblolly pine and cypress trees. Locals say the word "Pocomoke" is Native American for black water. People looking to hide out, in the old days, did so here, from bootleggers to slaves heading north to freedom. Heavy vegetation hangs over the river, with an almost tropical feeling. Wildlife officials estimate more than 27 species of mammals, 29 reptiles, 14 amphibians, and 172 varieties of birds have been seen in these wetlands. The park's Shad Landing area offers canoe rentals. Call 410-632-2566.

Elsewhere on the **Pocomoke River**, put in at **Whiton Crossing** near the **Wicomico County** line, and canoe on down to Snow Hill. Nassawango Creek, which feeds into the Pocomoke, has become crowded and many folks opt to go elsewhere.

Seasoned, adventurous canoeists can explore the salt marshes at **Janes Island State Park** in Somerset County near _Crisfield_. Work your way out to the edge of the great Tangier Sound. Take a map, a compass — and some good insect repellent. Call 410-968-1565.

Assateague Island National Seashore is also a good place to canoe, in the marshes and interior bays, although wildlife protection regulations must be followed. Canoe rentals. Call 410-641-3030.

CANOE RENTAL COMPANIES:

Pocomoke River Canoe Co. (312 N. Washington St., Snow Hill; 410-632-3971)
Daily rentals during summer; weekends during spring and fall.
Rainy Day (10441 Racetrack Rd./Rte. 589, Berlin; 410-641-5029)
Survival Products: (1116 N. Salisbury Blvd./Rte. 13, Salisbury; 410-543-1244)

· DIVING

For those who prefer the mysteries of the underwater world, there are various options in Chesapeake waters and practice pools. The following selection will lead you to scuba and other diving classes and excursions. Some dive operators hesitate to send newcomers into the Bay (because of its mucky bottom) and prefer to head straight for the Atlantic Ocean. If you're not experienced, don't go out untutored. Power boats and jet skis have already laid claim to many rivers and/or creeks, and they tend not to mix with diving. But if you do know what you're doing and you're lucky, you might hook up with somebody down Calvert Cliffs way who can show you where to dive for fossils.

HEAD OF THE BAY

East Coast Divers (331 St. John St.; Havre de Grace; 410-939-9030) Scuba classes, Atlantic Ocean dives, and free trips out on the Susquehanna for certified divers. What will you see there? "People have been out here for hundreds of years throwing stuff into the river," says co-owner Gene Weisheit, such as bottles and various other artifacts. "People always find something to take home."

ANNAPOLIS/WESTERN SHORE

Sea Dive & Cycle (Rte. 2/4, S&W Shopping Center, Solomons; 410-326-4385)
Mostly arranges charters out of the area, but can offer some advice to experienced divers who ask.
Point Lookout State Park (End of Rte. 235, in St. Mary's County; 301-872-5688)
With permission from the park, experienced divers can explore off the shore here.

UPPER EASTERN SHORE

Calypso Dive & Travel (Rte. 50 at Kent Narrows, at Mears Point Marina, Grasonville; 410-827-7000; 1-800-942-5977) Scuba classes, rentals.

LOWER EASTERN SHORE

Tidewater Aquatics (1147 South Salisbury Blvd. #7, Salisbury, 1-800-637-2102, 410-742-1992) Diving and snorkeling equipment; skin-diving school.

FISHING

From marshy creeks to wide open water, the Chesapeake and its tributaries comprise one of the greatest anglers' destinations anywhere. With the Bay the focus of so much environmental concern, catch-and-release fishing is becoming much more popular.

We attempt to cover the waterfront here, with information arranged in these categories: Chesapeake Fish Species (includes rockfish), the Best Fishing Guide, Fishing Licenses, Crabbing, Where to Drop Your Line (includes Free Fishing Areas), Charter Boats and Head Boats, and Boat Ramps.

CHESAPEAKE FISH SPECIES

There are 17 species of gamefish here to pursue from riverbanks, piers, skiffs, head boats, and charter boats. Bait your hook and go for bluefish, sea trout, white and yellow perch, spot, rockfish (also called striped bass), catfish, channel bass, and hardhead (croaker).

Bass fishing in the upper reaches of the Bay and the freshwater tributaries is so good that the 21st annual BASS Masters Classic was held there in the early '90s. Despite declines in other stocks due to deterioration in Bay water quality, this was the third best catch ever for the Bass Anglers Sportsmen's Society.

Anglers pursue the Bay's 17 species of recreational finfish.

David Trozzo

In Virginia, near Smith Point and Reedville, avid enthusiasts go out to the rich fishing grounds aboard the local charter boats. Says local Captain Billy Pipkin: "By May, the large, aggressive 'chopper' blues move up the Bay and should be bending the poles. These 6- to 20-lb. fighters will provide a thrill until the smaller, but just as ferocious, tailer blues come in." Feisty bluefish can be caught from May through November. Bottom fishing picks up by June and continues well into fall. "You can expect spot, croaker, flounder, and trout to be most plentiful. Spanish mackerel and drum often make special appearances during the season," says Captain Pipkin. September, when the bluefish and Norfolk spot are fattening up to head out into the ocean, offers some of the best Bay fishing.

Other good Bay quarry includes the black drum, a big old monster of a bottom fish. What this guy loses with its lack of fighting spirit, it makes up in sheer weight and size. It's a real line-tester: the Bay record is over a hundred pounds.

Shellfish include oysters (depleted because of disease, though *not harmful to humans*), clams, and crabs.

Crabbing

The number of Maryland blue crabs in the Bay is, alas, suffering during the mid-'90s. Some blame overharvesting of these ultra-tasty and stratospherically popular critters. Some cite other possible problems — including the natural up-and-down life cycle of any species. Whatever the reason, be kind to *callinectes sapidus*, and resist the urge to catch a couple dozen for yourself alone. Some people think it would be a good idea not to catch females, which have rounded, U-shaped aprons, unlike the pointed aprons of the males.

Catch a crab by tying chicken necks or eels in the bottom of a crab trap (widely available at hardware, fishing, or sporting goods stores) and drop the trap into the water. Or, you can dip with a minnow net. Just like Bay folks like to show newcomers how to eat — or pick — crabs, they'll also show you how to catch them. Just ask.

Both states regulate the spring-to-fall season, as well as the catch. Hardshells are limited to those that are five inches across from point-to-point. Check for the latest regulations, since management concerns are causing both states to rethink their usual rules.

Rockfish

The premiere Chesapeake gamefish, Maryland's Official State Fish, is striped bass, known locally as rockfish. Of North America's stripers, 90 percent spawn in the Bay. Concern was high when the fish declined dramatically from the '70s to the '80s, forcing a rockfish moratorium. The rockfish has made a terrific comeback, and charter boat captains now look for schools of them when out with fishing parties. Chesapeake Beach's Rod 'n' Reel Marina, home of a long-time charter operation, boasts "the last three records, going back to 1975,"

Fishing the Patuxent River, off Solomons Island.

David Trozzo

says Freddie Donovan, who co-owns the marina. Most recently, that was a 64.7 pound fish, caught May 14, 1992, by an angler aboard the appropriately named charter boat *Compensation*. Fly fishing for rock has caught on in the Bay in the last few years. If you're interested, check with charter operations.

The season in Maryland for this sport fish and delicacy is being extended from the two short fall seasons that governed its comeback years. Check sporting goods shops for up-to-date information.

THE BEST FISHING GUIDE

A complete county-by-county list of public boat ramps can be found in a booklet that no one coming to fish in Chesapeake country should be without: *A Fisherman's Guide to Maryland Piers and Boat Ramps*. It provides license details, creel limits, and seasonal limits for each species, maps highlighting the prime fishing grounds, and more. Dept. of Natural Resources, Fisheries Division, Tawes State Office Bldg., Annapolis MD 21401; 410-974-3365. For information on Virginia freshwater fishing, contact the Dept. of Game and Inland Fisheries, 4010 W. Broad St., Richmond VA 23230; 804-367-9369. Virginia saltwater anglers need to contact the Marine Resources Commission, 2600 Washington Ave., Newport News VA 23607; 804-247-2200.

FISHING LICENSES

Fishing licenses are required unless you're over 65 or under 16, and are widely available at fishing and sporting goods stores. A Chesapeake Bay Sport Fishing License issued by either state is good in Maryland or Virginia, although there are sometimes limits when it comes to fishing certain tributaries. If you're fishing from a chartered boat, you won't need a license. Nor do you need one if fishing as a nonpaying guest from private property. In addition, there are a number of Maryland-designated Free Fishing Areas; check with the Dept. of Natural Resources for locations.

WHERE TO DROP YOUR LINE

First, be aware of a unique Bay fishing spot — the one place you can expect to hook species that swim these waters. The Chesapeake Bay Bridge Tunnel encourages fishing off **Sea Gull Pier** at its manmade island, about midway out in the Bay, one of the East Coast's largest artificial reefs. There's plenty of parking and a restaurant. You will have to pay the tunnel's $10 fee — but only once. And consider these free fishing areas on Maryland's Eastern Shore:

UPPER EASTERN SHORE

Charlestown: The stone wharf at Conestoga and Water Sts.
Chestertown: Rte. 213 Bridge, over the Chester River.
Denton Crouse Memorial Park: N. of Md. Rte. 404 Bridge.

LOWER EASTERN SHORE

Cambridge: Long Wharf at the S. end of bulkhead near Municipal Docks. Also the old U.S. 50 bridge across the Choptank River.
Salisbury: Bulkhead between Mill and Division Sts.

CHARTER BOATS AND HEAD BOATS

Charter boat captains can be counted on to supply anglers with a rod and reel and bait, but plan on bringing lunch. You also may find that this is a fluid business — somebody who's running a boat this season may not be doing so next season. To contact the Maryland Charter Boat Association, call 410-639-2906 and leave a message.

Head boats are much larger, so named because they carry so many "heads" — thirty or more — out to the fishing grounds. Reservations are not generally necessary. Anglers generally pay a fee for use of rod and reel; bait may or may not be included. Fishing is confined to bottom fishing. Off southern Maryland, expect to catch white perch, Norfolk spot, and croaker. If the boat specializes in "chumming," you can catch bluefish and summer flounder. Some folks aren't in love with this fishing method, because crowded boats can mean tangled lines.

HEAD OF THE BAY

Havre de Grace

Penn's Beach Marina (411 Concord St.; 410-939-2060) Rent 15-ft. fiberglass boats with little 9.9 engines and go look for everything from rockfish to catfish. $40 for the day.

ANNAPOLIS/WESTERN SHORE

Annapolis

Samuel Middleton (410-263-3323) A wooden, Bay-built charter boat with a history. Back in the days when George Washington did his patriotic business in Annapolis, he'd cross the Chesapeake to Rock Hall by way of Mr. Middleton's ferry. Today, fishing enthusiasts can take just about the only charter out of downtown Annapolis. Up to six passengers. Equipment and bait furnished. Reservations.

Chesapeake Beach

Rod 'n' Reel Marina (Mears Ave. off Bayside Rd.; 301-855-8351) Sport fishing May–Nov. Half-day and full-day trips on 28-boat fleet of Coast Guard–licensed captains. Per-person rates also available for head-boat fishing. Long record of helping fishers find everything from spot to flounder to trophy rock.

Edgewater

Sportfishing on the Chesapeake Bay, Inc. (301-261-4207; 1-800-638-7871) Capt. Jerry Lastfogel has been running charter boat fishing expeditions for years. Former officer for the Maryland Charterboat Assoc. Fish aboard the 42-ft. *Belinda Gail III.*

Ridge

Scheible's Fishing Center (Wynne Rd.; 301-872-5185) Charter and head boats.

Solomons

Bunky's Charter Boat (Rte. 2/4; 410-326-3241) More than a dozen charter and head boats. Operated by the local guys who know the waters of the Patuxent River and the Bay. Coast Guard licensed to carry 49 passengers. Tackle, ice, and bait provided by most captains. Reservations.

Solomons Charter Captains Association (410-326-4456) Year-round charter boat fishing offered aboard 35 boats, all operated by U.S. Coast Guard–licensed captains.

Tall Timbers

Tall Timbers Marina (301-994-1508) Three charter fishing boats.

NORTHERN NECK/MIDDLE PENINSULA

Heathsville, Virginia

Kit II (804-453-3251) The 1986 Blue Fish Tournament Winner. Licensed for 26 passengers; Capt. Danny Crabbe.

Reedville, Virginia

The *Dudley* (804-453-3643) Capt. Fred M. Biddlecomb takes folks out aboard the 64-ft. charter boat.

Pittman's Charters Inc. (Rte. 1; 804-453-3643) Head out aboard the 42-ft. *Mystic Lady* May–mid-Dec.

Sunrise (804-453-4639) Up to 22 passengers; Capt. Bob Warren.

Wicomico Church, Virginia

Capt. Billy's Charters (Ingram Bay Marina, end of Rte. 609; 804-580-7292) Sail out of Ingram Bay aboard *Liquid Assets*, a 40-ft. vessel designed for fishing parties and sightseeing. Personalized service and instruction in fishing and cruising. Reservations.

Jimmick Jr. III (804-580-7744) Everything-supplied fishing and catered cruises for up to 24. Reservations. Capt. Jim Deibler.

UPPER EASTERN SHORE

Stevensville/Kent Island

Therapy Charters (215 Johnny Lane; 410-643-3276) Capt. Burton will take you out of Kent Narrows on his 39-ft. "Bay-built" traditional boat. 6 person limit, light tackle fishing. Apr.–Dec.

Tilghman

Harrison's Sport Fishing Ctr. (410-886-2121) One of the largest charter fleets on the Bay; many advantages for finding fish. Apr.–Nov.

LOWER EASTERN SHORE

Chincoteague, Virginia

Fish Tales (6531 Maddox Blvd.; 804-336-1875) Two charter vessels, both equipped for offshore angling, along with a bait and tackle shop. The bays behind Virginia's barrier islands are not a suitable sailing area owing to the shifting mud in shallow waters, but they offer some good fishing. In season, catch spot, flounder, and other edible species in sheltered waters; offshore, albacore, tuna, and shark are among the favorites. Capt. Pete Wallace.

Wachapreague, Virginia

Wachapreague Hotel & Marina (804-787-2105) Bottom and deep-sea fishing from a choice of several charter craft. They also rent small boats you can take out yourself.

BOAT RAMPS

Ask the Maryland Dept. of Natural Resources for *A Fisherman's Guide to Maryland Piers and Boat Ramps,* an excellent map showing every ramp in the state. Some easy launch points:

HEAD OF THE BAY

In *Cecil County,* try the Fredericktown boat launch on the Sassafras River (call Cecil County Parks and Recreation, 410-392-4537) or Elk Neck State Park (410-287-5333). Easy-to-find ramps onto the Susquehanna River in downtown *Havre de Grace* are Jean Roberts Memorial Park (year-round, 410-939-9448) and Tydings Park (6am–10pm, 410-939-1800). Small boats only.

ANNAPOLIS/WESTERN SHORE

In *Annapolis,* Sandy Point State Park (410-974-2149; fee or permit required) will get you right onto the Bay. Spa Creek access is at Truxtun Heights Park (410-263-7958) in the middle of town. In *Solomons,* use the Solomons Boat Ramp (410-535-1600 during the week; fee). Down *St. Mary's County* way, try

Waiting for the bluefish at Point Lookout, Maryland, where the Potomac River meets the Bay.

Dan Wolff

Forest Landing, Piney Point, St. Inigoes, and Point Lookout State Park (301-872-5688; fee).

UPPER EASTERN SHORE

In *Queen Anne's County* there's a one-day permit fee of $5 for Maryland residents, $10 for others; 410-758-0835. Try the ramps at Kent Narrows, Little Creek, Thompson Creek, Shipping Creek, Goodhand Creek (all on Kent Island) and Southeast Creek, Centreville, Crumpton, and Deep Landing (in the northern county).

LOWER EASTERN SHORE

Access here includes Choptank River Boat Ramps, 410-228-2090; the Fishing Bay Wildlife Management Area, near Blackwater Refuge, 410-376-3236; Janes Island State Park, 410-968-1565; Taylors Island Boat Ramp, 410-228-3234; and Messongo Creek Landing on Virginia's Lower Shore.

FOOTBALL

From the Naval Academy at Annapolis to the naval training stations on the Patuxent River, to the Norfolk Air Station, this is Navy country. People mean it when they say "Go, Navy!" Don't wait to buy tickets for the academy's home games until the day before the big event. Games at the **U.S. Naval Academy** are at the 30,000-seat Navy Marine Corps Memorial Stadium. Call 410-268-6060 for tickets.

GOLF

What to do if you're not out on the Chesapeake waters? Golf is a fine alternative here, with widely distributed courses of generally high quality on both of the Bay's shores. It's a longish season, too, given the mild mid-Atlantic climate. In fact, spring and fall may offer the most pleasant days on the links, if the Chesapeake summer's humidity is not to your liking. Most clubs have equipment for rent. Be sure to call ahead for tee times at these public courses, and be forewarned that semi-private clubs give first dibs to their members.

HEAD OF THE BAY

Brantwood Golf Club Course (Rte. 213, 1190 Augustine Herman Hwy., Elkton; 410-398-8848) 18-hole semi-private course.

ANNAPOLIS/WESTERN SHORE

Annapolis Golf Club (2638 Carrollton Rd.; 410-263-6771) Nice, local 9-hole course.

Bay Hills Golf Club (545 Bay Hills Dr., Arnold, north of Annapolis; 410-974-0669) 18 holes, semi-private. Reportedly improved in recent years.

Dwight D. Eisenhower Golf Course (Generals Hwy., Crownsville, just outside Annapolis; 410-222-7922) Public, 18-hole course with a special feature: bluebird houses set along the fairways. Very busy.

Swan Point Golf Club(11550 Swan Point Blvd., Issue; 301-259-0047) Where the serious players go. 12 holes on the water. Turn off Rte. 301 right before you head over the Potomac to Virginia.

Twin Shields Golf Club (Rte. 260, 2425 Roarty Rd., Dunkirk; 410-257-7800) 18 holes, semi-private. A local golf pro says he'd head here first among these Western Shore courses.

NORTHERN NECK/MIDDLE PENINSULA

Bushfield Golf Club (Mt. Holly, Virginia; 804-472-2602) At historic Bushfield Plantation. Nine holes, golf carts, driving range, par 72. Pro shop, snack bar.

Gloucester Country Club (Golf Club Rd. off Rte. 17, Gloucester, Virginia, 12 mi. N. of York River Bridge; 804-693-2662) Public 9-hole course. Good for beginners.

Golden Eagle Golf Course (At the Tides Inn, Irvington, Virginia; 804-438-5501) 18-hole championship golf course, said to be one of the top three in Virginia. Also a par 3 for inn and lodge guests. Part of the Tides Inn Resort, the course features professional instruction and a driving range. Par 72. Restaurant; hefty greens fees for non-guests.

Tartan Golf Course at Tides Lodge (Irvington, Virginia; 804-438-6200 or 1-800-248-4337) 18-hole course at an upscale resort. Par 72. Pro shop, game room, snack bar, restaurant. Although separately owned (by two brothers) Tides Lodge and Tides Inn (see above) are affiliated; guests at either resort can use facilities at the other. Reservations required.

The Village Green Golf Club (Rte. 360, Callao, Virginia; 804-529-6332) Public, 9-hole course. Par 36. Pro shop and restaurant year-round.

UPPER EASTERN SHORE

Hog Neck Golf Course (10142 Old Cordova Rd., off U.S. 50, Easton; 410-822-6079) Ranked by some golf experts as one of the top 25 public golf courses in the United States. 27 holes, with both 18-hole championship course and par 32 executive 9-hole.

Mears Great Oaks Landing Resort and Conference Center (22170 Great Oak Landing Rd., Chestertown; 410-778-2100) Par 3, executive 9-hole.

Queenstown Harbor Golf Links (310 Links Ln., off Rte. 301, Queenstown;

410-827-6611, 1-800-827-5257) A beautiful setting on the Chester River. 36 holes. Very busy, and recently voted "Best Public Golf Course in Maryland, Virginia and Washington, D.C." by readers of *Metro Golf*, distributed in the Baltimore-Washington area.

The Sports Trappe (Rte. 50, Trappe; 410-822-7345) A driving practice range. Nine miles south of Easton.

LOWER EASTERN SHORE

Captain's Cove (Rte. 679/Flemming Rd. off State Line Rd., Greenbackville, Virginia; 804-824-3465) Public, nine-hole course. Open water on four holes.

Eastern Shore Yacht and Country Club (Melfa, Virginia; 804-787-1525) Private club available to visitors by reciprocal agreement with other clubs. Reservations required. 18 holes. Open year-round.

Nassawango Country Club (River Rd., Snow Hill; 410-632-3114, 410-957-2262) Semi-private; 18 holes.

Northampton Country Club (Cape Charles, Virginia; 804-331-8423) Nine holes.

Nutters Crossing Golf Course & Driving Range (30827 Southampton Bridge Rd.; 410-860-4653) 18 holes.

Winter Quarters Golf Course (Pocomoke City; 410-957-1171) Two separate sets of tees to make a "front nine" and a "back nine."

HIKING

The beauty of the Chesapeake region is its diversity, and hikers here will find an intriguing range of habitat to explore. There are cypress swamps on both sides of the Bay, forests of loblolly pine or deciduous trees, the 21,000-acre Blackwater Wildlife Refuge on the Lower Shore, and the intriguing cliffs on the lower Western Shore, where sharks' teeth from prehistoric times still wash up on the beach.

Over 100 miles to the east of the Bay is the Atlantic Ocean, and Assateague Island — home to 44 different mammal species. Look out to the ocean during the summer, and you may see bottlenose dolphins. The flat beaches there are the southernmost point at which gray seals are born.

Less than 20 miles west of the Bay is the Patuxent River, home to Jug Bay, where wild rice and water hyacinths grow during summer. A sanctuary and a park on either side of the river allow access to visitors, from an easy boardwalk stroll past unfurling skunk cabbage in early spring at Patuxent River Park's Jug Bay Natural Area in Prince George's County, to the Otter Point Trail at 500-acre Jug Bay Wetlands Sanctuary in Anne Arundel County. If you're real quiet and even more lucky — you might see the river otters who live here.

But virtually all of the region's state parks, refuges, and wildlife management areas offer hiking opportunities. The observant walker may spot such rare species as the Delmarva fox squirrel, or catch a memorable eyeful when a bald eagle's immense wingspan glides over the cattails. For other hiking areas, check "Bird Watching" in this chapter.

HEAD OF THE BAY

Elk Neck State Park (4395 Turkey Point Rd., North East; 410-287-5333) Five different hiking trails, the most of any Maryland park east of the Bay. The well-kept paths take you along steep bluffs, through forests, and down to marshland and beaches. The wildlife is diverse and prolific. 2188 acres; camping is available.

Susquehanna State Park (410-836-6735, 410-557-7994; 801 Stafford Rd., Havre de Grace) Gently rolling hills are a departure from much of the flatlands that mark the Bay region. Spectacular spot along the river.

ANNAPOLIS/WESTERN SHORE

Calvert Cliffs State Park(Rte. 765, near Lusby; 301-888-1410) A great spot. This Bay-side park of 1313 acres offers 13 mi. of hiking trails with a bonus above and beyond the birds offshore: fossils dating 15 to 20 million years back to the Miocene Era may be collected by hikers if they've been uncovered by nature (no digging in the spectacular Calvert Cliffs is allowed). You have to hike back a couple of miles to the beach. Picnicking, fishing, and hunting. Open sunrise to sunset; swim at your own risk.

Jug Bay Wetlands Sanctuary (Lothian, on the tidal Patuxent River; 410-741-9330) Nine miles of nature-study and hiking trails. Pause along the river, and, if you're lucky, you might — and we mean *might* — catch a glimpse of the elusive river otter. A terrific, serene spot that is not over-crowded.

Point Lookout State Park (End of Rte. 235, St. Mary's County; 301-872-5688) Hike back along the beach to the ruins of the Civil War's Fort Lincoln.

Severn Run Natural Environment Area (next to Sandy Point State Park; call for access: 410-974-2149) Here the state has bought up 2,500 acres along the headwaters of the Severn River. Probably one of the few good hiking places near Annapolis. Closed to the general public, but may be accessed through adjacent Sandy Point State Park.

Smithsonian Environmental Research Center (Edgewater; 410-269-1412) Although hikers can use the trails only during business hours (8:30–4 weekdays), this is still pretty country. The Java History Trail is just over a mile long, meandering through an old farm named by a 19th-century naval officer whose ship sank the British frigate *Java* in the War of 1812.

NORTHERN NECK/MIDDLE PENINSULA

Chesapeake Nature Trail (W. of Kilmarnock on the south side of Rte. 3) For an easy hike in Lancaster County, try this 1.6-mile trail that passes the west branch of the Corrotoman River.

UPPER EASTERN SHORE

Eastern Neck Island National Wildlife Refuge (At the mouth of Chester River, Kent County, 410-639-7056) More than 2,000 acres of pristine wilds, only a portion of which is open to visitors. Among the plentiful wildlife here is the Delmarva fox squirrel, an endangered species found nowhere on the planet but on the Eastern Shore. Keep going out past Rock Hall till the road ends.

Horsehead Wetlands Center (Grasonville, just east of Kent Narrows; 410-827-6694) Operated by the Wildfowl Trust of North America. About a mile of trail winds through part of the 300-acre center, complete with blinds and towers to observe wildlife, as well as a boardwalk over the marsh. Public programs. Handicapped access; no pets; small fee; closed Christmas.

Other hiking options include **Tuckahoe State Park** (410-820-1668) near Denton, with a pretty lake to look at and lots of woods to walk through, including a marked fitness trail with exercises to be done at each station; **Martinak State Park**, on old Indian stomping grounds (Deep Shore Rd., off Rte. 404, 2 mi. S. of Denton; 410-479-1619); and **Idylwild Wildlife Management Area**, 3,000 acres of serenity and beauty (Houston Branch Rd., Federalsburg; 410-376-3236).

LOWER EASTERN SHORE

Blackwater National Wildlife Refuge (S. of Cambridge, Dorchester County; 410-228-2677) A couple of fairly short nature trails take visitors back into this bird watcher's paradise, where, in autumn, you'll see flocks of Canada geese and other waterfowl passing through. One of the last bastions of the Delmarva fox squirrel.

Pocomoke State Forest (Rte. 12, Snow Hill; 410-632-1565) Winding trails cut out by long-ago loggers.

HORSEBACK RIDING AND HORSE RACING

Chesapeake is indeed horse country, but you'll find your access limited due to liability issues if you don't have your own horse — or opt to take lessons. But there are a couple of good places to watch racing.

Delmarva Downs: Harness racing, nightly, Memorial Day–Labor Day. Junction of Rtes. 50 & 589, PO Box 11, Berlin; 410-641-0600.

Pimlico Race Course: Home to Baltimore's beloved Preakness Stakes. 5201 Park Heights Ave., Baltimore; 410-542-9400.

Wicomico Equestrian Center: The place to see a horse show. Winter Place Park, Old Ocean City Rd., Salisbury; 410-548-4900.

HUNTING

Native Americans and turn-of-the-century gentleman gunners alike pursued a sport synonymous with the Eastern Shore and Virginia's Tidewater: waterfowling. The honks of the Canada goose flying southwards in V-formation always signal the approach of another autumn. But Chesapeake hunting involves far more than the familiar Canada goose — whose numbers have declined in recent years. In the fall of '95, Maryland officials instituted a hunting ban on the geese, which may remain in effect for a couple of autumns until the birds' numbers go back up.

Seasons are complicated, but hunters in the Bay region typically are on the lookout for **ducks** (mallard, black duck, pintail, redhead, and wood duck), and for fast-flying **sea ducks** that make good sport and are hunted from charter boats (and with the right recipe, they're very good eating). **Snow geese** fly through Chesapeake in growing flocks these days, and their wiliness (they're harder to attract with decoys) and flavorfulness make them a pleasing challenge for waterfowlers.

Dove hunting is quite popular on the Shore and Northern Neck. The mourning dove, with its small size and zig-zagging flight, is a challenge: the national average is one dove per five shells spent. **Wild turkey** is another game bird on the rise on the Eastern Shore. The best turkey hunting is in Worcester County, but wild turkeys are stocked in almost every Eastern Shore county, and they're thriving. In 1995, Maryland opened the entire state to spring gobbler hunting for the first time ever, following extensive management efforts.

There are some good waterfowl hunting guides on the Chesapeake Shore. One of the best-known is Floyd Price, of Kennedyville (410-778-6412). Or, check with Dutch Swonger on Kent Island (410-643-2766). If these fellows are unavailable, maybe they'll recommend others. Guides' fees vary, but expect to pay about $100/day per person in your hunting party.

Beyond Chesapeake waterfowling, the **whitetail deer** hunting here is some of the best around. Quite a few Pope and Young Club record-book bucks have come out of the Shore, including a Kent County buck that held the national size record for two years. Kent and Queen Anne's counties are probably the best for whitetails. These Upper Shore counties are home to lots of large farms, and have plenty of cover and water — ideal conditions for trophy-size whitetails.

There's also a hunting season for an exotic expatriate. Years ago, the **Sika deer** was brought to the area from its native Japan by wealthy landowners who wanted unusual pets to roam their grounds. The Sikas escaped into the wild. Today they're prolific, especially in Dorchester County, and they're moving south. The Sika deer season often runs concurrent with the whitetail season. A small species, the Sika makes for excellent table game. Incidentally, the Sika is actually a member of the elk family.

Both Virginia and Maryland enforce extensive hunting regulations, set annually, regarding seasons, bag limits, and licensing — not to mention violations. For information on Maryland hunting licenses and regulations, contact Wildlife Division, E-1, Maryland Dept. of Natural Resources, 580 Taylor Ave., Annapolis; 410-974-3195. In Virginia, contact Dept. of Game and Inland Fisheries, 4010 W. Broad St., Richmond VA 23230; 804-367-1000.

RUNNING

With a relatively level landscape and plenty of country roads, Chesapeake is ideal running terrain: bring your Nikes. Running, as an organized sport, is a big deal in the Maryland half of Chesapeake, especially around Annapolis. Races are held practically every weekend for much of the year. Major events are the Annapolis ten-miler in mid-summer, and the 10-km Bay Bridge run in late spring. But there are many more races, such as the Oxford Triathlon. For information, call the Annapolis Striders running club; 410-268-1165.

SPORTING GOODS AND CAMPING SUPPLY STORES

Forgot your tent's sand stakes? Need a spare Styrofoam cooler? No sweat. Sporting- and outdoor-goods stores are your local repositories of information about where the fish are biting, how to obtain a hunting license, and other important details about recreation, in or outdoors. Some good bets:

HEAD OF THE BAY

Penn's Beach Marina (411 Concord St., Havre de Grace; 410-939-2060) Everything for the fisher.

ANNAPOLIS/WESTERN SHORE

Angler's Sport Center (Rte. 50, bet. Annapolis and Bay Bridge, S. Access Rd., just E. of Cape St. Claire; 410-757-3442) Hunting and fishing licenses, fishing gear, decoys, outdoor clothing. The dean of local fishing supply stores.

Marty's Sporting Goods (95 Mayo Rd., Edgewater; 410-956-2238) Everything for fishing.

Lining up for supplies at Tyler's Tackle Shop.

Tom Curley

Tyler's Tackle Shop (8210 Bayside Rd; Chesapeake Beach; 410-257-6610) A neat little place; rods, reels, whatever you need for fishing.

NORTHERN NECK/MIDDLE PENINSULA

Winter Harbor Seafood (Rte. 3, 1 mi. E. of Oak Grove, Virginia; 804-224-7779) This may be a seafood market, but it's also the place to get hunting and fishing gear and licenses. Game checking.

UPPER EASTERN SHORE

Albright's Gun Shop (36 E. Dover St., Easton; 410-820-8811)
Bear's Den (851 High St., Chestertown; 410-778-0087)
Shore Sportsman (Rte. 50, about 2 mi. S. of Easton; 410-820-5599, 410-476-3597)
Sportsman Service Center (Piney Creek Rd. and Rte. 50, Chester, Kent Island;
    410-643-4545; 1-800-342-3123 in MD only)
Towne Sporting Goods (Kent Plaza, Chestertown; 410-778-1501)
Toy's Outdoor Store (6274 Rock Hall Rd./Rte. 20, Rock Hall; 410-778-2561)

LOWER EASTERN SHORE

Assateague Village (Stephen Decatur Hwy./Rte. 611, near Assateague;
    410-641-3380) From donuts to kitchen magnets to camping supplies.
Bow Shack (Riverside Dr. extension, Salisbury; 410-749-9540)
Buck's Place (Stephen Decatur Hwy., near Assateague; 410-641-4177) Ponchos,
    some groceries, ice, and bottle openers; seafood house on premises.
Somerset Sporting Goods (537 Main St., Crisfield; 410-968-2822)
Welch's Country Deli (Stephen Decatur Hwy., near Assateague; 410-641-4733)
    Stocks most everything.

Parks and Wildlife Areas

Here's a quick compendium of good state, federal, and local parks and refuges
(and natural areas, too) arranged in geographical order for quick reference. All of
these wild areas offer an abundance of fishing, hiking, birding, or boating opportunities, and you've seen them listed elsewhere in the chapter under those headings.
However, for your convenience, we offer herewith a quick reference for some of
the region's favorite parks.

HEAD OF THE BAY

Elk Neck State Park (Rte. 272, 9 mi. S. of North East; 410-287-5333) 2,188 acres.
Susquehanna State Park (Gunpowder River Valley, Harford County;
    410-557-7994) 2,639 acres.

ANNAPOLIS/WESTERN SHORE

Calvert Cliffs State Park. (c/o Merkle Wildlife Sanctuary, 11704 Fenno Rd.; Upper
    Marlboro; 301-888-1410) 1,313 acres N. of Solomons, on Rte. 2/4.
Helen Avalynne Tawes Garden (Tawes State Office Building, Annapolis;
    410-974-3717; TTY 410-974-3683) Handicapped accessible six-acre garden
    designed to be touched.
Jug Bay Wetlands Sanctuary (Lothian; 410-741-9330) 9 miles of trails; uncrowded.
Point Lookout State Park (PO Box 48, Scotland; 301-872-5688) 528 acres.
St. Mary's River State Park (Off Rte. 5, St. Mary's; 301-872-5688) 2,176 acres.

→

Sandy Point State Park (100 E. College Pkwy, Annapolis; 410-974-2149) Rte. 50, near the last exit before the Bay Bridge; 786 acres. Ask about access to the **Severn Run Natural Environmental Area**, 2,500 acres.

Thomas Point Park (410-222-1969), a tiny spot at the end of the point; limited access.

NORTHERN NECK/MIDDLE PENINSULA

Belle Isle State Park (Off Rte. 354 on Rte. 683; 804-462-5030) 7 miles on the Rappahanock River.

Gloucester Point Beach Park (Rte. 17, Gloucester; 804-693-2355) 5 acres on the York River.

Westmoreland State Park (Off Rte. 3 E. outside Montross. 804-493-8821) 1,200 acres on the Potomac River.

UPPER EASTERN SHORE

Eastern Neck Wildlife Refuge (Rock Hall; 410-639-7056) 2,200 acres of island.

Idylwild Wildlife Management Area (Houston Branch Rd., Federalsburg; 410-376-3236) 2994 acres.

Martinak State Park (Off Rte. 404, 2 mi. S. of Denton; 410-479-1619) 107 acres.

Tuckahoe State Park (Rte. 480, off Rte 404, 6 mi. N. of Queen Anne; 410-820-1668) 3800 acres.

Wildfowl Trust of North America (Horsehead Wetlands Center, Grasonville; 410-827-6694) 310 acres.

Wye Island (Carmichael Rd., Queenstown; 410-827-7577)

LOWER EASTERN SHORE

Assateague Island National Seashore (Rte. 611, 7206 National Seashore Ln., Berlin; 410-641-3030) 13 mi. of barrier island.

Assateague State Park (7307 Stephen Decatur Hwy., Berlin; 410-641-2120)

Blackwater National Wildlife Refuge (2145 Key Wallace Dr., Cambridge; 410-228-2677) 21,000 acres.

Chincoteague National Wildlife Refuge (Chincoteague, Virginia ; 804-336-6122) 10 mi. of beach.

Deal Island Wildlife Management Area (Contact Salisbury's state DNR office; 410-543-6595)

Eastern Shore of Virginia National Wildlife Refuge 5003 Hallet Cir., Cape Charles, Virginia; 804-331-2760) 651 acres.

Ellis Bay Wildlife Management Area (Contact Deal Island number listed above)

Janes Island State Park (Rte. 2 just N. of Crisfield; 410-968-1565) About 3,000 acres, 2, 800 on the island.

Kiptopeke State Park (Off U.S. Rte. 13, 3 mi. N. of the Bay Bridge Tunnel; 804-331-2267)

Pocomoke River State Park (On Rte. 12 & also on Rte. 113, Snow Hill; 410-632-2566) Over 900 acres at two sites.

SWIMMING

Look to the public parks for some of the best swimming in the Chesapeake region, because swimming in the Bay itself is surprisingly limited due to restricted public access to the shoreline. A word about water quality: it's generally good but occasionally unpleasant or unacceptable. Diving randomly off your boat, particularly in smaller tributary creeks and rivers, is not recommended. One more dilemma: the annual problem of jellyfish, or stinging nettles. These not-so-welcome visitors show up in July or August in proportions inverse to the preceding spring's wetness. Lots of fresh rainwater discourages their growth, while a dry spring increases the saltiness of the Bay waters in which they thrive. Betterton Beach, on the Upper Eastern Shore, is beloved because it has no stinging nettles.

HEAD OF THE BAY

Elk Neck State Park (Rte. 272, North East; 410-287-5333) 9 mi. S. of North East.
North East Beach (Call Elk Neck phone number for information) Lifeguard, picnicking, bathhouse.

ANNAPOLIS/WESTERN SHORE

Arundel Olympic Swim Center (Riva Rd., Annapolis; 410-222-7933, 301-970-2216) Here's where you go for a good workout. Olympic-size pool. Operated by the Anne Arundel County Recreation Parks Dept. Seven days, Mon.–Fri. 6am–10pm, Sat. 8am–8pm, Sun. 10am–8pm. Nominal entrance fees.
Breezy Point (5 mi. S. of Chesapeake Beach in Calvert County; 410-535-0259) The county recently took over this formerly private Bay-side enclave. Nets off the beach protect swimmers from sea nettles. 6am–9pm, $4, Memorial–Labor Day.
Point Lookout State Park (Rte. 5, Point Lookout; 301-872-5688) The beach is nice for sunning, but there's also beach for surfcasting. Swim in designated areas.
Sandy Point State Park (Rte. 50, near the last exit before the Bay Bridge, Annapolis; 410-974-2149) One of the few sandy beaches on the Bay. It's fun to hang out here and watch what goes on out on the Bay; from the massive, coal-filled colliers headed for port in Baltimore to the crisp white sails of the yachting set in summer. You'll have an up close and personal view of the Bay Bridge, too.

NORTHERN NECK/MIDDLE PENINSULA

Gloucester Point Beach Park (Rte. 17, on the York River next to Coleman Bridge/York River Bridge, Gloucester, Virginia; 804-693-2355) Fishing pier, picnic area, horseshoe and volleyball courts, and swimming. Concession stand, restrooms open seasonally.

Westmoreland State Park (5 mi. N. of Montross, Virginia, off Rte. 3 E.; 804-493-8821) Olympic-size pool at this Potomac River-side park.

UPPER EASTERN SHORE

Betterton Beach (Rte. 292, Betterton, Kent County; contact Parks and Recreation, 410-778-1948) Reliable swimming conditions with a bonus: no stinging nettles. Lifeguard, picnicking, fishing jetty, bathhouse. Free.

LOWER EASTERN SHORE

Cedar Hill Park (Rte. 349, Bivalve; contact Dept. of Recreation, 410-548-4900) Beach, picnicking. Fee.

Great Marsh (Somerset Ave., Cambridge; contact Dorchester County Tourism, 410-228-1000) Boat ramp, picnicking. Free.

Shumaker Pond (Shumaker Dr., Salisbury; contact Dept. of Recreation, 410-548-4900) Lifeguard, picnicking, playground.

TENNIS

With a long warm season, Chesapeake is ideal tennis country. Chasing the ball is a great antidote for stiffened sea-legs or for hunter's legs cramped from crouching in a blind. Public courts abound throughout the Bay area. For locations, contact the recreation departments of the county in which you're staying. See Chapter Eight, *Information*, for county Chamber of Commerce phone numbers, listed under "Tourist Information."

ANNAPOLIS/WESTERN SHORE

In Anne Arundel County, 45 county parks have tennis courts; eight have lights for night-time play. Visitors to Annapolis — where court time is harder to find — may want to use courts in nearby towns in less-congested central or rural south county. Information: Anne Arundel County Dept. of Recreation and Parks, 410-222-7300. The city of Annapolis maintains courts at **Truxtun Park** in the middle of town. Call the city Recreation & Parks Dept.; 410-263-7958.

Indoor courts are available to a more limited audience; generally, those tourists who are staying at hotels in the area. Or you can try the following:

Totally Tennis (Rte. 2, N. of Annapolis; 410-544-2990) At the Big Vanilla Racquet Club, a private club accepting guests.

NORTHERN NECK/MIDDLE PENINSULA.

Windmill Point Marine Resort (End of Rte. 695, Lancaster County, Virginia; 804-435-1166) Courts available.

UPPER EASTERN SHORE

Cross Court Athletic Club (1180 S. Washington St. at Easton Pkwy., Easton; 410-822-1515)

LOWER EASTERN SHORE

Layton's Salisbury Sports Club (Court Plaza, Salisbury; 410-749-6923)

ZOOS

Hailed as one of America's finest small zoos, the **Salisbury Zoological Park** places animals in replicas of their natural habitats. On 12 acres along the Wicomico River, the zoo sells no peanuts or popcorn (neither of which is correct as animal food), and limits itself to North and South American species. Featured is a vast collection of waterfowl and other birds, from geese to American bald eagles, from pelicans to macaws. The spectacled bears of the South American highlands are a rare, endangered, and most endearing species. Animals indigenous to similar regions often share space at this well-conceived, naturalistic zoo. **Salisbury Zoo:** 750 S. Park Dr., next to City Park, Salisbury. Directions: just E. of Rte. 13 & S. of U.S. 50. 410-548-3188. Open Memorial–Labor days, daily 8am–7pm; rest of year 8:30–4:30. Free, but donations welcome.

NEARBY RECREATION

Ocean City, Maryland

Ocean City's major attraction is a 10-mile-long strip of golden sand that often is packed blanket to blanket on summer weekends. Over the years, government has engaged in a lengthy, some might say fruitless, battle to keep that sand in place by importing tons of sand from offshore to replace what the ocean's natural cycle washes away.

None of that worries visitors much, though. They come for the sun, the sand, the carnival rides, and the "World Famous French Fries" sold on Ocean City's boardwalk, and for lots of shops and restaurants. You can reach Ocean City, or "O.C.," from the Bay via three routes. Enter the oldest, southernmost part of the city on U.S. 50 from the west. Or take Md. 90 across the Assawoman Bay Bridge to what has become the city's center. Or, from the Delaware beach towns of Rehoboth, Dewey, and Bethany Beaches to the north, the Coastal Highway, Md. 528, is the best way in. For more information, call the Ocean City Convention and Visitor's Bureau at 410-289-8181.

Virginia Beach, Virginia

Rivaling the attractions of the Maryland shore, Virginia Beach draws revelers from all over Virginia and neighboring states. Virginia Beach proper offers 29 miles of sand beaches for sunning, swimming, and surf fishing, as well as waterskiing and boating. Atlantic Avenue, the major thoroughfare fronted by the boardwalk, has been revitalized as a pedestrian mall with public parks and benches. Outdoor entertainment is offered free daily during the summer, and Sunday fireworks displays are held from Memorial Day to Labor Day. To reach Virginia Beach, follow Va. Rtes. 58 or 44 E. from Norfolk. For more information call the area's visitor line at 804-490-1221, or 1-800-822-3224.

CHAPTER SEVEN
Antiques, Boutiques, and Inlet Outlets
SHOPPING

From ship's hardware to Anne Klein suits, shopping around the Chesapeake is, if nothing else, diverse. In some areas, such as the historic district in Annapolis or downtown St. Michael's, stores and boutiques cater to the tourist trade. Look for everything from T-shirts and crab refrigerator magnets to fine paintings and nature sculpture. Other towns, such as Havre de Grace or Solomons Island, have grown tourist trades in more recent years. That means fine arts and craft shops may well sit next to a decades-old downtown department store.

Chesapeake specialties include antiques, including decoys. Decoy hunters won't want to miss Havre de Grace, a former gunning sports-

Maryland State Archives

Shopping in Annapolis in the 1940s.

man paradise where decoys have become the folk art stock-in-trade. One local shop worker told of the old duck that came through at a rock-bottom price —

and sold at auction in New York for thousands. The Eastern Shore also offers ample opportunity for rummaging around for decoys.

Folks who think of "antique" as a verb should find plenty to keep themselves busy. Maryland Avenue in Annapolis continues to house upscale antiques shops, although bargain-hunters may want to meander south on Rte. 2 into Calvert County. As attics becoming increasingly picked over, however, you'll discover that antiques shops have assimilated into the "collectibles" trade, rendering your search for the perfect Queen Anne tea table less than a success. But by the same token, you'll find the dealers form a tight network. They'll know where to look for specific items.

Outlets also have sprung up, most notably in Queenstown, just over the Bay Bridge on Rte. 50. Shoppers will want to avoid the heavy-traffic Friday and Sunday hours when beach-goers headed to the Atlantic Ocean clog the highways — and the malls.

We concede that this is by no means a complete listing of the myriad stores along the Chesapeake, but we do think it's a good start. More detailed inquiries should be directed to area Chambers of Commerce (see Chapter Eight, *Information*). Note that most shops and stores are open five to seven days a week unless otherwise stated. You can almost count on the smaller and more remote businesses to be open only on weekends, especially during the winter. Be sure to call ahead.

ANTIQUES

From dusty barns to historic storefronts, Chesapeake has more than its quota of antiques shops. Prices can vary widely. If you're really a bargaineer, try an auction. One local institution on the Upper Shore is **Dixon's Furniture** in Queen Anne's County, better known as the Crumpton auction. People who live as sparingly as Thoreau at Walden Pond come back raving about the great finds at this vast affair. Starts at 8am sharp every Wednesday, Rtes. 290 and 544 (east of Chestertown) in Crumpton; 410-928-3006. Also, check out the big auction at **American Corner**, six miles north of Federalsburg on Md. 621. Every Thursday night, buildings full of stuff go on the block and you can find everything from outboard motors to furniture; 410-754-8826.

HEAD OF THE BAY

Havre de Grace

Bank of Memories (319 St. John St.; 410-939-4343) Range of estate and custom jewelry, antiques, appraisals. Housed in the old First National Bank in the center of town.

Franklin Street Antiques and Gifts (464 Franklin St.; 410-939-4220) Expansive range of stuff. Some decoys, that Havre de Grace icon from its days as a gunning mecca for sportsmen.

Golden Vein (408 N. Union Ave; 410-939-9595) Local institution features myriad dealers under one funky tin roof. Good browsing emporium.

Investment Antiques and Collectibles (123 S. Market St.; 410-939-1312) Still about the only local place to find hulking stone lions to sit beside the front doorstep, or street lamps to light the way. Less space in this roomy store is given over to architectural antiques than once was the case, but it's still a fine place to find a surprise.

The Photographer's Studio (131 N. Washington St., 410-939-6215) Wonderful used-book shop wherein the proprietor is likely to chat up customers to point out great bargains, including one recently overheard vis-à-vis E.R. Burroughs. Perhaps the only shop in town really worth a visit on its own.

Splendor In Brass (123 S. Market St.; 410-939-1312) Companion store to Investment Antiques, featuring brass beds.

Streets Uniques (2132 Pulaski Hwy.; 410-273-6778; Tues.–Sun.) Multi-dealer flea market means you might find just about anything. Antiques, collectibles.

North East

The Last Yankee Antiques (114 S. Main St.; 410-287-2252) A lighting shop, with custom lighting, shades, and antiques.

Perryville

Jackson Station (Rte. 40 & Jackson Station Rd.; 410-642-6579) Old and new furniture, and a range of collectibles, from dolls to brass.

The Lion at Blythedale (Rte. 222 bet. Rtes. 40 & I-95; 410-378-2287) An uncategorizable selection of antiques.

ANNAPOLIS/WESTERN SHORE

Annapolis

Annapolis Antique Gallery (2009 West St.; 410-266-0635) An emporium of 20 Annapolis-area dealers. Especially noted for furniture, including country, Victorian, and more. Formerly useful items gone decorative, like spinning wheels, and china, glass, silver, and jewelry. Take the Parole exit off Rte. 50, and you're there.

Baldwin & Claude Antiques (47 Maryland Ave; 410-268-1665) Been there for years. Maps, rare prints, books, and other antiques.

Cruets Cruets Cruets (47 Maryland Ave.; 410-263-4607) The name says it all. Also a very nice selection of glass and china, including full sets of Depression glassware.

The House of Orange (29-31 Maryland Ave.; 410-721-1808) One of the larger of Maryland Ave.'s antique shops, with two storefronts loaded with the usual china and household items. In back, though, handypeople will find a room filled with tools that are great fun to pick through, and the cooks among us will have quite a time in the kitchenware section. Catching the angler's eye, however, will be the old lures — includes those fabled poppers we all heard about when Grandpa told fish stories.

Joan's Gems (49 Maryland Ave.; 276-7830) Small shop filled with all kinds of antiques. Linens, china, jewelry.

Maryland Avenue Antiques (82 Maryland Ave.; 410-268-5158) Maryland Avenue's resident eccentric antiques shop, where credit cards are eschewed, but where an endless and mysterious array of antiques and other stuff will delight all browsers.

Pandora's Box Antiques & Collectibles (68 Maryland Ave.; 410-280-9144) Another browsable Maryland Ave. antiques shop, with china and other accessories.

The Ship and Soldier Shop (57 Maryland Ave.; 410-268-1141) Specializes in military miniatures. Appropriate here in the Navy's motherland.

Ron Snyder Antiques (2011 West St.; 410-266-5452) 18th- and 19th-century furniture. Right next to Annapolis Antique Gallery.

Third Millennium Designs (58 Maryland Ave.; 410-267-6428) An "antiques" shop in the "collectibles" sense of the term; a lot of 20th century.

Walnut Leaf Antiques (62 Maryland Ave.; 410-263-4885) Another of the venerable antiques shops on this antiques row — which is fast turning into Interior Design Row. Find a wide variety of lovely glass, china, and porcelains. Open every day.

West Annapolis Antiques & Consignment Shop (14 Annapolis St.; 410-268-8762) Delightful addition to the local antiques scene features a clutter of vintage jewelry (including good selection of costume brooches) dolls, and dressers. Where dealers shop, says co-owner Pat Blaser.

Huntingtown

Bowen's Garage Antique Center (Old Town, Rte. 524; 410-257-3105) Worth a detour off Rte. 2/4 into the old village center. Multi-dealer shop includes everything from a $155 Limoges oyster plate to Prince Albert's empty can. Some nice furniture, particularly oak. Open long weekends.

Southern Maryland Antique Center (Rte. 2/4 S.; 410-257-1677) Look for the red, white, and blue "antiques" flag flying on the highway; the center is in the back of a big cinderblock building. Fifteen shops under one roof sell everything from a 100-year-old walnut dentist's chest (replete with about a million little drawers) to an old framed saying not unlike the ones your grandmother used to hang on the kitchen wall. A dazzling array of glass. Thurs.–Sun.

North Beach

Nice & Fleazy Antiques (7th & Bay Ave.; 410-257-3044) Owner Dale Thomas can likely guide you through the sights of his eclectic little town as easily as through his eclectic three-shops-in-one emporium. Established, fun place. Also includes **Willetta's Antiques**.

Shady Side

Beachcomber Antiques (5560 Shady Side Rd. 410-867-2266) Big cinderblock place well worth a stop. Fewer gorgeous lamps than they once carried, but still a good place to look.

Solomons Island

Barb's Attic (14510 Main St.; 410-326-3720) Country furniture, country house-wares.

Grandmother's Store Antique Center (Dowell Rd., 2 $^1/_2$ miles north of the Thomas Johnson Bridge; 410-326-3366) Big browsable place in the old general store. Also has a smaller space in the **Harmon House** (see "Specialty Shops").

NORTHERN NECK/MIDDLE PENINSULA

Callao, Virginia

Larkins Antiques and Collectibles (Rte. 360, near junction of Rte. 202; 804-529-5916) This shop specializes in buying and selling, but you'll have to catch the proprietors by chance or appointment. Furniture, art, pottery, memorabilia, prints, glassware, lamps, books, china, Depression glass, guns, knives, clocks.

Gloucester, Virginia

In The Rough (Stagecoach Markets, Rte. 17; 804-693-9791) Buy, sell, or trade antiques, guns, and jewelry.

Olde Thyme Treasures (Hayes Plaza Shopping Center, Rte. 17; 804-642-4264) Here's where you can find one item you know you'll probably never find anywhere else: oil lamp replacement parts. Buy, sell, and trade antiques and collectibles. Weekend hours in winter.

The Peacock's Closet, Ltd. (Stagecoach Markets, Rte. 17; 804-694-0276) Nautical antiques and military memorabilia. Many other antiques and treasures.

The Stagecoach Markets and Antique Village (Rte. 17, 9 mi. N. of Yorktown, 1 mi. S. of Gloucester Courthouse; 804-693-3951) Emporium of more than 35 shops selling everything imaginable. Open only on Sat. & Sun.

Irvington, Virginia

Salmagundi (PO Box 401; 804-438-6006) The name refers to an exotically mixed salad, and that's what three partners have compiled here. Antiques include a huge, stunning hand-painted china bowl, while other pieces include whimsical constructions by a New York artist. Also fine gifts. Closed Jan.–Feb.

Hayes, Virginia

Lisburne Lane Antiques (4183 George Washington Memorial Hwy.; 804-642-3460) 18th- and 19th-century American and English furniture.

Kilmarnock, Virginia

Cap'n John's Antiques (Rte. 200; 804-435-6431) Repair, refinishing, and restoring of furniture, and variety of other antiques.

Lancaster, Virginia

Epping Forest Antiques & Gift Shoppe (Rte. 3; 804-462-7960) Carries primitives, sterling, jewelry, Art Deco, and furniture. Focus on shows means shop is real eclectic. Mon.–Sat. 10–5, Sun. noon–5.

Montross, Virginia

The Corner Store (Rtes. 3 & 214, near Stratford Hall; 804-493-8008) A good place to find Depression glass, old chests, or Avon bottles. Also a selection of contemporary ceramic gifts. In winter, switches to Thurs.–Sun. schedule.

Saluda, Virginia

Courthouse Antiques (Rte. 17 S. bypass; 804-758-4861) Antiques, collectibles, and quality antique reproductions.

Urbanna, Virginia

Miss Bettie's Antiques (Cross St.; 804-758-3831) Array of antique items.

Yorktown, Virginia

Swan Tavern Antiques (Main St., 804-898-3033) In an early 18th-century home, featuring, appropriately, 18th-century furniture, mostly English. Affiliated with **Lisburne Lane Antiques** in Hayes.

UPPER EASTERN SHORE

Easton

Foxwell's Antiques & Collectibles (Rte. 50; 410-820-9705) With 75 dealers in one location, you'll find a variety of items at this eminently browsable shop: glassware, china, antique advertising, and more.

Stockley Antiques (Mulberry Hill Farm on US 50 north of Easton; 410-822-9346) Not a store, exactly, but a restoration shop and historic replica furniture maker. There's a barn full of interesting pieces, and they'll custom-build period furniture.

Queenstown

Chesapeake Antique Center (Md. 18 & U.S. 301, behind Chesapeake Outlet Center; 410-827-6640) More than 70 dealers in a large exhibit space that almost entirely adheres to the "100-year rule": if it's not 100 years old or older, it's not sold here. Rules, of course, made to be broken, are excepted here for any 20th-century piece that is distinctly period, such as Art Deco.

Royal Oak

Oak Creek Sales (Rte. 329; 410-745-3193) An eclectic selection of all sorts of antiques and collectibles. This is where you find the figurine salt shaker sitting next to the Depression glass. Across the street, an entire barn is devoted to antique and used furniture.

St. Michaels

Pennywhistle Antiques (410-745-9771; 409 S. Talbot St.) Known for its exceptional collection of decoys, one room after another.

LOWER EASTERN SHORE

Cambridge

Mills Antiques & Used Furniture (Rte. 50; 410-228-9866) A treasure trove, and a habitual stopping point for those who know. Mills Antiques is like the ultimate attic: relics and detritus are piled haphazardly high, and you never know what you'll find. You'll also probably lose track of time while sifting through the aisles, but if the alarm goes off and you need to get going, check with the proprietors. Their sixth sense sees beneath the clutter. A separate book building (see "Books") is on the property.

Salisbury

Henrietta's Attic (205 Maryland Ave.; 410-546-3700, 1-800-546-3744) Collectibles, glassware, china, books, and genealogy materials.

Holly Ridge Antiques (1411 South Salisbury Blvd./U.S. 13); 410-742-4392) Specializing in 18th- and 19th-century furniture and accessories, and this time, a strict adherent to the "100-year rule" (see Chesapeake Antique Center, above). Not even any collectibles. Appraisals available. Closed Mon.

BOOKS

HEAD OF THE BAY

Havre de Grave

Courtyard Book Shop (313 St. John St.; 410-939-5150) Second-hand books to buy, sell, or trade. Quality only. Nice little location in the center of town.

ANNAPOLIS/WESTERN SHORE

Annapolis

Barnes & Noble Bookstores (Annapolis Harbour Center; 410-573-1115) This enormous store is ready-made for browsers; it features terrific children's section. A well-selected stock of Chesapeake area books fills the shelves.

B. Dalton Booksellers (Annapolis Mall; 410-266-6370) A knowledgeable staff and a good selection of local books, national bestsellers, audio books, and posters, calendars, and maps. Large selection of oversize illustrated books.

Briarwood Bookshop & Cards (88 Maryland Ave., 410-268-1440) Good selection of Maryland books. The literature selection, though small, is more adventurous than those found in most Annapolis bookstores. A quiet, handsome store, where conversation about books, the arts, and politics is often overheard.

Insight Concepts (155 Main St.; 410-263-1540; 1-800-935-BOOK) New Age central has moved downtown to the heart of Annapolis's historic district. The store is bigger, and the selection of self-help and spiritual books has grown alongside the wide selection of alternative accouterments. Browsers might overhear a psychic reading being given from behind the wood doors in back, but consider it part of the store's aura.

Mystery Tales (24 Annapolis St.; 410-280-0660) Mystery books and books on tape — even a selection of worn "Hardy Boys" titles that look as frayed as they did when we were kids. Browse while the resident black cat rubs up against your leg.

Step Forth Books & Healing Center (100 Annapolis St.; 410-263-8683) From a small collection of recovery books has grown a promising alternative center, where one can buy drums and aromatherapy oils, or find a good book on women's recovery issues. Owners Karen Mattison and Kathy Freeman bring abundant life experience to their business.

Solomons Island

Lazy Moon Book Shop (14510 Main St.; 410-326-3720) A favored used-book shop. More than 10,000 items, according to the store, and you'll be hard-pressed to argue. Rare and difficult-to-find titles, Thackeray's self-illustrated *Vanity Fair*, and a great nautical section on Chesapeake Bay. Good place to look for those out-of-print Bay books.

NORTHERN NECK/MIDDLE PENINSULA

Kilmarnock, Virginia

The Book Nook (W. Church St.; 804-435-3355) Great selection of Chesapeake Bay and Northern Neck specialty books, as well as all other topics. Gifts, too.

UPPER EASTERN SHORE

Centreville

Corsica Bookshop (101 Commerce St.; 410-758-1453) The Eastern Shore's most intelligently stocked bookstore, well-supplied in the classics, contemporary issues, regional and art books, and children's literature. There's a rare- and used-book section downstairs.

Chestertown

The Compleat Bookseller (301 High St.; 410-778-1480) Formerly a branch of the Corsica Bookshop, this fine store has a range of titles that you won't find in the big discount places.

Easton

The News Center (Talbottown Shopping Center; 410-822-7212) Reliable bookstore with friendly staff. Large paperback selection of everything from Dickens to bodice- and breeches-ripping romances, from cutting-edge contemporary fiction to paramilitary escapist yarns. Extensive horror, sci-fi, and mystery sections. Virtually complete section of regional writings. In addition, the News Center stocks the Shore's largest periodicals selection, with more than 1,000 titles. It's the only place in the area you'll find such publications as the *Village Voice*, *The Economist*, or Eurofashion mags. Even more, all of the above occupies but half the store. The rest is filled with cards and gifts.

Queenstown

Book Warehouse (Rtes. 50 & 301, Chesapeake Village Outlet Center; 410-827-8474) Hardcovers and paperbacks at 50% to 90% below retail. Good history, political science, literature, children's, and contemporary fiction sections, and a decent selection of deep discount coffee-table tomes. Good bargain store with a constantly changing inventory.

Trappe

Unicorn Book Shop (Rte. 50; 410-476-3838) This is an excellent rare and second-hand book shop. Bibliophiles looking for a seasoned but serviceable copy of *Wuthering Heights* or the serious antiquarian seeking the truly rare and precious will love this place. Prices are reasonable, especially when compared to prices at similar shops in an urban area. Owner Jim Dawson knows his stuff.

LOWER EASTERN SHORE

Berlin

Globe Café and Duck Soup Books (12 Broad St.; 410-641-0784) Good selection of Chesapeake region books, as well as cards and marine gift items (and a nice natural foods café, too). In the Old Globe Theater in this renovated little town near Assateague.

Cambridge

Mills Antiques & Used Furniture (U.S. 50; 410-228-9866) See this roadside gem in the "Antiques" section, too. There's also a book barn on the premises that warrants attention, packed and stacked to a dizzying degree. Low prices, unpredictable selection. Not for the claustrophobic. Also not for the person with a book-indifferent companion waiting in the car.

CHILDREN'S

ANNAPOLIS/WESTERN SHORE

Annapolis

Be Beep: A Toy Shop (Riva Rd., Riva; 410-224-4066) A fine selection of quality toys.

Building Blocks: A Children's Book Store (69 Maryland Ave.; 410-268-6848) Crammed with good books, including a selection of regional kids' books, and toys.

Poppets (Annapolis Harbour Center; 410-266-7713) Nice selection of collectible dolls. Array of picture books and unique toys.

UPPER EASTERN SHORE

Easton

Crackerjacks (7 S. Washington St.; 410-822-7716) Thoughtful toy store sells quality games, dolls, children's books, and stuffed animals. Imports.

CLOTHING

ANNAPOLIS/WESTERN SHORE

Annapolis

Elanne (27 Maryland Ave.; 410-263-3300) Excellent service from one of the city's long-lived specialty women's clothing shops. Regulars find the proprietors are willing to call if a favorite line comes in.

Fashnique (181 Main St.; 410-268-6778) Gauze, imports, 100% cotton and rayon clothing for women. Good selection, and the sales aren't bad, either. Lots of fun jewelry.

Ha! It fits! And so it goes at Hats in the Belfry in Annapolis.

David Trozzo

Hats in the Belfry (103 Main St.; 410-269-6670) Something of an impromptu performance space, because everybody has fun trying on hats — and management doesn't mind. Felt hats, straw hats (including genuine Panamas), funky hats, sporty hats, Easter bonnets, hats to garden in.

Hyde Park Annapolis Haberdashery (8 Dock St.; 410-263-0074) Classic men's clothing. Fairly conservative.

Johnson's on the Avenue (Maryland Ave. & State Cir.; 410-263-6390, 269-6390) Johnson's has reportedly made uniforms for Navy officers for decades, and shipped them all over the world. In the window hang traditional houndstooth wools and other classic menswear for civilians. Noted for fine service, they've been known to deliver to good customers in a pinch.

Laurance Clothing (232 Main St.; 410-263-1175) Great tie selection, nice summer clothes, French cuffs on 100% cotton shirts. Very helpful staff. Fine menswear.

The Leader (167 Main St.; 410-263-7507) Fine women's fashions. They even leave a pair of high heels in the dressing room if you're off the boat and browsing in your deck shoes (or off the street and browsing in your sneakers).

Leather and Fur Shoppe (65 Maryland Ave.; 410-263-5884) This shop has been there forever, and offers "fur remodeling," as well as sales of nice leather products.

South Moon Under (Annapolis Harbour Center; 410-224-1140) Breezy summer dresses, outdoor clothes by brands such as Patagonia.

The White House (129 Main St., 410-267-7747) Neat women's shop featuring gorgeous clothes in shades of white — and ecru, cream, and other shades of tawny fawn. Companion shop located in D.C.'s Union Station.

NORTHERN NECK/MIDDLE PENINSULA

Irvington, Virginia

The Dandelion (Rte. 200; 804-438-5194) Tailored women's clothing, near The Tides Inn.

Kilmarnock, Virginia

Jessica's (Rte. 3; 804-435-3125) Accessories and apparel, right in the middle of town.

Mathews, Virginia

Country Casuals (Main St.; 804-725-4050) Men's and women's casual and sports clothes.

Urbanna, Virginia

Cyndy's Bynn (Virginia St.; 804-758-3756) Clothing and gifts.

UPPER EASTERN SHORE

Easton

Rafters (Talbottown Shopping Center; 410-822-2111) Part women's clothing shop and part boutique. Formerly Hess Apparel.
Silk-N-Sanderson (35 N. Harrison St.; 410-822-2645) Upscale women's fashion. Good service; savvy inventory selection.

St. Michaels

Aileen Arader Boutique (201 Talbot St.; 410-745-9735) Tres sophisticated clothing boutique for women.
Bleachers (107 S. Talbot St.; 410-745-5676) Beachy boutique offers colorful, fun clothes for adults and children. Check out the shades.

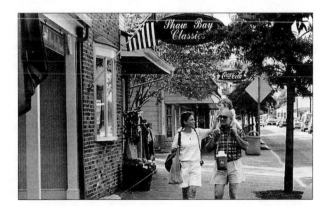

Shopping in St. Michaels.

David Trozzo

Chesapeake Bay Outfitters (100 Talbot St.; 410-745-3107) Sportsclothes, quality imprinted shirts, boat shoes. Clothing for men, women, and children.

Cindy's Ladies (300 Talbot St.; 410-745-9510) Contemporary fashions for plus-size women.

Shaw Bay Classics (208 S. Talbot St.; 410-745-3377) Fine women's clothing, very tasteful and traditional. A good place to find designer shoes.

LOWER EASTERN SHORE

Salisbury

Rafters (Salisbury Mall; 410-742-2111) See Rafters, in Easton, above.

FURNISHINGS AND HOME ACCESSORIES

ANNAPOLIS/WESTERN SHORE

Annapolis

Bishop's Gate (90 Maryland Ave.; 410-269-1740, 301-261-2474) A design piece in itself, this shop also serves as headquarters for an interior design business. Traditional items, reproductions, antique acquisitions.

Robert Row — Oriental Rugs and Carpets (55 Maryland Ave.; 410-626-0025) Antique rugs, tapestry pillows, imported necklaces, and an extremely loyal following. One of the Maryland Avenue stalwarts.

Solomons Island

Fine Things (Avondale Center, 14350 Solomons Island Rd.; 410-326-0546) High-end gifts (hand-painted water decanters, for instance) and home accessories, including mirrors and prints. Custom furniture and all interior decorating services available.

Grannie's Early Americana Gallery (10 Creston Ln.; 410-326-3326) The name describes the inventory; call for winter hours.

UPPER EASTERN SHORE

Denton

The Bartley Collection Ltd. (65 Engerman Ave., Denton Industrial Park; 410-479-4480, 1-800-227-8539) This nationally known company manufactures museum-quality 18th-century furniture reproductions. While its main avenue of business is in mail order kits for woodworking hobbyists, Bartley also sells finished products (for a steeper price), and has a showroom illustrating the quality of its furniture. Also sells a highly regarded line of stains and varnishes and decorative accessories.

St. Michaels

Higgins & Spencer Inc. (902 Talbot St.; 410-822-8256, 745-5192) For more than 50 years, this full-service furniture and carpet dealer has taken care of the Upper Eastern Shore, with pieces by Brown & Jordon, Henredon, Henkel-Harris, Craftique, Fitts Reed, and Kittinger, rugs and carpeting by Karastan, bedding and major-name appliances. They offer upholstering services, draperies made in its own workroom, carpet installation, and even complimentary interior-decorating services by a five-person designing staff.

LOWER EASTERN SHORE

Fruitland

The Unfinished Furniture Warehouse (Business Rte. U.S. 13, S. of Salisbury; 410-749-0889, 1-800-848-9878) Claims to be peninsula's largest selection of pine, oak, maple, and more. 10,000 feet of space. You select the stain or finish, and they'll custom-finish your piece.

Salisbury

Bozman's (503 E. Railroad Ave.; 410-749-5631) Longtime dealer in quality, hand-knotted Oriental rugs.

Classic Oriental Rugs & Imports (118-B N. Division St.; 410-546-3404) Oriental rugs bought, sold, cleaned, repaired, and appraised.

GALLERIES

HEAD OF THE BAY

Havre de Grace

Lloyd's Gallery and Eclections (200 N. Washington St. 410-939-2032) Local artist Valerie Lloyd's whimsical special edition prints of Bay life, like her "Redheads of the Chesapeake" featuring duck decoys, are sold side-by-side with all of the "eclectic collectibles" the owners of Eclections find in their travels among the region's auctions. Eclections, featuring everything from Elvis to Limoges, has two other nearby locations.

ANNAPOLIS/WESTERN SHORE

Annapolis

The Annapolis Pottery (40 State Cir.; 410-268-6153) Recently moved from its long-time but tiny wood-floored shop to far larger quarters right on State Circle. Stoneware pieces of all types; a well-loved local institution.

Aurora Gallery (67 Maryland Ave.; 410-263-9150) Very contemporary design pieces can be found here, along with paintings by local and regional artists, and fine crafts, including mouthblown glass, fiber, pottery, and wood. It's also a nice place to find different jewelry styles.

Baraka Art & Frame (196 Main St.; 410-268-8300) Prints, including a few featuring Navy planes and paraphernalia, and wide selection of frames.

Old-fashioned wood planks creak beneath visitors' feet at Dawson Gallery in Annapolis, where Tom Dawson displays fine works of art.

David Trozzo

Dawson Gallery (44 Maryland Ave.; 410-269-1299) A showcase for 19th-century American and European paintings, and a dealer for the works of Louis Feuchter, an early 20th-century Baltimore painter, whose small scenes of Eastern Shore life and Baltimore's Druid Park Zoo are exquisite. The space looks like galleries of the old school, with simple white walls and a wood-plank floor. Appraisals, frame restoration.

DeMatteis Gallery (209 West St.; 410-267-7860) Contemporary works by regional artists. One of the more experimental galleries in town.

La Petite Galerie (39 Maryland Ave.; 410-268-2425) Paintings from the 19th and 20th century, local artists. Mostly representational, traditional works. Weds.–Sun.

League of Maryland Craftsmen (54 Maryland Ave.; 410-626-1277) Photos, paintings, pottery by Maryland arts and craftspeople — check here for pictorial renderings of such state landmarks as Thomas Point Light. Wonderful wood turnings available here.

Maria's Picture Place (45 Maryland Ave.; 410-263-8282) Prints of Annapolis, the U.S. Naval Academy, and boats. Framing.

Maryland Federation of Art Gallery on the Circle (18 State Cir.; 410-268-4566) Changing exhibitions by members of this art association. Paintings, sculpture, wearable art, and photographs, by the accomplished artist to the Sunday painter. The place to look for a good deal on an undiscovered but talented artist's work. It's a great space in a historic old building, with exposed brick walls.

McBride Gallery (215 Main St.; 410-267-7077, 301-261-2124) Features traditional watercolors and oils by Mid-Atlantic artists. Exhibitions every two months.

Nancy Hammond Editions (64 State Cir.; 410-267-7711) This long-time area artist sells new renderings of old sights, especially for those who have tired of the usual Naval Academy scenes. Right across from the Statehouse.

West Annapolis Gallery (108 Annapolis St.; 410-269-5828) Liz Lind bought out her mother's share of the family business, moved her shop a few doors up, and is working to establish one of only a couple of contemporary galleries in town. A good person to ask about the local scene. Represents D.C. marble sculptor Claire McArdle.

Whitehall Gallery (57 West St., 410-269-6161) Contemporary prints, excellent frame shop.

Galesville

River Gallery, Ltd. (1000 Main St.; 410-867-0954) A gem of a cooperative in an old granary, where artists of varying talent turn out work of varying merit. Those in the market for original pieces will want to check here; some good works hang from time to time at excellent prices. Also, interesting handmade jewelry of clay or other media, prints. Open Fri.–Sun 11–5.

Leonardtown

The North End Gallery (18 Fenwick St.; 301-475-3130) Self-proclaimed as St. Mary;s County's Tiny Oasis of Culture, this artists co-op offers revolving exhibitions, and a range of talent that means you may find a good deal on a nice piece of original art. Open Weds.–Sun.

Prince Frederick

Main Street Gallery (486 Main St., 410-535-3334) A real fun find. Magenta mylar pinwheels whir beside the front porch — not far from the tree with the Mardi Gras beads and chimes. Castoff glass and potters' mistakes jumble along the gravel path. Inside, artists Nancy Collery and Jeff Klapper have turned the first floor of their home into a gallery — down to the art jewelry on the dining room table. Photography constructions, too. Shows regional and national artists. Open long weekends.

Solomons Island

Carmen's Gallery (Avondale Center, 14350 Solomons Island Rd.; 410-326-2549) Watercolors, serigraphs, Chesapeake scenes. Regional artists.

Chesapeake's back roads often yield the unexpected, like these artistic treasures at Main Street Gallery in Prince Frederick.

David Trozzo

West River

West River Artists (5504-B Muddy Creek Rd.; 410-867-1967) A variety of crafts, original art, and some antiques.

NORTHERN NECK/MIDDLE PENINSULA

Burgess, Virginia

Horn Harbor Studio (Rte. 810; 804-453-3728) Mary Lou Hann's original water-color paintings and limited edition prints of Chesapeake Bay and local scenes. Visitors are welcome at the artist's studio/workshop on Horn Harbor Creek.

Irvington, Virginia

Signum Gallery and Fine Line Designs (Rtes. 200 & 646; 804-438-5460) Paintings, pottery, jewelry, framing.

Kilmarnock, Virginia

The Cardinal's Nest (20 Main St., 804-435-1260) Art gallery, fine gifts, custom framing; also has a corner filled with Virginia-related gifts.

Lottsburg, Virginia

Bill Martz Impressions (Star Rte. Box 565; 804-529-7486) Features originals and prints as well as gift items such as notepaper (100 different kinds) and designer T-shirts and sweats by artist Bill Martz. Call for directions.

UPPER EASTERN SHORE

Chester/Kent Island

The Wood Duck Shoppe & Gallery (U.S. 50 & Cox Neck Rd; 410-643-4100) Waterfowl art and carvings.

Chestertown

Bittersweet (239 High St., 410-778-2289) An established antique store you might miss if you're not paying attention. Good variety and quality, and even the locals go here.

Massoni-Sommer Gallery (210 High Street; 410-778-4044) Run by the former owners of the Imperial Hotel next door, and they have retained close ties with the present hotel management. The conference room in the carriage house of the hotel is decorated with works by top Eastern Shore artists and also serves for special shows by the gallery.

Easton

Lu-Ev Framing Shop & Gallery (25-27 E. Dover St.; 410-822-5770) Local originals, and a healthy selection of prints, from Paul McGehee maritime period pieces to waterfowl art. Popular custom-frame shop.

LOWER EASTERN SHORE

Salisbury

The Gallery (Clairmont Shopping Center; 410-742-2880) Regional works in all media. The Gallery regularly holds one-person shows, and has an annual Christmas exhibit featuring four or five local artists. Custom framing and a range of gift items and crafts, such as decoys and shorebirds.

MacMillan Gallery (810 Beaglin Park Dr.; 410-749-2822) Prints and originals by local and nationally known artists. Custom framing.

Salisbury Art & Framing (213 North Blvd.; 410-742-9522) Works by local and nationally known artists depicting everything from Eastern Shore-scapes to the abstract. Prints, pottery, handmade jewelry. Custom framing.

Chincoteague, Virginia

Island Arts (6196 Maddox Blvd.; 804-336-5856) Owned by local artist Nancy West, the shop specializes in woven clothing and unique jewelry offerings. Also featured are Nancy's oil paintings, which have been exhibited nationwide.

Lott's Arts & Things (4281 Main St.; 804-336-5773) Features the silk-screen artistry of Welsh native Hal Lott, known to poster collectors for his works commemorating Pony-Pennings as well as the Island's noted Easter Decoy Festival.

Onley, Virginia

David Trozzo

At Turner Sculpture on the Lower Eastern Shore in Virginia, sculptor David Turner works a chunk of clay into an otter that will later be cast in bronze.

Turner Sculpture (Box 128; 804-787-2818) The drive down Rte. 13 gets a little long through Virginia's Eastern Shore, until you stumble upon this wonderful foundry, where William Turner, a dentist, and his son, David, create great blue herons, beluga whales — even a draft horse. Their wildlife sculpture is displayed throughout the country and, if you're lucky, they'll even show you the foundry where they do their bronze work. Terrific stop.

GIFT SHOPS

HEAD OF THE BAY

Chesapeake City

Maren's (200 Bohemia Ave.; 410-885-2475) Year-round Christmas shop. All sorts of cards, gifts, home accessories, collectibles, nautical items, works by area artisans.

ANNAPOLIS/WESTERN SHORE

Annapolis

Country Finds (103 Annapolis St.; 410-267-9366) Country accessories and antiques, and the most appropriate gift in town for the rootless Navy wife — a plaque that reads "Home is anywhere the Navy sends you."

The Gift Horse (77 Maryland Ave.; 410-263-3737) Countless small crystal pieces are all but hypnotizing. Pewter, figurines, and gifts.

The Manor House (Maryland Ave. at State Cir.; 410-268-0050) An eclectic shop. Stationery, and a hand-painted ceramic ottoman. A fun place to browse.

Sign o' the Whale (99 Main St.; 410-268-2161) Local landmark in historic former customs house. Terrific high-quality gift shop and women's sportswear. Some nice garden items.

NORTHERN NECK/MIDDLE PENINSULA

Irvington, Virginia

Wood-A-Drift Art Shop (Tidewater Dr.; 804-438-6913) Nautical gifts and art of the Chesapeake Bay. Music, either cassettes or compact discs, to suit any taste, from classical to semi-classical to New Age, and a good selection of sea songs.

UPPER EASTERN SHORE

Chestertown

Jenny Designs (103 Northgate Drive; 410-778-3433) Specializing in things ceramic: clocks, mugs, lamps, and more. Custom-made lampshades, too.

Rhodes (241 E. High St., 410-778-6688) High-end gift shop dealing in Spode and Waterford crystal, estate jewelry, Oriental carpets, and lamps.

Easton

Nilsen Gallery (15 N. Harrison St.; 410-820-8818) A fine, high-quality selection of Oriental arts both functional and decorative: ceramics, fabrics, jewelry, furnishings.

LOWER EASTERN SHORE

Crisfield

Rustic Charm (1104 W. Main St.; 410-968-3108) Various gifts with a country-regional flavor, in what claims to be the oldest country gift store on the Shore.

Salisbury

Salisbury Pewter (2611 N. Salisbury Blvd.; 410-546-1188, 800-824-4708) Keeping the metal-worker's craft alive, Salisbury Pewter handcrafts its famed hollow-ware pewter products while you watch. A showroom is here, too.

JEWELRY

ANNAPOLIS/WESTERN SHORE

Annapolis

La Belle Cezanne (117 Main St.; 410-263-1996) One of the best windows to shop in Annapolis. Great estate and other unique items.

Ron George Jewelers (205 Main St., 410-268-3651) Stalwart business near the City Dock features classic ruby, diamond, emerald, gold jewelry.

Tilghman Co. (44 State Cir.; 410-268-7855) The fine old Maryland name of this business tells you that this is a traditional jewelry store featuring classic gold and silver pieces, pearls. Lenox and Lladro, Waterford, and fine sterlingware.

Solomons Island

Solomons Mines (Avondale Center, 14350 Solomons Island Rd.; 410-326-6079) Custom, contemporary designs of gold and gemstones. Where the locals go to get their engagement rings.

UPPER EASTERN SHORE

Chester/Kent Island

Bay Country Jewelry (Rte. 18; 410-643-8040) New and antique jewelry. Appraisals.

Chestertown

Forney's Jewelers (106 S. Cross St.; 410-778-1966) Diamonds, gold, silver, pearls, colored gems, watches, as well as silverware, pewterware, china, brass.

Easton

Oscar Caplan & Sons Inc. (Loyola Federal Building, upstairs; 410-822-1553) They've been in business for almost 90 years; original designs a specialty. Diamond importers, gems, estate jewelry, watches.

Shearer the Jeweler (22 N. Washington St.; 410-822-2279) Diamonds, colored gems, watches, original designs.

Westphal Jewelers (19 N. Harrison St.; 410-822-7774) Diamonds, colored gems, watches, custom designs.

LOWER EASTERN SHORE

Princess Anne

Bailey Jewelers (30400 Mt. Vernon Rd.; 410-651-3073) Retired policeman Jonathan Bailey and his wife, Melissa, became master goldsmiths several years ago, garnered national and international awards for jewelry design, then settled down on the Eastern Shore to create trademark Chesapeake jewelry originals. Their handcrafted Bay-inspired designs include a crab, a skipjack, and an oyster, each rendered in 14- or 18-karat gold.

Salisbury

Kuhn's Jewelers (107 Downtown Plaza; 410-742-3256) Full line of quality jewelry from a company established in 1853.

KITCHENWARE

ANNAPOLIS/WESTERN SHORE

Annapolis

The Gourmet's Cup (104 Annapolis St.; 410-267-6544) Always a pot of gourmet coffee brewing, and a wide selection of coffees, mugs, pots, and other accouterments beloved by the java junkie. Variety of cooking gear, from fancy knives to Vidalia relish.

UPPER EASTERN SHORE

Easton

Rowen's Stationery Inc. (8-10 N. Washington St.; 410-822-2095) Along with all its supplies for the office and the art studio, the venerable Rowen's houses a nice selection of glassware, from tumblers to martini glasses; gourmet cooking supplies, and such things as serving trays with waterfowl scenes, etc.

Talbot Kitchens (31 N. Harrison St., 410-822-8877) Exhaustive range of kitchen accessories. Just the spot to buy that kiwi peeler for the chef who has everything.

MARINE SUPPLY

Also check with marinas (see Chapter Six, *Recreation*) for boat supplies, especially on the Eastern Shore.

HEAD OF THE BAY

Havre de Grace

Tidewater Marina (foot of Bourbon St.; 410-939-0950) Marine books and hardware, inside the marina. Keep going past the big boatyard; you'll find it.

ANNAPOLIS/WESTERN SHORE

Annapolis

Bacon & Assoc., Inc. (116 Legion Ave.; 410-263-4880) Nifty place for used equipment, especially used sails.
Boaters World (Annapolis Harbour Center; 410-266-7766, 301-970-2073) Discount marine supplies.
BOAT-US Marine Center (163 Jennifer Rd.; 410-573-5744) Recommended by sailors.

Find whatever it takes to keep that floating money pit going at Fawcett Boat Supplies in Annapolis.

David Trozzo

Fawcett Boat Supplies, Inc. (110 Compromise St.; 410-267-8681) Right at City Dock, Fawcett's stocks pretty much every boating thing you'll need, like all sizes of oarlocks — not always an easy item to find. A local institution and good source of local boating info. They have discount nautical books, and can find any nautical title you want.
West Marine (111 Hillsmere Dr.; 410-268-0129) Storefront of the big catalog chain service.

Solomons Island

Zahniser Yachting Center (Solomons, look for signs as you enter town on Rte. 2; 410-326-2166) Shop doubles as marine store stocking Ray-Bans to bottom paint, as well as fine women's clothing shop.

UPPER EASTERN SHORE

Stevensville/Kent Island

C& J Marine Discounters (Island Plaza; 410-643-7021)
L & B Marine Supply, Inc. (Thompson Creek Mall; 410-643-3600) Discount marine supply.

SPECIALTY SHOPS

HEAD OF THE BAY

Havre de Grace

Susquehanna Trading Co. (324 N. Union Ave.; 410-939-4252) Decoys are to Havre de Grace what hammocks are to Pawley's Island, and this shop sells an enormous selection of decoys across every price range, including pieces by local son and decoy carving star R. Madison Mitchell.
Top of the Bay (456 Franklin St.; 410-939-2138) Well-known place to hunt for decoys, especially those by Havre de Grace's best-known carvers from the first half of this century. Noon–5 daily.
Vincenti Decoys (353 Pennington Ave.; 410-734-7709) Supplies for the carver, including pre-cast feet, glass eyes, and an array of specialty paints. The owner also has his own carving shop in nearby Churchville.

ANNAPOLIS/WESTERN SHORE

Annapolis

A.L. Goodies (112 Main St.; 410-269-0071) The resident five-and-dime in the ever-more trendy City Dock area. They don't say they're peddling "collectibles" here, but you can still poke around for hours. Racks and racks of greeting cards, brass weathervanes . . . on your way out, don't forget to buy a peanut butter cookie.
Alley Cat (1 Craig St.; 410-267-9518) The dean of the local T-shirt trade. Always dependable.
Annapolis Country Store (53 Maryland Ave., 410-269-6773) The floors still creak in this upscale general store, which calls itself Maryland's oldest and largest wicker shop. Sure enough, there are tons of wicker baskets, trays, and anything else you can imagine. Also, Crabtree & Evelyn and other luxury toiletries, cookie tins, cards, and other gifts.
Annapolis Foundation Welcome Center and Museum Store (77 Main St.; 410-268-5576) Classic children's toys and museum-quality gifts, in a restored 18th-century warehouse, formerly the Maritime Museum.

Art Things (2 Annapolis St.; 410-268-3520) Great art supply shop, where the employees are perennially helpful and cheerful. Paints, brushes, paper, and such hard-to-find items as oversized mailing tubes.

Avoca Handweavers (141-143 Main St.; 410-263-1485) has been doing business in Ireland for decades, and continues to make a splash in the Annapolis historic district. Exquisite handiwork. Wools, cottons, and linens, clothing and other textiles, as well as Irish glass and pottery.

Chadwick's, The British Shoppe, Ltd. (10 Annapolis St.; 410-280-BRIT) Filled with all kinds of imported things British, including many foods, and Woods of Windsor toiletries.

Christmas Spirit (180 Main St.; 410-268-2600) The local holiday store. Includes ornaments and other Christmas items from around the world, as well as other gift selections.

Easy Street (8 Francis St.; 410-263-5556) A really nice fine crafts shop, featuring art glass and jewelry, and whimsical figurines doing things like flossing their brains. A bit different from the rest of the pack.

Enchanted Art (Annapolis Harbour Center on Rte. 2; 410-224-1155) Exceptional selection of Southwest jewelry for those who aren't headed for Santa Fe anytime soon, along with a wide array of Native American and other traditional crafts.

Gallery of Animal Art (1200 West St.; 410-267-7050) Prints and figurines of every imaginable animal or bird.

Irish Centre (105B Annapolis St.; 410-267-9001) The local reporters call down every St. Patrick's Day to find out what's what in this thoroughly Gaelic shoppe.

Merlin Trading Co. (75 Maryland Ave.; 410-263-4601) Fun place where row upon row of small beads fill tables in the back, where those so inclined can string beads to their hearts' content. Has expanded to include some fine crafts, and interesting jewelry, such as amber.

The Nature Co. (134 Main St.; 410-268-3909) PC shop for nature-lovers selling everything from whale posters and whiny, buzzing fly keychains to opal earrings and binocs. Always fun displays.

Pepper's (133 Main St., 410-267-8722, 301-261-1933) Navy T-shirt and sweatshirt central. Wide selection of Navy clothes. (Usually closed for a few weeks in February.)

Pris' Paper Parlor (11 Annapolis St.; 410-268-3011) Long-standing business prints your wedding invitations, and offers a terrific card selection.

Save the Bay Shop (188 Main St.; 410-269-1855) This is where you'll find photographs, books, maps, and discussions about the Bay. It's a tiny shop, but it stocks a lot, and the salesfolk are very knowledgeable.

The Ski Plateau (153 Main St.; 410-267-7705) Outdoorwear, snowboards, ski boot fittings.

The Smoke Shop (56 Maryland Ave.; 410-263-2066) Old-style tobacco shop with a variety of specialty tobaccos and tobacco-smoking paraphernalia, as well as tobacconists who can even take an educated stab at repairing old

Francis Keller weighs out a custom blend of tobacco at the nearly half-century-old Smoke Shop on Maryland Avenue in Annapolis.

David Trozzo

lighters. Spacious, fragrant humidor — and they've been known to let those who ask cart off the leftover cigar boxes, too.

Tiger's Eye (105 Annapolis St.; 410-268-5900) Bright shop, featuring fine jewelry, silk scarves, and such surprises as Chinese "mud men" — thoughtful little sculptures for only $5.

Twilite Zone (8 Fleet St.; 410-267-7222) Great selection of comics to buy, sell, or trade. All the classic heroes. Changing selection of used CDs and audio cassettes, from Jonathan Richman to J.S. Bach. An imaginative place.

Huntingtown

The Wright Touch (3150 Solomons Island Rd., Rte. 4; 410-535-5588) Country gift and furniture shop features such items as scented handmade candles and hand-painted country checkerboards. Right next to **Southern Maryland Antiques**.

Lexington Park

The Elephant's Trunk (Rte. 235; 301-862-1818) 3,000 square feet of international everything. Chinese imports, African and American crafts. Framed prints. A big emporium where people spend hours. Open 7 days.

Solomons

Harmon House (14538 Solomons Island Rd.; 410-326-6848) This four-shop co-op reflects very different tastes. Everything from crab tchotchkes to pottery art bowls by regional artists. A real mix, but seek and ye might find what you're looking for.

Sandpiper Gift Shop (Rte. 2/4; 410-326-3008) Upscale gifts; also has a shop in the lobby of the Holiday Inn.

Solomons Style (14560 Solomons Island Rd.; 410-326-0980) Mostly fancy sweatshirts for women, but some good jewelry and a few other togs.

NORTHERN NECK/MIDDLE PENINSULA

Heathville, Virginia

What's Nu? (Rte. 360, bet. Heathsville & Burgess; 804-580-3706) From the outside, this may look like the old general store it once was. Inside, this shop is both trendy and traditional, a showplace tempting to a variety of shopaholics. Antiques, handcrafted items, lamps, wicker, copper, brass, prints, nautical items, Oriental porcelain, and many more decorating accessories. The best news of all? Most items are below market prices. Buses welcome.

Mathews, Virginia

Sibley's General Store (Main St.; 804-725-5857) An "old-timey country store," where you can find whatever it is you can't find anyplace else.

Urbanna, Virginia

R.S. Bristow Store (Cross & Virginia Sts.; 804-758-2210) Here's an old-fashioned general store that didn't lose its character when new owners took over and modernized. Clothing, household goods, and more.

UPPER EASTERN SHORE

Chestertown

The Yardstick (111 S. Cross Street; 410-778-0049) This complete fabric store is also the place to find a good assortment of yarns and quilting supplies.
Twigs & Teacups (112 South Cross Street; 410-1708) With a collection of unusual gifts and cards, this is the place to find items you have never seen anywhere else. A good spot to pick up something unique for a friend back home.

Easton

American Pennyroyal (5 N. Harrison St.; 410-822-5030) A favorite among lovers of American country folk art. Everything from baskets and pottery to rugs, quilts, and jewelry.
The Cat's Meow (23 Goldsboro St.; 410-820-4220) The promised land for the felinophile: gifts, books, stationery, toys, clothing, jewelry, and supplies for cats and their human charges. Dogs now, too.
Eirinn Arts (21 N. Harrison St.; 410-822-9303) Quality imported Irish sweaters and other Irish items.

Queenstown

The Christmas Goose (US 50 across from Chesapeake Outlet Center; 410-827-5252) Handcrafted Christmas items — nutcrackers, ornaments, and more.

St. Michaels

Albright's St. Michaels (405 S. Talbot St.; 410-745-6388) Specializes in outdoor supplies, especially fly-fishing gear. Look closely and you will see they have a lot of antique decoys for sale, making this a real find for wooden duck seekers.

LOWER EASTERN SHORE

Cambridge

Bay Country Shop (U.S. 50; 410-221-0700) Rustic and goose-oriented Shore items.

Crisfield

Jane's Accents (345 W. Main St.; 410-968-0668) Baldwin brass, pewter, Yankee candles, Rowe Pottery, and Southern Craftsmen furniture.

Salisbury

The Country House (805 E. Main St.; 410-749-1959) This place bills itself as the "largest country store in the East" with the "largest collectible selection on the Shore." With 16,000 square feet filled with colonial-style country accents, pottery, collectibles, kitchenware, and furniture, it's easy to believe owners Mike and Norma Delano's claims.

MALLS AND OUTLETS

HEAD OF THE BAY

Perryville

Perryville Outlet Center (68 Heather Lane; exit 93 off I-95; 410-378-9399) Anne Klein, Sam & Libby Shoe Outlet, Capezio, and more.

ANNAPOLIS/WESTERN SHORE

Annapolis

Annapolis Harbour Center (Rte. 2 & Arist T. Allen Blvd.; 410-266-5857) This place has been packed since the day it opened. Tower Records, Office Depot, Fresh Fields, Starbucks, Barnes & Noble, and many specialty shops.

Annapolis Mall (Rte. 50, Jennifer & Bestgate Rds.; 410-266-5432) Newly renovated, with Nordstrom's to boot! All you'd expect: the Hecht Co., Montgomery Ward, clothing, book, record, shoe, drug, specialty stores.

UPPER EASTERN SHORE

Queenstown

Chesapeake Village Outlet Center (U.S. 50 & 301; 410-827-8699) Relatively new complex of factory-direct stores selling brand-name clothes, shoes, furnishings, and gift items at reduced prices. Stores here include Anne Klein, Bass, Brooks Brothers, Cape Isle Knitters, Geoffrey Beene, Izod, JH Collectibles, Liz Claiborne, Nike, Outer Banks, Van Heusen, VF Factory Outlet (Wrangler, Lee, Jantzen) and lots more. This place is big. Dansk devotees will find that store across the highway.

LOWER EASTERN SHORE

Crisfield

Carvel Hall Factory Outlet (Md. 413; 410-968-0500) Along with the famous Carvel Hall cutlery, there's crystal, silver, pewter, and housewares, and lots of good discount deals.

Salisbury

The Centre at Salisbury (2300 N. Salisbury Blvd.; 410-548-1600) A major mall, foodcourt and all. The anchor department stores are Boscov's, JC Penney, Hecht's, Montgomery Ward and Sears; a ten screen cinema.

Salisbury Mall (Glen Ave.; 410-749-1697) Salisbury's other, older, smaller mall. Peebles, B. Green warehouse food store, and a number of small shops, including antique stores.

CHAPTER EIGHT
The Right Connections
INFORMATION

Maryland State Archives

Plugging in to Annapolis in the good old days.

Anybody who travels likes to know a few rules the locals live by. Herewith, we offer an abbreviated encyclopedia of Bay-related information that will help you move easily through the region. This chapter provides guidance on the following subjects:

AMBULANCE AND EMERGENCY INFORMATION

Maryland

For police, fire, and ambulance emergencies in Maryland, call 911. Drivers with cellular phones can report accidents and other highway emergencies by calling #77 or 911. For additional information, contact the Maryland State Police, 410-486-3101, or 1201 Reisterstown Rd., Pikesville MD 21208.

The U.S. Coast Guard has had to clamp down in recent years on its search and rescue missions, which means you really must face danger to life and limb before they will come out to help. In other words, if you've run out of gas or fetched up on a sandbar, you'll have to settle for a Coast Guard referral to a marine service that takes care of such mishaps for a fee. Still, that does not mean you shouldn't call the Coast Guard if you think you need to:

U.S. Coast Guard Search and Rescue: Baltimore Group, 410-576-2520; Annapolis Station, 410-267-8107

Department of Natural Resources Police Emergency Dispatch: 410-974-3181 or 3186

Other emergency numbers:

Maryland Natural Resources Police, Marine & Inland: 410-267-7740 or 1-800-628-9944

Maryland Poison Center: 1-800-492-2414

Virginia

In Virginia, motorists with cellular phones who encounter highway emergencies may call 911, which serves the entire state.

On the Eastern Shore, 911 from any phone serves police, ambulance, and fire emergencies. In the rural Tidewater regions of the Northern Neck and Middle Peninsula, 911 service can be spotty, so call the local sheriff's office if you need immediate help. The state police in Virginia's Chesapeake region can be contacted by calling 804-424-6800. Write PO Box 1067, Chesapeake VA 23327. To reach the local sheriff, call the following:

Lancaster County Sheriff: 804-462-5111 (911 also works here)
Gloucester County Sheriff: 804-693-3890
Westmoreland County Sheriff: 804-493-8066

Mathews County Sheriff: 804-725-7177
Northumberland County Sheriff: 804-580-5221

As we stated in the Maryland emergency phone number section, the Coast Guard doesn't go out for garden-variety boating ailments, such as gasless boats or the embarrassment of running aground. However, don't hesitate to call if you feel you're in trouble on the water. The Coast Guard has a good record of taking care of folks who need help, even if it's only to make a referral to a commercial marine salvage business:

U.S. Coast Guard Search and Rescue (Hampton Roads Group): 804-483-8567
U.S. Coast Guard (Milford Haven: Smith Point to York River): 804-725-2125

For boating information, or to report environmental hazards, call the **Dept. of Game and Inland Fisheries** in Richmond at 804-367-1000 during weekday business hours.

Other emergency numbers:

Virginia Poison Center: 1-800-552-6337 or 804-828-9123.

AREA CODES

M*aryland*'s Chesapeake region is served by 410, although you may run across code 301 while making your plans. This area code serves the suburbs in the DC metro area, as well as part of the southern Western Shore. *Virginia*'s Bay Country (as well as Richmond and environs) use the 804 area code. In general, the 703 area codes you'll run across in this book serve Virginia numbers in the DC metro area.

BANKS

E lectronic teller system networks are found throughout the Chesapeake region, and you'll probably find the money machine of your choice with no problem. What with all the larger banks buying the smaller banks — and then merging with the competition — ATM services may change. For the latest information, check the most recent phone book and call the bank.

For information from the **1st National Bank of Maryland**, call the bank's main office in Baltimore: 410-347-6000. On the Lower Eastern Shore, contact the bank's Cambridge office at 405 Sunburst Highway (U.S. 50), 410-228-4400. Accepts MOST and Cirrus.

For the location of automatic teller machines operated by **NationsBank** throughout the state, call 1-800-235-8844, 8am to 10pm. Accepts MOST, Cirrus, Plus, MasterCard, and other systems in Maryland and Virginia.

Here are a few other local banks to call for information:

HEAD OF THE BAY

Havre de Grace

First Virginia Bank, Central Maryland: 233 St. Johns St., 410-939-4000
1st National Bank of Maryland: Juanita & Revolution Sts., 410-939-0020

ANNAPOLIS/WESTERN SHORE

Annapolis

Annapolis Bank & Trust Co.: Church Cir., 410-268-3366
Farmers Bank of Maryland: Church Cir., 410-263-2603
Nations Bank: 1713 West St., 410-260-6000
Nations Bank: 2530 Riva Rd., 410-224-4940

NORTHERN NECK/MIDDLE PENINSULA

While some leading banks have branches on the Northern Neck and Middle Peninsula, not all offer electronic banking. If they don't, they'll tell you, often directing customers to the nearest competitor offering electronic services.

Gloucester Point, Virginia

Crestar Bank: U.S. Rte. 17, near Coleman Bridge, 804-642-2141

UPPER EASTERN SHORE

Chestertown

Chestertown Bank of Maryland: High St., 410-778-7520; 410-778-2400

Easton

The Talbot Bank of Easton: 18 Dover St., 410-822-1400
St. Michaels Bank: 104 Marlboro Rd., 410-820-6080

Kent Island

First National Bank of Maryland: Rte. 50 & Dominion Rd., Kent Towne Mkt., Chester, 410-643-6101

LOWER EASTERN SHORE

Cambridge

First National Bank of Maryland: 405 Sunburst Hwy., 410- 228-4400

Salisbury

NationsBank: 1145 S. Salisbury Blvd., 410-742-8651

BIBLIOGRAPHY

BOOKS YOU CAN BUY

Children's Books

Henry, Marguerite. *Misty of Chincoteague*. Rand, 1947. (Many editions and publishers; this is original.)

Blackistone, Mick. *The Day They Left the Bay*. Acropolis, 1988.

Cummings, Priscilla. *Chadwick the Crab*. Tidewater Publishing, 1986. $6.95.

Frye, Harriet. *Look, a Lighthouse! Fact and Fancy* and *What Did They Say to Each
Other?* Little Pebble Press, 1975.

Holland, Jeffrey. *Chessie, The Sea Monster that Ate Annapolis*. Oak Creek Pub.,
1990.

Voigt, Cynthia. *Homecoming*. Fawcett, 1981.

Wolf, Bernard. *Amazing Grace: Smith Island and the Chesapeake Watermen*.
MacMillan, 1986. $14.95.

Cookbooks

Maryland Seafood Cookbooks, I, II, and III. Office of Seafood Marketing Division,
Maryland Dept. of Agriculture.

Kitching, Frances, and Dowell, Susan Stiles. *Mrs. Kitching's Smith Island Cookbook*. Tidewater Publishers, 1981. $9.50.

Fiction

Barth, John. *The Sot-Weed Factor*. Doubleday, 1987. $9.95.

Barth, John. *Tidewater Tales*. Fawcett, 1987. $15.

*Get your questions answered
at the Annapolis and Anne
Arundel Area Visitor Center
on West Street in Annapolis.*

David Trozzo

Michener, James A. *Chesapeake*. Random House, 1978. $6.99.

Styron, William. *A Tidewater Morning: Three Tales from Youth*. Random House, 1993. $17.

History and Lore

Brown, Alexander Crosby. *Steam Packets on the Chesapeake: A History of the Old Bay Line Since 1840*. Cornell Maritime, Tidewater Publishers, 1961.

Brown, Philip L. *The Other Annapolis, 1900-1950*. The Annapolis Publishing Co., 1994.

Brugger, Robert J. *Maryland: A Middle Temperament, 1634-1980*. Johns Hopkins University Press. $32.

Burgess, Robert H. *This Was Chesapeake Bay*. Cornell Maritime Press, 1963. 210 pp., illus., map, index. $25.95

Carr, Lois Green, Morgan, Philip D., and Russo, Jean B. *Colonial Chesapeake Society*. Univ. of N. Carolina, 1988.

DeGast, Robert. *The Lighthouses of the Chesapeake*. Johns Hopkins University Press, 1973.

Dize, Frances W. *Smith Island, Chesapeake Bay*. Tidewater Publishers, 1990. 214 pp., photographs, maps, notes. $22.95

Duda, Mark Damian. *Virginia Wildlife Viewing Guide*. Falcon Press Publishing, 1994.

Freeman, Roland L. *The Arabbers of Baltimore*. Tidewater Publishers, 1989. $19.95.

Keiper, Ronald R. *The Assateague Ponies*. Tidewater Publishers, 1985. Photographs, map, selected references, index. $6.

Lawson, Glen. *The Last Waterman: A True Story*. Crisfield Publishing Company, 1988. $9.95

Middleton, Arthur Pierce. *Tobacco Coast: A Maritime History of Chesapeake Bay in the Colonial Era*. Johns Hopkins University Press, 1984. $15.95.

Shomette, Donald. *Pirates on the Chesapeake: Being a True History of Pirates, Picaroons, and Sea Raiders on Chesapeake Bay, 1610-1807*. Tidewater Publishers, 1985. $18.50.

Travers, Paul J. *The Patapsco, Baltimore's River of History*. Tidewater Publishers, 1990.

Wennersten, John R. *The Oyster Wars of Chesapeake Bay*. Tidewater Publishers, 1981. $13.95.

Whitehead, John Hurt III. *The Watermen of the Chesapeake Bay*. Tidewater Publishers, 1979. 180 color photographs. $29.95.

Natural History and Field Guides

Hedeen, Robert A. *The Oyster: Life and Lore of the Celebrated Bivalve*. Tidewater Publishers, 1986. $16.95.

Horton, Tom. *Bay Country*. Johns Hopkins University Press, 1987.

Horton, Tom. *Turning the Tide: Saving the Chesapeake Bay*. Island Press, 1991.

Kent, Bretton W. *Fossil Sharks of the Chesapeake Bay Region.* Evergreen Rees & Boyer, 1994.

Lawrence, Susannah. *The Audubon Society Field Guide to the Natural Places of the Mid-Atlantic States: Coastal.* Pantheon Books, 1984.

Lippson, Alice J. & Robert L. *Life in the Chesapeake Bay.* Johns Hopkins University Press, 1984. $22.95.

Meanley, Brooke. *Birdlife at Chincoteague and the Virginia Barrier Islands.* Tidewater Publishers, 1981. $7.50.

Sherwood, Arthur W. *Understanding the Chesapeake: A Layman's Guide.* Tidewater Publishers, 1973.

Taylor, John W. *Birds of the Chesapeake Bay.* Johns Hopkins University Press, 1992. Paintings and musings by the author in coffee-table book.

Warner, William W. *Beautiful Swimmers: Watermen, Crabs and the Chesapeake Bay.* Penguin Books, 1976. $10.95.

White, Christopher P. *Chesapeake Bay: A Field Guide.* Tidewater Publishers, 1989. $12.95.

Williams, John Page Jr. *Chesapeake Almanac: Following the Bay through the Seasons.* Tidewater Publishers, 1993.

Photography and Essay

Fleming, Kevin. *Annapolis: The Spirit of the Chesapeake Bay.* Portfolio Press, Ltd., 1988. $37.50.

McWilliams, Jane Wilson, and Patterson, Carol Cushard. *Bay Ridge on the Chesapeake: An Illustrated History.* Brighton Editions, 1986. $26 and $30.

Jander, Anne Hughes. *Crab's Hole: A Family's Story of Tangier Island.* Literary House Press, Washington College, 1994. The story of an urban family who moved to the isolated island in the first half of the century.

Meyer, Eugene L. and Niemeyer, Lucian. *Chesapeake Country.* Abbeville Press, 1990.

Schubel, J.R. *The Living Chesapeake.* Johns Hopkins University Press, 1981. $19.95.

Snediker, Quentin, and Jensen, Ann. *Chesapeake Bay Schooners.* Tidewater Publishers, 1992. $44.95.

Warren, Mame. *Then Again . . . Annapolis, 1900-1965.* Time Exposure, 1990.

Warren, Marion, with Warren, Mame. *Bringing Back the Bay.* Johns Hopkins University Press, 1994.

White, Dan. *Crosscurrents in Quiet Water: Portraits of the Chesapeake.* Taylor Publishing, 1987. $35.

Recreation

Many overview books on sports and hobbies like sailing or fishing have sections that mention the Chesapeake Bay. Browse at your local library or book store.

Barton, Blair. *Best Bike Routes in Maryland: A County by County Guide.* Blair Barton, 1991. $29.95

Chesapeake Bay Magazine, *Guide to Cruising the Chesapeake Bay.* Annually.

Fisher, Alan. *Day Trips in Delmarva.* Rambler Books, Baltimore, 1992. $9.95.

Gillelan, G. Howard. *Gunning for Sea Ducks.* Tidewater Publishers, 1988. $14.95.

Shellenberger, William. *Cruising the Chesapeake: A Gunkholer's Guide.* International Marine Press, 1990.

Walters, Keith. *Chesapeake Stripers.* Aerie House, 1990.

Walters, Keith. *Chesapeake Bugaloo.* Aerie House, 1994. $17.95.

Travel

Anderson, Elizabeth B. *Annapolis: A Walk Through History.* Tidewater Publishers, 1984. $5.95

Meyer, Eugene L. *Maryland Lost and Found: People and Places from Chesapeake to Appalachia.* Johns Hopkins University Press, 1986. $16.95

Morrison, Russell, and Hansen, Robert. *Charting the Chesapeake.* Maryland State Archives, 1990. $25.

Papenfuse, Edward C., et al. *Maryland, A New Guide to the Old Line State.* A 1976 update of the Works Progress Administration writer's project travel guide, *A Guide to the Old Line State,* by the staff of the Maryland State Archives. Johns Hopkins University Press. $10.95 and $19.95.

Wiencek, Henry. *The Smithsonian Guide to Historic America, Virginia and the Capital Region.* Stewart, Tabori & Chang, 1989.

BOOKS YOU CAN BORROW

Barrick, Susan O. *The Chesapeake Bay Bibliography.* Virginia Institute of Marine Science, 1971. Scientific and natural history sources; look for the current volume under various authors.

Barrie, Robert and Barrie, George Jr. *Cruises, Mainly in the Bay of the Chesapeake.* Franklin Press, 1909. Subsequent reissue, 1956.

Bodine, A. Aubrey. *Chesapeake Bay and Tidewater.* Bodine and Assoc., 1954. Classic black-and-white photographs by noted Baltimore *Sunday Sun* photographer. Third edition, 1980.

Brewington, Marion Vernon. *Chesapeake Bay: A Pictorial Maritime History.* Cornell Maritime, 1956.

Burgess, Robert H. *This Was Chesapeake Bay.* Tidewater Publishers, 1963. Compendium of historic accounts of watermen and Bay vessels.

Byron, Gilbert. *Early Exploration of the Chesapeake Bay.* Maryland Historical Society, 1960.

Capper, John, et al. *Chesapeake Waters: Pollution, Public Health, and Public Opinion, 1607-1972.* Originally published by Environmental Protection Agency, contains historic account of Bay pollution. Republished 1983 by Tidewater.

Chapelle, Suzanne Ellery Greene, et al. *Maryland, A History of Its People.* Johns Hopkins University Press, 1986.

Dallam, Edith Stansbury. *St. James's Parish; Old Herring Creeke Parish: A History,*

1663-1799. Vestry of St. James' Parish, 1978. Discusses early Episcopal parishes in Anne Arundel County.

Earle, Swepson. *The Chesapeake Bay Country.* 1923. Reprinted by Weathervane Books, 1983.

Fiske, John. *Old Virginia and her Neighbours.* Houghton, Mifflin, & Co., 1897. Old-style account of founding of Chesapeake colonies.

Gibbons, Boyd. *Wye Island.* Johns Hopkins University Press, 1977. History and natural history of unspoiled island surrounded by Wye River on Maryland's Eastern Shore.

Hildebrand, Samuel F. *Fishes of Chesapeake Bay.* TFH Publications, 1972. Originally published in 1928 by the Govt. Printing Office.

Klingel, Gilbert C. *The Bay.* Tradition, 1966. Natural history essay.

Lippson, Alice Jane. *The Chesapeake Bay in Maryland: An Atlas of Natural Resources.* Johns Hopkins University Press, 1973. Sponsored by University of Maryland.

Metcalf, Paul. *Waters of Potowmack.* North Point Press, 1982. Natural and social history of Bay's most famous tributary, with excerpts from letters and diaries of historical figures, and interesting anecdotes.

Rothrock, Joseph T. *Chesapeake Odysseys: An 1883 Cruise Revisited.* Tidewater Publishers, 1984.

Schubel, J.R. *The Life and Death of the Chesapeake Bay.* University of Maryland. 1986.

Tawes, Leonard S. *Coasting Captain: Journals of Capt. Leonard S. Tawes, relating his career in Atlantic Coastwise Sailing Craft from 1868 to 1922.* Mariner's Museum, 1967.

Wilstach, Paul. *Tidewater Maryland.* The Bobbs-Merrill Co., 1931. Funky classic. Reprinted several times.

CLIMATE AND WEATHER

Chesapeake climate is generally mild, with winter temperatures averaging 40° F and summers averaging 76° F. The average annual rainfall amounts to a generous 43 inches.

But average temperatures tell only part of the story. Proximity to the 3,700-square-mile Bay often brings high humidity during the months of July and August, which can bring furious afternoon and evening thunderstorms in late summer, when daytime temperatures often reach the high 90s. Take these seriously; people have been struck and killed by lightning on and around the Bay. Even on the calmest day boaters **must always** keep an eye on the windward sky (and an ear on the marine weather forecast if possible).

By early September, humidity often has dropped considerably, although 80° days may continue. The average fall temperature is 62°. Sailors love it; a steady breeze blows in the 10- to 15-knot range.

Chesapeake winters tend to be mild — despite accounts of historic Bay freezes — with an average of fewer than 10 inches of snowfall and temperatures in the 30s. Wind chill near the water, however, can make the air seem considerably colder and may even produce dangerous chilling or frostbite.

Regardless of the season, remember that sunlight reflects brilliantly off the water. On the open Bay, rays are magnified by the water's surface, greatly increasing the risk of sunburn and sunstroke. A hat, lip balm, and sunscreen are always recommended. Also, keep in mind that alcoholic beverages are best consumed *after* your voyage. Enforcement of drunken-boater laws can be stringent on the Bay.

To obtain updated weather reports in Maryland, call 410-936-1212. In Virginia, call 804-877-1221 (Newport News) or 804-268-1212 (Richmond). Hotels served by cable television often carry a 24-hour weather channel with local forecasts.

COLLEGES AND UNIVERSITIES

For more information about St. John's College, the U.S. Naval Academy, St. Mary's College, and Washington College, see Chapter Four, *Culture*, "Historic Schools."

St. John's College: Annapolis, 410-263-2371
The U.S. Naval Academy: Annapolis, 410-293-1000
Saint Mary's College of Maryland: Saint Marys City, 301-862-0200
Salisbury State University: Salisbury, 410-543-6000
University of Maryland Eastern Shore: Princess Anne, 410-651-2200
Washington College: Chestertown, 410-778-2800

DAY CARE

Visitors can check with their hotels and innkeepers to find out about local folks who may be willing to take care of youngsters, and Yellow Pages directories list "Child Care" or "Child Day Care." For detailed inquiries about the quality and reliability of a particular program, we recommend that our readers turn to the state regulatory agencies.

In *Maryland*, an advocacy group called the **Maryland Committee for Children** runs a "Locate Line" Monday through Fridays, from 9:30am to 3:30pm, to help parents find dependable child care. Call 410-625-1111. Or call the **Child Care Administration** office at the state Human Resources Dept., 1-800-637-5561.

In *Virginia*, call the state's Dept. of Social Services, Div. of Licensing Programs, 804-692-1787.

ENVIRONMENT

S ave the Bay" is a rallying cry around the Chesapeake Bay, the focus of a massive cleanup effort by state and federal agencies since the late 1970s. If you really want to get into the issue, there's plenty of information. Local libraries often stock scientific studies on the Bay. Or you can contact a few point organizations.

The **Chesapeake Bay Foundation**, with offices in Maryland, Pennsylvania, and Virginia, is a non-profit organization that actively educates the three-state region about a range of Bay-related environmental issues. For more information, call the Annapolis headquarters at 410-268-8816.

The multi-agency umbrella that oversees the government cleanup, the **Chesapeake Bay Program**, also has a hotline. Call 1-800-YOUR-BAY. Finally, try the **Chesapeake Regional Information Service**, or CRIS, at 1-800-662-CRIS. The 24-hour, 7-days-per-week hotline is the place to call for facts and figures on the Bay, or to report an illegal dumping. For those online, contact the CRIS e-mail address, at cris@igc.apc. Sponsored by the Alliance for the Chesapeake Bay.

GUIDED TOURS AND CRUISES

F or information about guided tours and walking tours, see Chapter Four, *Culture*. For information about cruises and water tours, see Chapter Six, *Recreation*, in the "Cruises and Excursion Boats" section under "Boating."

HANDICAPPED SERVICES

B oth Maryland and Virginia, well accustomed to welcoming tourists, put forth significant effort to ensure pleasant and enjoyable visits for wheelchair-bound or other disabled visitors. In _Maryland_, the *Maryland Travel Guide*, published by Maryland's Division of Tourism and Promotion, contains information about services and access for disabled persons. Free copies may be ordered from the **Division of Tourism and Promotion** by calling 410-333-6611 or 1-800-445-4558 ext. 103, Mon.–Fri., 8–5. Ask for the Destination Maryland brochure, which is keyed to indicate handicapped accessibility (it's also available by calling 1-800-543-1036).

In _Virginia_, call the **Division of Tourism** in Richmond for information about services for the disabled: 804-786-4484. Or, for $5, purchase a copy of *The Virginia Travel Guide for the Disabled*, a 300-page directory written by William and

Cheryl Duke, whose son has muscular dystrophy. The Dukes describe every-thing from where people with emphysema can find oxygen to the exact loca-tion of buttons on elevators. Contact The Opening Door, Inc., Route 2, Box 1805, Woodford VA 22580; 804-633-6752.

·HOSPITALS AND HEALTH CARE

S hould a serious health problem arise, you are, fortunately, near some of the nation's top medical facilities. These include the following:

Baltimore, Maryland

The Johns Hopkins Hospital: 600 N. Wolfe St., 410-955-2280 (main emergency); **Johns Hopkins Children's Center:** 410-955-5680 (emergency); **Johns Hopkins Bayview Medical Center:** 4940 Eastern Ave., 410-550-0350 (emergency).

University of Maryland Medical Center University Hospital: Redwood & Greene Sts., 410-328-6722 (adult emergency) or 410-328-6677 (pediatric emergency).

Washington, DC area

The George Washington University Medical Center: 901 23rd St. NW, Wash-ington DC, 202-994-1000; emergency room, 202-994-3211.

Georgetown University Medical Center: 3800 Reservoir Rd. NW, Washington DC, 202-687-2000; emergency services, 202-784-2118.

Washington Adventist Hospital: 7600 Carroll Ave., Takoma Park MD, 301-891-7600 or 301-891-5070 (emergency dept.).

Richmond, Virginia

Medical College of Virginia Hospitals: 401 N. 12th St., 804-828-9000.

Norfolk, Virginia

Children's Hospital of the King's Daughters: 601 Children's Lane, 804-668-7000; emergency room 804-668-7188. Emergency room open 24 hours.

The following local hospitals offer comprehensive medical services. All operate emergency rooms 24 hours a day, 7 days a week, unless otherwise noted.

HEAD OF THE BAY

Union Hospital of Cecil County: 106 Bow St., Elkton, 410-398-4000; emergency room, 410-392-7061.

ANNAPOLIS/WESTERN SHORE

Anne Arundel Medical Center: Franklin & Cathedral Sts., Annapolis, 410-267-1000; emergency, 410-267-1275.
North Arundel Hospital: 301 Hospital Drive, Glen Burnie, 410-787-4000; emergency room 410-787-4565.

NORTHERN NECK/MIDDLE PENINSULA

Riverside Walter Reed Hospital: Highway 17, Gloucester VA, 804-693-8800 or 804-693-8899 (emergency room).
Rappahannock General Hospital: Rte. 1036, Kilmarnock VA, 804-435-8000 or 804-435-8544 (emergency room).

UPPER EASTERN SHORE

Kent & Queen Anne's Hospital, Inc.: 100 Brown St., Chestertown, 410-778-3300; emergencies, ext. 2500.
Memorial Hospital at Easton: 219 South Washington St., Easton, 410-822-1000.

LOWER EASTERN SHORE

Dorchester General Hospital: 300 Byrn St., Cambridge MD, 410-228-5511; emergency room, ext. 360 or 361.
Edward W. McCready Memorial Hospital: Hall Highway, Crisfield MD, 410-968-1200.
Peninsula Regional Medical Center: 100 E. Carroll St., Salisbury MD, 410-546-6400; emergency, 410-543-7101.

LATE NIGHT FOOD AND FUEL

ANNAPOLIS/WESTERN SHORE

Chesapeake Exxon (fuel) Rtes. 50 & 450, Annapolis; 410-266-7475. Open 24 hours.
Chick and Ruth's Delly (food) 165 Main St., Annapolis; 410-269-6737. Open 24 hours. See Chapter Five, *Restaurants,* for more information.

UPPER EASTERN SHORE

Royal Farm Stores (food) 5th & Market Sts., Denton; 410-479-3422. 5am to midnight.
Fast Stop (food and gas) Cordova Road & Rte. 50, Easton; 410-822-3333. Open 24 hours.

Faulkner's Exxon Service Station Rtes. 50 & 331, Easton; 410-822-8219. Open 24 hours.

LOWER EASTERN SHORE

Cambridge Amoco (fuel) Rte. 50, Cambridge; 410-376-3634. 6am to 10pm.
Dunkin Donut (food) Sunburst Highway, Cambridge; 410-228-6197.
Shore Stop (food) 811 Priscilla St., Salisbury; 410-548-3385. 6am to midnight.

Keep an eye out for the Shore Stop stores, which are convenience store–gas stations scattered all along the Delmarva Peninsula — often a welcome sight for weary travelers heading through the sparse lower shore. Among those open 24 hours along the Virginia shore:

Chincoteague, corner of Church and N. Main St.; 804-336-6380.
Accomac, 23135 Lankford Hwy. (Rte. 13); 804-787-3688.
Cape Charles, 22177 Lankford Hwy. (Rte 13); 804-331-4008
Nassowadox, 7410 Lankford Hwy. (Rte. 13); 804-442-5170.

NEWSPAPERS AND MAGAZINES

The Chesapeake's proximity to major cities mean folks deep in Chesapeake Country are as likely to read the *Washington Post* as their local paper. Still, the local papers are filled with information about everything from tides to interesting local festivals. Don't overlook them.

Maryland

Chesapeake Bay Magazine: 1819 Bay Ridge Ave., Annapolis; 410-263-2662. A monthly magazine featuring stories about the Bay, fishing, boating, and other water-related issues.

The (Annapolis) Capital: 2000 Capital Dr., Annapolis; 410-268-5000. The state capital's newspaper covers state politics as well as a variety of local issues affecting the residents of Anne Arundel County. The paper publishes a comprehensive Friday *Entertainment* section focusing on Annapolis-area events. The paper is owned by Capital-Gazette newspapers, which also publishes other papers in the area: the weekly **Crofton News-Crier**, **Bowie Blade-News**, and the nation's oldest newspaper, the biweekly **Maryland Gazette**, which concentrates on northern Anne Arundel County.

Publick Enterprise: PO Box 4520, Annapolis; 410-268-3527. Hefty free news magazine published twice a month; found in shops and banks in downtown Annapolis. Focuses on upcoming cultural events, boating news, and local personalities and history.

New Bay Times: PO Box 358, Deale; 410-867-0304. An eclectic freebie that offers information on entertainment, nature, and other topics of interest to

Bay readers. Look for it around Maryland's Western Shore and Kent Island. Thurs.

The (Easton) Star-Democrat: 29088 Airpark Dr., Airport Industrial Park, Easton; 410-822-1500. Published Mon.–Fri.

The (Salisbury) Daily Times: Times Square, Salisbury; 410-749-7171.

The (Cambridge) Daily Banner: PO Box 580, 1000 Goodwill Ave., Cambridge; 410-228-3131. Published Mon.–Fri.

The (Baltimore) Sun, The Sunday Sun: 501 N. Calvert St., Baltimore; 410-332-6000 or 1-800-829-8000. The recently merged morning *Sun* and *Evening Sun* offers blanket coverage of Maryland as well as a weekly entertainment tabloid on Fri.

Baltimore Afro-American: 2519 N. Charles St., Baltimore. 410-554-8200. Coverage of local events with an emphasis on issues affecting the African-American community. Biweekly, Weds. and Fri.

Washington, DC

The Washington Post: 1150 15th St. NW; 202-334-6000. The nationally-oriented morning daily includes a Friday *Weekend* section focusing on events in and around Washington — and often, on the Bay.

The Washington Times: 3600 New York Ave. NE; 202-636-3000. The morning daily includes a weekly entertainment section that appears on Thurs.

Virginia

The (Gloucester-Mathews) Gazette-Journal: Main St. & Lewis Ave., Gloucester; 804-642-2191 in Gloucester Point; 804-693-3101 in Mathews. A local weekly published Thurs.

The Daily Press: 7505 Warwick Blvd., Newport News; 804-247-4600, 1-800-543-8908.

The Northern Neck News: 5 Court St., Warsaw; 804-333-NEWS, 333-3655 (published Weds.).

The Virginian-Pilot-Ledger-Star: 150 W. Brambleton Ave., Norfolk; 804-446-2000. The major 7-day-a-week paper serving the Tidewater area.

The Richmond Times Dispatch: 333 E. Grace St., Richmond; 804-649-6000. The Virginia capital's morning and evening dailies, published 7 mornings a week.

REAL ESTATE

Affordable land is at a premium in Chesapeake country. During the real estate boom of the '80s, prices were driven up by the increasing popularity of the Bay area among city dwellers willing to commute, as well as new development regulations that restrict building in "critical areas" near the Bay.

Information about buying in the area is available from the many real estate agencies in the region, most of whom offer free listings through area chambers of commerce, and who can offer you access to the multiple listing service, or MLS. For more information, contact the **Maryland Association of Realtors** at 410-841-6080 or 301-261-8290, or the **Virginia Association of Realtors** at 804-264-5033.

RELIGIOUS SERVICES AND ORGANIZATIONS

Some of the nation's most historic churches are located within the Chesapeake region. There's a broad range: Christ Church in Kilmarnock, Virginia, is considered an excellent example of colonial church architecture, while the only Catholic to sign the Declaration of Independence started St. Mary's Parish in Annapolis in 1822. The present-day St. Mary's Church, on Duke of Gloucester Street, is an impressive Gothic building constructed in 1859. But Annapolis began as a Church of England capital for the colony, and St. Anne's Episcopal Church, in Church Circle, was a focus of the town plan in the late 17th century. Wye Episcopal Church, in Wye Mills on the Eastern Shore, dates from 1721.

For a directory of local church services, often the most ready reference is the Saturday edition of local newspapers. Places of worship, of course, also are listed in local telephone directories. Some local inns and hotels also post schedules of worship services for the convenience of guests. In Annapolis, for example, **Loew's Annapolis Hotel** maintains a list of services at the concierge desk; the **Waterfront Marriott** posts services just off the lobby; and **Historic Inns of Annapolis** provides listings on request. On Virginia's Northern Neck, check at the **Tides Inn** on Rte. 3 in Warsaw.

Chesapeake Bay headquarters for three states and the District of Columbia: the Chesapeake Bay Foundation, in Annapolis.

David Trozzo

ROAD SERVICE

For a complete listing of AAA phone numbers for the region, check "Getting Around the Chesapeake Bay Area by Car" in Chapter Two, *Transportation*.

HEAD OF THE BAY

Morgan's Chevron: 218 W. Pulaski Hwy., Elkton; 410-398-1288. 24-hour.

ANNAPOLIS/WESTERN SHORE

Darden's 24-Hour Towing: Annapolis; 410-269-1046, 410-263-9210, 1-800-870-1046.

NORTHERN NECK/MIDDLE PENINSULA

Gloucester Towing: Ark VA; 804-693-4244.
Curtis Texaco Station: Heathsville VA; 804-580-8888.

UPPER EASTERN SHORE

Mullikin's Auto Body, Inc.: Easton; 410-820-8676. 24-hour.

LOWER EASTERN SHORE

Sonny and Dan Towing: Salisbury; 410-749-7712.

TIDES

If you're going for a sail or leaving your crab pot in the water for a few hours, you may want to check the tide. Typical Chesapeake tidefalls are only 1.5 to 2 feet, but it can make a big difference in the Bay's shallow waters. Keep an eye out for extra high tides if a storm is in the forecast. For ready information, check local newspapers, broadcast weather reports, or the monthly *Chesapeake Bay Magazine*. The *New Bay Times* also publishes weekly tides. Information is also available at any marina or tackle shop.

TOURIST INFORMATION

Both Virginia and Maryland offer extensive tourist information services. Tourist information centers are scattered throughout Maryland's Chesapeake region, but are less available in Virginia's Northern Neck and Middle

Peninsula. Your best bets in Virginia are the center next to the Potomac River Bridge on Rte. 301, or in the urban Tidewater area. For more information about the Bay, contact the following:

Maryland Division of Tourism: 410-333-6611 or 1-800-543-1036.

HEAD OF THE BAY

Harford County Tourism Office: 220 South Main St., Bel Air MD 21014; 410-638-3339; Mon.–Fri. 8:30–4:30.

ANNAPOLIS/WESTERN SHORE

Annapolis and Anne Arundel County Conference and Visitors Bureau: 26 West St., Annapolis MD 21401; 410-268-8687, 410-280-0445.
Calvert County Dept. of Economic Development & Tourism: Courthouse, Prince Frederick MD 20678; 1-800-331-9771, 410-535-4583, 301-855-1880.
St. Mary's County Chamber of Commerce: 6260 Leonardtown Rd., Mechanicsville MD 20659; 301-884-5555.

NORTHERN NECK/MIDDLE PENINSULA

Northern Neck Visitor Information Service: Rte. 301, Dahlgren VA 22448; 800-453-6167.
Gloucester Chamber of Commerce: Main St., Gloucester VA 23061; 804-693-2425.
Mathews Chamber of Commerce: PO Box 1126, Mathews VA 23109; 804-725-9029.
The Virginia Division of Tourism: 901 E. Byrd St., Richmond VA 23219; 804-786-4484.

UPPER EASTERN SHORE

Queen Anne's County Visitors Service: 3100 Main St., Grasonville MD 21638; 410-827-4810.
Kent County Chamber of Commerce: 118 N. Cross St., Chestertown MD 21620; 410-778-0416; 9–4 daily.
Caroline County Commissioner's Office: PO Box 207, Denton MD 21629; 410-479-0660.
Talbot County Conference and Visitor's Bureau: PO Box 1366, Easton MD 21601; 410-822-4606; fax 410-822-7922; for St. Michael's, Easton, Oxford, Tilghman.

LOWER EASTERN SHORE

Dorchester Chamber of Commerce: 203 Sunburst Highway, PO Box 205, Cambridge MD 21613; 410-228-3575

Somerset County Tourism Office: Rte. 13, PO Box 243, Princess Anne MD 21853; 410-651-2968; 9–6 daily.

Wicomico County Convention and Visitors Bureau: Civic Center, 500 Glen Ave., Salisbury MD 21801; 410-548-4914.

Chincoteague Chamber of Commerce: PO Box 258, Chincoteague VA 23336; 804-336-6161.

U.S. Fish and Wildlife Service: PO Box 62, Chincoteague VA 23336; 804-336-6122; for information on Chincoteague Island.

Eastern Shore of Virginia Chamber of Commerce: PO Box R, Melfa VA 23410; 804-787-2460.

CHAPTER NINE
Bay Neighbors
BALTIMORE AND
NEARBY ATTRACTIONS

David Trozzo

Baltimore's expansive Inner Harbor, with modern shopping plazas, the historic frigate Constellation, *and more.*

We pride ourselves on knowing the back way through Chesapeake's towns and rural areas, but the Bay boasts cities, too. None is more Chesapeake than Baltimore. We offer herewith an abbreviated, best-of-the-city guide — as well as selected suggestions for additional places to visit in the region.

BALTIMORE

The Chesapeake's major sea-going port for 200 years shed its blue-collar image in the 1980s after undergoing a renaissance that cities nationwide still try to emulate.

The city transformed a decaying waterfront warehouse district into the now-famous **Inner Harbor**, a dizzying array of shops, restaurants, and attractions. A weekend is hardly enough time to catch it all: from the world-class **National Aquarium** (described below) to the **Maryland Science Center**, a hands-on science museum perfect for families with its IMAX Theater, Davis Planetarium, and Hubble Space Telescope Visitor Center (601 Light St.; 24-info line, 410-685-5225 or -5222; open daily; admission fee). Feast on everything from

Maryland crab cakes to the latest Cal-Ital trends at the **Harborplace pavilions,** three malls that also offer dozens of upscale shops.

But there's much more to Charm City, as it's affectionately called, than the Inner Harbor. Tourists who don't realize this miss out on some great opportunities for sightseeing, eating, and shopping.

Baltimore is a city of neighborhoods, whether it's the highbrow **Mount Vernon Place,** the city's cultural heart; **Little Italy,** a charming slice of Italian-Americana with large and small Italian restaurants on every corner; or **Fells Point,** the 18th-century fishing village now known for its boutiques and active night life.

Food lovers must explore the city's public markets. The most famous is **Lexington Market** (400 W. Lexington St.) established circa 1782 with 140 merchants still going strong. You can still find sandwiches here for under $2 and fresh produce at well below supermarket prices. Or, the cheapest cut flowers in town flourish at the **Cross Street Market** (bet. Charles & Light Sts., Federal Hill). Finally, **Broadway Market** (on Broadway, Fells Point) offers fresh gourmet breads. Call 410-837-4636 for general information about these markets.

While you're exploring, take a stroll up **Charles Street,** Baltimore's "Main Street" and home to many shops, galleries, and ethnic eateries. Less than a mile up from the Inner Harbor, picturesque **Mount Vernon Square** shows off landscaped parks and the nation's first monument to George Washington. The physically fit might want to head up the monument's 228 steps for a terrific, 360-degree view of the city.

In the neighborhood, you'll find the **Walters Art Gallery,** with its centuries-old collection, and the **Peabody Institute,** the famed music conservatory. Farther up the street, in Charles Village, look for the **Baltimore Museum of Art,** adjacent to the sprawling main campus of **Johns Hopkins University.**

The lovers of America's pastime also will want to visit the **Babe Ruth Museum,** dedicated to the city's native son. It's at 216 Emory St. (410-727-1539), just "a long slideball from Camden Yards," as one local put it. Camden Yards is, of course, officially called **Oriole Park at Camden Yards,** the city's new, old-fashioned baseball park that's drawn rave reviews from architecture critics and fans alike. It's the most widely sold-out stadium in the country. (For Baltimore Orioles game info: 410-685-9800.)

Easily accessible by Interstate 95 (or I-97 if you're headed north from Annapolis), Baltimore proper is simple to navigate. The city has expansive bus service, but its light rail and subway service are very limited. Sometimes, you just can't get a regular taxicab in Baltimore, but the water taxis that cruise the harbor are a great way to travel the waterfront. They charge as little as $2 for an all-day pass and offer a fabulous view of the city's illuminated skyline.

For more information about Baltimore's sights, contact:

Baltimore Office of Promotion: 200 W. Lombard St., Baltimore MD 21201; 410-752-8632.

Baltimore Area Visitor Center: 300 W. Pratt St., Baltimore MD 21201; 410-837-4636, 1-800-282-6632. Ask for "Baltimore Attractions," an excellent brochure guide.

BALTIMORE'S MAJOR ATTRACTIONS

B&O RAILROAD MUSEUM
410-752-2490.
901 W. Pratt St.
Hours: Daily 10–5.
Admission: $6 adults, $5 seniors, $3 ages 5–12.

The museum is the oldest railroad station in the country and the birthplace of the Baltimore & Ohio Railroad. America's first passenger trains headed west to Ellicott's Mills from here in 1830.

Today, visitors can see over 120 pieces of full-sized railroad equipment as well as displays of railroad artifacts, model trains, and exhibits. Even those who aren't railroad aficionados will likely find themselves awed by the building's Roundhouse. Built in 1884, it measures nearly 240 feet across and 123 feet high. Surrounded by locomotives of the era, it's a crowd pleaser.

BALTIMORE MUSEUM OF ART
410-396-7100.
Art Museum Dr.
Hours: Weds.–Fri. 10–4;
Sat. & Sun. 11–6.
Admission: $5.50 adults, $3.50 seniors & full-time students, $1.50 ages 7–18.

Maryland's oldest and largest art museum has been expanded to include a new wing of modern art. However, the museum's best-known collection is the Cone Collection, artworks collected by two Baltimore sisters who amassed one of the world's great selections of Matisse paintings. The BMA was a major contributor to the Matisse exhibit that caused a New York sensation in the early '90s; enjoy a meal in its restaurant overlooking a sculpture garden.

BALTIMORE ZOO
410-396-7102.
Druid Hill Park.
Hours: 10–4 daily; weekends 10–5:30 Memorial Day–Labor Day.
Admission: $7.50 adults, $4 children 2–15 & adults 62 and older.

The county's favorite children's zoo, open year-round, features such exhibits as the six-acre African Watering Hole, where the rhinos roam, and the Leopard Lair, where a new African leopard lives. Look also for the indoor Chimpanzee Forest.

FORT McHENRY NATIONAL MONUMENT

Marylander Francis Scott Key wrote the words to "The Star Spangled Banner" after watch-

410-962-4290.
End of East Fort Ave.
Hours: Daily 8am–5pm.
Admission: $2 adults, 16 and under free

ing the nation's flag fly high above Fort McHenry during the War of 1812.

Although historians dispute that Key actually saw the flag, there's no doubt that Fort McHenry remains one of the most popular tourist meccas in Baltimore. Situated in the industrial neighborhood of South Baltimore, Fort McHenry's expansive grounds and brick fort and ramparts lie adjacent to the Baltimore Harbor. This peaceful setting provides a perfect picnic spot and a haven for joggers and cyclists. The fort itself allows visitors many opportunities to explore a variety of exhibits. Don't miss the movie in the visitor center. A dramatic retelling of the fort's defense of Baltimore during the British invasion ends with a patriotic surprise.

NATIONAL AQUARIUM IN BALTIMORE
410-576-3800; TTY 410-625-0720.
501 E. Pratt St.
Hours: July & Aug.:
Sun.–Thurs. 9–6; Fri. & Sat. 9–8; otherwise Sat.–Thurs. 10–5, Fri. 10–8.
Admission: $11.50 adults; $9.50 seniors, $7.50 ages 3–11.

The two-toed sloth high in the trees of the Tropical Rainforest and the sharks and dolphins in their watery homes are just a few of the 5,000 creatures to be found at the National Aquarium.

Just as impressive is the Coral Reef. A winding, downward path takes you up close to the huge tank containing the reef, with its sharks, tortoises, and other colorful inhabitants. The Marine Mammal Pavilion features performing dolphins, with shows usually on the hour.

The aquarium's biggest drawback is its crowds. Lines start forming early on the weekends, and the crush of people can make viewing the exhibits rather uncomfortable. Try visiting on Friday nights during the spring and summer, when the aquarium stays open until 8pm.

WALTERS ART GALLERY
410-547-9000
600 N. Charles St.
Hours: Tues.–Sun. 11–5.
Admission: $4 adults, $3 seniors & full-time students, under 18 free.

With a collection of 30,000 pieces spanning three wings, the Walters presents buildings as impressive as the masterpieces they contain. The landmark Italian Renaissance Revival 1904 Gallery building, the four-story 1974 building, and the Hackerman House, a Greek Revival mansion, all sit at the foot of the Washington Monument in historic Mount Vernon Square.

The collections include Fabergé eggs; Oriental porcelains; Egyptian, Greek and Roman pieces; and 19th-century artworks, including paintings by Monet, Delacroix, and Pisarro.

BALTIMORE LODGINGS

With the growth of Baltimore's tourist trade has come a wealth of lodgings. Here are a few of our favorites.

THE ADMIRAL FELL INN
410-522-7377.
888 S. Broadway; Market
Square at Thames St.
Price: Very Expensive.
Credit Cards: AE, D, DC,
MC, V.

Fells Point, Baltimore's original port, maintains much of its 18th-century charm, with its Belgian-brick streets, tugboats, salty taverns, and red brick homes.

The Admiral Fell Inn has become one of its most popular landmarks, known for its formal restaurant as well as its hotel. That popularity propelled the owners to expand from 37 rooms to 80 rooms in 1995.

Staying at the Admiral Fell puts you right in the center of all the action of Fells Point, where weekends can get hectic after dark. But by day, shoppers can delight in everything from upscale art galleries to chic boutiques and punk rock stores.

Even though the inn is within yards of dozens of local restaurants and bars, guests may find they don't want to leave. The Admiral Fell offers an English pub, a casual restaurant called The Point, and its Admiral Fell Inn restaurant, where — what else? — Maryland crab cakes top the menu.

**A HOUSE BY THE SIDE
OF THE ROAD**
410-539-0652.
134 Birckhead St.; off
William St. S. of Federal
Hill.
Price: Expensive.
Credit Cards: None.

Its name evokes images of winding country roads and wraparound porches. But Susan Belisle's two-story brick rowhouse sits seven blocks past Baltimore's Inner Harbor, just on the outskirts of historic Federal Hill.

This isn't an ordinary bed & breakfast. Belisle rents the entire house, which includes two bedrooms and one bath. Situated on a quiet, tiny street, the house is decorated in a bright and sort of frilly Victorian-meets-country style. Light blue and peach colored walls, tulle and lace curtains, along with dried and fresh flowers, accent each room.

The real draw, however, is the French canopy wedding bed, with its lace and pearls woven through the arches above a queen-sized bed. You get your choice: down or regular pillows. And Belisle has been known to spread fresh flowers across the bed for her visiting brides and grooms. When honeymooners are hungry, they can have their gingerbread pancakes in bed, downstairs, or out on the secluded patio.

**INN AT GOVERNMENT
HOUSE**
410-539-0566.

This 1800s-era mansion in the picturesque Mount Vernon neighborhood captures the feel-

1125-1129 N. Calvert St.;
13 blocks N. of Inner
Harbor.
Price: Expensive.
Credit Cards: AE, DC, MC,
V.

ing of what it must have been like to be rich and successful in Victorian Baltimore.

Everything at the inn — from its 1897 Louis Prague lithographs adorning the hallways to its 10-foot mahogany dining room table — is authentic. A former hostess's ghost is even said to haunt the mansion.

But the five-story townhouse also offers guests the luxury and comfort of a modern hotel. The 20 bedrooms each come with their own baths and their own identities. Sun lovers might enjoy "the room with the big windows," replete with seven windows lining nearly half of this room on the building's turret.

Downstairs, guests are free to make themselves at home in the formal living room, library, or dining room. It might even be worthwhile to ask for an informal tour of the mansion's many treasures, which include its original lead glass and stained glass, numerous bronze statues, and the chandelier made of armor.

Full breakfasts are offered each morning; wine is brought to your room each afternoon.

MR. MOLE BED & BREAKFAST
410-728-1179.
1601 Bolton St.
Price: Expensive.
Credit Cards: AE, D, MC,
V.

Mr. Mole carries the distinction of being the only lodging establishment in Baltimore to win the Mobile Travel Guide's 1995 four-star rating. It's easy to see why.

Elegantly decorated in English country fashion, this 1870s townhouse in the historic, tree-lined neighborhood of Bolton Hill boasts 14-foot ceilings, marble fireplaces, and scores of 18th- and 19th-century antiques.

Each of the five suites has its own style and name. Owners Paul Bragaw and Collin Clarke try to match up their guests with the rooms.

The Garden Suite, a favorite among newlyweds for its bright sun room and floral decor, includes a queen-sized bed and a sitting area. The Print Room, with both a queen and full-sized bed, stands out for its immense size and the understated formality of gray and white paint and 18th-century silhouettes and engravings.

The Explorer Suite seems almost out of place, with its leopard skin bed coverings, African masks, and zebra skin rug. But it might be perfect for someone tired of tried-and-true Laura Ashley prints.

All of the rooms include spacious and sparkling clean white bathrooms. Hairdryers, Caswell-Massey toiletries, and thick terry robes are available in each. A Danish buffet breakfast of sliced meats, cheeses, fresh fruit, and homemade baked goods is served each morning.

**UNION SQUARE HOUSE
BED & BREAKFAST**
410-233-9064.
23 S. Stricker St.
Price: Moderate to
  Expensive.
Credit Cards: AE, D, MC,
  V.

It's Christmas all year at the Union Square House, a Victorian Italianate home on the city's "Millionaires' Row" where the city's wealthy railroad families lived in the 19th century. Nowadays, the nearby neighborhoods are a bit rough. But Union Square, and its namesake park, have been renovated to much of their original splendor. The bed & breakfast is within walking distance of Hollins Market, one of the city's historic fresh food markets, as well as Oriole Park at Camden Yards.

Period furnishings and a formal living room adorned with original plaster moldings and woodwork highlight Claire and Joe Debes's B&B. A huge Christmas tree standing next to the bay window is decorated according to the season: pumpkin lights at Halloween, bunnies for Easter and, of course, ornaments at Christmas.

If bed size is a consideration, be forewarned that these are antiques — and the biggest size is always full-sized. There are three rooms with private baths although only one adjoins its accompanying bedroom. However, privacy is assured in the other two because guests are given keys to "their" bathrooms.

Following is a selection of hotels in Baltimore:

Doubletree Inn at the Colonnade: 410-235-5400; 4 W. University Pkwy.
Harbor Court Hotel: 410-234-0550; 550 Light St.
Henderson's Wharf Inn: 410-522-7777; 1000 Fell St.
Stouffer Renaissance Hotel: 410-547-1200; 202 E. Pratt St.
Hyatt Regency Baltimore: 410-528-1234; 300 Light St.

With the Baltimore skyline in the background, Oriole Park at Camden Yards supplies one of the country's best places to take in a ballgame. With your favorite beverage, of course.

David Trozzo

BALTIMORE RESTAURANTS

**BANJARA
RESTAURANT**
410-962-1554.
1017 S. Charles St.
Open: Daily.
Price: Inexpensive to
   Moderate.
Cuisine: Indian.
Serving: L, D.
Credit Cards: All major
   accepted.
Reservations: Accepted.

Black-tie waiters open doors for shorts-clad patrons at this attractive, authentic Indian eatery, where midweek rarely finds empty dinner tables and weekends folks willingly stand in lines. That's saying something in Federal Hill, where lots of popular restaurants serve lots of different cuisines, all drawing their share of customers.

Start with a bowl of mulligatawny, a lentil and tomato broth spiced slightly with mustard seed. Vegetable pakora also makes a nice starter if you like crispy chunks of cauliflower, spinach, and potato deep-fried in a light chick-pea batter.

Chicken tikka masala — grilled boneless chunks of chicken sautéed in a tangy sauce, is among the most popular dishes here, although we also recommend grilled salmon prepared with yogurt, lemon juice, cumin, and green chili. It's cooked over charcoal.

Vegetarians find plenty to choose from on Banjara's reasonably priced menu, and servers aren't bashful about making recommendations. If spicy Indian cuisine is virgin territory to you, don't feel intimidated. Specify spice levels from mild to excessive, and cool your tongue with iced tea or Indian beer.

DONNA'S AT THE BMA
410-467-3600.
10 Art Museum Dr.
Open: Daily.
Price: Moderate.
Cuisine: Californian-Italian.
Serving: L, D, SB.
Credit Cards: AE, DC, MC,
   V.
Reservations: Accepted at
   dinner, or for parties
   over five at lunch and
   Sunday brunch.

Donna's is quickly becoming a household name in Baltimore, so maybe it's no wonder they took over the cafe at the Baltimore Museum of Art. This one, like other locations, has that easily recognizable Donna's decor of black and metal accents. But this restaurant offers something the others don't: a view of the museum's sculpture garden and bragging rights to being in the same building with the great works of Matisse, Rodin, and Picasso.

Former *Baltimore Sun* design director Donna Crivello, partner in the business and mastermind behind the food, insists that what comes from her kitchen is fresh, not too fussed over, and not heavily masked in sauces.

Salads start as simply as mixed greens tossed with a balsamic vinaigrette, and run up to more complex concoctions like poached pears, gorgonzola, and walnuts. And by now, Donna's roasted vegetables of eggplant, red peppers, artichoke hearts, onions, and potatoes are nearly famous. Try them on focaccia at lunch. Other entrées center around fish or meat, such as a lean breast of duck touched with a sweet sauce of brandied fig, apple, and raisin, as are the accompanying risotto pancakes. Braciola may appeal to heartier appetites. Served with a red pepper garlic sauce, the thin beef slices hug goat cheese and spinach.

GERMANO'S TRATTORIA
410-752-4515.
300 High St.
Open: Daily.
Price: Moderate to Expensive.
Cuisine: Italian, specializing in Tuscan.
Serving: L, D.
Credit Cards: AE, CB, D, DC, MC, V.
Reservations: Recommended.

Mention Germano's Trattoria to some folks, and they'll go on about a tomato or vegetable soup served in a boule of crusty bread. Then they'll go on about it again.

This two-story restaurant is one of the great reasons to come to Little Italy — as if you needed any more excuses to venture to this part of town. Follow burgundy-carpeted stairs upstairs and curve around through one dining room into another. Large windows give the room a surprisingly airy feeling, despite dark walls.

Mussels get a high rating here and are available in appetizer and entrée form. The same goes for pastas. From the 10 first-course pastas offered, we chose ravioli stuffed with ricotta and spinach in walnut sauce, and angel hair tossed with fresh tomatoes, garlic, oil, and herbs. Each can be ordered as appetizers or side dishes for half the price plus $2. But the menu doesn't stop there. Choose from a variety of fish, seafood, and veal. Save room for dessert, though. Chocolate lovers should order the marengo cioccolato. This combination of rich chocolate and light meringue is an achievement few can claim.

Valet parking is offered.

SPIKE & CHARLIE'S RESTAURANT & WINE BAR
410-752-8144.
1225 Cathedral St.
Open: Tues.–Sun.
Serving: L (except Sat.), D, SB.
Price: Moderate to Expensive.
Cuisine: Contemporary American.
Credit Cards: AE, D, DC, MC, V.
Reservations: Highly recommended.

Smack in the midst of Baltimore's "Cultural Center," Spike & Charlie's has become a popular dining spot for the pre- and post-theater crowd, who pack this trendy Art Deco restaurant on performance nights. The owners call their cuisine "progressive American," but we call it some of Baltimore's most imaginative food — served alongside a varied and affordable wine selection.

The menu changes every few weeks, and the chef adapts seasonal fruits and vegetables to the dishes of the moment. Take, for instance, Vidalia onion season. Those sweet Georgia onions made it into two early summer dishes, including one of the gourmet pizzas.

We sampled Vidalia onion soup with fennel-seed croutons, a lighter and definitely less gooey version of the standard French onion soup. Then the creative kitchen sent a seared tuna steak laid over black olive pasta and mixed with salt-preserved lemons and oven-cured tomatoes. The tuna was perfectly cooked; the pasta a flawless al dente. And Spike & Charlie's doesn't skimp. After savoring lots of big, fat shrimp in the sautéed shrimp and sugar snap peas, red pepper pesto, and green onion trenette, only one question remained. Was there room for some of the prettiest and tastiest desserts in town? Homemade chocolate chip mint ice cream arrived between thin chocolate cookie layers sat on a dish drizzled with orange sauce. It looked almost too beautiful to eat — but we forced ourselves. Touché!

HISTORIC TRIANGLE: WILLIAMSBURG, JAMESTOWN, AND YORKTOWN

Perhaps all Americans should visit **Colonial Williamsburg**, in Virginia, a living-history town that for the price of admission for a day truly will send you back in time. In all, 88 original buildings still stand among the village of 500 structures, all sited accurately with the help of archaeologists. Along Duke of Gloucester Street stand the restored homes and workshops of the 18th and early 19th century.

Restored in 1926 with the aid of John D. Rockefeller, Jr., Williamsburg originally was established as Virginia's capital in 1699. In 1780, the capital was moved to Richmond. Now you can see everything from the Governor's Palace to four nearby museums (including one of the gorgeous James River plantations), and don't forget to stop in at a tavern for a tankard of ale.

Williamsburg is a great place in any season, with fireplace woodsmoke and bayberry candle aromas filling the winter air, and dogwood, daffodils, and lilacs in spring. Also, the formal English gardens, restored to period symmetry, will keep the kids busy; don't miss the maze. People in period costumes are everywhere, and if they're not demonstrating the fine art of smithing, they may be part of a fife-and-drum exhibition.

With a huge variety of restaurants (gourmets: dine at The Trellis in town) and lodging opportunities, Williamsburg is midway between Richmond and Norfolk off I-64. Ticket costs range from about $15 for children to $30 for adults, with a wide variety of packages available. There's also a shuttle to help you get around. Call 1-800-HISTORY.

Only a few miles away is the **Jamestown Settlement**, which combines indoor gallery exhibits and outdoor living history to tell the story of the early English colonists who came here in 1607. Along the river banks of the settlement are docked full-size replicas of the *Susan Constant, Godspeed,* and *Discovery* that brought the early colonists. Onboard, sailors in colonial dress describe the four-month voyage from England. There's also a fort and an Indian village. The Jamestown Settlement is just off Rte. 31, six miles from Williamsburg, and can also be reached via the Colonial Parkway. The museum is open 9–5, except Christmas and New Year's Day. Seasonal restaurant, gift shop. Call 804-253-4838.

Former President George Bush helped reopen the new and $3.9-million-worth-of-improved **Yorktown Victory Center** not so long ago, an enterprise drawing rave reviews for nearly 1,000 different artifacts from the Revolutionary War. The museum offers a re-created history of the era, down to the life of the ordinary man. Costumed interpreters help tell the tale. Call 804-253-4838. Nearby **Yorktown Battlefield** is the site of the last, climactic battle that ended the Revolutionary War.

Also in the Historic Triangle region are the **Busch Gardens** theme park, the daunting bargainland at the **Williamsburg Pottery Factory**, and much, much more. The area's tourism trade is well served by an excellent publicity/customer service machine, and questions can be directed to the Williamsburg Area Convention & Visitor's Bureau, PO Box 3585, Williamsburg, VA 23187; 804-253-0192.

URBAN VIRGINIA TIDEWATER: HAMPTON, NORFOLK, NEWPORT NEWS

Virginia's Tidewater region officially includes the entire tidal shoreline of the Bay and its tributaries, from the Norfolk area to Maryland. If, however, you were to ask a Virginian down on the Northern Neck about the Tidewater, he or she would send you south. Tidewater, to those folks, has come to mean the urban part of the Bay, which we address here.

Here the Chesapeake Bay meets its final tributary, the James River, and joins waters with the Atlantic Ocean. The naturally secure harbors have drawn not only commercial vessels, but much of the U.S. Navy. A variety of cruises and harbor tours ply these waters between **Hampton**, **Newport News**, and **Norfolk**, including some on 19th-century-style schooners and riverboats.

One particularly interesting Bay-related attraction is the **Mariners Museum** (100 Museum Dr., Newport News; 804-596-2222). Herein see perhaps the finest display of model ships you're ever likely to view, showcased in a dramatic black room with spotlighted cases and magnifiers that show the detailing of the miniature vessels. This was a lifetime project by artist August F. Crabtree. Several other galleries, including the Chesapeake Bay Gallery, are also here.

New in nearby Norfolk is **NAUTICUS, the National Maritime Center** (804-664-1007) on the city's waterfront. Aquariums and interactive simulators let visitors check out life beneath the sea or on a naval battleship. Art lovers in Norfolk will want to see the **Chrysler Museum** (245 West Olney Rd.; 804-664-6200; 804-622-ARTS) with its terrific collection that includes gorgeous Tiffany pieces in the glass collection, and French and Italian paintings.

For more information, contact the Newport News Tourism Development Office (1-800-333-7787) and the Norfolk Convention and Visitors Bureau (1-800-368-3097).

WASHINGTON, DC

Highlights for a visit to The Nation's Capital, about 50 miles west of Annapolis on the tidal Potomac River, include the **Kennedy Center for the Performing Arts**; the **Lincoln, Washington, and Jefferson Memorials**; and the **Capitol** and the **Mall**, along which are the many museums of the **Smithsonian Institution**. Many of the museums, galleries, and other cultural or historical sites are free. For more information about what to see and do in DC, contact the Convention and Visitor Information Center, 202-789-7000; 1450 Pennsylvania Avenue NW, Washington DC 20004.

IF TIME IS SHORT

G iven the summer-country/winter-city yin and yang of Chesapeake life — particularly in Maryland, where all but the deepest of low-land Dorchester dwellers can get to Annapolis for a day — we offer here-with a seasonal tasting of the region's best.

In summer, there's no choice about the mainstay of how you'll spend your day. You'll spend it on the water. We suggest a day of fishing aboard a boat chartered out of **Harrison's Sport Fishing Center** on _Tilghman Island_. They've been renting boats forever over there, know the local captains — and know where the fish are schooling. No reason not to come home with your full complement of rockfish. After you return to shore, swing by **Dogwood Harbor** to see the famed sailing skipjacks, moored there until the oyster season starts in fall. Then take a scenic, 21-mile drive en route to dinner: go back up through _St. Michaels_ (stop if the **Chesapeake Maritime Museum** is still open), and branch off to the right through _Royal Oak_ to _Bellevue_. Catch the famed **Oxford-Bellevue Ferry** across the Tred Avon River to _Oxford_, where you'll join the cruising sailor set at the historic Robert Morris Inn. Order crab cakes, and strawberry pie in summer.

As the days cool down, we think of poking around the three-centuries-old streets of _Annapolis_. Stop by the historic **Maryland Statehouse**, and learn about the signing of the Treaty of Paris there. Amble across **State Circle** to **Maryland Avenue**, and snoop amongst the high-end designer and antique shops as the foliage fades to autumn. At the **Naval Academy** two blocks over, see the chapel — and don't forget to go downstairs and view John Paul Jones's magnificent tomb. Then stroll down toward **City Dock** via **Prince George Street**, examining three centuries' worth of architecture along the way. The ambitious might want to learn more; **Historic Annapolis, Inc.'s** recorded walking tour — narrated by Walter Cronkite himself — can be rented for a small fee at the **Annapolis Foundation Welcome Center and Museum Store** at the foot of Main St. by City Dock. Or, take one of **Chesapeake Marine Tours** excursion boats from City Dock out to Annapolis Roads — a journey that may inspire you to charter a sailboat from one of the venerable local sailing schools, like **Annapolis Sailing School**.

If it's lunch or dinnertime, try either tiny little **Joss Café and Sushi Bar** (195 Main St.), or cross Spa Creek to **Café La Mouffe** on Bay Ridge Ave.

→

in **_Eastport_**. (We suggest you drive at night; during the day, why not catch a water taxi?)

When spring warmth begins to chase winter away, it's time for a dose of ocean. No place could be finer than **_Assateague Island_**, also known as **Assateague National Seashore**. Pack your binoculars, pull on your hiking boots, and head off down 13 miles of beach. Keep an eye out for the wild ponies, who shouldn't bother you if you don't bother them. Assateague National Seashore rents canoes seasonally; you should be able to head out into Sinepuxent Bay come mid-April. Hard-core birders will want to drive over to Virginia, to **_Chincoteague_** (same island; different management), generally considered the better birding spot of the two.

Index

LODGING BY PRICE CODE

Inexpensive: Up to $55
Moderate: $56 to $85
Expensive: $86 to $125
Very Expensive: $126 and above

HEAD OF THE BAY

Inexpensive
Comfort Inn

Inexpensive–Moderate
Super 8

Moderate–Expensive
Spencer-Silver Mansion
Vandiver Inn

Moderate to Very Expensive
Inn at the Canal

ANNAPOLIS/WESTERN SHORE

Inexpensive
Days Inn, Lexington Park

Inexpensive–Moderate
Howard Johnson's Lodge
Patuxent Inn

Inexpensive–Very Expensive
Back Creek Inn B&B

Moderate
Magnolia House

Moderate–Expensive
Ark and Dove
By-the-Bay B&B

Chez Amis
Comfort Inn, Solomons
The Corner Cupboard Inn
Courtyard by Marriott
The Doll's House B&B
Gibson's Lodgings
Holiday Inn, Annapolis
Holiday Inn, Solomons
Jonas Green House
Prince George Inn B&B

Moderate–Very Expensive
The William Page Inn

Expensive
American Heritage B&B
Chesapeake Bay Lighthouse B&B

Expensive–Very Expensive
Annapolis Marriott Waterfront
Flag House Inn
Harborview Boat & Breakfast
Historic Inns of Annapolis
Lowes Annapolis Hotel
Reynold's Tavern
Wyndham Garden Hotel

Variable by Length of Stay
Residence Inn by Marriott

NORTHERN NECK/MIDDLE PENINSULA

Inexpensive
Whispering Pines Motel

Inexpensive–Moderate
Bay Motel
Dockside Inn

RESTAURANTS BY PRICE CODE

RESTAURANTS BY CUISINE

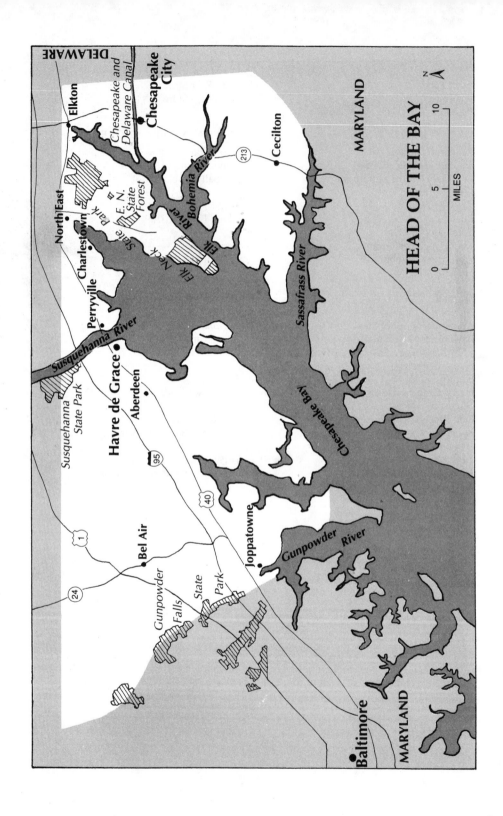

HEAD OF THE BAY

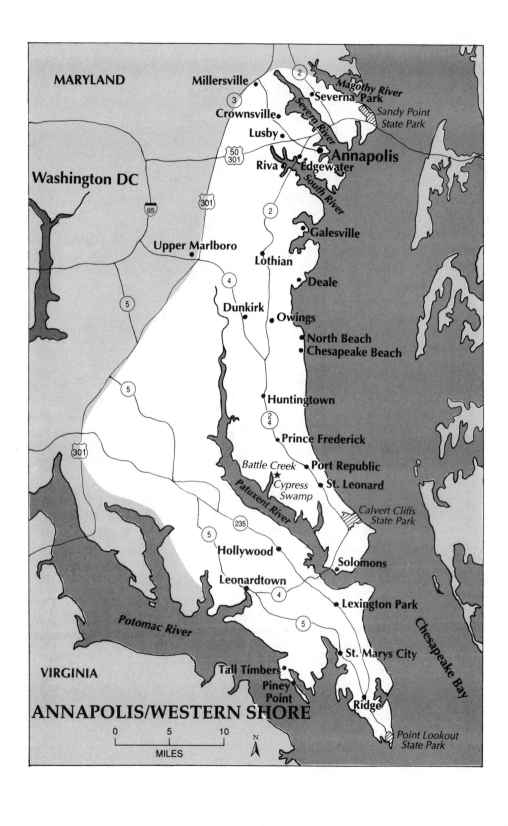

MARYLAND

Millersville

3

Crownsville

Magothy River

Severna Park

2

Severn River

Sandy Point State Park

Lusby

50 301

Annapolis

Riva

Edgewater

South River

Washington DC

95

301

2

Galesville

Upper Marlboro

Lothian

4

Deale

5

Dunkirk

Owings

North Beach

Chesapeake Beach

5

Huntingtown

2 4

Prince Frederick

301

Battle Creek

Port Republic

Cypress Swamp

St. Leonard

Patuxent River

Calvert Cliffs State Park

235

5

Hollywood

Solomons

Leonardtown

4

Lexington Park

Potomac River

5

St. Marys City

Chesapeake Bay

VIRGINIA

Tall Timbers

Piney Point

Ridge

ANNAPOLIS/WESTERN SHORE

Point Lookout State Park

0   5   10

MILES

N

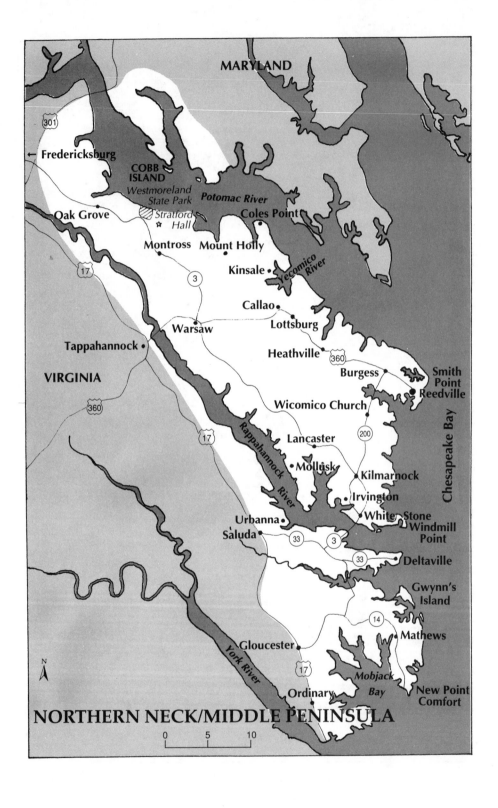

NORTHERN NECK/MIDDLE PENINSULA

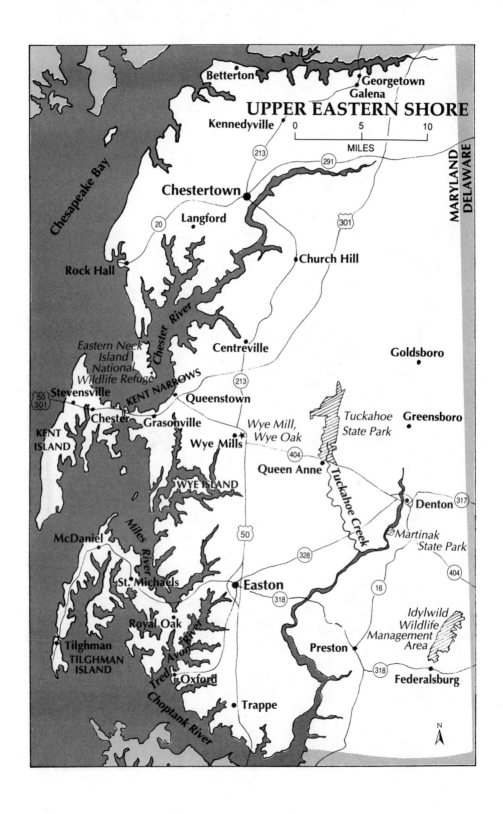

UPPER EASTERN SHORE

Betterton
Georgetown
Galena
Kennedyville
0   5   10
MILES

213

291

Chesapeake Bay

Chestertown
20
Langford

301

Church Hill

Rock Hall

Chester River

Goldsboro

Eastern Neck
Island
National
Wildlife Refuge

KENT NARROWS

Centreville

213

Tuckahoe
State Park

Greensboro

50
301
Stevensville

Queenstown

Chester   Grasonville

KENT
ISLAND

Wye Mill,
Wye Oak

Wye Mills

404

Queen Anne

Tuckahoe Creek

Denton   317

WYE ISLAND

Miles River

50

Martinak
State Park

McDaniel

328

404

St. Michaels

16

Easton
318

Idylwild
Wildlife
Management
Area

Royal Oak

Tilghman
TILGHMAN
ISLAND

Tred Avon River

Preston

318

Oxford

Federalsburg

Choptank River

Trappe

MARYLAND
DELAWARE

N

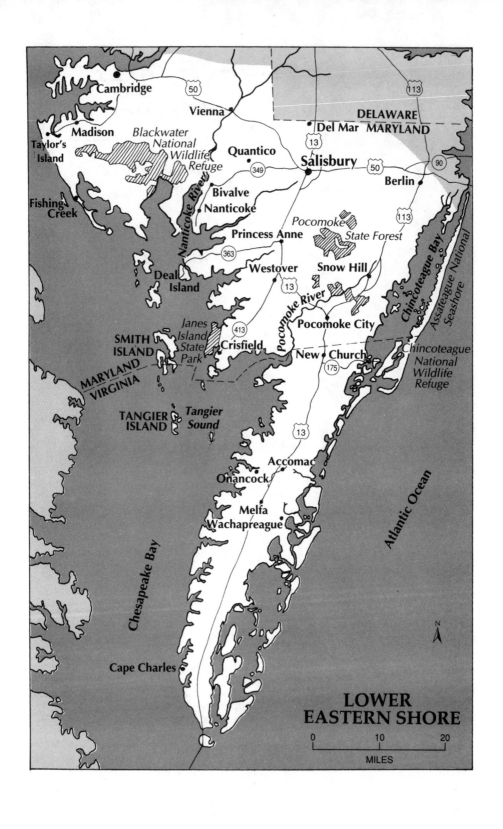

Cambridge
Vienna
50
Madison
Blackwater
Taylor's
Island
National
Wildlife
Refuge
Quantico
Fishing
Creek
Bivalve
Nanticoke
Princess Anne
Deal
Island
Westover
13
Pocomoke
State Forest
Snow Hill
Pocomoke River
Pocomoke City
SMITH
ISLAND
Janes
Island
State
Park
Crisfield
MARYLAND
VIRGINIA
New Church
TANGIER
ISLAND
Tangier
Sound
Accomac
Onancock
Melfa
Wachapreague
DELAWARE
Del Mar MARYLAND
13
Salisbury
50
Berlin
113
90
113
Chincoteague Bay
Assateague National
Seashore
Chincoteague
National
Wildlife
Refuge
Atlantic Ocean
Chesapeake Bay
Cape Charles
N
363
413
175
349

**LOWER
EASTERN SHORE**

0   10   20

MILES

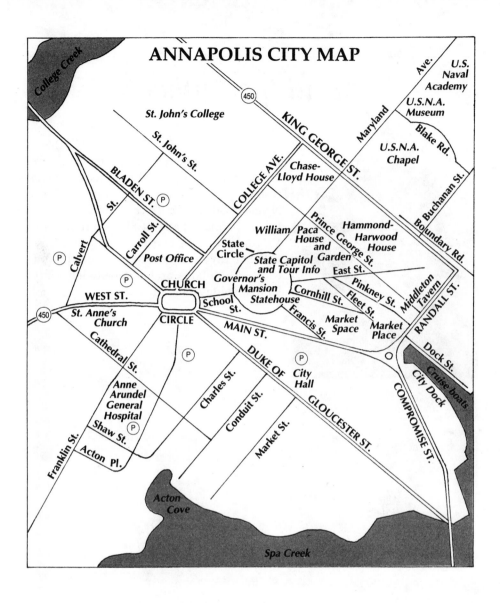

ANNAPOLIS CITY MAP

About the Author

The Chesapeake Bay Book author Allison Blake, a former feature writer for *The Capital* in Annapolis, has written about travel, restaurants, and lodgings for *Baltimore*, *National Geographic Traveler*, and *New England Monthly* magazines. She is a reporter in Virginia, and she and her husband, Joshua Gillelan, divide their time between the Blue Ridge Mountains and Mitchellville, Maryland, outside Annapolis.